Generations

..

Your Family
in Modern American History

Second Edition

Jim Watts
The City College of the City University of New York

Allen F. Davis
Temple University

Alfred A. Knopf
NEW YORK

THIS IS A BORZOI BOOK
PUBLISHED BY ALFRED A. KNOPF, INC.

Second Edition
987654321
Copyright © 1974, 1978 by Alfred A. Knopf, Inc.

Library of Congress Cataloging in Publication Data

Watts, Jim, 1935–   comp.
    Generations : your family in modern American history.

    Bibliography: p.
    1. United States—Social conditions—Addresses,
essays, lectures.   2. United States—Genealogy—
Addresses, essays, lectures.   I. Davis, Allen
Freeman, 1931–   II. Title.
HN57.W354   1978   309.1'73   77-27098
ISBN 0-394-32075-1

Cover photo: The Staten Island Historical Society, Richmondtown, Staten Island, N.Y. 10306. Photo by E. Alice Austen.

Manufactured in the United States of America

From "Heroism: 'Commando' Kelly's One Man War" by Sergeant Charles E. Kelly [and Pete Martin]. Reprinted by permission from *The Saturday Evening Post.* © 1944 by The Curtis Publishing Company.

From *Pacific War Diary, 1942–1945* by James J. Fahey. © 1963 by James J. Fahey. Reprinted by permission of Houghton Mifflin Company.

From *State of the Nation* by John Dos Passos. Copyright by Elizabeth H. Dos Passos. Reprinted by permission of Houghton Mifflin Company.

Abridged from *A Choice of Weapons* by Gordon Parks, pp. 252, 256–259, 261–264, 265–267, 269–272. Copyright © 1965, 1966 by Gordon Parks. Reprinted by permission of Harper & Row, Publishers, Inc.

Japanese American Evacuation and Relocation Records, The Bancroft Library, University of California, Berkeley. Published by permission of the Director, The Bancroft Library, University of California, Berkeley.

From *The Organization Man* by William H. Whyte, Jr., pp. 69–71, 73–81, 83, 85. Copyright © 1956 by William H. Whyte, Jr. Reprinted by permission of Simon & Schuster, a Division of Gulf & Western Corporation.

From *Stinking Creek* by John Fetterman. Copyright © 1967 by John Fetterman. Reprinted by permission of the publishers, E. P. Dutton.

Excerpted from *Coming of Age in Mississippi* by Anne Moody. Copyright © 1968 by Anne Moody. Reprinted by permission of The Dial Press.

From *What Really Happened to the Class of '65?* by Michael Medved and David Wallechinsky. Copyright © 1976 by Michael Medved and David Wallechinsky. Reprinted by permission of Random House, Inc.

From *Future Shock* by Alvin Toffler. Copyright © 1970 by Alvin Toffler. Reprinted by permission of Random House, Inc.

"A Russian Immigrant Remembers" by Isadore Ross. Published by permission of the author.

" 'My Family's History Begins in Edmondson, Arkansas' " by Norene Dove. Published by permission of the author.

"Biography of a Grandmother" by Linda K. Schilke. Permission granted by Linda Schilke Balmer.

ILLUSTRATION SOURCES

6 *top and bottom* U.S. Information Agency/National Archives; 7 Bureau of Agricultural Economics/National Archives; 8 Neil Benson; 12 National Archives; 14 U.S. Information Agency/National Archives; 19 *top and bottom* Neil Benson; 22 *top and bottom* Harvey Stein; 23 *top* Philip Teuscher; 23 *bottom* Charles Gatewood; 24 Neil Benson; 26 Roger Lubin; 27 *left* Philip Teuscher; 27 *right* Charles Gatewood; 28 *top* Harvey Stein; 28 *bottom* Ellen Pines/Woodfin Camp; 31 *top* Roger Lubin; 31 *bottom* Philip Teuscher; 37 U.S. Information Agency/National Archives; 39 U.S. Information Agency/National Archives; 40 *top and bottom* U.S. Information Agency/National Archives; 42 Museum of the City of New York, Photo by Charles von Urban; 43 Brown Brothers; 45 Roger Lubin; 46 *left* Wide World Photos; 46 *right* UPI; 47 *top and bottom* Bruce Davidson/Magnum; 49 Brown Brothers; 51 The National Galleries; 53 Courtesy, Ford Motor Company; 54 Danny Lyon/Magnum; 55 New York Public Library/Picture Collection; 57 *top* Library of Congress; 57 *bottom* Brown Brothers; 61 Thomas Hopker/Woodfin Camp; 63 *right and left* New York Public Library/Picture Collection; 64 New York Public Library/Picture Collection; 65 Courtesy, Mrs. William Goldberg; 66 Dan Budnik/Woodfin Camp; 72 New York Public Library; 75 The Granger Collection; 80 Library of Congress; 83 Office of the Secretary of Agriculture/National Archives; 86 Lin Caufield Photographers, Inc.; 91 Library of Congress; 102 Library of Congress; 106 Library of Congress; 109 Public Health Service/National Archives; 117 Library of Congress; 125 Library of Congress; 127 Library of Congress; 128 Photograph by Jacob A. Riis, The Jacob A. Riis Collection, Museum of the City of New York; 129 Library of Congress; 132 Photograph by Jacob A. Riis, The Jacob A. Riis Collection, Museum of the City of New York; 133 Photo by Lewis Hine, George Eastman House; 136 Library of Congress; 137 Library of Congress; 139 Brown Brothers; 144 *top and bottom* Library of Congress; 145 *top and bottom* Library of Congress; 150 *top and bottom* Library of Congress; 151 *top and bottom* Library of Congress; 159 *top and bottom* Library of Congress; 161 Library of Congress; 168 Library of Congress; 170 U.S. Information Agency/National Archives; 172 *top* U.S. Coast Guard/National Archives; 172 *bottom* U.S. Information Agency/National Archives; 173 Library of Congress; 176 Library of Congress; 177 Courtesy, Raymond & Malvina Phillips; 179 *left and right* Library of Congress; 180 U.S. Office of War Information/National Archives; 184 Library of Congress; 187 Franklynn Peterson/Black Star; 190 *top and bottom* Library of Congress; 191 *top and bottom* Library of Congress; 197 Women's Bureau/National Archives; 199 Figure © 1976 by The New York Times Company. Reprinted by permission; 201 Figure © 1976 by The New York Times Company. Reprinted by permission; 204 Library of Congress; 207 Figure © 1976 by The New York Times Company. Reprinted by permission; 208 Department of Housing and Urban Development; 209 Department of Housing and Urban Development; 213 *top and bottom* U.S. Information Agency/National Archives; 219 ACTION; 221 *top left and top right* Neil Benson; 221 *bottom* UPI; 225 Department of Housing and Urban Development; 227 Both figures © 1977 by The New York Times Company. Reprinted by permission; 229 Neil Benson; 231 Neil Benson; 239 The Balch Institute, Philadelphia; 240 *left* Allen F. Davis; 240 *right* Smithsonian Institution Photo No. 75-149; 242 *top right* Allen F. Davis; 242 *top right* Jim Watts; 242 *bottom* Allen F. Davis; 243 *left and right* Courtesy, Elizabeth D. Flynn; 244 *right* Allen F. Davis; 245 Allen F. Davis; 248 National Archives.

Acknowledgments

My contributions to this book grow out of twelve years of teaching experience at the City College of New York, a singular institution whose successes are ever sweeter as the odds lengthen. In 1973 a National Endowment for the Humanities Younger Humanist Fellowship gave me the opportunity to study and reflect upon an experimental mode of teaching history. Colleagues at City College who initially participated in the planning and teaching of a course in family history included Bob Hajdu, Gail Kaplan, Sue Levine, Lucy Quimby, and Bob Twombly. Georgette Kagan and John Jucovy have more recently contributed greatly as wise and energetic teaching assistants. The excellent staff of City College's Cohen Library has been of enormous help over the years, particularly Professor Sheila Herstein and Mr. Robert Fueglein, each of whose technical knowledge and general wisdom has helped me out of innumerable self-created problems.

Our search for photographs in Washington was facilitated by many resourceful and courteous federal government people, among whom we would especially like to thank Thomas Oglesby, reference chief of the Still Picture Branch of the National Archives, and Beatrice Menchaca of that staff; David A. Murdock, of the Printing and Visual Arts Division of HUD; and Anne Bringsjord, director of photo services of ACTION.

I also gladly acknowledge the inspiration provided, sometimes knowingly, often not, by Mary Sullivan Hughes Watts, and by Maurice Bice, Manny Chill, Herbert Nechin, Adrienne Rich, Marty Waldman, and Mike Weisser. My mentor at the University of Missouri, the late Walter V. Scholes, was an inspiring human being, and I do not forget him. My understanding of the importance of knowing what I came from is most associated with an extraordinary man, my late father, James F. (Jake) Watts, of Oswego, New York. My own family is adorned with the riches of Jimmy, Jennifer, and Nathaniel, and with the remarkable Judy Humphry Watts.

JIM WATTS

A number of students at Temple University have contributed to *Generations* by studying the history of their families and sharing their discoveries with me. This book also owes a great debt to my family—Harold F. Davis, my father, who talked to me about my own family and helped me relate the past to the present, and Greg, Paul, and Bobbie, who went on many expeditions in search of ancestors. Leone Cobb not only taught me how to use the semicolon, but also helped me rediscover my hometown. Barry Kramer, Sally Benson, and Hannah Newman listened and made suggestions, while William Cutler and Ronald Grele gave advice on oral history, and Alice Kessler, who read the manuscript at one point, made some important changes.

This edition has profited from the criticism and the suggestions of John Hayes, Susan Marcus, Lindsay Nauen, Nora Burgess, as well as the students who attended the American Studies summer institutes at Emory University and Skidmore College. Stuart Sprague of Morehead State University and Kirk Jeffrey of Carleton College have offered their support and encouragement. Philip Mooney of the Balch Institute allowed me to search his collections for illustrations and Neil Benson graciously provided many of his own photographs. Norene Dove, Isadore Ross, and Linda K. Schilke gave us permission to reproduce their own fascinating family stories. We want especially to thank James Dent Walker, genealogist and local history specialist at the National Archives, who took time from his own busy schedule to help us in many ways.

Finally Jim and I would like to express appreciation to the staff at Alfred A. Knopf for their thoughtful and efficient work. In particular, we would like to thank Lynn Goldberg, who contributed to the book with her imagination and her search for pictures, and to Elaine Romano, who copyedited this edition. She has worked so closely with us during the life of this book that she should in truth be listed as a co-author.

ALLEN F. DAVIS

Contents

Introduction

If you have grown up and gone to school in the United States, you have studied American history for almost as long as you can remember. From the first or second grade when you colored pictures of Lincoln and cut out cherry trees and hatchets, to later grades when you memorized the special meaning of dates like 1607 or 1863, American history has been a required subject. You have been buffeted by facts about Puritans, the westward movement, the age of Jackson, Civil War battles, overseas expansion, the New Deal, and the New Frontier, but the facts have probably had little meaning and surely have been forgotten more quickly than they were memorized. Although there is a certain intellectual excitement in sorting out the conflicting interpretations of past events, that kind of intellectual game often leaves out the human element.

Perhaps a few historical facts have remained with you because of a personal experience—a visit to a local battle site or a historic house, a tour of a restored village, coming across some old news clippings or letters preserved by a relative, or perhaps just seeing some striking old pictures. They gave you a glimpse of a different kind of past, one remote from that in history books and inhabited by real people with problems and hopes and desires. But the glimpse was, no doubt, fleeting and soon disappeared. Perhaps while reading a novel or watching a movie, you got another brief look at the past as a panorama of human suffering, lust and love, failure and triumph; but that is not supposed to be history—or is it?

All of us, through our parents, grandparents, great-grandparents, and other ancestors, are a part of history stretching back into a dim and distant past. You will probably search in vain for a really famous person in your family background. Everyone, however, has ancestors whose lives were altered by the forces of history—by wars, depressions, population movements, shifts in national boundaries, changes in farming methods, the process of industrialization. You can begin to understand some of the dimensions of human existence, some of the process of change, by looking at your own family, studying your own particular ethnic group, and examining the community in which you live.

The best way to begin the study of the past is with yourself. Where do you fit in? What makes you similar to your friends? What makes you different? How do you explain your own special situation? Does it have something to do with the generation in which you were born? The accident of birth, for example, caused those born in the 1930s, a time of low birth rate, to have had much greater employment opportunities than you can expect to have if you were born in the early 1960s, a time of high birth rate. Perhaps it is not so much time and generation as sex, race, or religion that you see as crucial in defining your place and identity. Then, being a woman or being a black, an Italian or a Jew will become the most important fact in your life. And social class, too, can be significant in defining your life style, especially if you are either very rich or very poor.

Probably the most crucial influence on your life was your own family. Whether you grew up in a nuclear family (made up of husband, wife, and children) or an extended family (a group of assorted relatives living together and functioning as a unit), you have, no doubt, been radically affected by your interaction with your parents, brothers and sisters, and other relatives. These interactions constitute a unique story, a history. There are "official" records of this history—deeds, marriage certificates, divorce decrees, various court records, the discharge papers of one released from the army. But behind these recorded events are human stories of pathos and triumph and tragedy. A baby dies, a son leaves home, a daughter marries, children rebel against their parents. There is bitterness and remorse and failure, or perhaps resignation. All of these are universals which touch every family at one point or another.

Both continuity and change characterize these universal human experiences. To put it another way, over the past five generations in your family, sixty-two people participated in your creation. Your thirty-two great-, great-, great-grandparents must seem like characters out of ancient history to you, yet they lived only about a century and a half ago, a short period in historical time. They—and even your more distant ancestors as well—were in some ways just like you. Survival, after all, has always compelled men and women to find the means to acquire food, shelter, and clothing. And being human has always required confronting births and deaths, experiencing pleasure and enduring pain, seeking both solitude and association. In the latter regard, peoples over the centuries have tended to identify themselves with others, with family or community, by region or nationality, with ethnic groups, or religion. Although your thirty-two great-, great-, great-grandparents may remain beyond your knowledge in most ways, you may be sure that they shared with you many of the experiences of the human condition.

We tend to forget the continuities of existence because of the extraordinary changes the world has undergone in the relatively recent past. Indeed, your ancestors beyond the third and fourth generations past lived in a world amazingly different from what you have known. Their world began to disappear when machines became the primary factor in the production and distribution of goods and services. The age-old patterns of life that were rather quickly destroyed by industrialization offer a striking contrast to the way we live today. Our material progress has thus been acquired at the cost of the destruction of much that was valuable, as an examination of the days of our preindustrial ancestors will reveal.

Industrialization is just one of the ways the life style of your family has been affected by the events of the past. Another event of major importance was the movement of peoples. Perhaps your family came from Ireland in the great migration after the potato famine in the 1840s; or maybe they were Jews who left Russia in the early 1900s. Possibly you are descended from the slaves who survived the passage from Africa, or perhaps you can trace your ancestry back to the migration from England in the seventeenth and eighteenth centuries. Whatever your own special background, unless you are a pure-blooded Indian, your ancestors went through the process of being uprooted from one culture and establishing themselves in another. (Even if your background can be traced to the native Americans, you too have a heritage of movement and change.) The wrenching moves from one land to another that your parents or grandparents made, the hopes and fears, dreams and heartaches they had, constitute a widely shared American experience.

There are, of course, some for whom the effects of immigration are too distant to be felt. But even if your parents or grandparents are not recent immigrants, the chances are that your family has moved from farm to city, from small city to metropolis, from East to West, or from South to North. Americans have always been a mobile people and they continue to be so even today. It is now an unusual American family that has lived for more than two generations in the same community, let alone in the same house. Every move meant leaving friends and often possessions, although it did not necessarily mean leaving the memories of a place behind. The human dimension of American mobility can be probed by asking questions of your family.

Just as geographic mobility has helped shape the American character, so too has belief in the American Dream, the notion that America is a land of opportunity

where poor men and women, if they work hard, can improve their situation or at least create a better life for their children. Almost everyone, except those who came as slaves, believed this dream in the past, but how many really succeeded in creating a better life in a new land?

A person's success, or lack of it, has been affected by many factors, not the least of which, in the twentieth century, have been the Great Depression and the war that followed it. These large historical forces are much discussed in history books, mainly from the viewpoint of their effect on political processes and society in the abstract. Both events had very personal sides to them, however, as any member of your family who lived through those decades can attest. For nearly everyone who experienced the depression of the thirties, the hope for a continuously improving life was shattered. True, that hope was revived for some of the prosperity and sense of purpose that World War II gave back to the country. But not everyone shared in this wartime optimism—certainly not those black Americans who fought for a freedom they did not have at home, nor those Japanese-Americans interned in concentration camps for the accident of their ethnic heritage—and even for those who did, the memory of bad times was too vivid to ever allow them freedom from naggingly practical concerns. If there is a gap between generations today manifested in what parents and children are concerned with and in what their expectations for the future are, surely it has been conditioned by the differences between the periods of history through which the two generations have lived. Those differences can be laid out and, if not reconciled, at least understood through a comparison of your own family's recollections of living through the past and your remembrances of the time during which you grew up.

The strategy of this book, then, is to help you gather information and to ask questions about yourself and your family and about the movements and events that have influenced your history. After an initial inquiry into the value of studying family history, we ask you to examine yourself and then to find out about your parents' generation and the generations that preceded theirs. We then ask you to contemplate the experience of movement and disruption that is almost universal in the country's history. Next, we ask that you study the impact of those two major events of the twentieth century —the depression and World War II—on your family and community. At the end we try to get you to look at the world you are presently living in and to ask questions about it. So the structure of this book is roughly circular. It starts with you and the present, goes back several generations, and then comes forward to the present again.

Generations
..
Your Family in Modern American History

one

Why Study Family History?

Why should I be interested in studying my ancestors? you may ask. My family is not important. My grandfather and great-grandmother cannot be very interesting, because I know they were poor and "ordinary"—common people. Is it not more important and usually more interesting to study famous people, the kings, presidents, and generals who really made a difference in history? Or, if we must study families, why not the famous ones, such as the Adams family, the Roosevelts, or the Rockefellers?

These are natural questions, and there are many answers to them. Perhaps the most basic reason to explore your family's history is that in finding out where you came from, you may learn more about who you are. To discover where your parents were born, to appreciate the struggles that your great-grandfather endured, to re-create what it felt like to live in another time and place, and to imagine what it must have been like for those who came before you is to uncover something important about yourself.

Studying your family's history is much more than a self-serving exercise, however. Until recently, most historical writing has been the story of the famous and the infamous. All too often, it has been the story of famous white men. Even genealogy (i.e., the careful investigation of family lineage) has been reserved for those who came from an Anglo-Saxon Protestant background and could trace their family at least to the American Revolution and perhaps even to the arrival of the *Mayflower* in 1620. Most of us are from ordinary families (as were most of those who sailed on the *Mayflower* and fought in the Revolution five generations later). By tracing our past we can learn something about the ways anonymous Americans lived in the past. We can begin to appreciate what travel across the ocean or across the continent really meant to the men, women, and children who made those voyages. We can observe depressions and

wars not from the point of view of the leaders but from the vantage point of the people who had to suffer and die. We may come to understand how the passage of time has changed the way we live, altered the landscape, and transformed work and transportation and housing. We can also learn that some things stay the same.

There is something exciting, even exhilarating, about discovering your own past. Perhaps the following essays will help to stimulate your imagination and make you think about the ways you can discover your lost heritage. The first selection is a brief essay by Ray Jenkins, an Alabama journalist who returned to his hometown in Georgia accompanied by his daughter, Nancy. As he strolls the fields that had once belonged to his family, he contemplates the changes that have occurred in his lifetime. He suddenly asks the girl if she realizes that her ancestors as far back as her great-great-grandfather had all worked these fields. She replies: "Well, so what?"

Perhaps that is your own reaction at this point to studying your family's past. Or, perhaps you have already experienced the thrill of discovering a piece of your special history. In any case, you can certainly appreciate the changes that have occurred in Ray Jenkins' lifetime, and the sadness he experienced in breaking a cultural chain by moving from one kind of life to another. Should we not be aware of the family chains, both broken and unbroken, in our own past?

The next selection is the now famous story of how Alex Haley traced his family's slave ancestors. The popular success of his book, *Roots,* and the eight-part television series based on the book, has made his one of the most famous families in America. Of course, in some ways Haley's story is a unique one, and you will not be able to duplicate his success. Yet every family has an oral tradition that can be explored and built on. Your time and resources will be more limited than Haley's, but the same excitement and thrill of discovery await you as you uncover your own family history, find one of your ancestors listed in an official government document, or visit a place where one of your people lived.

Some families, of course, are easier to trace than others, but at some point every family disappears into a great unknown. There are some family roots that are impossible to discover. Every successful search also consists of a certain amount of luck. Even if you fail to trace your family's roots for many generations, you will have experienced something of the thrill of historical research and learned something about the reality of the way ordinary people lived.

A Georgian Remembers
Ray Jenkins

Have you ever returned to a town, a neighborhood, or a house where you once lived? If you have, you will understand some of the mixed emotions that Ray Jenkins felt in returning to his ancestral home. You may also appreciate the excitement he felt in discovering a dusty book in a library that contained the record of his family. Perhaps you can have a similar experience.

The author makes a major point of the fact that he broke a cultural and family chain by moving off the land, away from the family homestead, to continue his education. He never went back. Almost every family in America has someone who broke that cultural chain—the immigrant who first moved to America or the person who left the farm to go to the city. Who broke the cultural chain in your family? When? Why?

If you head south from Plains over the country roads through the peanut fields of southwestern Georgia, you soon will come to Jenkins' Crossing.

It is not so famous a place nowadays as Plains, the home of my neighbor Jimmy Carter. In fact, Jenkins' Crossing no longer has any geographic importance at all, except perhaps to the engineer of the little train which slows down as it crosses the highway at that point on its clickety-clack daily run over decrepit tracks, hauling fertilizer, cottonseed, lumber and other essentials of the region.

It is, however, of considerable importance to me. If scant available records are any guide, that land first came into the possession of someone named Jenkins sometime around the turn of the 19th century, scarcely 25 years after the issue of the great Declaration whose 200th anniversary we are celebrating.

It is not fashionable in these days of that ever-renascent, ever-elusive "New South" to speak much about ancestry, but if you strip us to our essential core, you will find that most Southerners feel some small measure of kinship with the Rev. Gail Hightower, the half-mad cuckolded preacher of Faulkner's world who used to see ghosts of his ancestors thundering across the night sky.

So it was that when I stumbled upon a small, romanticized history of my county—among the volumes in Widener Library at Harvard, of all unlikely places, never before opened since it was put on its obscure shelf 30 years before—my fascination quickly turned into eager anticipation when I reached the section drawn from my own family's Bible records.

One of the earliest entries recorded the birth of one Royal Jenkins, in 1787, and I vaguely wondered if the name reflected latent Tory [pro-British] sympathies.

Why is the Bible a good source of family history?

Then I came upon a series of deaths in rapid succession. "Russell F. Jenkins departed this life March 30, 1853 . . . Sarah Jenkins departed this life April 9, 1853 . . . Alexander Daniel Jenkins departed this life April 27, 1853. . . ." And so on.

At the conclusion of this melancholy recitation was a solemn note of explanation: "The

What differences do you see in these two pictures? How has modern technology changed the nature of farming? How do these photos explain the virtual disappearance of the "hired hand"? Is it still possible to feel close to the land in the last part of the twentieth century?

above five were poisoned by a slave." Not even the name of this individual, who had made known in so dramatic a way grievances against the Jenkins family, is recorded. Nor are we told what happened to this stealthy rebel.

My visits to Jenkins' Crossing—I still call it "home"—are infrequent these days, and they are usually hurried trips, to handle some business matter involving the land which finally passed into my absentee ownership. On one such visit a few weeks ago, I took along Nancy Jenkins, who is six, for companionship on the drive through this dreary and desolate region, a countryside dotted by sad gray shacks, many almost taken over by the ubiquitous kudzu vine, populated now only by ghosts like those of Hightower's dying reverie.

It is rare these days even to see a mule, that worthy and uncomplaining beast of burden whose energy so long sustained the agriculture of this region. I recall, not long ago, chuckling when I saw a young man on a modern tractor with air-conditioned, glass-enclosed cab, listening to high-volume rock-'n'-roll stereo music as he drove the great machine so effortlessly over the cotton field, doing the work that would have required a dozen men, women and children just a generation back. Can there be, I asked myself, any kinship between this young "farmer" and one who had grappled with a strong weed with his bare hands, had watered the soil with his sweat?

In an idle moment Nancy and I strolled in the fields, now luxuriant with this year's peanut crop. Overwhelmed by the heavy presence of the past, I tried to communicate my feelings to my small daughter.

"Nancy," I began, "did you know that your father, your grandfather, your great-grandfather and your great-great-grandfather all worked in these fields when they were little like you?"

Her curiosity was aroused, and she waited expectantly for some point to my story. But, alas, there was none. Then, sensing my uncertainty, this slip of an offspring of all those celebrated ancestors closed the matter with a shrug and a murmur, more bewildered than impertinent, "Well, so what?"

What place do you call "home"? Is it the same place in which you reside now?

Is modern life so different that the past is incomprehensible?

What can you tell about this family from the photograph? What social class do they come from? What occupation does the man engage in? How are the four people related? Is there any significance in the way they pose, separated from each other?

Is the Carter family a typical Southern family? Why do we expect our Presidents and other public officials to have close-knit families and to project an image of family loyalty and solidarity? Why did this brief walk on Inauguration Day attract so much favorable attention?

Indeed, so what? How could she understand what the place had meant to me, a child growing up nine miles from the nearest paved road? Like her older brothers who had also grown up in the city, she did not even know the color of a cotton bloom.

Unless a man has picked cotton all day in August; has sat in an outhouse in 20 degrees in January and passed this time of necessity by reading last year's Sears Roebuck catalogue; has eaten a possum and liked it; has castrated a live pig with a dull pocket knife and has wrung a chicken's neck with his own hands; has learned at least a few chords on a fiddle and guitar; has tried to lure a sharecropper's daughter into the woods for mischievous purposes; has watched a man who had succeeded in doing just that have his sins washed away in the Blood of the Lamb in a baptism in a muddy creek; has been kicked by a mean milch cow and kicked her back; has drunk busthead likker knowing full well it might kill him; has wished the next day it had killed him; has watched a neighbor's house burn down; has drawn a knife on an adversary in fear and anger; has half-soled his one pair of shoes with a tire-repair kit; has gone into a deep dark well to get out a dead chicken that had fallen in; has waited beside a dusty road in the midday heat, hoping the R.F.D. postman would bring some long-coveted item ordered from the catalogue; has been in close quarters with a snake; has, in thirsty desperation, drunk water that worked alive with mosquito larvae called wiggletails; has eaten sardines out of a can with a stick; has killed a cat just for the hell of it; has felt like a nigger was mistreated but was afraid to say so; has stepped in the droppings of a chicken and not really cared; has been cheated by someone he worked hard for; has gone to bed at sundown because he could no longer endure the crushing isolation; has ridden a bareback mule three miles to visit a purty girl who waited in a clean, flimsy cotton dress—unless he has done these things, then he cannot understand what it was like in my South.

Can people of different backgrounds ever really understand one another, then?

It is a definition, I hasten to add, which conveys neither superiority nor inferiority; it is morally neutral. It is just that my experience was different from that of my children. Jimmy Carter will understand, but not my children.

When I was Nancy's age, I had no reason to believe that I would ever leave the farm; indeed, I had every reason to believe that my children and grandchildren would be born there, just as my parents and grandparents had been born there.

But there were forces at work which would not permit this orderly plan of nature to be carried out. Our little country school—whose cornerstone bore the name of some visionary forebear who valued education—closed in the 1940's, its enrollment decimated by the great trek from the farms to the cities.

Arrangements had to be made for me to continue my education. (Like Jimmy Carter, I was later to become the first member of my family to graduate from college.) So I went to live with an aunt, in a little town called Camilla, so that I could finish high school.

The distance was only about 20 miles but, culturally, it was a different universe. It is no exaggeration to say that the cultural leap from the farm to Camilla, a town of only 3,000, was greater than the leap from Camilla to New York City would have been.

So I was the link in the cultural chain which broke. This is not all that unusual in America, really. Anyone in Boston with an Irish name, anyone in Chicago with a Polish name, anyone in New York with an Eastern European Jewish name can probably tell you precisely when the same thing happened in their own families, usually a couple of generations back.

And yet, this event comes rather hard for those who must make the break. And it was all the more so in my own case because it was a chain which had not been broken since some poor wretch named Jenkins, given the option of spending his life in a debtor's prison in England or coming to the new colony of Georgia, boarded one of Gen. James Oglethorpe's ships and set sail into the perilous unknown in the first third of the 18th century.

Except for the introduction of the internal-combustion engine, itself scarcely more than a novelty in the rural milieu of the 1930's and 1940's, my childhood was not unlike that of my forefathers for five generations back. But it was radically different from my children's childhood.

About the time I was leaving the farm for good, to go to the state university to take up what my mother surely thought was the odd career of journalism, a small, fragile piece of humanity was being blown about by storms of a different kind which beset Europe in those same years that I was growing up on the farm. In due course that orphaned child from Germany came to rest in Georgia. There, the two broken links came together, and the boys and little Nancy were born in due course. They are, I am sure, not even aware today that they are among that 1.4 percent of Alabama citizens listed in the official Census of the United States as being of "foreign stock." In fact, they are scarcely even aware that they are the second links in the new chain.

Was your early life rooted? What attitudes might this early experience have fostered?

What changes might the author have experienced?

At what point in your family history did the chain snap?

9

My Furthest-Back Person—the African
ALEX HALEY

How do you explain the enormous success of *Roots,* both as a book and as a television series? Is it because Alex Haley is dealing with the slave experience, or is it because we all have a need to find our own roots? Might it be because America has developed to the point where no part of its historical experience, no matter how painful, need now be ignored?

Because your resources will be more limited than Haley's, you probably will not be able to duplicate this method. Still, you may be able to uncover a very exciting story. By reading this essay carefully, you should participate in Haley's thrill of discovery while at the same time coming to understand what is useful to your own work in the method that he uses.

My Grandma Cynthia Murray Palmer lived in Henning, Tenn. (pop. 500), about 50 miles north of Memphis. Each summer as I grew up there, we would be visited by several women relatives who were mostly around Grandma's age, such as my Great Aunt Liz Murray who taught in Oklahoma, and Great Aunt Till Merriwether from Jackson, Tenn., or their considerably younger niece, Cousin Georgia Anderson from Kansas City, Kan., and some others. Always after the supper dishes had been washed, they would go out to take seats and talk in the rocking chairs on the front porch, and I would scrunch down, listening, behind Grandma's squeaky chair, with the dusk deepening into night and the lightning bugs flicking on and off above the now shadowy honeysuckles. Most often they talked about our family—the story had been passed down for generations—until the whistling blur of lights of the southbound Panama Limited train *whooshing* through Henning at 9:05 P.M. signaled our bedtime.

So much of their talking of people, places and events I didn't understand: For instance, what was an "Ol' Massa," an "Ol' Missus" or a "plantation"? But early I gathered that white folks had done lots of bad things to our folks, though I couldn't figure out why. I guessed that all that they talked about had happened a long time ago, as now or then Grandma or another, speaking of someone in the past, would excitedly thrust a finger toward me, exclaiming, "Wasn't big as *this* young'un!" And it would astound me that anyone as old and grey-haired as they could relate to my age. But in time my head began both a recording and picturing of the more graphic scenes they would describe, just as I also visualized David killing Goliath with his slingshot, Old Pharaoh's army drowning, Noah and his ark, Jesus feeding that big multitude with nothing but five loaves and two fishes, and other wonders that I heard in my Sunday school lessons at our New Hope Methodist Church.

The furthest-back person Grandma and the others talked of—always in tones of awe, I noticed—they would call "The African." They said that some ship brought him to a

Can you recall any such discussions of your family history?

Who is the "furthest-back" person that is still remembered in your family?

place that they pronounced " 'Naplis." They said that then some "Mas' John Waller" bought him for his plantation in "Spotsylvania County, Va." This African kept on escaping, the fourth time trying to kill the "hateful po' cracker" slave-catcher, who gave him the punishment choice of castration or of losing one foot. This African took a foot being chopped off with an ax against a tree stump, they said, and he was about to die. But his life was saved by "Mas' John's" brother—"Mas' William Waller," a doctor, who was so furious about what had happened that he bought the African for himself and gave him the name "Toby."

Crippling about, working in "Mas' William's" house and yard, the African in time met and mated with "the big house cook named Bell," and there was born a girl named Kizzy. As she grew up her African daddy often showed her different kinds of things, telling her what they were in his native tongue. Pointing at a banjo, for example, the African uttered, "*ko*"; or pointing at a river near the plantation, he would say, "*Kamby Bolong*." Many of his strange words started with a "*k*" sound, and the little, growing Kizzy learned gradually that they identified different things.

When addressed by other slaves as "Toby," the master's name for him, the African said angrily that his name was "*Kin-tay*." And as he gradually learned English, he told young Kizzy some things about himself—for instance, that he was not far from his village, chopping wood to make himself a drum, when four men had surprised, overwhelmed, and kidnapped him.

Is the foreign language you know that of your ancestors? If not, why didn't you learn that language?

So Kizzy's head held much about her African daddy when at age 16 she was sold away onto a much smaller plantation in North Carolina. Her new "Mas' Tom Lea" fathered her first child, a boy she named George. And Kizzy told her boy all about his African grandfather. George grew up to be such a gamecock fighter that he was called "Chicken George," and people would come from all over and "bet big money" on his cockfights. He mated with Matilda, another of Lea's slaves; they had seven children, and he told them the stories and strange sounds of their African great-grandfather. And one of those children, Tom, became a blacksmith who was bought away by a "Mas' Murray" for his tobacco plantation in Alamance County, N.C.

Tom mated there with Irene, a weaver on the plantation. She also bore seven children, and Tom now told them all about their African great-great grandfather, the faithfully passed-down knowledge of his sounds and stories having become by now the family's prideful treasure.

The youngest of that second set of seven children was a girl, Cynthia, who became my maternal Grandma (which today I can only see as fated). Anyway, all of this is how I was growing up in Henning at Grandma's, listening from behind her rocking chair as she and the other visiting old women talked of that African (never then comprehended as *my* great-great-great-great-grandfather) who said his name was "*Kin-tay*," and said "*ko*" for banjo, "*Kamby Bolong*" for river, and a jumble of other "*k*"-beginning sounds that Grandma privately muttered, most often while making beds or cooking, and who also said that near his village he was kidnapped while chopping wood to make himself a drum.

The story had become nearly as fixed in my head as in Grandma's by the time Dad and Mama moved me and my two younger brothers, George and Julius, away from Henning to be with them at the small black agricultural and mechanical college in Normal, Ala., where Dad taught.

To compress my next 25 years: When I was 17 Dad let me enlist as a mess boy in the U.S. Coast Guard. I became a ship's cook out in the South Pacific during World War II, and at night down by my bunk I began trying to write sea adventure stories, mailing them off to magazines and collecting rejection slips for eight years before some editors began purchasing and publishing occasional stories. By 1949 the Coast Guard had made me its first "journalist"; finally with 20 years' service, I retired at the age of 37, determined to make a full time career of writing. I wrote mostly magazine articles; my first book was "The Autobiography of Malcolm X."

Then one Saturday in 1965 I happened to be walking past the National Archives building in Washington. Across the interim years I had thought of Grandma's old stories —otherwise I can't think what diverted me up the Archives' steps. And when a main reading room desk attendant asked if he could help me, I wouldn't have dreamed of admitting to him some curiosity hanging on from boyhood about my slave forebears. I kind of mumbled that I was interested in census records of Alamance County, North Carolina, just after the Civil War.

The microfilm rolls were delivered, and I turned them through the machine with a

Have you ever tried to research your own family history? Why or why not?

11

REPORT and MANIFEST of the LADING of the *Sloop Polly* — burthen *Thirty Six & Seventy two* 95 Tons, American built, from *the Isle of Goree* being the Port from whence she last sailed, _____ Master during the Voyage *Joshua Smith* — the present Master, and is owned by *Cyprian Sterry of Providence Rhode Island*,

Marks	Numbers	Contents of each Package, &c. or Quantity, if stowed loose.	By whom shipped.	Where destined.	To whom consigned.	Port or Place where laden.
	1–40	Forty Slaves	Isaac Gorham	Savannah in Georgia	Robert Watts	The River of Goree
		Stores				
		One Barrel Beef				
		One half Barrel Pork				
		Two Barrels Corn				
		Ten Gallons Rum				

What is the significance of this document, written in such prosaic language? Can you locate on a map the embarkation point and compare it with the location of the stated kidnapping of Kunte Kinte at about the same time? Is there any significance in the eventual forced settling of many Africans in the exact same area as inhabited by the ancestors of Jimmy Carter and Ray Jenkins?

building sense of intrigue, viewing in different census takers' penmanship an endless parade of names. After about a dozen microfilmed rolls, I was beginning to tire, when in utter astonishment I looked upon the names of Grandma's parents: Tom Murray, Irene Murray . . . older sisters of Grandma's as well—every one of them a name that I'd heard countless times on her front porch.

It wasn't that I hadn't believed Grandma. You just *didn't* not believe my Grandma. It was simply so uncanny actually seeing those names in print and in official U.S. Government records.

During the next several months I was back in Washington whenever possible, in the Archives, the Library of Congress, the Daughters of the American Revolution Library. (Whenever black attendants understood the idea of my search, documents I requested reached me with miraculous speed.) In one source or another during 1966 I was able to document at least the highlights of the cherished family story. I would have given anything to have told Grandma, but, sadly, in 1949 she had gone. So I went and told the only survivor of those Henning front-porch storytellers: Cousin Georgia Anderson, now in her 80's in Kansas City, Kan. Wrinkled, bent, not well herself, she was so overjoyed, repeating to me the old stories and sounds; they were like Henning echoes: "Yeah, boy, that African say his name was '*Kin-tay*'; he say the banjo was '*ko*,' an' the river '*Kamby Bolong*,' an' he was off choppin' some wood to make his drum when they grabbed 'im!" Cousin Georgia grew so excited we had to stop her, calm her down, "You go 'head, boy! Your grandma an' all of 'em—they up there watching what you do!"

That week I flew to London on a magazine assignment. Since by now I was steeped in the old, in the past, scarcely a tour guide missed me—I was awed at so many historical

Why have blacks in particular become so conscious of their heritage? Would other groups do well to follow their example?

places and treasures I'd heard of and read of. I came upon the Rosetta stone in the British Museum, marveling anew at how Jean Champollion, the French archaeologist, had miraculously deciphered its ancient demotic and hieroglyphic texts . . .

The thrill of that just kept hanging around in my head. I was on a jet returning to New York when a thought hit me. Those strange, unknown-tongue sounds, always part of our family's old story . . . they were obviously bits of our original African "*Kin-tay's*" native tongue. What specific tongue? Could I somehow find out?

Back in New York, I began making visits to the United Nations Headquarters lobby; it wasn't hard to spot Africans. I'd stop any I could, asking if my bits of phonetic sounds held any meaning for them. A couple of dozen Africans quickly looked at me, listened, and took off—understandably dubious about some Tennesseean's accent alleging "African" sounds.

My research assistant, George Sims (we grew up together in Henning), brought me some names of ranking scholars of African linguistics. One was particularly intriguing: a Belgian- and English-educated Dr. Jan Vansina; he had spent his early career living in West African villages, studying and tape-recording countless oral histories that were narrated by certain very old African men; he had written a standard textbook, "The Oral Tradition."

So I flew to the University of Wisconsin to see Dr. Vansina. In his living room I told him every bit of the family story in the fullest detail that I could remember it. Then, intensely, he queried me about the story's relay across the generations, about the gibberish of "*k*" sounds Grandma had fiercely muttered to herself while doing her housework, with my brothers and me giggling beyond her hearing at what we had dubbed "Grandma's noises."

Dr. Vansina, his manner very serious, finally said, "These sounds your family has kept sound very probably of the tongue called 'Mandinka.'"

I'd never heard of any "Mandinka." Grandma just told of the African saying "*ko*" for banjo, or "*Kamby Bolong*" for a Virginia river.

Among Mandinka stringed instruments, Dr. Vansina said, one of the oldest was the "*kora.*"

"*Bolong,*" he said, was clearly Mandinka for "river." Preceded by "*Kamby,*" it very likely meant "Gambia River."

Dr. Vansina telephoned an eminent Africanist colleague, Dr. Philip Curtin. He said that the phonetic "*Kin-tay*" was correctly spelled "*Kinte,*" a very old clan that had originated in Old Mali. The Kinte men traditionally were blacksmiths, and the women were potters and weavers.

I knew I must get to the Gambia River.

The first native Gambian I could locate in the U.S. was named Ebou Manga, then a junior attending Hamilton College in upstate Clinton, N. Y. He and I flew to Dakar, Senegal, then took a smaller plane to Yundum Airport, and rode in a van to Gambia's capital, Bathurst. Ebou and his father assembled eight Gambia government officials. I told them Grandma's stories, every detail I could remember, as they listened intently, then reacted. "'*Kamby Bolong*' of course is Gambia River!" I heard. "But more clue is your forefather's saying his name was '*Kinte.*'" Then they told me something I would never even have fantasized—that in places in the back country lived very old men, commonly called *griots,* who could tell centuries of the histories of certain very old family clans. As for *Kintes,* they pointed out to me on a map some family villages, Kinte-Kundah, and Kinte-Kundah Janneh-Ya, for instance.

The Gambian officials said they would try to help me. I returned to New York dazed. It is embarrassing to me now, but despite Grandma's stories, I'd never been concerned much with Africa, and I had the routine images of African people living mostly in exotic jungles. But a compulsion now laid hold of me to learn all I could, and I began devouring books about Africa, especially about the slave trade. Then one Thursday's mail contained a letter from one of the Gambian officials, inviting me to return there.

Monday I was back in Bathurst. It galvanized me when the officials said that a *griot* had been located who told the *Kinte* clan history—his name was Kebba Kanga Fofana. To reach him, I discovered, required a modified safari; renting a launch to get upriver, two land vehicles to carry supplies by a roundabout land route, and employing finally 14 people, including three interpreters and four musicians, since a *griot* would not speak the revered clan histories without background music.

The boat Baddibu vibrated upriver, with me acutely tense: Were these Africans maybe viewing me as but another of the pith-helmets? After about two hours, we put

How did looking for his own history help the author's appreciation of history?

What would drive a man to such lengths to find his past?

How has increased black consciousness changed the image of African history?

13

African tribes often assign one of their members the highly honored task of mentally keeping their history. What need might the retelling of the past serve?

in at James Island, for me to see the ruins of the once British-operated James Fort. Here two centuries of slave ships had loaded thousands of cargoes of Gambian tribespeople. The crumbling stones, the deeply oxidized swivel cannon, even some remnant links of chain seemed all but impossible to believe. Then we continued upriver to the left-bank village of Albreda, and there put ashore to continue on foot to Juffure, village of the *griot*. Once more we stopped, for me to see *toubob kolong*, "the white man's well," now almost filled in, in a swampy area with abundant, tall, saw-toothed grass. It was dug two centuries ago to "17 men's height deep" to insure survival drinking water for long-driven, famishing coffles of slaves.

Why would these remnants of the past have affected him so?

Walking on, I kept wishing that Grandma could hear how her stories had led me to the "*Kamby Bolong.*" (Our surviving storyteller Cousin Georgia died in a Kansas City hospital during this same morning, I would learn later.) Finally, Juffure village's playing children, sighting us, flashed an alert. The 70-odd people came rushing from their circular, thatch-roofed, mud-walled huts, with goats bounding up and about, and parrots squawking from up in the palms. I sensed him in advance somehow, the small man amid them, wearing a pillbox cap and an off-white robe—the *griot*. Then the interpreters went to him, as the villagers thronged around me.

How has his growing sense of African heritage affected his self-image as an American black?

And it hit me like a gale wind: every one of them, the whole crowd, was *jet black*. An enormous sense of guilt swept me—a sense of being some kind of hybrid . . . a sense of being impure among the pure. It was an awful sensation.

14

The old *griot* stepped away from my interpreters and the crowd quickly swarmed around him—all of them buzzing. An interpreter named A. B. C. Salla came to me; he whispered: "Why they stare at you so, they have never seen here a black American." And that hit me: I was symbolizing for them twenty-five millions of us they had never seen. What did they think of me—of us?

Then abruptly the old *griot* was briskly walking toward me. His eyes boring into mine, he spoke in Mandinka, as if instinctively I should understand—and A. B. C. Salla translated:

"Yes . . . we have been told by the forefathers . . . that many of us from this place are in exile . . . in that place called America . . . and in other places."

I suppose I physically wavered, and they thought it was the heat; rustling whispers went through the crowd, and a man brought me a low stool. Now the whispering hushed —the musicians had softly begun playing *kora* and *balafon*, and a canvas sling lawn seat was taken by the *griot*, Kebba Kanga Fofana, aged 73 "rains" (one rainy season each year). He seemed to gather himself into a physical rigidity, and he began speaking the *Kinte* clan's ancestral oral history; it came rolling from his mouth across the next hours . . . 17th- and 18th-century *Kinte* lineage details, predominantly what men took wives; the children they "begot," in the order of their births; those children's mates and children.

Events frequently were dated by some proximate singular physical occurrence. It was as if some ancient scroll were printed indelibly within the *griot's* brain. Each few sentences or so, he would pause for an interpreter's translation to me. I distill here the essence:

The *Kinte* clan began in Old Mali, the men generally blacksmiths ". . . who conquered fire," and the women potters and weavers. One large branch of the clan moved to Mauretania from where one son of the clan, Kairaba Kunta Kinte, a Moslem Marabout holy man, entered Gambia. He lived first in the village of Pakali N'Ding; he moved next to Jiffarong village; ". . . and then he came here, into our own village of Juffure."

In Juffure, Kairaba Kunta Kinte took his first wife, ". . . a Mandinka maiden, whose name was Sireng. By her, he begot two sons, whose names were Janneh and Saloum. Then he got a second wife, Yaisa. By her, he begot a son, Omoro."

The three sons became men in Juffure. Janneh and Saloum went off and found a new village, Kinte-Kundah Janneh-Ya. "And then Omoro, the youngest son, when he had 30 rains, took as a wife a maiden, Binta Kebba.

"And by her, he begot four sons—Kunta, Lamin, Suwadu, and Madi . . ."

Sometimes, a "begotten," after his naming, would be accompanied by some later-occurring detail, perhaps as ". . . in time of big water (flood), he slew a water buffalo." Having named those four sons, now the *griot* stated such a detail.

"About the time the king's soldiers came, the eldest of these four sons, Kunta, when he had about 16 rains, went away from this village, to chop wood to make a drum . . . and he was never seen again . . ."

Goose-pimples the size of lemons seemed to pop all over me. In my knapsack were my cumulative notebooks, the first of them including how in my boyhood, my Grandma, Cousin Georgia and the others told of the African "*Kin-tay*" who always said he was kidnapped near his village—while chopping wood to make a drum . . .

I showed the interpreter, he showed and told the *griot*, who excitedly told the people; they grew very agitated. Abruptly then they formed a human ring, encircling me, dancing and chanting. Perhaps a dozen of the women carrying their infant babies rushed in toward me, thrusting the infants into my arms—conveying, I would later learn, "the laying on of hands . . . through this flesh which is us, we are you, and you are us." The men hurried me into their mosque, their Arabic praying later being translated outside: "Thanks be to Allah for returning the long lost from among us." Direct descendants of Kunta Kinte's blood brothers were hastened, some of them from nearby villages, for a family portrait to be taken with me, surrounded by actual ancestral sixth cousins. More symbolic acts filled the remaining day.

When they would let me leave, for some reason I wanted to go away over the African land. Dazed, silent in the bumping Land Rover, I heard the cutting staccato of talking drums. Then when we sighted the next village, its people came thronging to meet us. They were all—little naked ones to wizened elders—waving, beaming, amid a cacophony of crying out; and then my ears identified their words: *"Meester Kinte! Meester Kinte!"*

Let me tell you something: I am a man. But I remember the sob surging up from my

What caused their excitement? Might it have had something to do with finding a piece of their own lost history?

15

feet, flinging up my hands before my face and bawling as I had not done since I was a baby . . . the jet-black Africans were jostling, staring . . . I didn't care, with the feelings surging. If you really knew the odyssey of us millions of black Americans, if you really knew how we came in the seeds of our forefathers, captured, driven, beaten, inspected, bought, branded, chained in foul ships, if you really knew, you needed weeping . . .

Back home, I knew that what I must write, really, was our black saga, where any individual's past is the essence of the millions'. Now flat broke, I went to some editors I knew, describing the Gambian miracle, and my desire to pursue the research; Doubleday contracted to publish, and Reader's Digest to condense the projected book; then I had advances to travel further.

In what sense is everyone's personal history the story of millions?

What ship brought Kinte to Grandma's " 'Naplis" (Annapolis, Md., obviously)? The old *griot's* time reference to "king's soldiers" sent me flying to London. Feverish searching at last identified, in British Parliament records, "Colonel O'Hare's Forces," dispatched in mid-1767 to protect the then British-held James Fort whose ruins I'd visited. So Kunta Kinte was down in some ship probably sailing later that summer from the Gambia River to Annapolis.

Now I feel it was fated that I had taught myself to write in the U.S. Coast Guard. For the sea dramas I had concentrated on had given me years of experience searching among yellowing old U.S. maritime records. So now in English 18th-century marine records I finally tracked ships reporting themselves in and out to the Commandant of the Gambia River's James Fort. And then early one afternoon I found that a Lord Ligonier under a Captain Thomas Davies had sailed on the Sabbath of July 5, 1767. Her cargo: 3,265 elephants' teeth, 3,700 pounds of beeswax, 800 pounds of cotton, 32 ounces of Gambian gold, and 140 slaves; her destination: "Annapolis."

That night I recrossed the Atlantic. In the Library of Congress the Lord Ligonier arrival was one brief line: "Shipping In The Port Of Annapolis—1748–1775." I located the author, Vaughan W. Brown, in his Baltimore brokerage office. He drove to Historic Annapolis, the city's historical society, and found me further documentation of her arrival on Sept. 29, 1767. (Exactly two centuries later, Sept. 29, 1967, standing, staring seaward from an Annapolis pier again I knew tears.) More help came in the Maryland Hall of Records. Archivist Phebe Jacobsen found the Lord Ligonier's arriving customs declaration listing, "98 Negroes"—so in her 86-day crossing, 42 Gambians had died, one among the survivors being 16-year-old Kunta Kinte. Then the microfilmed Oct. 1, 1767, Maryland Gazette contained, on page two, an announcement to prospective buyers from the ship's agents, Daniel of St. Thos. Jenifer and John Ridout (the Governor's secretary): "from the River GAMBIA, in AFRICA . . . a cargo of choice, healthy SLAVES . . ."

Assignment 1

BEGINNING YOUR STUDY OF FAMILY HISTORY

Your first assignment is to begin the process of generating data on your own family's history. The Appendix of this book provides a number of aids for this task. The most logical starting point is the section in the Appendix entitled "Researching and Writing Your Family History" (pp. 235–253), which supplies clues on how to go about finding information. The papers also found in the Appendix (pp. 254–268) show the kinds of essays you may turn out after completing this book and your research.

After reading these sections, you should start collecting information. First, fill in the form on "Yourself" (p. 280) and as much of the genealogical chart (either one of the two supplied on pp. 277 and 279) as you can. Next, if you live at home, gather information requested about the other members of your family on the remaining forms

(pp. 281–288). If you are living away from home, write a letter explaining what you are doing, and ask that the information be sent to you. At your next opportunity, see what you can discover around your house. (Ask permission when appropriate!) You may turn up photographs, certificates, wills, deeds, diaries, family bibles, and so on. Try to find out the specific places where your ancestors spent their lives, both in this country and, if possible, in the society of their birth if other than the United States. Where feasible, write letters to officials in those places (to the city or county clerk, probate court, or foreign consulates in the United States) to find out how to obtain pertinent family documents. Let your librarian or instructor help you to locate these places on a map and suggest ways of establishing contacts.

two

The Self Examined

Everyone, regardless of his background or position in life, is interested in himself. Part of the fascination of reading a novel or watching a movie is, after all, the feeling of identification with the characters depicted. Autobiography has much the same appeal, for in following the author's memories and self-analysis, it is easy to move to one's own memories and to probe for meaning and understanding from one's own past. Usually autobiographies are written by the famous, but certainly one does not have to be famous to write and think autobiographically. In fact, without realizing it, we do it every day. The old man recalling stories of his youth for his grandson; the mother suggesting in pride or in anger that when she was a girl, "things were different"; brothers and sisters sharing their conflicting memories of the same event—all are examples of thinking in this manner.

The two selections that follow—one by a girl who grew up in an affluent suburb, the other by a boy raised in an inner-city slum—are examples of autobiographic accounts by ordinary people. In one sense they are unrepresentative of the kind of self-evaluation that most people undertake in trying to make sense out of their backgrounds: in general, people do not take the trouble to write down their family legends or their recollections of childhood and adolescence. But in another, more important sense they are typical because the factors that they represent as having had the most influence on their lives have probably had a similar impact on lives like our own. For both, the influence of the community where they were born and grew up was a marked one. It determined, for instance, how they spent their free time—in front of a television set or on the streets with a gang. Their

respective socioeconomic classes, too, played a recognizable part in shaping their lives and their expectations for the future, since, obviously, being affluent or very poor affects not only the physical conditions of life but attitudes that grow from these conditions. And, although both are not consciously aware of it, the sex roles they were expected to assume had a large influence on the course of their actions.

Perhaps you will find that you have little in common with either of the authors. If, for example, you have moved many times, you may lack their sense of belonging to a particular community. But, then, examining the differences that you feel between yourself and the authors may prove just as significant in providing clues to yourself as recognizing those social factors that you share with them. And, there are many other factors besides. In the past, religion and ethnicity were important in establishing the identities of a vast number of immigrant Americans and, with race, continue to have an influence—for some, a major one—on the quality of life. In the end, of course, our experience is shaped not only by abstract social forces but also by the people with whom we associate. Perhaps, then, you can point to a particular individual—a parent, teacher, or friend—who gave your life its particular impetus.

Obviously, your life is too complex to be totally explained in terms of a few social factors. Yet by studying and thinking about some of the intertwined lines of influence, you can begin to appreciate the history of which you are a part. Through this self-examination, moreover, you will be taking the first step toward understanding your society.

an 18-year-old looks back on life
JOYCE MAYNARD

What kinds of things do you remember from your first year in high school? What do you think of when you fix your mind on your hometown? Do you remember the words to songs, or the best place you ever lived, or a special friend, or a scary movie or television show? What do you recall about the big events, like the Vietnam War or riots on college campuses and in city streets?

Everyone has his or her own special memories, and each generation shares certain experiences that are in detail different from the memories of both older and younger generations. Even within the same generation, experiences and the influences that shaped those experiences tend to be very different, as the following essay makes clear.

The author, born in 1953, is probably older than you. She is quite convinced that the thousands of hours that she spent watching television had an enormous effect on how she came to understand the world. Has it been much the same for you? Has the impact of television contributed to separating the life you lead from that of your parents who grew into adolescence before the television era? Do you ever worry about the dire predictions of critics who fear that immersion in television is producing a passive, semiliterate generation with a distorted set of values and skewed sense of reality?

As you read the following essay, consider too the ways in which the essayist's ideas reflect her social class. Why do people in secure and comfortable lives tend to have very different concerns and interests from people with fewer advantages? Can you specify the factors that determine your social class and how and where you live?

Every generation thinks it's special—my grandparents because they remember horses and buggies, my parents because of the Depression. The over-30's are special because they knew the Red Scare of Korea, Chuck Berry and beatniks. My older sister is special because she belonged to the first generation of teen-agers (before that, people in their teens were *adolescents*), when being a teen-ager was still fun. And I— I am 18, caught in the middle. Mine is the generation of unfulfilled expectations. "When you're older," my mother promised, "you can wear lipstick." But when the time came, of course, lipstick wasn't being worn. "When we're big, we'll dance like that," my friends and I whispered, watching Chubby Checker twist on "American Bandstand." But we inherited no dance steps, ours was a limp, formless shrug to watered-down music that rarely made the feet tap. "Just wait till we can vote," I said, bursting with 10-year-old fervor, ready to fast, freeze, march and die for peace and freedom as Joan Baez, barefoot, sang "We Shall Overcome." Well, now we can vote, and we're old enough to attend rallies and knock on doors and wave placards, and suddenly it doesn't seem to matter any more.

My generation is special because of what we missed rather than what we got, because in a certain sense we are the first and the last. The first to take technology for granted. (What was a space shot to us, except an hour cut from Social Studies to gather before a TV in the gym as Cape Canaveral counted down?) The first to grow up with TV. My sister was 8 when we got our set, so to her it seemed magic and always somewhat foreign. She had known books already and would never really replace them. But for me, the TV set was, like the kitchen sink and the telephone, a fact of life.

We inherited a previous generation's hand-me-downs and took in the seams, turned up the hems, to make our new fashions. We took drugs from the college kids and made them a high-school commonplace. We got the Beatles, but not those lovable look-alikes in matching suits with barber cuts and songs that made you want to cry. They came to us like a bad joke—aged, bearded, discordant. And we inherited the Vietnam war just after the crest of the wave—too late to burn draft cards and too early not to be drafted. The boys of 1953—my year—will be the last to go.

Do you share her feeling that politics is irrelevant?

Is TV as essential as the kitchen sink in American life?

The roles acceptable to many women have changed enormously just in your own lifetime. In the 1960s feminists took to the streets to make their concerns known to the public. But how much has the Women's Movement changed national attitudes? Are the majorettes or the advocates more typical of the young women you know? Is it possible to be both a costumed sex symbol and a believer in equality for women?

So where are we now? Generalizing is dangerous. Call us the apathetic generation and we will become that. Say times are changing, nobody cares about prom queens and getting into the college of his choice any more—say that (because it sounds good, it indicates a trend, gives a symmetry to history) and you make a movement and a unit out of a generation unified only in its common fragmentation. If there is a reason why we are where we are, it comes from where we have been.

Like overanxious patients in analysis, we treasure the traumas of our childhood. Ours was more traumatic than most. The Kennedy assassination has become our myth: Talk to us for an evening or two—about movies or summer jobs or Nixon's trip to China or the weather—and the subject will come up ("Where were *you* when you heard?"), as if having lived through Jackie and the red roses, John-John's salute and Oswald's on-camera murder justifies our disenchantment.

Does the Kennedy assassination have special significance only for those who have first-hand memories of it?

We haven't all emerged the same, of course, because our lives were lived in high-school corridors and drive-in hamburger joints as well as in the pages of Time and Life, and the images on the TV screen. National events and personal memory blur so that, for me, Nov. 22, 1963, was a birthday party that had to be called off and Armstrong's moonwalk was my first full can of beer. If you want to know who we are now; if you wonder how we'll vote, or whether we will, or whether, 10 years from now, we'll end up just like all those other generations that thought they were special—with 2.2 kids and a house in Connecticut—if that's what you're wondering, look to the past because, whether we should blame it or not, we do.

. . .

If I had spent at the piano the hours I gave to television, on all those afternoons when I came home from school, I would be an accomplished pianist now. Or if I'd danced, or read, or painted . . . But I turned on the set instead, every day, almost, every year, and sank into an old green easy chair, smothered in quilts, with a bag of Fritos beside me and a glass of milk to wash them down, facing life and death with Dr. Kildare, laughing at Danny Thomas, whispering the answers—out loud sometimes—with "Password" and "To Tell the Truth." Looking back over all those afternoons, I try to convince myself they weren't wasted. I must have learned something; I must, at least, have changed.

Why this concern over wasting time? Is this a middle-class attitude?

What I learned was certainly not what TV tried to teach me. From the reams of trivia collected over years of quiz shows, I remember only the questions, never the answers. I loved "Leave It to Beaver" for the messes Beaver got into, not for the inevitable lecture from Dad at the end of each show. I saw every episode two or three times, witnessed Beaver's aging, his legs getting longer and his voice lower, only to start all over again with young Beaver every fall. (Someone told me recently that the boy who played Beaver Cleaver died in Vietnam. The news was a shock—I kept coming back to it for days until another distressed Beaver fan wrote to tell me that it wasn't true after all.)

I got so I could predict punch lines and endings, not really knowing whether I'd seen the episode before or only watched one like it. There was the bowling-ball routine, for instance: Lucy, Dobie Gillis, Pete and Gladys—they all used it. Somebody would get his finger stuck in a bowling ball (Lucy later updated the gimmick using Liz Taylor's ring) and then they'd have to go to a wedding or give a speech at the P.T.A. or have the boss to dinner, concealing one hand all the while. We weren't supposed to ask questions like "Why don't they just tell the truth?" These shows were built on deviousness, on the longest distance between two points, and on a kind of symmetry which decrees that no loose ends shall be left untied, no lingering doubts allowed. (The Surgeon General is off the track in worrying about TV violence, I think. I grew up in the days before lawmen became peacemakers. What carries over is not the gunfights but the memory that everything always turned out all right.) Optimism shone through all those half hours I spent in the dark shadows of the TV room—out of evil shall come good.

Does TV still reflect the same optimism today?

Most of all, the situation comedies steeped me in American culture. I emerged from years of TV viewing indifferent to the museums of France, the architecture of Italy, the literature of England. A perversely homebound American, I pick up paperbacks in bookstores, checking before I buy to see if the characters have foreign names, whether the action takes place in London or New York. Vulgarity and banality fascinate me. More intellectual friends (who watch no TV) can't understand what I see in "My Three Sons." "Nothing happens," they say. "The characters are dull, plastic, faceless. Every show is the same." I guess that's why I watch them—boring repetition is, itself, a rhythm—a steady pulse of flashing Coca-Cola signs, McDonald's Golden Arches and Howard Johnson roofs.

What human need does repetitiveness or predictability satisfy?

20

I don't watch TV as an anthropologist, rising loftily above my subject to analyze. Neither do I watch, as some kids now tune in to reruns of "The Lone Ranger" and "Superman" (in the same spirit they enjoy comic books and pop art) for their camp. I watch in earnest. How can I do anything else? Five thousand hours of my life have gone into this box.

• • •

Ask us whose face is on the $5 bill and we may not know the answer. But nearly everyone my age remembers a cover of Life magazine that came out in the spring of 1965, part of a series of photographs that enter my dreams and my nightmares still. They were the first shots ever taken of an unborn fetus, curled up tightly in a sack of veins and membranes, with blue fingernails and almost transparent skin that made the pictures look like double exposures. More than the moon photographs a few years later, that grotesque figure fascinated me as the map of a new territory. It was often that way with photographs in Life—the issue that reported on the "In Cold Blood" murders; a single picture of a boy falling from an airplane and another of a woman who had lost 200 pounds. (I remember the faces of victims and killers from seven or eight years ago, while the endless issues on Rome and nature studies are entirely lost.)

Photographs are the illustrations for a decade of experiences. Just as, when we think of "Alice in Wonderland," we all see Tenniel's drawings, and when we think of the Cowardly Lion, we all see Bert Lahr, so, when we think of Lyndon Johnson's airborne swearing-in as President in 1963, we have a common image furnished by magazines, and when we think of fetuses, now, those cabbages we were supposed to have come from and smiling, golden-haired cherubs have been replaced forever by the cover of Life. Having had so many pictures to grow up with, we share a common visual idiom and have far less room for personal vision. The movie versions of books decide for us what our heroes and villains will look like, and we are powerless to change the camera's decree. So, while I was stunned and fascinated by that eerie fetus (where is he now, I wonder, and are those pictures in his family album?) I'm saddened too, knowing what it did to me. If I were asked to pinpoint major moments in my growing up, experiences that changed me, the sight of that photograph would be one.

Do TV, movies, and magazines kill personal imagination?

• • •

Everyone is raised on nursery rhymes and nonsense stories. But it used to be when you grew up, the nonsense disappeared. Not for us—it is at the core of our music and literature and art and, in fact, of our lives. Like characters in an Ionesco play, we take absurdity unblinking. In a world where military officials tell us "We had to destroy the village in order to save it," Dylan lyrics make an odd kind of sense. They aren't meant to be understood; they don't jar our sensibilities because we're used to *non sequiturs*. We don't take anything too seriously these days. (Was it a thousand earthquake victims or a million? Does it matter?) The casual butcher's-operation in the film "M*A*S*H" and the comedy in Vonnegut and the album cover showing John and Yoko, bareback, are all part of the new absurdity. The days of the Little Moron joke and the elephant joke and the knock-knock joke are gone. It sounds melodramatic, but the joke these days is life.

Are teen-agers today as cynical as they are portrayed here?

You're not supposed to care too much any more. Reactions have been scaled down from screaming and jelly-bean-throwing to nodding your head and maybe—if the music really gets to you (and music's the only thing that does any more)—tapping a finger. We need a passion transfusion, a shot of energy in the veins. It's what I'm most impatient with, in my generation—this languid, I-don't-give-a-s——— -ism that stems in part, at least, from a culture of put-ons in which any serious expression of emotion is branded sentimental and old-fashioned. The fact that we set such a premium on being cool reveals a lot about my generation; the idea is not to care. You can hear it in the speech of college students today: cultivated monotones, low volume, punctuated with four-letter words that come off sounding only bland. I feel it most of all on Saturday morning, when the sun is shining and the crocuses are about to bloom and, walking through the corridors of my dorm, I see there isn't anyone awake.

Is music the only thing that gets to you?

• • •

We feel cheated, many of us—the crop of 1953—which is why we complain about inheriting problems we didn't cause. (Childhood notions of justice, reinforced by Perry Mason, linger on. Why should I clean up someone else's mess? Who can I blame?) We're

An American born in the 1950s who lives to be seventy may watch more than 50,000 hours of television in his or her lifetime. People, regardless of age or class, seem mesmerized by its offerings—no matter how thin. What common need does TV seem to satisfy? What function does it serve for you?

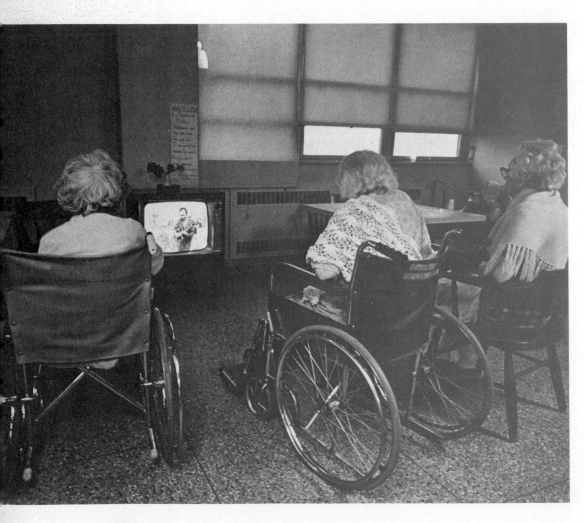

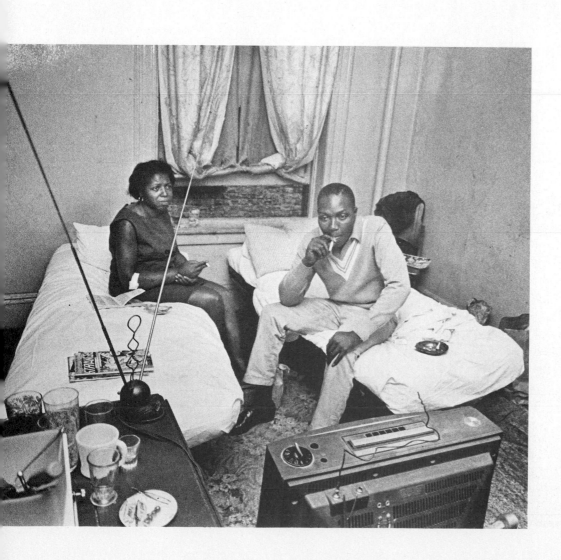

Demonstration, especially antiwar protest, was a common form of social activism in the 1960s. Do you think this kind of activism died because of a lack of causes or because people came to regard mass protest as ineffective? Do you feel politically effective now? Long hair was a form of protest for young men in the 1960s. Do hair styles and clothes still transmit signals of protest?

excited also, of course: I can't wait to see how things turn out. But I wish I weren't quite so involved, I wish it weren't my life that's being turned into a suspense thriller.

When my friends and I were little, we had big plans. I would be a famous actress and singer, dancing on the side. I would paint my own sets and compose my own music, writing the script and the lyrics and reviewing the performance for the New York Times. I would marry and have three children (they don't allow us dreams like that any more) and we would live, rich and famous (donating lots to charity, of course, and periodically adopting orphans), in a house we designed ourselves. When I was older I had visions of good works. I saw myself in South American rain forests and African deserts, feeding the hungry and healing the sick, with an obsessive selflessness, I see now, as selfish, in the end, as my original plans for stardom.

Now my goal is simpler. I want to be happy. And I want comfort—nice clothes, a nice house, good music and good food, and the feeling that I'm doing some little thing that matters. I'll vote and I'll give to charity, but I won't give myself. I feel a sudden desire to buy land—not a lot, not as a business investment, but just a small plot of earth so that whatever they do to the country I'll have a place where I can go—a kind of fallout shelter, I guess. As some people prepare for their old age, so I prepare for my 20's. A little house, a comfortable chair, peace and quiet—retirement sounds tempting.

Is the desire for selfless service ultimately selfish?

Have your goals been scaled down from what they were five years ago?

24

Down These Mean Streets
Piri Thomas

Growing up affluent in suburbia as Joyce Maynard did is one extreme in the range of possible American experiences. There are millions of Americans, however, who have lived at the other extreme, growing up poor in the city. In the following article, Piri Thomas gives an account of coming of age on the mean streets of Spanish Harlem. His world is one of gangs, drugs, and violence, where mere survival is a day-to-day struggle. To what extent is your experience similar to that of Piri Thomas? The constant need to assert one's rights and to establish one's identity through gangs and fighting is primarily a male experience. Yet everyone, in one way or another, must announce, as the author does, "Hey, World—here I am."

YEE-AH!! Wanna know how many times I've stood on a rooftop
   and yelled out to anybody
"Hey, World—here I am. Hallo, World—this is Piri. That's me.
"I wanna tell ya I'm here—you bunch of mother-jumpers—I'm here, and I want
   recognition, whatever that mudder-fuckin word means."

Man! How many times have I stood on the rooftop of my broken-down building
   at night and watched the bulb-lit world below.
Like somehow it's different at night, this my Harlem. There ain't no bright sunlight
   to reveal the stark naked truth of garbage-lepered streets.
Gone is the drabness and hurt, covered by a friendly night.
It makes clean the dirty-faced kids.

This is a bright *mundo* [world], my streets, my *barrio de noche* [ghetto of night],
With its thousands of lights, hundreds of millions of colors
Mingling with noises, swinging street sounds of cars and curses,
Sounds of joys and sobs that make music.
If anyone listens real close, he can hear its heart beat—

YEE-AH! I feel like part of the shadows that make company for me in this warm
   amigo darkness.
I am "My Majesty Piri Thomas," with a high on anything and like a stoned king,
   I gotta survey my kingdom.
I'm a skinny, dark-face, curly-haired, intense Porty-Ree-can—
Unsatisfied, hoping, and always reaching.

Have you ever felt ambivalent about the place where you grew up?

I got a feeling of aloneness and a bitterness that's growing and growing
Day by day into some kind of hate without *un nombre* [a name].
Yet when I look down at the streets below, I can't help thinking
It's like a great big dirty Christmas tree with lights but no fuckin presents.
And man, my head starts growing bigger than my body as it gets crammed full of
   hate.

And I begin to listen to the sounds inside me.
Get angry, get hating angry, and you won't be scared.
What have you got now? Nothing.
What will you ever have? Nothing.
. . . Unless you cop for yourself!

Is his experience of alienation the same as Joyce Maynard's?

    Hanging around on the block is a sort of science. You have a lot to do and a lot of nothing to do. In the winter there's dancing, pad combing, movies, and the like. But summer is really the kick. All the blocks are alive, like many-legged cats crawling with fleas. People are all over the place. Stoops are occupied like bleacher sections at a game, and beer flows like there's nothing else to drink. The block musicians pound out gone beats on tin cans and conga drums and bongos. And kids are playing all over the place —on fire escapes, under cars, in alleys, back yards, hallways.

    We rolled marbles along the gutter edge, trying to crack them against the enemy marbles, betting five and ten marbles on being able to span the rolled distance between your marbles and the other guy's. We stretched to the limit skinny fingers with dirty gutter water caked between them, completely oblivious to the islands of dog filth, people filth, and street filth that lined the gutter.

    That gutter was more dangerous than we knew. There was a kid we called Dopey, a lopsided-looking kid who was always drooling at the mouth. Poor Dopey would do anything you'd tell him, and one day somebody told him to drink dirty street water. He got sick, and the ambulance from City Hospital came and took him away. The next time we saw Dopey, he was in a coffin box in his house. He didn't look dopey at all; he looked like any of us, except he was stone dead.

Is hanging around restricted to the ghetto? If not, how does it differ elsewhere?

Where you grew up may have had an influence on what you did. Even the smallest details, for example, how you got to school, were probably influenced by your locale. The sum of these details gave a distinctive pace or beat to your life. What rhythms are implicit in these three photos of school transportation? Which suggests your own background, and do you identify or rebel against that rhythm?

All of us went to Dopey's funeral. We were sweeter to him in death than we ever had been in life. I thought about death, that bogeyman we all knew as kids, which came only to the other guy, never to you. You would live forever. There in front of Dopey's very small, very cheap coffin I promised myself to live forever; that no matter what, I'd never die.

For a few days after Dopey's funeral we talked about how Dopey now was in a big hole in the ground till his bones grew rotten and how none of us was afraid of death or dying. I even described how I'd die and breathe my last. I did the whole bit, acting out every detail. I had a kid hold my head in his lap while I spoke about leaving for the last roundup in the ranch house up yonder, an idea I got from a Johnny Mack Brown cowboy flicker. It was swell acting. I ended with a long, shuddering expelling of breath, a rolling of the eyeballs, whites showing carefully, and jaws falling slack amidst cries of "Holy Jesus" and "Man, what a fuckin' actor that guy is!" Then I arose from my flat sidewalk slab of death, dusted myself off, looked around and said "Hey, man, let's play Johnny-on-the-Pony, one-two-three."

At thirteen or fourteen we played a new game—copping girls' drawers. It became part of our street living—and sometimes a messy part. Getting yourself a chick was a rep builder. But I felt that bragging to other fellas about how many cherries I'd cracked or how many panties came down on rooftops or back yards was nobody's business but my own, and besides, I was afraid my old lady would find out and I'd get my behind wasted. And anyway it was better to play mysterious with the guys at bullshit sessions, just play it cool as to who and how you copped.

It was all part of becoming *hombre* [a man], of wanting to have a beard to shave, a driver's license, a draft card, a "stoneness" which enabled you to go into a bar like a man. Nobody really digs a kid. But a man—cool. Nobody can tell you what to do—and nobody better. You'd smack him down like Whiplash does in the cowboy flick or really light him up like Scarface in that gangster picture—swoon, crack, bang, bang, bang—short-nose, snub-nose pistol, and a machine gun, and a poor fuckin' loud-mouth is laid out.

Does the idea of death affect you in the same way?

What does "becoming a man" mean to you? Is there anything comparable in "becoming a woman"?

Games sometimes acquire a distinctive character because of their surroundings. How might this basketball game be transformed if it were played in uniforms, in a gymnasium? How would the baseball game pictured below be played on a city street?

That was the way I felt. And sometimes what I did, although it was real enough, was only a pale shadow of what I felt. Like playing stickball . . .

I stood at the side of the sewer that made home plate in the middle of the street, waiting impatiently for the Spalding ball to be bounced my way, my broomstick bat swinging back and forth.

"Come on, man, pitch the ball!" I shouted.

"Take it easy, buddy," the pitcher said.

I was burning, making all kinds of promises to send that rubber ball smashing into his teeth whenever he decided to let it go.

"Come on, Piri, lose that ball—smack it clear over to Lexington Avenue."

"Yeah, yeah, watch me."

The ball finally left that hoarder's hand. It came in on one bounce, like it was supposed to, and slightly breaking into a curve. It was all mine.

"Waste it, *panín* [pal]," shouted my boy Waneko.

I gritted my teeth and ran in to meet the ball. I felt the broomstick bat make connection and the ball climb and climb like it was never coming back. It had "home run" all over it. One runner came in and I was right behind him. My boys pushed out their hands to congratulate me. We had twelve *bolos* [dollars] on the game. I slapped skin with them, playing it cool all the way. Man, that was the way to be.

Does "making it" in sports still confer status for boys?

• • •

We were moving—our new pad was back in Spanish Harlem—to 104th Street between Lex and Park Avenue.

Moving into a new block is a big jump for a Harlem kid. You're torn up from your hard-won turf and brought into an "I don't know you" block where every kid is some kind of enemy. Even when the block belongs to your own people, you are still an outsider who has to prove himself a down stud with heart.

Why do all groups have initiation rites?

As the moving van rolled to a stop in front of our new building, number 109, we were all standing there, waiting for it—Momma, Poppa, Sis, Paulie, James, José, and myself. I made out like I didn't notice the cats looking us over, especially me—I was gang age. I read their faces and found no trust, plenty of suspicion, and a glint of rising hate. I said to myself, *These cats don't mean nothin'. They're just nosy.* But I remembered what had happened to me in my old block, and that it had ended with me in the hospital.

This was a tough-looking block. That was good, that was cool; but my turf had been tough, too. *I'm tough,* a voice within said. *I hope I'm tough enough. I am tough enough. I've got* mucho corazón [*much heart*], *I'm king wherever I go. I'm a killer to my heart. I not only can live, I will live, no punk out, no die out, walk bad; be down, cool breeze, smooth.* My mind raced, and thoughts crashed against each other, trying to reassemble themselves into a pattern of rep. I turned slowly and with eyelids half-closed I looked at the rulers of this new world and with a cool shrug of my shoulders I followed the movers into the hallway of number 109 and dismissed the coming war from my mind.

The next morning I went to my new school, called Patrick Henry, and strange, mean eyes followed me.

"Say, pops," said a voice belonging to a guy I later came to know as Waneko, "where's your territory?"

In the same tone of voice Waneko had used, I answered, "I'm on it, dad, what's shaking?"

What part does language play in establishing your identity?

"Bad, huh?" He half-smiled.

"No, not all the way. Good when I'm cool breeze and bad when I'm down."

"What's your name, kid?"

"That depends. 'Piri' when I'm smooth and 'Johnny Gringo' when stomping time's around."

"What's your name now?" he pushed.

"You name me, man," I answered, playing my role like a champ.

He looked around, and with no kind of words, his boys cruised in. Guys I would come to know, to fight, to hate, to love, to take care of. Little Red, Waneko, Little Louie, Indio, Carlito, Alfredo, Crip, and plenty more. I stiffened and said to myself, *Stomping time, Piri boy, go with heart.*

I fingered the garbage-can handle in my pocket—my homemade brass knuckles. They were great for breaking down large odds into small, chopped-up ones.

Waneko, secure in his grandstand, said, "We'll name you later, *panín.*"

I didn't answer. Scared, yeah, but wooden-faced to the end, I thought, *Chevere, panín* [Great, pal].

29

It wasn't long in coming. Three days later, at about 6 p.m., Waneko and his boys were sitting around the stoop at number 115. I was cut off from my number 109. For an instant I thought, *Make a break for it down the basement steps and through the back yards—get away in one piece!* Then I thought, *Caramba! Live punk, dead hero. I'm no punk kid. I'm not copping any pleas.* I kept walking, hell's a-burning, hell's a-churning, rolling with cheer. *Walk on, baby man, roll on without fear. What's he going to call?*

"Whatta ya say, Mr. Johnny Gringo?" drawled Waneko.

Think, man, I told myself, *think your way out of a stomping. Make it good.* "I hear you 104th Street coolies are supposed to have heart," I said. "I don't know this for sure. You know there's a lot of streets where a whole 'click' is made out of punks who can't fight one guy unless they all jump him for the stomp." I hoped this would push Waneko into giving me a fair one. His expression didn't change.

"Maybe we don't look at it that way."

Crazy, man. I cheer inwardly, the cabrón [*chump*] *is falling into my setup. We'll see who gets messed up first, baby!* "I wasn't talking to you," I said. "Where I come from, the pres is president 'cause he got heart when it comes to dealing."

Waneko was starting to look uneasy. He had bit on my worm and felt like a sucker fish. His boys were now light on me. They were no longer so much interested in stomping me as in seeing the outcome between Waneko and me. "Yeah," was his reply.

I smiled at him. "You trying to dig where I'm at and now you got me interested in you. I'd like to see where you're at."

Waneko hesitated a tiny little second before replying, "Yeah."

I knew I'd won. Sure, I'd have to fight; but one guy, not ten or fifteen. If I lost I might still get stomped, and if I won I might get stomped. I took care of this with my next sentence. "I don't know you or your boys," I said, "but they look cool to me. They don't feature as punks."

I had left him out purposely when I said "they." Now his boys were in a separate class. I had cut him off. He would have to fight me on his own, to prove his heart to himself, to his boys, and most important, to his turf. He got away from the stoop and asked, "Fair one, Gringo?"

"Uh-uh," I said, "roll all the way—anything goes." I thought, *I've got to beat him bad and yet not bad enough to take his prestige all away.* He had *corazón.* He came on me. *Let him draw first blood,* I thought, *it's his block.* Smish, my nose began to bleed. His boys cheered, his heart cheered, his turf cheered. "Waste this chump," somebody shouted.

Okay, baby, now it's my turn. He swung. I grabbed innocently, and my forehead smashed into his nose. His eyes crossed. His fingernails went for my eye and landed in my mouth—crunch, I bit hard. I punched him in the mouth as he pulled away from me, and he slammed his foot into my chest.

We broke, my nose running red, my chest throbbing, his finger—well, that was his worry. I tied up with body punching and slugging. We rolled onto the street. I wrestled for acceptance, he for rejection or, worse yet, acceptance on his terms. It was time to start peace talks. I smiled at him. "You got heart, baby," I said.

He answered with a punch to my head. I grunted and hit back, harder now. I had to back up my overtures of peace with strength. I hit him in the ribs, I rubbed my knuckles in his ear as we clinched. I tried again. "You deal good," I said.

"You too," he muttered, pressuring out. And just like that, the fight was over. No more words. We just separated, hands half up, half down. My heart pumped out, *You've established your rep. Move over, 104th Street. Lift your wings, I'm one of your baby chicks now.*

Five seconds later my spurs were given to me in the form of introductions to streetdom's elite. There were no looks of blankness now; I was accepted by heart.

"What's your other name, Johnny Gringo?"

"Piri."

"Okay, Pete, you wanna join my fellows?"

"Sure, why not?"

But I knew I had first joined their gang when I cool-looked them on moving day. *I was cool, man,* I thought. *I could've wasted Waneko any time, I'm good, I'm damned good, pure* corazón. *Viva me!* Shit, I had been scared, but that was over. I was in; it was *my* block now.

Not that I could relax. In Harlem you always lived on the edge of losing rep. All it takes is a one-time loss of heart.

30

Is facing violence mainly a ghetto experience or is it a universally male one?

What else is involved here besides a physical challenge?

Why these rules and emphasis upon fair play in an essentially chaotic situation?

What do you think of the idea of "coolness" —emotionless strength —as a male ideal?

When you were in high school, what kind of activity was most important to you? Was it, as the picture above suggests, an informal activity like "hanging out" on a street corner? Or was it spending time in classes or other more formal groups? How did your community, economic and social class, or sex influence how you spent your time?

...

"You wan' some?" I heard a voice near me say.

I opened my eye a little. I saw a hand, and between its fingers was a stick of pot. I didn't look up at the face. I just plucked the stick from the fingers. I heard the feminine voice saying, "You gonna like thees pot. Eet's good stuff."

I felt its size. It was king-sized, a bomber. I put it to my lips and began to hiss my reserve away. It was going, going, going. I was gonna get a gone high. I inhaled. I held my nose, stopped up my mouth. I was gonna get a gone high . . . a gone high . . . a gone high . . . and then the stick was gone, burnt to a little bit of a roach.

Were drugs a part of your experience of growing up?

I got to thinking way-out thoughts on a way-out kick. The words went wasting each other in a mad race inside my head. *Hey world, do you know these mean streets is like a clip machine? It takes, an' keeps on taking, till it makes a cat feel like every day is something that's gotta be forgotten. But there's good things, too, man. Like standing together with your boys, and feeling like king. Like being down for anything, even though you're scared sweat will stand out all over you and your brave heart wants to crawl out through your pores.*

Man! You meet your boys and make it to a jump, where you can break night dancing. You walk down them streets and you feel tall and tough. You dig people watching you an' walk a little more boppy. You let your tailormade hang cool between tight lips, unlit, and when you talk, your voice is soft and deep. Your shoulders brush against your boys. Music pours out of candy stores, restaurants and open windows and you feel good-o at the greatness of the sounds. You see the five-story crumbling building where the dance is happening. You flick your eyeballs around from force of habit, to see if any of the Jolly Rogers [another gang] are around. The shit's on. But nobody like that's around, so you all make it up the stairs, and the sounds of shoes beating them long, dead wooden steps make it sound like a young army going to war. It's only nine guys, but each is a down stud. You think about how many boys you got an' it's more than you need.

The set is on the fifth floor and the floor is creaking an' groaning under the weight of all the coolies that are swinging. You dig the open door of the roof and smell burning pot. It smells like burned leaves. You and your boys dig each other for the same idea and, like one, make it up to the roof. Joints are pulled out of the brims of hats and soon there's no noise except the music and the steady hiss of cats blasting away on kick-sticks.

Then it comes—the tight feeling, like a rubber band being squeezed around your forehead. You feel your Adam's apple doing an up-an'-down act—gulp, gulp, gulp—and you feel great—great, dammit! So fine, so smooth. You like this feeling of being air-light, with your head tight. You like the sharpness of your ears as they dig the mambo music coming up the stairs. You hear every note clear. You have the power to pick out one instrument from another. Bongos, congas, flute, piano, maracas, marimba. You keep in time with your whole body and swinging soul, and all of a sudden you're in the middle, hung up with a chick; and the music is soft and she's softer, and you make the most of grinding against her warmth. Viva, viva, viva!

Then the Jolly Rogers walk in and everybody starts dealing. Your boys are fighting and you fall in with them. Bottles are hitting everything but the walls. You feel somebody put his damn fist square in your damn mouth and split your damn lip and you taste your own sweet blood—and all of a sudden you're really glad you came. You're glad you smoked pot, you're glad somebody punched you in the mouth; you're glad for another chance to prove how much heart you got. You scream mad and your mouth is full of "motherfuckers!" and you swing out hard. Ah, chevere! *That broke his fuckin' nose.*

Everybody's screaming; there's sounds of feet kicking fallen bad men; there's sounds of chicks screaming "Po-leece" outta open windows. Then the police siren is heard. It sounds like a stepped-on bitch. A blank is put on the rumble and everybody puts the law into effect. The fight stops and everybody makes it outta the place like it had caught fire. We still hate each other, but we hate the cops worse.

Everybody splits and beats it over hills and over dales—and over rooftops. You feel so good that when the cops make it up them five flights, they ain't gonna find nothing but a sad Puerto Rican record playing a sad bolero called "Adiós, motherfuckers."

Yeah. But the best is the walk back to the block, with the talk about the heart shown in the rumble, the questions put down and the answers given. The look of pride and the warmth of hurts received and given. And each cat makes it to his pad to cop a nod and have his dreams, sweetened by his show of corazón. *Yeah, man, we sure messed them Jolly Rogers up . . .*

Is there anything in this fantasy ideal with which you can identify?

32

A BRIEF AUTOBIOGRAPHICAL ESSAY

Turn to the Appendix and on page 280, if you have not already done so, fill out the form "Yourself." Since these notes are your own personal possessions, you can feel totally free to respond to the categories. This is so with all of the information requested in the Appendix. Its only purpose is to serve as a convenient way of thinking about and gathering significant information for your studies.

After you have filled out the form, let a day pass before beginning the written part of this assignment. Then, review in your mind the influences that both Maynard and Thomas cited as being most significant in their lives. Now, look again at what you have written.

Worlds separate Joyce Maynard and Piri Thomas—the comfortable if uninspiring middle-class suburbs and the violent mean streets of the inner city. Yet as different as their experiences are, both essayists share a common link: each has been able to identify key factors that explain his or her life. What about you?

Unlike Piri Thomas, you may have grown up in an environment fairly free of physical danger. And perhaps you do not, like Joyce Maynard, see television as a dominating force in your development. Yet, if you think about it, you will recall significant experiences—events, people, places, ideas—that have shaped and defined you. You may even have discovered some overriding personal meaning in social class, racial, or ethnic self-identification, or struggled through a crisis that represented a dramatic turning point in your life.

Write a brief account of your own life. Follow the method used by Maynard and Thomas; that is, select pertinent factual material, put it in narrative form, and give it some interpretation. Do not just list bareboned facts in chronological order. Be selective, in the manner of the two essayists, and focus your thinking and writing on what you believe to be major influences on your own development. As a guide, aim for about 1,000 words, though you may certainly write more if you get carried away.

three

The American Dream

For generations America was the land of legendary promise and opportunity. Of course, the promise often turned to disappointment, the opportunity to defeat. Still, until very recently the myth persisted that anyone in America, regardless of race, creed, or sex, had an equal opportunity to achieve success. The events of the recent past have weakened this reverential faith in success as the automatic reward for effort and talent. But even today this American Dream remains an article of faith for many Americans.

Belief in the American Dream was particularly strong among the tens of millions of immigrants who came to these shores, particularly those who arrived in the late nineteenth and early twentieth centuries. Anxious to be free of the fetters of class and caste in traditional societies, many men and women found in America cheap land in abundance. Some sent letters home encouraging friends and relatives to leave the old country, where landholding patterns were very restrictive. Those who were less successful and who found life hard in America, were no less thankful for they found safety here from the ravages of discrimination and disease. However mean existence became in a grimy tenement, life here was preferable to the sure death of the potato famine or pogroms, or to the grinding oppression of feudalism. If the American Dream of the first generation was survival and personal freedom, their dream for their children and their children's children became much grander.

The American Dream expanded with the economic development of the nation. In the twentieth century industrialization became tied to a buildup of a consumer-oriented market, demanding an increasingly educated citizenry for ever more specialized jobs. Expectations of life proceeded apace. New industries mushroomed. Supersonic transportation systems, sophisticated communications networks, and a pervasive national media all quickly developed. For the children and grandchildren of the immigrant masses of seventy-five years ago, the dream was redefined: higher education would be the key to achieving a material life beyond the imagination of grandparents. Upward social mobility changed from a possibility to a probability, and then approached a birthright.

So strong was the faith in America to deliver on its ostensible promise that even the disastrous Great Depression of the 1930s failed to obstruct the vision. Indeed, the innumerable Hollywood "war movies" of the 1940s could unblushingly portray the average G.I. as fighting for the opportunity to return to Main Street, the girl next door, a house of his own, a good job, and a college education for the kids.

It may be necessary to explain the American Dream to many of today's students, whose own education and experience have produced a degree of skepticism generally unshared by previous generations of American young people. Some contemporary social critics even argue that the long-established American drive for success has declined markedly. Young people today, they contend, are more interested in security than in opportunity, in comfortable life styles than in the high risks and tensions that may lead to success. This turnabout may be related to a gradual disappearance of the American Dream as a motivating force.

As you read the following selections, written by people who are roughly of your parents' generation, ask yourself if you have anything in common with the goals and experiences related in them. Martha Weinman Lear emphasizes the simple but fervent patriotism of her immigrant father as a dominating influence in the shaping of her American Dream. The other three people tell of their experiences in finding that key elements of the dream were false, even nightmarish.

Mario Puzo speaks of the role of ethnic identity in defining his ideas of success, contrasting the supportive function of his family with the narrowness of their world view. Malcolm X describes the nightmare of a boy trapped in racism, poverty, and despair. Betty Friedan tells of how her dreams for the future were narrowly constricted by the role of wife and mother that she felt she had to assume.

How have the social forces these authors discuss affected your life? Has ethnicity or racial consciousness been important? Patriotism and faith in "the American way of life"? Do these factors help explain your parents' ideas concerning "making it" in American society? Have you been stung by discrimination because of ethnicity, race, sex, or religion? Is discrimination a less heavy burden today than a generation ago? Or is the old notion of the American Dream of success fading in your own generation because of the persistence of these or other injustices?

Many other questions will come to mind as you delve into what has constituted the American Dream and how it has evolved. Try to determine for yourself if there is anything of value worth retaining of the dream, or whether a new dream for the future is needed.

Of Thee I Sing

Martha Weinman Lear

Nearly every American over thirty years of age was brought up to believe that whatever the injustices and hard knocks of the past, useful work and a bit of luck would bring good fortune. As recently as a few years ago, faith in "the American way of life" often approached mystical dimensions, cushioning failures and absorbing the shock of periodic bad economic times, while at the same time promising the eventual disappearance of poverty, racism, and other persistent injustices from the land. This faith was so strong that doubters and dissenters risked much by questioning the ability of the American system to deliver on its promise.

For the vast majority of peaceful, hard-working, ordinary Americans, upward social mobility was relatively limited and hard won. Yet even the failure to discover streets filled with gold did not diminish the gratitude felt by the first generations to America nor their faith that this country would provide an abundant future for their children. The American Dream, once fully realized, would bring political freedom, educational opportunity, economic advancement, and contentment. For men, this meant secure jobs at decent wages under good working conditions. For women, the tasks of keeping house and raising children after marriage were prescribed.

This selection describes the effect of an immigrant father's patriotism in the shaping of his young daughter's sense of what was valuable in life. Notice how this strong parental nationalism was reinforced by the public school, where the girls and boys learned life's patterns for becoming "good Americans."

They still tell in our family how the 14-year-old, my father, came off the boat with a rope around his waist to hold up his pants. When he bent to kiss the ground, the rope loosened and his pants fell down. "America!" he cried.

My God, how he believed. He carried his faith into the country like baggage and hung onto it, with that fierce urgent immigrant's grip, through the sweatshops, through the Crash, through the wars, the political scandals, the Coughlins, the Ku Klux Klanners, the lynchings, whatever. They were all temporary aberrations from the eternal goodness of America, which was second only to the goodness of God.

American cops were honest (though intimidating; he never overcame that Old-Country tremor; once, when he was stopped for speeding, he went white and I thought he would faint), American politicians were omniscient and incorruptible, American millionaires were benevolent, The American Dream was real and it was upon him. It was not jingoism, never anything like that, and it was surely no belief in capitalism, of which he knew nothing. It was simply a celebration of that *safety* that shone like sun upon his home, his children, his religion, his pennies in the bank.

Once he took us from Boston to see the Statue of Liberty. It was important, he said, for the children to understand what America meant. We stood at the top of that colossus in the bay and he gestured outward with the pride of a host.

Why do you think safety was so important to immigrants?

The Boy Scouts have been an important organization for the teaching of male sex roles, patriotism and loyalty, service to the community, and other values cherished by the middle class throughout the twentieth century. Are they as important today in the community where you grew up as they once were? If not, why not? What other organizations are important in the process of socialization?

"This is the melting pot of the world," he said.

"What does it melt?" I asked.

"People," he said.

He could never understand other immigrants' complaints about the hardness of life. "You should thank God to work here," he said. "There could never be a Hitler here."

And to his children, whenever we whined about anything we couldn't have, or refused to finish the food set before us: "Shame. Think of the poor children in Europe." We were fattened on visions of the poor children in Europe.

World War II was a holy war. F.D.R. was a saint. (When he invited us in for a fireside chat, no one was allowed to speak. When he died, we cried. I don't know why, except that our elders cried. What better reason?) Truman was a *very* good person. Ike was Homeric, beyond politics. The Checkers speech was suspect, and it was true that the man was not likable, but out of this possible breach of faith my father salvaged a peculiarly American ethic. "A man deserves another chance," he said. "You can see he's sorry." Joe McCarthy was bad, but American goodness triumphed. "Have you no sense of decency, sir?" Joseph Welch intoned, and my father applauded wildly and thumped the table. "Decency!" he said. He was so proud that Joseph Welch came from Boston.

Our earliest perceptions of what it meant to be American were filtered through his own. We moved with him in a magnetic field of verities: God blesses America. A chicken in every pot. The land of plenty. The land of opportunity. Streets paved with gold (he lived poor and died poor but assumed, cheerfully, that he simply had not found the right streets. "Money doesn't buy happiness," he said). The cradle of liberty. Our boys in blue.

What elements of the American Dream does this paragraph enumerate?

Our cause is just. The land of the free and the home of the brave. Brothers under the skin. All men are created equal. Anyone can grow up to be President.

My father voted Democratic by rote, and by some cultural imperative that he only dimly understood; I never knew a Republican until I got to college. But he loved the *sound* of "two-party system," it tinkled like a soft clear bell in his ear, and in fervent lectures to his friends around our kitchen table, over the coffee, after the pinochle, he defended the right of Republicans to exist.

"Freedom means that you can pick from different things," he said. "I do not agree with what you say, but I will defend with my life . . . How does the rest of it go? You know, that saying by George Washington."

"Nathan Hale, Daddy," I said (and so believed for many years).

He beamed triumphantly around the table. "There! You see what it means to get an American education? Where else could she get an education like that."

Why did most immigrants revere education? What part of the American Dream could be achieved by education?

Thus his faith informed us, and we never had reason to doubt. It was everywhere corroborated. Each morning in school we prayed as mechanically as we brushed our teeth, invoking God's blessing upon this land. We stood, facing the flag, put our hands to our hearts and chirped: ". . . one nation, indivisible, with liberty and justice for all."

One girl brought a note from home requesting that she be excused from reciting the Pledge of Allegiance. This was wartime. She was suspended for a week, and when she returned—on condition that she recite the Pledge—we ostracized her. "Traitor!" we shrieked in the school cafeteria. I cannot imagine what we thought it meant. A teacher reprimanded us. "It's not her fault that her parents are traitors," she said.

Is it a legitimate function of schools to teach patriotism?

At assemblies we sang "America the Beautiful," rendering it, as we had been taught, up-tempo and with a great operatic rolling of the R's: ". . . And cr-r-rown thy good with br-r-rother-r-rhood/Fr-r-rom sea to shining sea!" And then, after school, we would go out into the streets of Roxbury, where the black kids were forever beating up on the Jewish kids and the Irish kids on the black kids and the police on them all. We heard no dissonance. We sensed no irony.

We went to the movies and watched our brave boys yield nothing to the Nazi torturers beyond name, rank and serial number. We hissed the Jap savages impaling infants on their bayonets. In downtown Boston we watched the grown women, the 17-year-olds, strolling on the arms of acned boys in uniform, and ached to be old enough to stroll with them. To comfort them.

We made brownies and sent them to our friends' older brothers. I won a good-citizenship contest and got to sit in the window of Filene's specialty shop, selling war bonds, wearing an Uncle Sam hat and a red, white and blue ribbon across my chest which said: "Miss Roxbury for Victory."

The son of my parents' friends was killed in action. We sat and mourned with them, and with the pregnant young widow, and someone pointed to her belly and said: "He died so his child and his grandchildren would live in peace." It was comforting. It was beyond doubt.

Why do you think this sentiment did not prevail in the 1960s?

Our school was an architectural entity split down the middle by slapped-up walls and double-locked doors, with honor students standing guard: girls' side, boys' side. On our side, we learned.

"Cleanliness is next to godliness," the home-economics teacher told us. And on the blackboard she wrote:

"The way to a man's heart is through his stomach."

We sewed pink-and-white gingham aprons. We balanced imaginary food budgets. We made chicken pot pie. We learned how to set tables and how to lift coffee stains from tablecloths.

Our American-history teacher, who had absorbed her history from others as we absorbed it from her, without question, retired to get married (imagine, we said to each other, getting married *so old;* she was 27). We gave her a farewell party. The principal, who always wore a tiny American flag in his lapel, came and told us: "Most of you girls will grow up to be wives and mothers. For a woman, there is no higher calling. . . ."

Did your mother share this conviction? Do you?

The slyness with which we prepared for that calling astounds me still. It was, after all, a war game. Battle plans, camouflages, hide-and-seek. We thought it was marvelous. We pouted, Hollywood-style. We giggled, even the smartest of us, like twits. We wriggled when we walked and wore contrivances to push whatever was there up to make a cleavage and out to make pencil-sharp points, and made our lips glisten dark and lush, like Rita Hayworth's lips, and said: "No . . . *Don't!*"

The first of the engagements was announced after the war. She came to school bearing

Americans have always had faith that their schools would turn out good citizens as well as teach the three Rs and open the doors to opportunity. An equal education for all was part of the American Dream. Can you tell something about the social, economic, and ethnic background of these children? Do you suppose these youngsters were always this alert and happy? What do today's different-looking classrooms reflect in contrast to what you see in this photo? Have the schools failed over the last generation?

on her ring finger a glinting chip that was almost lost in the baby fat of her knuckle, and we all stared as though it were the Hope diamond. He was the boy next door. They had a blueprint for life: She would drop out after this junior year and work until she had saved enough for a trousseau. He would finish high school. Then they would marry—she had planned, already, every detail of her wedding gown; she described the bits of lace and the placement of seed pearls and we all closed our eyes envisioning—and settle into an apartment in Roxbury and save for a home in Brookline. They would have four children. He would go into the insurance business, and his goal was to earn $10,000 a year, which would buy one hell of a house. We all blinked at the force of his ambition.

Is this vision of the American Dream still widely shared?

My own ambition was to study journalism. My guidance counselor advised against it. "Be an English teacher," he said. "Journalism is not for women. It makes them tough."

We were graduated in a fine postwar euphoria. It said beneath my picture in the yearbook: "Her voice is ever soft and low, an excellent thing in a woman." I was pleased.

I gave the Class Speech and spoke, soft and low, of the sacrifices that had been made for democracy and of our mission, now, to go forth into the world and assure that they would not have been made in vain: to be good Americans, to marry good Americans, to raise good Americans. My parents cried a little. The graduation ceremony ended with "God Bless America," and it echoed so that, as we filed out into the sun, we could hear nothing but America singing.

The cataclysmic assaults upon faith and myth, innocence, invincibility all came after my father's death. I cannot imagine what he would think today, but I suspect that he would still hear America singing. It was a sound so sweet that he could never have borne to relinquish it.

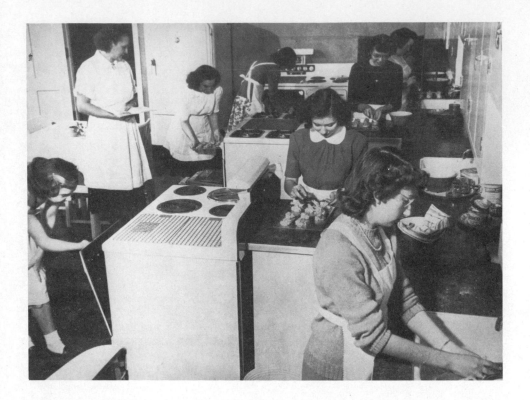

What can you tell about sex roles and the future expectations of the students in these home economics and shop classes? How have your schools reinforced traditional values? Why do you think it is so threatening for a boy to take home economics or a girl shop? How is the situation different today?

40

Choosing a Dream:
Italians in Hell's Kitchen
Mario Puzo

In this essay, Mario Puzo, the author of *The Godfather,* looks back at his youth in New York City and tries to depict some of the forces that had an impact on his life. Not everyone grew up in an Italian neighborhood and dreamed of becoming a writer, but Puzo does recall attitudes and incidents that have a universal appeal. For example, he has an ambivalent attitude toward his family, both loving and resenting them, and he looks back nostalgically on his earlier life as a happier period. He recalls things that perhaps your parents and others from their generation will remember—trolley cars, crowding around the crystal radio set, and how World War II provided one way of escaping family and background. Do you share his optimism about the American experience? Did your father or mother have similar dreams and aspirations? Do you feel that he is right in stating that although a great deal has changed in forty years, one thing has remained the same—"The contempt of the young for their elders"?

As a child and in my adolescence, living in the heart of New York's Neapolitan ghetto, I never heard an Italian singing. None of the grown-ups I knew were charming or loving or understanding. Rather they seemed coarse, vulgar, and insulting. And so later in my life when I was exposed to all the clichés of lovable Italians, singing Italians, happy-go-lucky Italians, I wondered where the hell the moviemakers and storywriters got all their ideas from.

At a very early age I decided to escape these uncongenial folk by becoming an artist, a writer. It seemed then an impossible dream. My father and mother were illiterate, as were their parents before them. But practising my art I tried to view the adults with a more charitable eye and so came to the conclusion that their only fault lay in their being foreigners; I was an American. This didn't really help because I was only half right. I was the foreigner. They were already more "American" than I could ever become.

But it did seem then that the Italian immigrants, all the fathers and mothers that I knew, were a grim lot; always shouting, always angry, quicker to quarrel than embrace. I did not understand that their lives were a long labor to earn their daily bread and that physical fatigue does not sweeten human natures.

And so even as a very small child I dreaded growing up to be like the adults around me. I heard them saying too many cruel things about their dearest friends, saw too many of their false embraces with those they had just maligned, observed with horror their paranoiac anger at some small slight or a fancied injury to their pride. They were, always, too unforgiving. In short, they did not have the careless magnanimity of children.

In my youth I was contemptuous of my elders, including a few under thirty. I thought my contempt special to their circumstances. Later when I wrote about these illiterate men and women, when I thought I understood them, I felt a condescending pity. After

Why had his family remained illiterate over the generations?

What could he mean by this?

Italians, like other immigrant groups, tended to cluster in ethnic ghettos. This one, on New York's Lower East Side, is much like the one Puzo inhabited in the 1930s, but there were other Little Italy's in dozens of large American cities. In what ways might a person raised in an ethnic ghetto be significantly different from someone who grew up without ethnic reinforcement?

all, they had suffered, they had labored all the days of their lives. They had never tasted luxury, knew little more economic security than those ancient Roman slaves who might have been their ancestors. And alas, I thought, with new-found artistic insight, they were cut off from their children because of the strange American tongue, alien to them, native to their sons and daughters.

Already an artist but not yet a husband or father, I pondered omnisciently on their tragedy, again thinking it special circumstance rather than a constant in the human condition. I did not yet understand why these men and women were willing to settle for less than they deserved in life and think that "less" quite a bargain. I did not understand that they simply could not afford to dream; I myself had a hundred dreams from which to choose. For I was already sure that I would make my escape, that I was one of the chosen. I would be rich, famous, happy. I would master my destiny.

And so it was perhaps natural that as a child, with my father gone, my mother the family chief, I, like all the children in all the ghettos of America, became locked in a bitter struggle with the adults responsible for me. It was inevitable that my mother and I became enemies.

Is it inevitable for parents and children to become enemies?

As a child I had the usual dreams. I wanted to be handsome, specifically as cowboy stars in movies were handsome. I wanted to be a killer hero in a world-wide war. Of if no wars came along (our teachers told us another was impossible), I wanted at the very least to be a footloose adventurer. Then I branched out and thought of being a great artist, and then, getting ever more sophisticated, a great criminal.

My mother, however, wanted me to be a railroad clerk. And that was her *highest* ambition; she would have settled for less. At the age of sixteen when I let everybody know that I was going to be a great writer, my friends and family took the news quite calmly, my mother included. She did not become angry. She quite simply assumed that I had gone off my nut. She was illiterate and her peasant life in Italy made her believe that only a son of the nobility could possibly be a writer. Artistic beauty after all could spring only from the seedbed of fine clothes, fine food, luxurious living. So then how was it possible for a son of hers to be an artist? She was not too convinced she was wrong even after my first two books were published many years later. It was only after the commercial success of my third novel that she gave me the title of poet.

My family and I grew up together on Tenth Avenue, between Thirtieth and Thirty-first streets, part of the area called Hell's Kitchen. This particular neighborhood could have been a movie set for one of the Dead End Kid flicks or for the social drama of the East Side in which John Garfield played the hero. Our tenements were the western wall of the city. Beneath our windows were the vast black iron gardens of the New York Central Railroad, absolutely blooming with stinking boxcars freshly unloaded of cattle and pigs for the city slaughterhouse. Steers sometimes escaped and loped through the heart of the neighborhood followed by astonished young boys who had never seen a live cow.

The railroad yards stretched down to the Hudson River, beyond whose garbagey waters rose the rocky Palisades of New Jersey. There were railroad tracks running downtown on Tenth Avenue itself to another freight station called St. Johns Park. Because of this, because these trains cut off one side of the street from the other, there was a wooden bridge over Tenth Avenue, a romantic-looking bridge despite the fact that no sparkling water, no silver flying fish darted beneath it; only heavy dray carts drawn by tired horses, some flat-boarded trucks, tin lizzie automobiles and, of course, long strings of freight cars drawn by black, ugly engines.

What was really great, truly magical, was sitting on the bridge, feet dangling down, and letting the engine under you blow up clouds of steam that made you disappear, then reappear all damp and smelling of fresh ironing. When I was seven years old I fell in love for the first time with the tough little girl who held my hand and disappeared with me in that magical cloud of steam. This experience was probably more traumatic and damaging to my later relationships with women than one of those ugly childhood adventures Freudian novelists use to explain why their hero has gone bad.

What kind of memories do you have of the place where you grew up? What memories do your parents have?

Immigrants may have dreamed of more opportunity in America but, like these Italian-American builders of the New York, Boston & Westchester railroad, they often had to settle for the lowest-paid, least-respected jobs. Few had the skills for more desirable work, though they often hoped their children would do better. Is upward socioeconomic mobility as important to you as it may have been to your parents and grandparents?

43

My father supported his wife and seven children by working as a trackman laborer for the New York Central Railroad. My oldest brother worked for the railroad as a brakeman, another brother was a railroad shipping clerk in the freight office. Eventually I spent some of the worst months of my life as the railroad's worst messenger boy.

My oldest sister was just as unhappy as a dressmaker in the garment industry. She wanted to be a school teacher. At one time or another my other two brothers also worked for the railroad—it got all six males in the family. The two girls and my mother escaped, though my mother felt it her duty to send all our bosses a gallon of homemade wine on Christmas. But everybody hated their jobs except my oldest brother who had a night shift and spent most of his working hours sleeping in freight cars. My father finally got fired because the foreman told him to get a bucket of water for the crew and not to take all day. My father took the bucket and disappeared forever.

Nearly all the Italian men living on Tenth Avenue supported their large families by working on the railroad. Their children also earned pocket money by stealing ice from the refrigerator cars in summer and coal from the open stoking cars in the winter. Sometimes an older lad would break the seal of a freight car and take a look inside. But this usually brought down the "Bulls," the special railroad police. And usually the freight was "heavy" stuff, too much work to cart away and sell, something like fresh produce or boxes of cheap candy that nobody would buy.

Was there an occupation that one or both of your parents were shunted into because of their racial or ethnic background? Did they resent the lack of opportunity?

The older boys, the ones just approaching voting age, made their easy money by hijacking silk trucks that loaded up at the garment factory on Thirty-first Street. They would then sell the expensive dresses door to door, at bargain prices no discount house could match. From this some graduated into organized crime, whose talent scouts alertly tapped young boys versed in strongarm. Yet despite all this, most of the kids grew up honest, content with fifty bucks a week as truck drivers, deliverymen, and white-collar clerks in the civil service.

I had every desire to go wrong but I never had a chance. The Italian family structure was too formidable.

I never came home to an empty house; there was always the smell of supper cooking. My mother was always there to greet me, sometimes with a policeman's club in her hand (nobody ever knew how she acquired it). But she was always there, or her authorized deputy, my older sister, who preferred throwing empty milk bottles at the heads of her little brothers when they got bad marks on their report cards. During the great Depression of the 1930s, though we were the poorest of the poor, I never remember not dining well. Many years later as a guest of a millionaire's club, I realized that our poor family on home relief ate better than some of the richest people in America.

My mother would never dream of using anything but the finest imported olive oil, the best Italian cheeses. My father had access to the fruits coming off ships, the produce from railroad cars, all before it went through the stale process of middlemen; and my mother, like most Italian women, was a fine cook in the peasant style.

How important do you think the family is in determining a child's conduct in life?

My mother was as formidable a personage as she was a cook. She was not to be treated cavalierly. My oldest brother at age sixteen had his own tin lizzie Ford and used it to further his career as the Don Juan of Tenth Avenue. One day my mother asked him to drive her to the market on Ninth Avenue and Fortieth Street, no more than a five-minute trip. My brother had other plans and claimed he was going to work on a new shift on the railroad. Work was an acceptable excuse even for funerals. But an hour later when my mother came out of the door of the tenement she saw the tin lizzie loaded with three pretty neighborhood girls, my Don Juan brother about to drive them off. Unfortunately there was a cobblestone lying loose in the gutter. My mother dropped her black leather shopping bag and picked up the stone with both hands. As we all watched in horror, she brought the boulder down on the nearest fender of the tin lizzie, demolishing it. Then she picked up her bag and marched off to Ninth Avenue to do her shopping. To this day, forty years later, my brother's voice still has a surprised horror and shock when he tells the story. He still doesn't understand how she could have done it.

My mother had her own legends and myths on how to amass a fortune. There was one of our uncles who worked as an assistant chef in a famous Italian-style restaurant. Every day, six days a week, this uncle brought home, under his shirt, six eggs, a stick of butter, and a small bag of flour. By doing this for thirty years he was able to save enough money to buy a fifteen-thousand-dollar house on Long Island and two smaller houses for his son and daughter. Another cousin, blessed with a college degree, worked as a chemist in a large manufacturing firm. By using the firm's raw materials and equipment he con-

Do you think mothers play as important a role in the family structure now?

cocted a superior floor wax which he sold door to door in his spare time. It was a great floor wax and with his low overhead, the price was right. My mother and her friends did not think this stealing. They thought of it as being thrifty.

The wax-selling cousin eventually destroyed his reputation for thrift by buying a sailboat; this was roughly equivalent to the son of a Boston brahmin spending a hundred grand in a whorehouse.

As rich men escape their wives by going to their club, I finally escaped my mother by going to the Hudson Guild Settlement House. Most people do not know that a settlement house is really a club combined with social services. The Hudson Guild, a five-story field of joy for slum kids, had ping pong rooms and billiard rooms, a shop in which to make lamps, a theater for putting on amateur plays, a gym to box and play basketball in. And then there were individual rooms where your particular club could meet in privacy. The Hudson Guild even suspended your membership for improper behavior or failure to pay the tiny dues. It was a heady experience for a slum kid to see his name posted on the billboard to the effect that he was suspended by the Board of Governors.

• • •

The Hudson Guild was also responsible for absolutely the happiest times of my childhood. When I was about nine or ten they sent me away as a Fresh Air Fund kid. This was a program where slum children were boarded on private families in places like New Hampshire for two weeks.

As a child I knew only the stone city. I had no conception of what the countryside could be. When I got to New Hampshire, when I smelled grass and flowers and trees, when I ran barefoot along the dirt country roads, when I drove the cows home from pasture, when I darted through fields of corn and waded through clear brooks, when I gathered warm brown speckled eggs in the henhouse, when I drove a hay wagon drawn by two great horses—when I did all these things—I nearly went crazy with the joy of it. It was quite simply a fairy tale come true.

The family that took me in, a middle-aged man and woman, childless, were Baptists and observed Sunday so religiously that even checker playing was not allowed on the Lord's day of rest. We went to church on Sunday for a good three hours, counting Bible

Was the American notion of thrift and hard work exaggerated among recent immigrants?

For many Americans of immigrant descent, success has meant earning enough money to be able to leave a ghetto for the suburbs. By this standard these Italian-Americans, enjoying a game of boccie on a court by their suburban homes, have "made it." Would your parents agree with this assessment? Do you share that value?

class, then again at night. On Thursday evenings we went to prayer meetings. My guardians, out of religious scruple, had never seen a movie. They disapproved of dancing, they were no doubt political reactionaries; they were everything that I came later to fight against.

And yet they gave me those magical times children never forget. For two weeks every summer from the time I was nine to fifteen I was happier than I have ever been before or since. The man was good with tools and built me a little playground with swings, sliding ponds, seesaws. The woman had a beautiful flower and vegetable garden and let me pick from it. A cucumber or strawberry in the earth was a miracle. And then when they saw how much I loved picnics, the sizzling frankfurters on a stick over the wood fire, the yellow roasted corn, they drove me out on Sunday afternoons to a lovely green grass mountainside. Only on Sundays it was never called a picnic, it was called "taking our lunch outside." I found it then—and now—a sweet hypocrisy.

• • •

From this Paradise I was flung into Hell. That is, I had to help support my family by working on the railroad. After school hours of course. This was the same railroad that had supplied free coal and free ice to the whole Tenth Avenue when I was young enough to steal with impunity. After school finished at 3 P.M. I went to work in the freight office as a messenger. I also worked Saturdays and Sundays when there was work available.

I hated it. One of my first short stories was about how I hated that job. But of course what I really hated was entering the adult world. To me the adult world was a dark enchantment, unnatural. As unnatural to the human dream as death. And as inevitable.

The young are impatient about change because they cannot grasp the power of time itself; not only as the enemy of flesh, the very germ of death, but time as a benign cancer. As the young cannot grasp really that love must be a victim of time, so too they cannot grasp that injustices, the economic and family traps of living, can also fall victim to time.

• • •

America may be a fascistic, warmongering, racially prejudiced country today. It may deserve the hatred of its revolutionary young. But what a miracle it once was! What has happened here has never happened in any other country in any other time. The poor who had been poor for centuries—hell, since the beginning of Christ—whose children had inherited their poverty, their illiteracy, their hopelessness, achieved some economic dignity and freedom. You didn't get it for nothing, you had to pay a price in tears, in suffering, but why not? And some even became artists.

Not even my gift for retrospective falsification [remembering the good and not the

Why have Americans traditionally distrusted city life and glorified simple country living?

Do you accept this view of time and the young?

Has this country become less than it once was?

46

Many Italian Americans of your parents' generation viewed Frank Sinatra and Joe DiMaggio (pictured on the preceding page) as symbols of the American Dream come true. Few of that generation, however, achieved the wealth and fame of these two superstars. Like the people shown here, most settled for considerably less. By their own standards, were the men and women who failed to reach that height of success failures? Did they, in fact, settle for less?

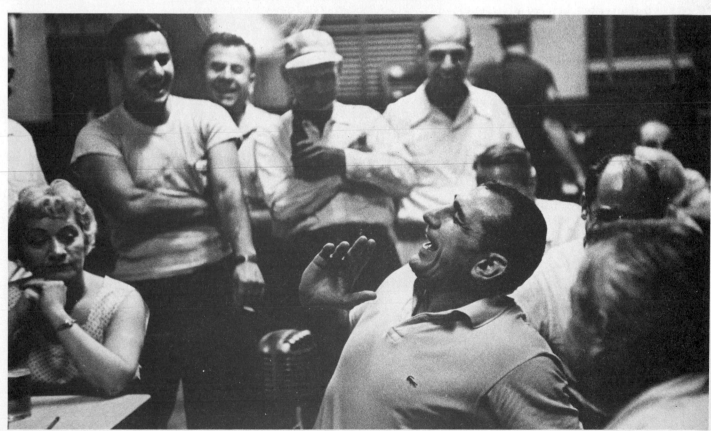

bad] can make my eighteenth to twenty-first years seem like a happy time. I hated my life. I was being dragged into the trap I feared and had foreseen even as a child. It was all there, the steady job, the nice girl who would eventually get knocked up, and then the marriage and fighting over counting pennies to make ends meet. I noticed myself acting more unheroic all the time. I had to tell lies in pure self-defense, I did not forgive so easily.

But I was delivered. When World War II broke out I was delighted. There is no other word, terrible as it may sound. My country called. I was delivered from my mother, my family, the girl I was loving passionately but did not love. And delivered WITHOUT GUILT. Heroically. My country called, ordered me to defend it. I must have been one of millions, sons, husbands, fathers, lovers, making their innocent getaway from baffled loved ones. And what an escape it was. The war made all my dreams come true. I drove a jeep, toured Europe, had love affairs, found a wife, and lived the material for my first novel. But of course that was a just war as Vietnam is not, and so today it is perhaps for the best that the revolutionary young make their escape by attacking their own rulers.

Did any member of your family serve in a war? Did he or she experience the war in this way?

Then why five years later did I walk back into the trap with a wife and child and a civil service job I was glad to get? After five years of the life I had dreamed about, plenty of women, plenty of booze, plenty of money, hardly any work, interesting companions, travel, etc., why did I walk back into that cage of family and duty and a steady job?

For the simple reason, of course, that I had never really escaped, not my mother, not my family, not the moral pressures of our society. Time again had done its work. I was back in my cage and I was, I think, happy. In the next twenty years I wrote three novels. Two of them were critical successes but I didn't make much money. The third novel, not as good as the others, made me rich. And free at last. Or so I thought.

Then why do I dream of those immigrant Italian peasants as having been happy? I remember how they spoke of their forebears, who spent all their lives farming the arid mountain slopes of Southern Italy. "He died in that house in which he was born," they say enviously. "He was never more than an hour from his village, not in all his life," they sigh. And what would they make of a phrase like "retrospective falsification"?

No, really, we are all happier now. It is a better life. And after all, as my mother always said, "Never mind about being happy. Be glad you're alive."

When I came to my "autobiographical novel," the one every writer does about himself, I planned to make myself the sensitive, misunderstood hero, much put upon by his mother and family. To my astonishment my mother took over the book and instead of my revenge I got another comeuppance. But it is, I think, my best book. And all those old-style grim conservative Italians whom I hated, then pitied so patronizingly, they also turned out to be heroes. Through no desire of mine. I was surprised. The thing that amazed me most was their courage. Where were their Congressional Medals of Honor? Their Distinguished Service Crosses? How did they ever have the balls to get married, have kids, go out to earn a living in a strange land, with no skills, not even knowing the language? They made it without tranquillizers, without sleeping pills, without psychiatrists, without even a dream. Heroes. Heroes all around me. I never saw them.

Was it more "heroic" to have been living then than now?

But how could I? They wore lumpy work clothes and handlebar moustaches, they blew their noses on their fingers and they were so short that their high-school children towered over them. They spoke a laughable broken English and the furthest limit of their horizon was their daily bread. Brave men, brave women, they fought to live their lives without dreams. Bent on survival, they narrowed their minds to the thinnest line of existence.

It is no wonder that in my youth I found them contemptible. And yet they had left Italy and sailed the ocean to come to a new land and leave their sweated bones in America. Illiterate Colombos, they dared to seek the promised land. And so they, too, dreamed a dream.

• • •

But maybe the young are on the right track this time. Maybe they know that the dreams of our fathers were malignant. Perhaps it is true that the only real escape is in the blood magic of drugs. All the Italians I knew and grew up with have escaped, have made their success. We are all Americans now, we are all successes now. And yet the most successful Italian man I know admits that though the one human act he never could understand was suicide, he understood it when he became a success. Not that he ever would do such a thing; no man with Italian blood ever commits suicide or becomes a

Puzo speaks of the immigrant generation of Italians as "happy" though their lives were grim. Can you detect anything in this photograph of an Italian-American religious festival in 1915 that suggests what he means? Is happiness, in Puzo's sense, part of the American Dream of success?

homosexual in his belief. But suicide has crossed his mind. And so to what avail the finding of the dream? He went back to Italy and tried to live like a peasant again. But he can never again be unaware of more subtle traps than poverty and hunger.

There is a difference between having a good time in life and being happy. My mother's life was a terrible struggle and yet I think it was a happy life. One tentative proof is that at the age of eighty-two she is positively indignant at the thought that death dares approach her. But it's not for everybody that kind of life.

Thinking back I wonder why I became a writer. Was it the poverty or the books I read? Who traumatized me, my mother or the Brothers Karamazov? Being Italian? Or the girl sitting with me on the bridge as the engine steam deliciously made us vanish? Did it make any difference that I grew up Italian rather than Irish or black?

No matter. The good times are beginning, I am another Italian success story. Not as great as DiMaggio or Sinatra but quite enough. It will serve. Yet I can escape again. I have my retrospective falsification (how I love that phrase). I can dream now about how happy I was in my childhood, in my tenement, playing in those dirty but magical streets —living in the poverty that made my mother weep. True, I was a deposed dictator at fifteen but they never hanged me. And now I remember, all those impossible dreams strung out before me, waiting for me to choose, not knowing that the life I was living then, as a child, would become my final dream.

Is Puzo advocating abandoning the dream of success? Do you agree?

the autobiography of Malcolm X
Malcolm X and Alex Haley

For many Americans, especially those born black, the American Dream almost always became a nightmare. Malcolm X, in this excerpt from his autobiography, describes the horror of his youth. He recalls pistol shots and a burning house, the murder of his father, the moves and uprooting, and the poverty, conflict, and insanity that led to the breakup of his family. And yet he has some fond memories along with a sense of family loyalty and pride. Is this kind of nightmare, this perversion of the American Dream, unique to the black experience? Have you seen it happening in your own family? Is there any experience in your family background that would contribute to a greater understanding of the nightmare Malcolm X describes here?

When my mother was pregnant with me, she told me later, a party of hooded Ku Klux Klan riders galloped up to our home in Omaha, Nebraska, one night. Surrounding the house, brandishing their shotguns and rifles, they shouted for my father to come out. My mother went to the front door and opened it. Standing where they could see her pregnant condition, she told them that she was alone with her three small children, and that my father was away, preaching, in Milwaukee. The Klansmen shouted threats and warnings at her that we had better get out of town because "the good Christian white people" were not going to stand for my father's "spreading trouble" among the "good" Negroes of Omaha with the "back to Africa" preachings of Marcus Garvey.

My father, the Reverend Earl Little, was a Baptist minister, a dedicated organizer for Marcus Aurelius Garvey's U.N.I.A. (Universal Negro Improvement Association). With the help of such disciples as my father, Garvey, from his headquarters in New York City's Harlem, was raising the banner of black-race purity and exhorting the Negro masses to return to their ancestral African homeland—a cause which had made Garvey the most controversial black man on earth.

Still shouting threats, the Klansmen finally spurred their horses and galloped around the house, shattering every window pane with their gun butts. Then they rode off into the night, their torches flaring, as suddenly as they had come.

My father was enraged when he returned. He decided to wait until I was born—which would be soon—and then the family would move. I am not sure why he made this decision, for he was not a frightened Negro, as most then were, and many still are today. My father was a big, six-foot-four, very black man. He had only one eye. How he had lost the other one I have never known. He was from Reynolds, Georgia, where he had left school after the third or maybe fourth grade. He believed, as did Marcus Garvey, that freedom, independence and self-respect could never be achieved by the Negro in America, and that therefore the Negro should leave America to the white man and

Why didn't his father turn to the law?

The Ku Klux Klan, a white terrorist group that originated in the South during Reconstruction, went through a second period of growth directly after World War I. Catholics, Jews, and foreigners, as well as blacks, were subject to its attacks. Has your family ever been under attack by a similar group?

return to his African land of origin. Among the reasons my father had decided to risk and dedicate his life to help disseminate this philosophy among his people was that he had seen four of his six brothers die by violence, three of them killed by white men, including one by lynching. What my father could not know then was that of the remaining three, including himself, only one, my Uncle Jim, would die in bed, of natural causes. Northern white police were later to shoot my Uncle Oscar. And my father was finally himself to die by the white man's hands.

It has always been my belief that I, too, will die by violence. I have done all that I can to be prepared.

How did Malcolm X die?

· · ·

. . . The teaching of Marcus Garvey stressed becoming independent of the white man. We went next, for some reason, to Lansing, Michigan. My father bought a house and soon, as had been his pattern, he was doing free-lance Christian preaching in local Negro Baptist churches, and during the week he was roaming about spreading word of Marcus Garvey.

He had begun to lay away savings for the store he had always wanted to own when, as always, some stupid local Uncle Tom Negroes began to funnel stories about his revolutionary beliefs to the local white people. This time, the get-out-of-town threats came from a local hate society called The Black Legion. They wore black robes instead of white. Soon, nearly everywhere my father went, Black Legionnaires were reviling him as an "uppity nigger" for wanting to own a store, for living outside the Lansing Negro district, for spreading unrest and dissension among "the good niggers."

Why weren't blacks more united at this time?

As in Omaha, my mother was pregnant again, this time with my youngest sister. Shortly after Yvonne was born came the nightmare night in 1929, my earliest vivid memory. I remember being suddenly snatched awake into a frightening confusion of pistol shots and shouting and smoke and flames. My father had shouted and shot at the two white men who had set the fire and were running away. Our home was burning down around us. We were lunging and bumping and tumbling all over each other trying to escape. My mother, with the baby in her arms, just made it into the yard before the house crashed in, showering sparks. I remember we were outside in the night in our underwear, crying and yelling our heads off. The white police and firemen came and stood around watching as the house burned down to the ground.

· · ·

After that, my memories are of the friction between my father and mother. They seemed to be nearly always at odds. Sometimes my father would beat her. It might have had something to do with the fact that my mother had a pretty good education. Where she got it I don't know. But an educated woman, I suppose, can't resist the temptation to correct an uneducated man. Every now and then, when she put those smooth words on him, he would grab her.

My father was also belligerent toward all of the children, except me. The older ones he would beat almost savagely if they broke any of his rules—and he had so many rules it was hard to know them all. Nearly all my whippings came from my mother. I've thought a lot about why. I actually believe that as anti-white as my father was, he was subconsciously so afflicted with the white man's brainwashing of Negroes that he inclined to favor the light ones, and I was his lightest child. Most Negro parents in those days would almost instinctively treat any lighter children better than they did the darker ones. It came directly from the slavery tradition that the "mulatto," because he was visibly nearer to white, was therefore "better."

Is it plausible that a man so conscious of his black heritage would think this way?

· · ·

Back when I was growing up, the "successful" Lansing Negroes were such as waiters and bootblacks. To be a janitor at some downtown store was to be highly respected. The real "elite," the "big shots," the "voices of the race," were the waiters at the Lansing Country Club and the shoeshine boys at the state capitol. The only Negroes who really had any money were the ones in the numbers racket, or who ran the gambling houses, or who in some other way lived parasitically off the poorest ones, who were the masses. No Negroes were hired then by Lansing's big Oldsmobile plant, or the Reo plant. (Do you remember the Reo? It was manufactured in Lansing, and R. E. Olds, the man after whom it was named, also lived in Lansing. When the war came along, they hired some Negro janitors.) The bulk of the Negroes were either on Welfare, or W.P.A., or they starved.

· · ·

My mother at this time seemed to be always working—cooking, washing, ironing, cleaning, and fussing over us eight children. And she was usually either arguing with or not speaking to my father. One cause of friction was that she had strong ideas about what she wouldn't eat—and didn't want *us* to eat—including pork and rabbit, both of which my father loved dearly. He was a real Georgia Negro, and he believed in eating plenty of what we in Harlem today call "soul food."

Can you explain her distaste for these foods?

I've said that my mother was the one who whipped me—at least she did whenever she wasn't ashamed to let the neighbors think she was killing me. For if she even acted as though she was about to raise her hand to me, I would open my mouth and let the world know about it. If anybody was passing by out on the road, she would either change her mind or just give me a few licks.

Thinking about it now, I feel definitely that just as my father favored me for being lighter than the other children, my mother gave me more hell for the same reason. She was very light herself but she favored the ones who were darker. Wilfred, I know, was particularly her angel. I remember that she would tell me to get out of the house and "Let the sun shine on you so you can get some color." She went out of her way never to let me become afflicted with a sense of color-superiority. I am sure that she treated me this way partly because of how she came to be light herself.

· · ·

One afternoon in 1931 when Wilfred, Hilda, Philbert, and I* came home, my mother and father were having one of their arguments. There had lately been a lot of tension around the house because of Black Legion threats. Anyway, my father had taken one of the rabbits which we were raising, and ordered my mother to cook it. We raised rabbits, but sold them to whites. My father had taken a rabbit from the rabbit pen. He had pulled off the rabbit's head. He was so strong, he needed no knife to behead chickens or rabbits. With one twist of his big black hands he simply twisted off the head and threw the bleeding-necked thing back at my mother's feet.

How did racial prejudice help weaken the fabric of family life?

My mother was crying. She started to skin the rabbit, preparatory to cooking it. But my father was so angry he slammed on out of the front door and started walking up the road toward town.

It was then that my mother had this vision. She had always been a strange woman in this sense, and had always had a strong intuition of things about to happen. And most of her children are the same way, I think. When something is about to happen, I can

*Malcolm X was one of eight children.—Ed.

When Malcom X was a child, blacks were largely excluded from automobile assembly-line work. Now they make up a sizable proportion of automobile workers. Is this an indication that the American Dream is becoming accessible to blacks? Is this an improvement?

feel something, sense something. I never have known something to happen that has caught me completely off guard—except once. And that was when, years later, I discovered facts I couldn't believe about a man who, up until that discovery, I would gladly have given my life for.

My father was well up the road when my mother ran screaming out onto the porch. *"Early! Early!"* She screamed his name. She clutched up her apron in one hand, and ran down across the yard and into the road. My father turned around. He saw her. For some reason, considering how angry he had been when he left, he waved at her. But he kept on going.

She told me later, my mother did, that she had a vision of my father's end. All the rest of the afternoon, she was not herself, crying and nervous and upset. She finished cooking the rabbit and put the whole thing in the warmer part of the black stove. When my father was not back home by our bedtime, my mother hugged and clutched us, and we felt strange, not knowing what to do, because she had never acted like that.

I remember waking up to the sound of my mother's screaming again. When I scrambled out, I saw the police in the living room; they were trying to calm her down. She had snatched on her clothes to go with them. And all of us children who were staring knew without anyone having to say it that something terrible had happened to our father.

My mother was taken by the police to the hospital, and to a room where a sheet was over my father in a bed, and she wouldn't look, she was afraid to look. Probably it was wise that she didn't. My father's skull, on one side, was crushed in, I was told later. Negroes in Lansing have always whispered that he was attacked, and then laid across some tracks for a streetcar to run over him. His body was cut almost in half.

He lived two and a half hours in that condition. Negroes then were stronger than they are now, especially Georgia Negroes. Negroes born in Georgia had to be strong simply to survive.

It was morning when we children at home got the word that he was dead. I was six. I can remember a vague commotion, the house filled up with people crying, saying bitterly that the white Black Legion had finally gotten him. My mother was hysterical. In the bedroom, women were holding smelling salts under her nose. She was still hysterical at the funeral.

I don't have a very clear memory of the funeral, either. Oddly, the main thing I remember is that it wasn't in a church, and that surprised me, since my father was a

Almost 5,000 blacks were the victims of lynchings in the fifty years following Reconstruction, many in the North and West. Most died by hanging, but there were other hideous mob actions, like that against Malcom X's father. Is the decline in such overt violence a sign of improved race relations?

preacher, and I had been where he preached people's funerals in churches. But his was in a funeral home.

And I remember that during the service a big black fly came down and landed on my father's face, and Wilfred sprang up from his chair and he shooed the fly away, and he came groping back to his chair—there were folding chairs for us to sit on—and the tears were streaming down his face. When we went by the casket, I remember that I thought that it looked as if my father's strong black face had been dusted with flour, and I wished they hadn't put on such a lot of it.

What effect might this have had on a young boy?

• • •

So there we were. My mother was thirty-four years old now, with no husband, no provider or protector to take care of her eight children. But some kind of a family routine got going again. And for as long as the first insurance money lasted, we did all right.

Wilfred, who was a pretty stable fellow, began to act older than his age. I think he had the sense to see, when the rest of us didn't, what was in the wind for us. He quietly quit school and went to town in search of work. He took any kind of job he could find and he would come home, dog-tired, in the evenings, and give whatever he had made to my mother.

Hilda, who always had been quiet, too, attended to the babies. Philbert and I didn't contribute anything. We just fought all the time—each other at home, and then at school we would team up and fight white kids. Sometimes the fights would be racial in nature, but they might be about anything.

Reginald came under my wing. Since he had grown out of the toddling stage, he and I had become very close. I suppose I enjoyed the fact that he was the little one, under me, who looked up to me.

My mother began to buy on credit. My father had always been very strongly against credit. "Credit is the first step into debt and back into slavery," he had always said. And then she went to work herself. She would go into Lansing and find different jobs—in housework, or sewing—for white people. They didn't realize, usually, that she was a Negro. A lot of white people around there didn't want Negroes in their houses.

She would do fine until in some way or other it got to people who she was, whose widow she was. And then she would be let go. I remember how she used to come home crying, but trying to hide it, because she had lost a job that she needed so much.

What options were open to his mother? Do black women have more options today?

Once when one of us—I cannot remember which—had to go for something to where she was working, and the people saw us, and realized she was actually a Negro, she was fired on the spot, and she came home crying, this time not hiding it.

When the state Welfare people began coming to our house, we would come from school sometimes and find them talking with our mother, asking a thousand questions. They acted and looked at her, and at us, and around in our house, in a way that had about it the feeling—at least for me—that we were not people. In their eyesight we were just *things*, that was all.

My mother began to receive two checks—a Welfare check and, I believe, a widow's pension. The checks helped. But they weren't enough, as many of us as there were. When they came, about the first of the month, one always was already owed in full, if not more, to the man at the grocery store. And, after that, the other one didn't last long.

We began to go swiftly downhill. The physical downhill wasn't as quick as the psychological. My mother was, above everything else, a proud woman, and it took its toll on her that she was accepting charity. And her feelings were communicated to us.

She would speak sharply to the man at the grocery store for padding the bill, telling him that she wasn't ignorant, and he didn't like that. She would talk back sharply to the state Welfare people, telling them that she was a grown woman, able to raise her children, that it wasn't necessary for them to keep coming around so much, meddling in our lives. And they didn't like that.

But the monthly Welfare check was their pass. They acted as if they owned us, as if we were their private property. As much as my mother would have liked to, she couldn't keep them out. She would get particularly incensed when they began insisting upon drawing us older children aside, one at a time, out on the porch or somewhere, and asking us questions, or telling us things—against our mother and against each other.

. . .

Then, about in late 1934, I would guess, something began to happen. Some kind of psychological deterioration hit our family circle and began to eat away our pride. Perhaps it was the constant tangible evidence that we were destitute. We had known other families who had gone on relief. We had known without anyone in our home ever expressing it that we had felt prouder not to be at the depot where the free food was passed out. And, now, we were among them. At school, the "on relief" finger suddenly was pointed at us, too, and sometimes it was said aloud.

It seemed that everything to eat in our house was stamped Not To Be Sold. All Welfare food bore this stamp to keep the recipients from selling it. It's a wonder we didn't come to think of Not To Be Sold as a brand name.

Sometimes, instead of going home from school, I walked the two miles up the road into Lansing. I began drifting from store to store, hanging around outside where things like apples were displayed in boxes and barrels and baskets, and I would watch my chance and steal me a treat. You know what a treat was to me? Anything!

Or I began to drop in about dinnertime at the home of some family that we knew. I knew that they knew exactly why I was there, but they never embarrassed me by letting on. They would invite me to stay for supper, and I would stuff myself.

Especially, I liked to drop in and visit at the Gohannas' home. They were nice, older people, and great churchgoers. I had watched them lead the jumping and shouting when my father preached. They had, living with them—they were raising him—a nephew whom everyone called "Big Boy," and he and I got along fine. Also living with the Gohannas was old Mrs. Adcock, who went with them to church. She was always trying to help anybody she could, visiting anyone she heard was sick, carrying them something. She was the one who, years later, would tell me something that I remembered a long time: "Malcolm, there's one thing I like about you. You're no good, but you don't try to hide it. You are not a hypocrite."

The more I began to stay away from home and visit people and steal from the stores, the more aggressive I became in my inclinations. I never wanted to wait for anything.

. . .

When I began to get caught stealing now and then, the state Welfare people began to focus on me when they came to our house. I can't remember how I first became aware that they were talking of taking me away. What I first remember along that line was my mother raising a storm about being able to bring up her own children. She would whip me for stealing, and I would try to alarm the neighborhood with my yelling. One thing I have always been proud of is that I never raised my hand against my mother.

In the summertime, at night, in addition to all the other things we did, some of us boys would slip out down the road, or across the pastures, and go "cooning" watermelons. White people always associated watermelons with Negroes, and they sometimes called Negroes "coons" among all the other names, and so stealing watermelons became "cooning" them. If white boys were doing it, it implied that they were only acting like Negroes. Whites have always hidden or justified all of the guilts they could by ridiculing or blaming Negroes.

One Halloween night, I remember that a bunch of us were out tipping over those old country outhouses, and one old farmer—I guess he had tipped over enough in his day —had set a trap for us. Always, you sneak up from behind the outhouse, then you gang together and push it, to tip it over. This farmer had taken his outhouse off the hole, and set it just in *front* of the hole. Well, we came sneaking up in single file, in the darkness, and the two white boys in the lead fell down into the outhouse hole neck deep. They smelled so bad it was all we could stand to get them out, and that finished us all for that

What statement is the author making about the effects of welfare on the recipient and the donor? Do you agree?

Mario Puzo looks upon his poverty-stricken childhood as one of the happiest times of his life. Account for the difference of attitude in Malcolm X.

How is his growing aggressiveness related to his poverty?

In 1895 Booker T. Washington, a leading black intellectual, proposed that black advancement would come only if blacks carved out a place of economic service for themselves in their communities that would not antagonize whites. Toward this end he established Tuskegee Institute (pictured on the right) as a training ground for black farmers, mechanics, and domestic servants. The black shown here—a trainman—is in a line of work that Washington would have approved.

In the 1930s, the period Malcom X recalls here, unemployment was a much more severe problem for blacks than for whites, with three to four times as many blacks forced onto relief rolls as whites. Do you see any correlation between the kinds of jobs blacks occupied and why they were so hard-hit by the depression? What do you think of the philosophy that blacks should concentrate on making small economic gains?

Halloween. I had just missed falling in myself. The whites were so used to taking the lead, this time it had really gotten them in the hole.

Thus, in various ways, I learned various things. I picked strawberries, and though I can't recall what I got per crate for picking, I remember that after working hard all one day, I would up with about a dollar, which was a whole lot of money in those times. I was so hungry, I didn't know what to do. I was walking away toward town with visions of buying something good to eat, and this older white boy I knew, Richard Dixon, came up and asked me if I wanted to match nickels. He had plenty of change for my dollar. In about a half hour, he had all the change back, including my dollar, and instead of going to town to buy something, I went home with nothing, and I was bitter. But that was nothing compared to what I felt when I found out later that he had cheated. There is a way that you can catch and hold the nickel and make it come up the way you want. This was my first lesson about gambling: if you see somebody winning all the time, he isn't gambling, he's cheating. Later on in life, if I were continuously losing in any gambling situation, I would watch very closely. It's like the Negro in America seeing the white man win all the time. He's a professional gambler; he has all the cards and the odds stacked on his side, and he has always dealt to our people from the bottom of the deck.

Is this an accurate analogy?

• • •

It was about this time that the large, dark man from Lansing began visiting. I don't remember how or where he and my mother met. It may have been through some mutual friends. I don't remember what the man's profession was. In 1935, in Lansing, Negroes didn't have anything you could call a profession. But the man, big and black, looked something like my father. I can remember his name, but there's no need to mention it. He was a single man, and my mother was a widow only thirty-six years old. The man was independent; naturally she admired that. She was having a hard time disciplining us, and a big man's presence alone would help. And if she had a man to provide, it would send the state people away forever.

We all understood without ever saying much about it. Or at least we had no objection. We took it in stride, even with some amusement among us, that when the man came, our mother would be all dressed up in the best that she had—she still was a good-looking woman—and she would act differently, lighthearted and laughing, as we hadn't seen her act in years.

It went on for about a year, I guess. And then, about 1936, or 1937, the man from Lansing jilted my mother suddenly. He just stopped coming to see her. From what I later understood, he finally backed away from taking on the responsibility of those eight mouths to feed. He was afraid of so many of us. To this day, I can see the trap that Mother was in, saddled with all of us. And I can also understand why he would shun taking on such a tremendous responsibility.

What does this say about why, in many black families, the mother is the head of the household?

But it was a terrible shock to her. It was the beginning of the end of reality for my mother. When she began to sit around and walk around talking to herself—almost as though she was unaware that we were there—it became increasingly terrifying.

The state people saw her weakening. That was when they began the definite steps to take me away from home. They began to tell me how nice it was going to be at the Gohannas' home, where the Gohannas and Big Boy and Mrs. Adcock had all said how much they liked me, and would like to have me live with them.

I liked all of them, too. But I didn't want to leave Wilfred. I looked up to and admired my big brother. I didn't want to leave Hilda, who was like my second mother. Or Philbert; even in our fighting, there was a feeling of brotherly union. Or Reginald, especially, who was weak with his hernia condition, and who looked up to me as his big brother who looked out for him, as I looked up to Wilfred. And I had nothing, either, against the babies, Yvonne, Wesley, and Robert.

As my mother talked to herself more and more, she gradually became less responsive to us. And less responsible. The house became less tidy. We began to be more unkempt. And usually, now, Hilda cooked.

We children watched our anchor giving way. It was something terrible that you couldn't get your hands on, yet you couldn't get away from. It was a sensing that something bad was going to happen. We younger ones leaned more and more heavily on the relative strength of Wilfred and Hilda, who were the oldest.

When finally I was sent to the Gohannas' home, at least in a surface way I was glad. I remember that when I left home with the state man, my mother said one thing: "Don't let them feed him any pig."

Eventually my mother suffered a complete breakdown, and the court orders were finally signed. They took her to the State Mental Hospital at Kalamazoo.

It was seventy-some miles from Lansing, about an hour and a half on the bus. A Judge McClellan in Lansing had authority over me and all of my brothers and sisters. We were "state children," court wards; he had the full say-so over us. A white man in charge of a black man's children! Nothing but legal, modern slavery—however kindly intentioned.

My mother remained in the same hospital at Kalamazoo for about twenty-six years. Later, when I was still growing up in Michigan, I would go to visit her every so often. Nothing that I can imagine could have moved me as deeply as seeing her pitiful state. In 1963, we got my mother out of the hospital, and she now lives there in Lansing with Philbert and his family.

It was so much worse than if it had been a physical sickness, for which a cause might be known, medicine given, a cure effected. Every time I visited her, when finally they led her—a case, a number—back inside from where we had been sitting together, I felt worse.

My last visit, when I knew I would never come to see her again—there—was in 1952. I was twenty-seven. My brother Philbert had told me that on his last visit, she had recognized him somewhat. "In spots," he said.

But she didn't recognize me at all.

She stared at me. She didn't know who I was.

Her mind, when I tried to talk, to reach her, was somewhere else. I asked, "Mama, do you know what day it is?"

She said, staring, "All the people have gone."

I can't describe how I felt. The woman who had brought me into the world, and nursed me, and advised me, and chastised me, and loved me, didn't know me. It was as if I was trying to walk up the side of a hill of feathers. I looked at her. I listened to her "talk." But there was nothing I could do.

I truly believe that if ever a state social agency destroyed a family, it destroyed ours. We wanted and tried to stay together. Our home didn't have to be destroyed. But the Welfare, the courts, and their doctor, gave us the one-two-three punch. And ours was not the only case of this kind.

I knew I wouldn't be back to see my mother again because it could make me a very vicious and dangerous person—knowing how they had looked at us as numbers and as a case in their book, not as human beings. And knowing that my mother in there was a statistic that didn't have to be, that existed because of a society's failure, hypocrisy, greed, and lack of mercy and compassion. Hence I have no mercy or compassion in me for a society that will crush people, and then penalize them for not being able to stand up under the weight.

On the whole, has society been more destructive or supportive of your family? In what ways?

I have rarely talked to anyone about my mother, for I believe that I am capable of killing a person, without hesitation, who happened to make the wrong kind of remark about my mother. So I purposely don't make any opening for some fool to step into.

Back then when our family was destroyed, in 1937, Wilfred and Hilda were old enough so that the state let them stay on their own in the big four-room house that my father had built. Philbert was placed with another family in Lansing, a Mrs. Hackett, while Reginald and Wesley went to live with a family called Williams, who were friends of my mother's. And Yvonne and Robert went to live with a West Indian family named McGuire.

Do you think the state could have acted differently?

Separated though we were, all of us maintained fairly close touch around Lansing—in school and out—whenever we could get together. Despite the artificially created separation and distance between us, we still remained very close in our feelings toward each other.

The Feminine Mystique
betty friedan

The American Dream of success has usually been assumed to be a masculine idea. To make a lot of money or rise to a position of power and influence, to dream of changing the world, or even merely to have a career has usually been the male prerogative. Prior to the contemporary women's liberation movement, the woman was left to dream of becoming a wife and mother. In the following selection, Betty Friedan, one of the early leaders of the women's movement, describes the problems of identity and self-image for women today. Has it always been this way? Is it easier for women now to find a sense of identity and purpose than it was for your mother's generation? Or do you still see a particular dilemma faced by women when they are twenty-one and have to decide what to do with their lives? Also, given the strength of the liberation movement, how do you think males are reacting—is there more resistance than understanding? Give this some thought as you read what Betty Friedan has to say.

I discovered a strange thing, interviewing women of my own generation over the past ten years. When we were growing up, many of us could not see ourselves beyond the age of twenty-one. We had no image of our own future, of ourselves as women.

I remember the stillness of a spring afternoon on the Smith campus in 1942, when I came to a frightening dead end in my own vision of the future. A few days earlier, I had received a notice that I had won a graduate fellowship. During the congratulations, underneath my excitement, I felt a strange uneasiness; there was a question that I did not want to think about.

"Is this really what I want to be?" The question shut me off, cold and alone, from the girls talking and studying on the sunny hillside behind the college house. I thought I was going to be a psychologist. But if I wasn't sure, what did I want to be? I felt the future closing in—and I could not see myself in it at all. I had no image of myself, stretching beyond college. I had come at seventeen from a Midwestern town, an unsure girl; the wide horizons of the world and the life of the mind had been opened to me. I had begun to know who I was and what I wanted to do. I could not go back now. I could not go home again, to the life of my mother and the women of our town, bound to home, bridge, shopping, children, husband, charity, clothes. But now that the time had come to make my own future, to take the deciding step, I suddenly did not know what I wanted to be.

I took the fellowship, but the next spring, under the alien California sun of another campus, the question came again, and I could not put it out of my mind. I had won another fellowship that would have committed me to research for my doctorate, to a

An entire industry has grown up around a woman's "need" for cosmetics. A trip to the beauty salon was, and in some cases still is, a weekly ritual. Why might women of your mother's generation have participated in this ritual?

career as professional psychologist. "Is this really what I want to be?" The decision now truly terrified me. I lived in a terror of indecision for days, unable to think of anything else.

Why was she afraid of success? Are men ever indecisive in this way?

The question was not important, I told myself. No question was important to me that year but love. We walked in the Berkeley hills and a boy said: "Nothing can come of this, between us. I'll never win a fellowship like yours." Did I think I would be choosing, irrevocably, the cold loneliness of that afternoon if I went on? I gave up the fellowship, in relief. But for years afterward, I could not read a word of the science that once I had thought of as my future life's work; the reminder of its loss was too painful.

I never could explain, hardly knew myself, why I gave up this career. I lived in the present, working on newspapers with no particular plan. I married, had children, lived according to the feminine mystique as a suburban housewife. But still the question haunted me. I could sense no purpose in my life, I could find no peace, until I finally faced it and worked out my own answer.

What does she mean by "feminine mystique"?

I discovered, talking to Smith seniors in 1959, that the question is no less terrifying to girls today. Only they answer it now in a way that my generation found, after half a lifetime, not to be an answer at all. These girls, mostly seniors, were sitting in the living room of the college house, having coffee. It was not too different from such an evening when I was a senior, except that many more of the girls wore rings on their left hands. I asked the ones around me what they planned to be. The engaged ones spoke of weddings, apartments, getting a job as a secretary while husband finished school. The

Is this question equally terrifying today?

others, after a hostile silence, gave vague answers about this job or that, graduate study, but no one had any real plans. A blonde with a ponytail asked me the next day if I had believed the things they had said. "None of it was true," she told me. "We don't like to be asked what we want to do. None of us know. None of us even like to think about it. The ones who are going to be married right away are the lucky ones. They don't have to think about it."

But I noticed that night that many of the engaged girls, sitting silently around the fire while I asked the others about jobs, had also seemed angry about something. "They don't want to think about not going on," my ponytailed informant said. "They know they're not going to use their education. They'll be wives and mothers. You can say you're going to keep on reading and be interested in the community. But that's not the same. You won't really go on. It's a disappointment to know you're going to stop now, and not go on and use it."

In counterpoint, I heard the words of a woman, fifteen years after she left college, a doctor's wife, mother of three, who said over coffee in her New England kitchen:

> The tragedy was, nobody ever looked us in the eye and said you have to decide what you want to do with your life, besides being your husband's wife and children's mother. I never thought it through until I was thirty-six, and my husband was so busy with his practice that he couldn't entertain me every night. The three boys were in school all day. I kept on trying to have babies despite an Rh discrepancy. After two miscarriages, they said I must stop. I thought that my own growth and evolution were over. I always knew as a child that I was going to grow up and go to college, and then get married, and that's as far as a girl has to think. After that, your husband determines and fills your life. It wasn't until I got so lonely as the doctor's wife and kept screaming at the kids because they didn't fill my life that I realized I had to make my own life. I still had to decide what I wanted to be. I hadn't finished evolving at all. But it took me ten years to think it through.

The feminine mystique permits, even encourages, women to ignore the question of their identity. The mystique says they can answer the question "Who am I?" by saying "Tom's wife . . . Mary's mother." But I don't think the mystique would have such power over American women if they did not fear to face this terrifying blank which makes them unable to see themselves after twenty-one. The truth is—and how long it has been true, I'm not sure, but it was true in my generation and it is true of girls growing up today—an American woman no longer has a private image to tell her who she is, or can be, or wants to be.

The public image, in the magazines and television commercials, is designed to sell washing machines, cake mixes, deodorants, detergents, rejuvenating face creams, hair tints. But the power of that image, on which companies spend millions of dollars for television time and ad space, comes from this: American women no longer know who they are. They are sorely in need of a new image to help them find their identity. As the motivational researchers keep telling the advertisers, American women are so unsure of who they should be that they look to this glossy public image to decide every detail of their lives. They look for the image they will no longer take from their mothers.

In my generation, many of us knew that we did not want to be like our mothers, even when we loved them. We could not help but see their disappointment. Did we understand, or only resent, the sadness, the emptiness, that made them hold too fast to us, try to live our lives, run our fathers' lives, spend their days shopping or yearning for things that never seemed to satisfy them, no matter how much money they cost? Strangely, many mothers who loved their daughters—and mine was one—did not want their daughters to grow up like them either. They knew we needed something more.

But even if they urged, insisted, fought to help us educate ourselves, even if they talked with yearning of careers that were not open to them, they could not give us an image of what we could be. They could only tell us that their lives were too empty, tied to home; that children, cooking, clothes, bridge, and charities were not enough. A mother might tell her daughter, spell it out, "Don't be just a housewife like me." But that daughter, sensing that her mother was too frustrated to savor the love of her husband and children, might feel: "I will succeed where my mother failed, I will fulfill myself as a woman," and never read the lesson of her mother's life.

Recently, interviewing high-school girls who had started out full of promise and talent, but suddenly stopped their education, I began to see new dimensions to the problem

KEEP YOUR SHIRT ON

'TILL YOU SEE

hartog

I'M JUST HIS WIFE

BUT AFTER ALL, it was my idea that he get himself a smoother, Barbasol Face. Now I have to compete with other women at parties to get near that handsome man! It's unfair. I married him despite the rough skin and bristly beard he used to have because of old-fashioned shaving methods.

THAT CHEEK TO CHEEK WALK is hard to resist when a man has a Barbasol Face. For modern Barbasol contains beneficial oils that not only soften the beard, but also soothe the skin, helping to leave it soft and fresh and smooth.

YOU FACE YOUR MIRROR every morning with a smile when Barbasol's handy. Tender skin? Don't worry. Here's the coolest, smilingest, most comforting shave a man can have. You'll agree after a trial of ten days or so. 25¢ and 50¢ tubes. 75¢ jar. Barbasol Blades, 5 for 10¢, 15 for 25¢.

Barbasol

For modern shaving—
No Brush—No Lather—No Rub-in

Some of the advertising copy of a generation ago, particularly that directed toward men, presented a clear picture of women as sexual objects. The advertisement for men's shirts on the left is a blatant example. More subtle is the advertisement for shaving cream that suggests that a man who uses the product will be the cause of intense sexual rivalry among women—with the man's wife making a poor showing in the match. How does such advertising illustrate the point that women of Friedan's generation lacked an identity of their own?

of feminine conformity. These girls, it seemed at first, were merely following the typical curve of feminine adjustment. Earlier interested in geology or poetry, they now were interested only in being popular; to get boys to like them, they had concluded, it was better to be like all the other girls. On closer examination, I found that these girls were so terrified of becoming like their mothers that they could not see themselves at all. They were afraid to grow up. They had to copy in identical detail the composite image of the popular girl—denying what was best in themselves out of fear of femininity as they saw it in their mothers. One of these girls, seventeen years old, told me:

Are there any ethnic, regional, or religious differences in how girls grow up to be women in America?

Women may not have wanted their daughters to grow up like them, but they often reinforced stereotyped roles through what they permitted their children to do. Thus, a boy's free time might be filled with a job like a paper route, while a girl was expected to help with the housework. Compare your upbringing in this respect with that of your mother or father.

I want so badly to feel like the other girls. I never get over this feeling of being a neophyte, not initiated. When I get up and have to cross a room, it's like I'm a beginner, or have some terrible affliction, and I'll never learn. I go to the local hangout after school and sit there for hours talking about clothes and hairdos and the twist, and I'm not that interested, so it's an effort. But I found out I could make them like me—just do what they do, dress like them, talk like them, not do things that are different. I guess I even started to make myself not different inside.

I used to write poetry. The guidance office says I have this creative ability and I should be at the top of my class and have a great future. But things like that aren't what you need to be popular. The important thing for a girl is to be popular.

Is this still important today?

Now I go out with boy after boy, and it's such an effort because I'm not myself with them. It makes you feel even more alone. And besides, I'm afraid of where it's going to lead. Pretty soon, all my differences will be smoothed out, and I'll be the kind of girl that could be a housewife.

I don't want to think of growing up. If I had children, I'd want them to stay the same age. If I had to watch them grow up, I'd see myself growing older, and I wouldn't want to. My mother says she can't sleep at night, she's sick with worry over what I might do. When I was little, she wouldn't let me cross the street alone, long after the other kids did.

I can't see myself as being married and having children. It's as if I wouldn't have any personality myself. My mother's like a rock that's been smoothed by the waves, like a void. She's put so much into her family that there's nothing left, and she resents us because she doesn't get enough in return. But sometimes it seems like there's nothing there. My mother doesn't serve any purpose except cleaning the house. She isn't happy, and she doesn't make my father happy. If she didn't care about us children at all, it would have the same effect

What is your image of motherhood?

as caring too much. It makes you want to do the opposite. I don't think it's really love. When I was little and I ran in all excited to tell her I'd learned how to stand on my head, she was never listening.

Lately, I look into the mirror, and I'm so afraid I'm going to look like my mother. It frightens me, to catch myself being like her in gestures or speech or anything. I'm not like her in so many ways, but if I'm like her in this one way, perhaps I'll turn out like my mother after all. And that terrifies me.

And so the seventeen-year-old was so afraid of being a woman like her mother that she turned her back on all the things in herself and all the opportunities that would have made her a different woman, to copy from the outside the "popular" girls. And finally, in panic at losing herself, she turned her back on her own popularity and defied the conventional good behavior that would have won her a college scholarship. For lack of

Is refusing the opportunity for a career a retreat?

In the version of the American Dream permitted to women of past generations, success in life was measured by the kind of marriage they made. To what extent is this still the case?

an image that would help her grow up as a woman true to herself, she retreated into the beatnik vacuum.

• • •

The only other kind of women I knew, growing up, were the old-maid high-school teachers; the librarian; the one woman doctor in our town, who cut her hair like a man; and a few of my college professors. None of these women lived in the warm center of life as I had known it at home. Many had not married or had children. I dreaded being like them, even the ones who taught me truly to respect my own mind and use it, to feel that I had a part in the world. I never knew a woman, when I was growing up, who used her mind, played her own part in the world, and also loved, and had children.

Are there more role models for women today?

• • •

Can the role of housewife and mother give women an identity as a human being, in Friedan's sense?

Mine was the first college generation to run head-on into the new mystique of feminine fulfillment. Before then, while most women did indeed end up as housewives and mothers, the point of education was to discover the life of the mind, to pursue truth and to take a place in the world. There was a sense, already dulling when I went to college, that we would be New Women. Our world would be much larger than home. Forty per cent of my college class at Smith had career plans. But I remember how, even then, some of the seniors, suffering the pangs of that bleak fear of the future, envied the few who escaped it by getting married right away.

The ones we envied then are suffering that terror now at forty. "Never have decided what kind of woman I am. Too much personal life in college. Wish I'd studied more science, history, government, gone deeper into philosophy," one wrote on an alumnae questionnaire, fifteen years later. "Still trying to find the rock to build on. Wish I had finished college. I got married instead." "Wish I'd developed a deeper and more creative life of my own and that I hadn't become engaged and married at nineteen. Having expected the ideal in marriage, including a hundred-per-cent devoted husband, it was a shock to find this isn't the way it is," wrote a mother of six.

Did your mother go to college? Do you think that fact made a difference in her outlook?

• • •

It is my thesis that the core of the problem for women today is not sexual but a problem of identity—a stunting or evasion of growth that is perpetuated by the feminine mystique. It is my thesis that as the Victorian culture did not permit women to accept or gratify their basic sexual needs, our culture does not permit women to accept or gratify their basic need to grow and fulfill their potentialities as human beings, a need which is not solely defined by their sexual role.

What does the author mean by "a problem of identity"?

• • •

The search for identity is not new . . . in American thought—though in every generation, each man who writes about it discovers it anew. In America, from the beginning, it has somehow been understood that men must thrust into the future; the pace has always been too rapid for man's identity to stand still. In every generation, many men have suffered misery, unhappiness, and uncertainty because they could not take the image of the man they wanted to be from their fathers. The search for identity of the young man who can't go home again has always been a major theme of American writers. And it has always been considered right in America, good, for men to suffer these agonies of growth, to search for and find their own identities. The farm boy went to the city, the garment-maker's son became a doctor, Abraham Lincoln taught himself to read—these were more than rags-to-riches stories. They were an integral part of the American dream. The problem for many was money, race, color, class, which barred them from choice—not what they would be if they were free to choose.

Even today a young man learns soon enough that he must decide who he wants to be. If he does not decide in junior high, in high school, in college, he must somehow come to terms with it by twenty-five or thirty, or he is lost. But this search for identity is seen as a greater problem now because more and more boys cannot find images in our culture —from their fathers or other men—to help them in their search. The old frontiers have been conquered, and the boundaries of the new are not so clearly marked. More and more young men in America today suffer an identity crisis for want of any image of man worth pursuing, for want of a purpose that truly realizes their human abilities.

If liberated, won't women encounter the same problem—the lack of anything worth pursuing—as men? Would this be desirable?

But why have theorists not recognized this same identity crisis in women? In terms of the old conventions and the new feminine mystique women are not expected to grow up to find out who they are, to choose their human identity. Anatomy is woman's destiny, say the theorists of femininity; the identity of woman is determined by her biology.

But is it? More and more women are asking themselves this question. As if they were waking from a coma, they ask, "Where am I . . . what am I doing here?" For the first time in their history, women are becoming aware of an identity crisis in their own lives, a crisis which began many generations ago, has grown worse with each succeeding generation, and will not end until they, or their daughters, turn an unknown corner and make of themselves and their lives the new image that so many women now so desperately need.

In a sense that goes beyond any one woman's life, I think this is the crisis of women growing up—a turning point from an immaturity that has been called femininity to full human identity. I think women had to suffer this crisis of identity, which began a hundred years ago, and have to suffer it still today, simply to become fully human.

An Interview and Outline: Social Forces and Your Family

The autobiographical statements in this chapter cut across ethnic, racial, class, sex, and geographical lines, and reflect the ideals of four very different young people of a generation ago. Try to define in your own terms what their aspirations were. What, for instance, was the dream of Lear as she left high school? or of Puzo on the streets of Hell's Kitchen? or of Malcolm X after his father's death? or of Friedan in her college years? If you come to some understanding of these dreams, you are on your way to grasping what your parents might have felt. You can then compare the dreams of an earlier generation of young people with your own and those of your friends.

To help you formulate the similarities and differences, contrast the basic social forces emphasized in the four essays with the recollections of your parents. To what extent did patriotism, ethnicity, racism, or sexism affect their lives? If your parents are not immediately available for ques-

tioning, find someone at school or in the community who is about their age. What were their hopes in their youth? Were they achieved? If so, how? If not, why not? Before undertaking such an interview, you may find it helpful to refer again to the Appendix for suggestions on interviewing techniques (pp. 235–237) and for specific questions you might ask (pp. 269–271).

From the information that you gather, construct an outline on the theme "Changes in self-perception, in ideals, and in society over the past generation."

This is a good time, as well, to check yourself on the letters you have written in search of documents. Have you heard from the local governments or other respondents concerning the availability of public records on your ancestors? These things take time, and you cannot let these inquiries wait until the last moment.

four

The World We Have Lost

Think for a moment about your grandparents. Imagine if you can the time when they were your age. They were, once, you know. If you begin to count the ways in which their world differed from your world, you will realize how profound many of the changes are, or at least seem to be. No television or radio, probably no automobiles or electricity or indoor plumbing. Certainly no suburbs, Super Bowls, or supermarkets. And no toothpaste in a tube or *Time* magazine, rock music or six-packs.

Now imagine your great-grandparents and great-great-grandparents, and on to those anonymous ancestors even further back in time. We all have eight great-grandparents and sixteen great-great-grandparents. If you could go back nine generations beyond your parents, you would have 1,024 direct ancestors. How did all those people, especially the ones born before the middle of the nineteenth century, think about their lives? How did they spend their days?

There are, of course, some things that remain constant over the many centuries—birth, death, childhood, old age, marriage, and sexual relationships, as well as work, obtaining food, eating, and sleeping. But even here, differences between you and your distant relatives can be discerned. Attitudes toward childhood, death, and sex, for example, have changed dramatically over 200 years. The kind of work most people do and the processes of growing and preparing food have also been altered by time. Even family living has changed. Although recent historical investigation reveals that in the Western world, at least from the seventeenth century, most people have lived in nuclear rather than in extended families (i.e., they have lived in a household with mother, father, and children, with few people from another generation), still family relationships and the ways families live have certainly changed markedly over three centuries.

Generations vary a great deal in length, but if you could discover your sixty-four great-great-great-great-grandparents they would probably have lived about the time of the American Revolution. Where they lived would have influenced their life style, their hopes and fears and dreams. But whether they were members of an African tribe, peasants in eastern Europe, farmers in Ireland or Italy, or millers and merchants in America, they probably would have much more in common with each other than any of them would have with your generation.

For centuries, most men and women in all parts of the world lived close to the land. They probably died near where they were born, and they knew little of what went on beyond their village. They raised almost all they needed, and their work was closely related to their home and family. Their days and years were bounded and controlled by climate, weather, and the seasons.

We should not be overly nostalgic about this world of small communities where work was closely related to family routines and the rhythm of the seasons, for it was also a world of disease and early death, of constant struggle and frequent disaster. Then, more commonly than now, a strong religious faith provided both explanation and sustenance in the face of inevitable tragedies.

Wealth, position, and class have always made a difference in life style and even in life expectancy. To be a big landowner or a merchant was always to have an advantage over a peasant or an indentured servant. But even the wealthy in the seventeenth century fell victim to yellow fever epidemics and had to use candles for light, a fireplace for heat, and an outdoor privy.

Everyday life has been transformed in the last 150 years by a series of accelerating revolutions that are sometimes lumped together and called "industrialism." These revolutions have influenced every area of life, not just the process of manufacturing and production. Contemplate for a moment the changes that have occurred in transportation. Before the railroad began to connect cities in the mid–nineteenth century, the only way to travel overland was on horseback or in a horse-drawn vehicle (or, in some parts of the world, a vehicle drawn by another animal). People were limited to a distance of twenty-five or thirty miles a day. Travel was difficult and dangerous. The railroad, the automobile, and the airplane have made it possible to travel great distances with ease and comfort. It may now be impossible to find a person who remembers when the first railroad was built, but there are many who can remember when travel by train was still somewhat novel, and many others can recall the first automobile in town or the first airplane they ever saw. You probably have vivid memories of the first man to land on the moon. The rocket has not yet altered our daily lives to any great extent, but the railroad, the automobile, and the airplane make our lives very different from those who lived in the eighteenth century.

A similar revolution has occurred in communication. In the eighteenth century a letter or a newspaper sometimes took three months to go from Boston to London, and those living in the small communities away from the urban centers were even more isolated from news. The nineteenth-century inventions of the telegraph, the cable, and the telephone, and the twentieth-century inventions of radio and television, make any news event today instantly available in almost every part of the world and have certainly had a visual and audible impact on our lives that those living in the eighteenth century could not have imagined.

Other developments, such as electricity, indoor plumbing, food processing, refrigeration, the growth of large industry, and advertising also make our lives very different from those of our ancestors. Artificial heat, light, and air conditioning together with our great concern with the clock and the division of the day into hours and minutes have divorced our lives from the natural rhythm of climate, weather, and the seasons.

The revolutions that have transformed daily existence have taken place more rapidly in some parts of the world than in others. There are still pockets even in the United States where life has not changed a great deal since the eighteenth century. Perhaps you can discover such a place, or at least some people born in the 1880s or 1890s who remember life before electricity, indoor plumbing, and the internal-combustion engine. If you try you can recover something of the world we have lost. Just as important, you may come to appreciate how history has shaped your life and the lives of your ancestors.

THE PREINDUSTRIAL FAMILY
Peter Laslett

In the following essay Peter Laslett tries to re-create the life of a family of bakers in London in the early seventeenth century. It was a time when work was closely related to family life, when children were also workers, and when a wife was clearly subservient to her husband. It was surely no golden age, but it was a time quite unlike our own. Most of our ancestors were probably not bakers in London, but wherever they lived and whatever their occupations they probably had much more in common with these bakers than with anyone living in the last quarter of the twentieth century.

As you read this essay notice how much the author is able to read into one document. That technique may be useful to you as you attempt to recover the history of your own family. Try to determine how the life style of these men, women, and children differs from your own. Whether you decide that we have made great progress since 1619 or have in some ways declined, you will agree with the author that things have changed dramatically. We are, as the author notes at the end, "very different from our ancestors."

In the year 1619 the bakers of London applied to the authorities for an increase in the price of bread. They sent in support of their claim a complete description of a bakery and an account of its weekly costs. There were thirteen or fourteen people in such an undertaking: the baker and his wife, four paid employees who were called journeymen, two apprentices, two maidservants and the three or four children of the master baker himself. Six pounds ten shillings a week was reckoned to be the outgoings of this establishment of which only eleven shillings and eightpence went for wages: half a crown a week for each of the journeymen and tenpence for each of the maids. Far and away the greatest expense was for food: two pounds nine shillings out of the six pounds ten shillings, at five shillings a head for the baker and his wife, four shillings a head for their helpers and two shillings for their children. It cost much more in food to keep a journeyman than it cost in money; four times as much to keep a maid. Clothing was charged up too, not only for the man, wife and children, but for the apprentices as well. Even school fees were claimed as a justifiable charge on the price of bread for sale, and sixpence a week was paid for the teaching and clothing of a baker's child.

A London bakery was undoubtedly what we should call a commercial or even an industrial undertaking, turning out loaves by the thousand. Yet the business was carried on in the house of the baker himself. There was probably a *shop* as part of the house, *shop* as in *workshop* and not as meaning a retail establishment. Loaves were not ordinarily sold over the counter: they had to be carried to the open-air market and displayed on stalls. There was a garner behind the house, for which the baker paid two shillings a week in rent, and where he kept his wheat, his *sea-coal* for the fire and his store of

> What conclusions do you draw about the structure of the family 350 years ago from the fact that workers were fed by their employers?

What does this illustration suggest about the nature of family life and its relationship to work? What time of day might this be? How do you explain the scene in terms of Laslett's emphasis on the small scale of urban life?

salt. The house itself was one of those high, half-timbered overhanging structures on the narrow London street which we always think of when we remember the scene in which Shakespeare, Pepys or even Christopher Wren lived. Most of it was taken up with the living-quarters of the dozen people who worked there.

It is obvious that all these people ate in the house since the cost of their food helped to determine the production cost of the bread. Except for the journeymen they were all obliged to sleep in the house at night and live together as a family.

The only word used at that time to describe such a group of people was "family." The man at the head of the group, the entrepreneur, the employer, or the manager, was then known as the master or head of the family. He was father to some of its members and in place of father to the rest. There was no sharp distinction between his domestic and his economic functions. His wife was both his partner and his subordinate, a partner because she ran the family, took charge of the food and managed the women-servants, a subordinate because she was woman and wife, mother and in place of mother to the rest.

Was the wife's role more central to the workings of the family in the past than now? Why or why not?

The paid servants of both sexes had their specified and familiar position in the family, as much part of it as the children but not quite in the same position. At that time the family was not one society only but three societies fused together; the society of man and wife, of parents and children and of master and servant. But when they were young, and servants were, for the most part, young, unmarried people, they were very close to children in their status and their function. Here is the agreement made between the parents of a boy about to become an apprentice and his future master. The boy covenants to dwell with his master for seven years, to keep his secrets and to obey his commandments.

> Taverns and alehouses he shall not haunt, dice, cards or any other unlawful games he shall not use, fornication with any woman he shall not commit, matrimony with any woman he shall not contract. He shall not absent himself by night or by day without his master's leave but be a true and faithful servant.

On his side, the master undertakes to teach his apprentice his *"art, science or occupation with moderate correction."*

> Finding and allowing unto his said servant meat, drink, apparel, washing, lodging and all other things during the said term of seven years, and to give unto his said apprentice at the end of the said term double apparel, to wit, one suit for holydays and one suit for worken days.

Apprentices, therefore, and many other servants, were workers who were also children, extra sons or extra daughters (for girls could be apprenticed too), clothed and educated as well as fed, obliged to obedience and forbidden to marry, often unpaid and dependent until after the age of twenty-one. If such servants were workers in the position of sons and daughters, the sons and daughters of the house were workers too. John Locke laid it down in 1697 that the children of the poor must work for some part of the day when they reached the age of three. The children of a London baker were not free to go to school for many years of their young lives, or even to play as they wished when they came back home. Soon they would find themselves doing what they could in *bolting,* that is sieving flour, or in helping the maidservant with her panniers of loaves on the way to the market stall, or in playing their small parts in preparing the never-ending succession of meals for the whole household.

Why do you think childhood education was so little valued then?

We may see at once, therefore, that the world we have lost, as I have chosen to call it, was no paradise or golden age of equality, tolerance or loving kindness. It is so important that I should not be misunderstood on this point that I will say at once that the coming of industry cannot be shown to have brought economic oppression and exploitation along with it. It was there already. The patriarchal arrangements which we have begun to explore were not new in the England of Shakespeare and Elizabeth. They were as old as the Greeks, as old as European history, and not confined to Europe. And it may well be that they abused and enslaved people quite as remorselessly as the economic arrangements which had replaced them in the England of Blake and Victoria. When people could expect to live for so short a time, how must a man have felt when he realized that so much of his adult life must go in working for his keep and very little more in someone else's family?

But people very seldom recognize facts of this sort, and no one is content to expect to live as long as the majority in fact will live. Every servant in the old social world was probably quite confident that he or she would some day get married and be at the head of a new family, keeping others in subordination. If it is legitimate to use the words exploitation and oppression in thinking of the economic arrangements of the pre-industrial world, there were nevertheless differences in the manner of oppressing and exploiting. The ancient order of society was felt to be eternal and unchangeable by those who supported, enjoyed and endured it. There was no expectation of reform. How could there be when economic organization was domestic organization, and relationships were rigidly regulated by the social system, by the content of Christianity itself?

Here is a vivid contrast with social expectation in Victorian England, or in industrial countries everywhere today. Every relationship in our world which can be seen to affect our economic life is open to change, is expected indeed to change of itself, or if it does not, to *be* changed, made better, by an omnicompetent authority. This makes for a less stable social world, though it is only one of the features of our society which impels us all in that direction. All industrial societies, we may suppose, are far less stable than their predecessors. They lack the extraordinarily cohesive influence which familial relationships carry with them, that power of reconciling the frustrated and the discontented by emotional means. Social revolution, meaning an irreversible changing of the pattern of social relationships, never happened in traditional, patriarchal, pre-industrial human society. It was almost impossible to contemplate.

With the breakdown of the family today, is more social revolution inevitable?

• • •

73

... There are reasons why a baker's household might have been a little out of the ordinary, for baking was a highly traditional occupation in a society increasingly subject to economic change. [And] ... a family of thirteen people, which was also a unit of production of thirteen, less the children still incapable of work, was quite large for English society at that time. Only the families of the really important, the nobility and the gentry, the aldermen and the successful merchants, were ordinarily as large as this. In fact, we can take the bakery to represent the upper limit in size and scale of the group in which ordinary people lived and worked. Among the great mass of society which cultivated the land, ... the family group was smaller than a substantial London craftsman's entourage. There are other things we should observe about the industrial and commercial scene.

It is worth noticing to begin with, how prominently the town and the craft appear in the folk-memory we still retain from the world we have lost. Agriculture and the countryside do not dominate our recollections to anything like the extent that they dominated that vanished world. We still talk to our children about the apprentices who married their master's daughter: these are the heroes. Or about the outsider who marries the widow left behind by the father/master when he comes to die: these unwelcome strangers to the family are the villains. We refer to bakers as if they really baked in their homes; of spinsters who really sit by the fire and spin. A useful, if a rather arbitrary and romantic guide to the subject in hand, is the famous collection of Fairy Tales compiled by the brothers Grimm in Germany nearly 150 years ago, where the tales we tell to our children mostly have their source. Even in the form given to them by Walt Disney and the other makers of films and picture-books for the youngest members of our rich, leisurely, powerful, puzzled world of successful industrialization, stories like Cinderella are a sharp reminder of what life was once like for the apprentice, the journeyman, the master and all his family in the craftsman's household. Which means, in a sense, that we all know it all already.

Are there other stories and expressions we have inherited to remind us of this lost life?

• • •

... Let us emphasize again the scale of life in the working family of the London baker. Few persons in the old world ever found themselves in groups larger than family groups, and there were few families of more than a dozen members. The largest household so far known to us, apart from the royal court and the establishments of the nobility, lay and spiritual, is that of Sir Richard Newdigate, Baronet, in his house of Arbury within his parish of Chilvers Coton in Warwickshire, in the year 1684. There were thirty-seven people in Sir Richard's family: himself; Lady Mary Newdigate, his wife; seven daughters, all under the age of sixteen; and twenty-eight servants, seventeen men and boys and eleven women and girls. This was still a family, not an institution, a staff, an office or a firm.

Everything physical was on the human scale, for the commercial worker in London, and the miner who lived and toiled in Newdigate's village of Chilvers Coton. No object in England was larger than London Bridge or St. Paul's Cathedral, no structure in the Western World to stand comparison with the Colosseum in Rome. Everything temporal was tied to the human life-span too. The death of the master baker, head of the family, ordinarily meant the end of the bakery. Of course there might be a son to succeed, but the master's surviving children would be young if he himself had lived only as long as most men. Or an apprentice might fulfil the final function of apprenticehood, substitute sonship, that is to say, and marry his master's daughter, or even his widow. Surprisingly often, the widow, if she could, would herself carry on the trade.

This, therefore, was not simply a world without factories, without firms, and for the most part without economic continuity. Some partnerships between rich masters existed, especially in London, but since nearly every activity was limited to what could be organized within a family, and the lifetime of its head, there was an unending struggle to manufacture continuity and to provide an expectation of the future.

Is the need to provide a sense of continuity as great today?

• • •

When we insist on the tiny scale of life in the pre-industrial world, especially on the small size of the group in which nearly everybody spent their lives, there are, of course, certain occasions and institutions which we must not overlook. There were the military practices, an annual muster of the ablebodied men from every county, which took place after harvest in Tudor times. There were regular soldiers too, though not very many of them; variegated bands of the least promising of men straggling behind the banner of some noble adventurer. Much more familiar to Englishmen, at least in the maritime areas, must have been the sailors; twenty, thirty, even fifty men at sea, sometimes for days, or even weeks on end.

Lilliputian, we must feel, when we compare such details with the crowds we meet in our society. The largest crowd recorded for seventeenth-century England, that is the Parliamentary Army which fought at Marston Moor, would have gone three, four or even five times into the sporting stadium of today. Other organizations and purposes which brought groups of people together were the Assizes in the County Towns; the Quarter Sessions of the County Justices; the meetings of the manorial courts in the villages, of the town councils in the towns, of the companies or craftsmen there, each one to a trade or occupation; the assemblies which sometimes took place of clergy or of nonconformist ministers. Most regular of all, and probably largest in scale and most familiar to ordinary men and women were the weekly market days and the annual fairs in each locality. Then there were the 2,000 schools in England, one for every fifth parish but very few large enough to have more than a single teacher, and the two universities, with less than 10,000 men between them. Then there was Parliament itself. All these occasions and institutions assembled men in some numbers for purposes which could not be called familial. Women too assembled, though, save to the markets, they came as spectators rather than as participants.

The fact that it is possible to name most of the large-scale institutions and occasions in a sentence or two makes the contrast with our own world more telling than ever. We have only to think of the hundreds of children sitting every day, all over the country, in their classrooms, the hundreds and thousands together in the factories, the offices, the shops, to recognize the difference. The detailed study of the pre-industrial social world makes this question of scale more critical still. Wherever the facts of economic life and technology required a working group different in size and constitution from the working family, there was discontinuity. Hence the crew of a ship, the team of workers on a building, the fifty or sixty grown men who might be required to work a mine or an

How is the scene in this preindustrial bakery similar to other productive facilities prior to industrialization? What does the picture suggest about the quality and quantity of the work? What does a modern bakery look like?

armaments manufactory, were all looked upon as exceptional. As indeed they were, so much so that the building trade had had its own society from medieval times, and the miners were a community apart wherever they were found.

Not only did the scale of their work and the size of the group which was engaged make them exceptional, the constitution of the group did too. In the baking household we have chosen as our standard, sex and age were mingled together. Fortunate children might go out to school, but adults did not usually go out to work. There was nothing to correspond to the thousands of young men on the assembly line, the hundreds of young women in the offices, the lonely lives of housekeeping wives, which we now know only too well. We shall see that those who survived to old age in the much less favourable conditions for survival which then were prevalent, were surprisingly often left to live and die alone, in their tiny cottages or sometimes in the almshouses which were being built so widely in the England of the Tudors and the Stuarts. Poor-law establishments, parochial in purpose and in size, had begun their melancholy chapter in the history of the English people. But institutional life was otherwise almost unknown. There were no hotels, hostels, or blocks of flats for single persons, very few hospitals and none of the kind we are familiar with, almost no young men and women living on their own. The family unit where so great a majority lived was what we should undoubtedly call a "balanced" and "healthy" group.

When we turn from the hand-made city of London to the hand-moulded immensity of rural England, we may carry the same sentimental prejudice along with us. To every farm there was a family, which spread itself over its portion of the village lands as the family of the master-craftsman filled out his manufactory. When a holding was small, and most were small as are the tiny holdings of European peasants today, a man tilled it with the help of his wife and his children. No single man, we must remember, would usually take charge of the land, any more than a single man would often be found at the head of a workshop in the city. The master of a family was expected to be a householder, whether he was a butcher, a baker, a candlestick maker or simply a husbandman, which was the universal name for one whose skill was in working the land. Marriage we must insist, and it is one of the rules which gave its character to the society of our ancestors, was the entry to full membership, in the enfolding countryside, as well as in the scattered urban centres.

But there was a difference in scale and organization of work on the land and in the town. The necessities of rural life did require recurrent groupings of households for common economic purposes, occasionally something like a crowd of men, women and children working together for days on end. Where the ground was still being tilled as open fields, and each household had a number of strips scattered all over the whole open area and not a compact collection of enclosures, ploughing was co-operative, as were many other operations, above all harvesting, and this continued even after enclosure. We do not yet know how important this element of enforced common activity was in the life of the English rural community on the eve of industrialization, or how much difference enclosure made in this respect. But whatever the situation was, the economic transformation of the eighteenth and nineteenth centuries destroyed communality altogether in English rural life. The group of men from several farmsteads working the heavy plough in springtime, the bevy of harvesters from every house in the village wading into the high standing grass to begin the cutting of the hay, had no successors in large-scale economic activity. For the arrangement of these groups was entirely different in principle from the arrangement of a factory, or a firm, or even of a collective farm.

Both before and after enclosure, some peasants did well: their crops were heavier and they had more land to till. To provide the extra labour needed then, the farming householder, like the successful craftsman, would extend his working family by taking on young men and women as servants to live with him and work the fields. This he would have to do, even if the land which he was farming was not his own but rented from the great family in the manor house. Sometimes, we have found, he would prefer to send out his own children as servants and bring in other children and young men to do the work. This is one of the few glimpses we can get into the quality of the emotional life of the family at this time, for it shows that parents may have been unwilling to submit children of their own to the discipline of work at home. It meant, too, that servants were not simply the perquisites of wealth and position. A quarter, or a third, of all the families in the country contained servants in Stuart times, and this meant that very humble

Does living in a mass society encourage or discourage personal relationships?

Is marriage as essential to maintaining society and sustaining the individual today?

76

people had them as well as the titled and the wealthy. Most of the servants, moreover, male or female, in the great house and in the small, were engaged in working the land.

The boys and the men would do the ploughing, hedging, carting and the heavy, skilled work of the harvest. The women and the girls would keep the house, prepare the meals, make the butter and the cheese, the bread and the beer, and would also look after the cattle and take the fruit to market. At harvest-time, from June to October, every hand was occupied and every back was bent. These were the decisive months for the whole population in our damp northern climate, with its single harvest in a season and reliance on one or two standard crops. So critical was the winning of the grain for bread that the first rule of gentility (a gentleman never worked with his hands for his living) might be abrogated.

We have hinted that a fundamental characteristic of the world we have lost was the scene of labour, which was universally supposed to be the home. It has been implied in the case of industry and in towns, that the hired man who came in to work during the day and went home to his meals at night was looked on as exceptional. Apart from the provisions about journeymen, who were, in fact, the focus of whatever difficulty in "labour relations" was experienced at this time in the towns, no standard arrangement has been found which contemplated any permanent division of place of living and place of employment. That such divisions existed, and may even have been commonplace in town and in country, cannot be in doubt. There is evidence that a clothmaker in a big way, in the city of Beauvais in France at any rate, would have machinery in his house for more men than could possibly have lived there. It is thought that men walked in from the villages to Beauvais to do their day's work, just as men used to walk from the villages to the towns to work on the building sites in Victorian England. In those areas of England which first became industrial, there are signs that, like those in Beauvais, they too must have contained economic units which had to be supplied by daily wage labour. It came also, maybe, from the surrounding country, but certainly from the grown sons of families living in the town as well, young men, perhaps, even older men and married men, who cannot have been working where they lived. But when all this is said, the division of dwelling place and working place was no recognized feature of the social structure of the towns which our ancestors inhabited. The journey to work, the lonely lodger paying his rent out of a factory wage or office salary, are the distinguishing marks of our society, not of theirs. We are forced to suppose that in industrial and commercial matters the working family was assumed to be self-sufficient in its labour, in spite of the vicissitudes of the market.

But the level of activity in agriculture is fundamentally rhythmic, and its labour demands inevitably vary with the time of the year, the weather in the week, as well as with the prices of its products on the market. To work the land at all, especially as we have already hinted with the climate and geology of England, provision had to be made for a pool of labour, which the farming family could use or not as the farmer himself should decide. The manner in which this economic necessity was provided for shows how well the traditional, patriarchal structure of society could be adapted to meet the needs of a particular economy. It has to be traced in the life stories of the men and the women who lived in the villages and worked the land, or who pursued those occupations which were settled in the countryside, and were as much a part of its life as what went on in the stables and the barns. Let us begin with the life cycle of a poor inhabitant of an English village.

A boy, or a girl, born in a cottage, would leave home for service at any time after the age of ten. A servant-in-husbandry, as he might be called if he were a boy, would usually stay in the position of servant, though very rarely in the same household, until he or she got married. Marriage, when and if it came, would quite often take place with another servant. All this while, and it might be twelve, fifteen or even twenty years, the servant would be kept by the succession of employers in whose houses he dwelt. He was in no danger of poverty or hunger, even if the modest husbandman with whom he lived was worse housed than his landlord's horses, and worse clothed than his landlord's servants. "His landlord's horses," wrote a contemporary of the lowly husbandman, "lie in finer houses, than he, and his meanest servant wears a cloth beyond him." But the husbandman had his own servant, nevertheless, for when he said family prayers after a day's exhausting toil "the wife is sleeping in one corner, the child in another, the servant in a third."

But poverty awaited the husbandman's servant when he got married, and went him-

Why did industrialization foster commuting and apartment dwelling?

self to live in just such a labourer's cottage as the one in which he had been born. Whoever had been his former master, the labourer, late servant in husbandry, would be liable to fall into want directly [after] his wife began to have children and he lost the earnings of his companion. Once he found himself outside the farming household his living had to come from his wages, and he, with every member of his family, was subject for his labour to the local vagaries in the market. Day-labourer was now his full description, for he earned what money came his way by contracting for work a day at a time with the gentlemen, yeomen, and husbandmen of his village. This was a source of the variable casual labour needed to keep agriculture going, and the poor cottager could expect mainly seasonal employment at a wage fixed, as indeed his wage as a servant had been fixed, by the justices of the peace. Two forms of wage were laid out in the published tables, with and without meat and drink. The day-labourer visiting a farm for his work could claim his place at the table along with the servants living-in; it might be said that he was made a member of the working family for that day by breaking bread with the permanent members. It was almost a sacramental matter.

But his own casual earnings were not the only fund on which the labourer had to live. There was the produce of the little plot of land lying round his cottage to begin with. Elizabeth's government had decreed that it should be four acres in size though this cannot have been anything like a general rule. Then there were the pennies thrown to his children for bird scaring, or catching vermin, or minding sheep—the little boy blue who burst into tears in the nursery rhyme might easily have been of nursery age. But above all, there were the earnings of his wife and the whole of his little family at "industrial" occupations. A little family because every grown child would have to leave, and because death came quickly. It was the cottagers of England who carried on the great woollen industry of England, spinning the yarn which the capitalist clothiers brought to their doors. Industry, in fact, kept the poor alive in the England of our ancestors, and the problem of poverty in their own opinion could only have been solved by the spread of industrial activity. Though men did not seem to have seen it in quite this way, the existence of industry also helped to ensure that enough people lived on the land to meet the seasonal demands of agriculture.

The men and women whose livelihood came from crafts, agricultural and industrial, lived under the same system of servanthood until marriage. So indeed did the merchants and the shopkeepers. Not all households took part in this system all the time. At any moment a quarter or a third of the households of a community would contain servants, and a similar proportion would have children absent from home and in service. The households which remained would at that point in time be unaffected by the system of service, but many of them, perhaps most, would at other stages of their development either yield up or take in servants. This is the sense in which it could be said that service was practically a universal characteristic of pre-industrial English society.

Industry at this time was carried on not only by individual productive units, like the bakery in London, but by the *putting-out* system, in which several households were set on work by one middleman, the clothier-capitalist we have referred to. Much of it was done in the spare time of the farming population, not simply by the labourers, but by the farmers and their families as well, the simpler operations, that is to say, the sorting and carding and spinning of the wool. But the weaving, the dyeing and dressing of the cloth was usually the work of families of weavers, shearmen or dyers who did nothing else for nine months of the year. If they worked on the land of the villages where they lived it was only in harvest-time, from late June, when the haymaking began, till late September when the last of the wheat or the barley would be brought home.

Hence it came about that the English village contained not simply the husbandmen, the labourers and their families, with the smith, the ploughwright, the miller and the men who plied the agricultural trades, but textile workers too. In the Midlands there were nailers and miners, and everywhere everyone might also work on the land, during the crisis of harvest-time. Such are the rough outlines of the system whereby the independent household was preserved, yet made to collaborate with other independent households in the working of the land, and in the production of cloth. Capitalism, we must notice, was a feature of the system, that store of wealth and raw materials in the hands of the clothier which made it possible for him to give work to the villagers and yet not move them from the village. In the world we have lost, then, industry and agriculture lived together in some sort of symmetry, and the unity of the family was in no way in jeopardy.

In what sense was the preindustrial family "patriarchal" if women and children played such key roles in sustaining it?

78

...

The word alienation is part of the cant of the mid-twentieth century and it began as an attempt to describe the separation of the worker from his world of work. We need not accept all that this expression has come to convey in order to recognize that it does point to something vital to us all in relation to our past. Time was when the whole of life went forward in the family, in a circle of loved, familiar faces, known and fondled objects, all to human size. That time has gone for ever. It makes us very different from our ancestors.

Is the reintegration of work life and family life possible? Is it desirable?

The Estate of Michael D. Davis, 1800-1837
Vermont Sheep Farmer

One technique historians use to reconstruct the everyday life of the past is to examine the estate inventories that are preserved in probate records. Michael D. Davis, a sheep farmer in Vermont, died unexpectedly in 1837, leaving a widow and two small children. Before his estate could be settled, an inventory was conducted listing all his possessions.

His one cash crop was probably wool, although he might in addition have sold or traded some of his grain, potatoes, and hay. If he had died in the spring rather than in the fall, he would not have had such a large supply of these items on hand. His large kettle, which was broken and awaiting repair, had many uses, including the separation from hardwood ashes of potash, a product used in the manufacture of soap and glass that also might be sold.

Davis seems to have raised most of the food he needed, even making his own maple sugar. His meat was salted and stored in one of the barrels, the most common means for storing and transporting all products in his day. His wife used the two spinning wheels to make most of the clothes the family wore. Notice that the only book he owned was a Bible and that one of his most valuable possessions was a bay mare that, among other things, provided him transportation to the Congregational Meeting House on Sunday. When his horse and wagon took him to town, he could visit the miller, the blacksmith, the harness maker, or the cooper. He might purchase salt at the store, for that was one of the few items he could not grow. His best shoes may have been made by the shoemaker, his best pantaloons by a tailor. But he probably made the boots himself, and his wife made the rest of the clothes—even coats, vests, and hats. For a man his age, in that part of the country, he was reasonably well off. Notice, however, that most of his wealth was in land.

How would a list of your possessions compare with his?

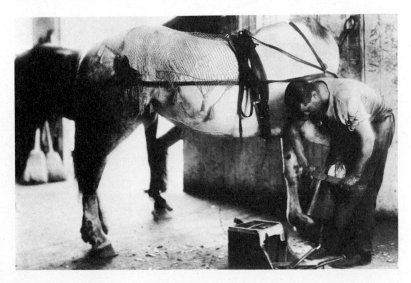

In the era in which Michael Davis lived, every town, no matter how small, had a blacksmith. Why was he essential in an age when people were so self-sufficient?

55 acres of land off from Lot no 74 first division of
    the original Right of John Pyanger in the
    township of Wolcott together with the buildings
    attached thereto at $700.00
The whole of Lot no 69 first Division of the Right of
    Derrick L. Goes supposed to contain one
    hundred acres being in said Wolcott at   400.00
3 Pews in the Congregational Meeting House in
    said Wolcott at 10 Dollars each   30.00

1 Brindle Cow	16.00
1 Red Cow	14.00
1 2 year old Bull	10.00
3 calves @ 4.00	12.00
27 sheep	40.50
23 sheep	33.75
28 sheep	28.00
20 lbs sugar	1.80
1 saddle	5.00
200 old sap buckets	8.00
70 new " "	5.60
1 gun and equipment	4.00
4 pelts	2.00
1 new axe	1.50
1 1/2 B salt	1.67
1 Linnen Wheel	1.00
1 Woollen "	1.00
2 meat Barrells	1.00
1 bushel Basket	.34
1 Large Bible	3.00
1 Over Coat	5.00
1 Light "	5.00
1 pr blue Pantaloons	1.00
1 pr grey "	2.00
1 pr blue "	2.75
1 thick vest	2.00
1 thin vest	2.00
1 pr thin boots	1.50
1 " " shoes	1.50
1 " horse hyde shoes	.50
1 neck stock	1.00
3 soft hats	6.00
Lot Pine Lumber	25.00
1 wood saw	1.00
a hay knife	.75
1 iron square	.38
1 set of bench planes	1.25
a auger	.34
1 pr Large Steel yards	1.00
1 pr Small " "	.50
1 Cook Stove, pipe etc	20.00

1 Bay Mare	57.50
20 Tons Hay	120.00
18 B. Wheat	25.50
25 B. Oats	8.75
200 B. Potatoes	40.00
500 lb pork in the hog	37.50
1 Single Sleigh	18.00
1 old "	4.00
1 harness	3.25
1 no. 1 caldron kettle (broken)	3.50
1 cart	6.00
1 gig wagon	12.00
3 shoats	15.00
1 chain	1.67
1 single harness & bells	8.00
244 lbs wool	85.40
1 wood clock	8.00
a pail pot	1.00
1 tea kettle	.75
1 Spider	.50
1 broken kettle	.20
1 tin Baker	.50
1 4 foot table fall leaf	2.00
1 pine leaf table	.50
1 light stand	1.00
7 dining chairs	3.50
6 kitchen "	1.50
1 old desk	2.00
1 bureau	6.00
1 looking glass	.50
1 trunk	1.75
1 dozen printed plates	1.25
1 " edged "	.42
1 Tea set	1.00
1 Nappy	.17
1 pitcher	.20
1 stone cream pot	.50
1 stone preserve pot, tin pans	1.45
2 earthen pans, 1 shaker pail	.62
1 case knives and forks	.50
1 Bed and Bedding	15.00
1 Bed and Bedding	12.00
1 small Bed and Bedding	3.00

Debts due the estate Book note, some doubtful
                              150.00

Isaac Pennock Jr., Ephram Ladd appraisers

	$2067.96
Whole Amount of Real Estate	1130.00
Whole Amount of Personal Estate	937.96

NINETEENTH-CENTURY SELF-SUFFICIENCY: A PLANTER'S AND HOUSEWIFE'S "DO-IT-YOURSELF" ENCYCLOPEDIA

JO ANN CARRIGAN

Most rural women living in the nineteenth century, or for that matter anytime before the nineteenth century, in addition to being wives and mothers often ran a domestic factory and served as nurse, pharmacist, veterinarian, and engineer. The way many women actually lived contrasted sharply with the image of women in their day as weak, submissive, pure, and defenseless. This essay is based on a family manuscript and illustrates many aspects of everyday life. Perhaps you can find a similar document among your own family's papers or, by talking to your grandparents, you may be able to recover an oral tradition that includes home remedies, recipes, and a family folklore.

... **T**he nineteenth-century rural housewife baked her own bread, cakes, and pies; preserved the food products of the farm; made her own soap, candles, furniture polish, and other basic household items, as well as her feminine luxuries such as cologne and curling liquid. In addition to his basic knowledge of farming, the planter needed considerable information at his fingertips regarding the care of his farm animals and the treatment of diseases to which they might fall victim. Furthermore, it was not at all uncommon for farmers to practice medicine among their families, and slaves if they owned any, during the ante bellum period. Since the nearest physician ordinarily was many miles away and licensing requirements were practically nonexistent, manuals of instruction in "Domestic Medicine" as well as the drugs used in regular medical practice were readily available to all who had the price. An intelligent planter who had read and absorbed several medical handbooks and incorporated with that knowledge his own common sense and empirical outlook could be expected to have at least as much success as many self-styled doctors or poorly trained ones. From the baking of one's own bread to the practice of one's own medicine, the rural individual of the nineteenth century supplied his needs and solved his problems in an essentially different fashion from that of the participants in today's interdependent socio-economic framework.

Do you think we have given up too much of our self-reliance?

A manuscript discovered in southwest Arkansas several years ago provides a good reflection of this nineteenth-century rural self-sufficiency through hundreds of specific illustrations which it contains. Filed away in an old bookcase in the home of Mrs. Carrie Carrigan in Ozan (Hempstead County), Arkansas, this small hard-backed composition book had been forgotten and unopened for many years. It seems that this two-hundred-page handwritten compilation of medical remedies, cooking recipes and other practical information was brought to Arkansas from North Carolina in the 1850's by Alfred H. Carrigan and his young bride, Mary E. Moore, along with a number of other books from the Moore family library. Containing a wealth of information arranged topically, in alphabetical order, and even partially indexed, the little manual must have been exceed-

82

Can you imagine what life was like for a family on the so-called "sod house frontier" of the plains? Does the family portrait suggest a close-knit family? Do you feel any great tension with everyone in the small house living so close together? Can you imagine month after month of frozen winter in that house? Why are so many family members dressed in the same cloth? What was the woman's life like? From where do you suppose these people came to the frontier?

ingly helpful to that young couple settling in a place relatively distant from their former homes. In fact, for a time it was probably the most useful reference book in their entire library.

Approximately the first quarter of the manuscript consists of remedies for the diseases and ailments of man—asthma, bilious fever, bruises, burns, chills and fevers, colds, deafness and earache, hydrophobia, hiccups, itch, nettle rash, poisoning, rheumatism, ringworm, sore throat, toothache, warts, whooping cough, and worms—to list only a few. The treatments described in the handbook incorporated some of the valid procedures as well as the fallacious practices of early and mid-nineteenth-century medicine, in addition to a generous selection of folk remedies, some of value and some absurd.

Immediately following the remedies for human ailments is a section dealing with veterinary medicine, classified under these headings: Horses, Cows, Sheep, Hogs, and Chickens. The first entry relating to horses set forth a detailed description of their teeth at various ages—information which any person wishing to become a good horse trader needed to know. Other entries prescribed remedies for such horse ailments as bots or grubs, breaking-out, colic, founder, galls, heaves, strains, and wounds.

Treatments for diseases and disorders among cows included measures for colic, hoven,

What home remedies for diseases has your family passed down to you?

83

kicking, lice, milk fever, sprains, and worms. One of the several alternative entries for colic suggested this course of action:

> Make a band of twisted straw and place it in its mouth and make it fast on top of the head just behind the horns, in the act of chewing the band she will open the gullet & let the air out.

A simple but ingenious method designed to solve the problem of a kicking cow was to "ty a rope round her horns and draw it over a beam, then draw it until it raises her head pretty high but do not raise her fore feet of[f] the ground ..." According to the handbook, "she will not only be disabled from kicking but also will let dow[n] the milk."

Under the heading "Sheep," the first item stated that "The seed of broom corn is better than indian corn to fatten sheep." Following that entry, appropriate treatments were listed for apoplexy, blackmuzzle, rot, flies, wounds, and other sheep disorders. To prevent sheep rot, the manual advised quite sensibly that the sheep "always have a lump of salt to lick in their troughs." The one general medicine prescribed "For the common diseases of pigs" consisted of a compound of sulphur, madder, saltpeter, and black antimony.

To fatten chickens, the little encyclopedia instructed that they be fed on a mixture of half-cooked rice, milk, and sugar, noting that "The rice will give a delicate whiteness to the flesh." Furthermore, that entry advised that "charcoal broken in small peaces increases the appetite & promotes digestion"—among chickens, that is. For a poultry ailment called the "Gaps," one might either "smoke them with tobacco untill they quit crying," or "put asefedity in the water & in the meal," or "strip a feather except 1 1/2 inches at the end, lay the chicken on its back, stretch out its neck, put the feather in its windpipe, twist it round, pull it out." One rather quaint, if seemingly meaningless, remedy for "Chip" among chickens recommended that one "shut them up for 24 hours without food or raiment."

In the handbook's section on veterinary medicine a total of seventy-four separate entries dealt with preventive as well as remedial measures for various animal diseases and proper care of the farm stock. With such information readily at hand, presumably a farmer could have handled most medical problems which might have risen among his animals. The remainder of the manual consists of cooking recipes and assorted information of obvious value to both the head of the household and his wife.

A highly practical entry entitled "To ascertain the weight of live stock" described a method by which one might figure the weight of his animals without the use of a scale:

> Multiply the length from the root of the tail to the front of the shoulder by the girt and this by 23 if it is less than 7 feet & more than five in girt. By 31 when it is less than 9 & more than 7. By 16 when less than 5 & more than 3, by a leven when less than 3 feet. For a half fatted calf, or a cow which has had a calf, deduct 1 stone in 20, allowing 14 lbs to be a stone.

In a similar fashion the farmer was also able to "weigh" his corn (both shelled and unshelled) by measuring the length, breadth, and thickness of the container.

From a scheme for weighing corn and livestock to helpful hints on transplanting cabbage and removing moss from the housetop, the manuscript supplied an abundance of miscellaneous information to engage the attention and serve the interests of the young agriculturalist. His encyclopedia even recorded detailed instructions for hunting wild bees:

> Provide your self with a tin box that will hold about a pt, put into it a piece of dry honey comb, carry in your pocket, a phial of 1/2 honey & 1/2 water, go to piece of new ground at a distance from any tame bees, open the box, and pour some of the mixture, on the comb, & then hunt among the flowers for a bee, if a bee is found catch it by shuting the lid over it, wate untill it becomes still, then open the box, it will fly round the box a few times & fly away, wate & in a few minutes it will return with 2 or 3 others, & in 1/2 hour they will have a line formed between you & the tree, then set the box over as many as possible, then go the edge of the next wood and wait untill they are still then open the box etc, untill the tree is found, a pocket spy glass is usefull to see a bee from the top of a tree, the time for hunting them is in September or October or in the spring, if a bee cannot be found to commence operations with burn some honey on a stone & maby some wanderer may smell it....

Since the time of agriculture's primitive beginnings, sowers and reapers have had to concern themselves with the question of the weather, a vital factor in the regulation of farm activities. Unable to control it, the farmer could only adapt his planting and harvesting to its normal course, always with the hope that climatic conditions would work with him and not against him. Naturally, an ability to predict the weather would serve as a decided advantage in planning for the day-to-day activity, and long before the time of scientific meteorology a kind of weather lore—part observation, part superstition—was developed. The handbook included a weather chart listing the probabilities for summer and for winter depending on the "time of the Moon's Change." In addition to the chart, several entries set forth other guides for the weather prophet:

> When the sun sets in a cloud, or rises clear & soon pases behind a cloud look out for foul weather, when a storm clears off in the night time look for rain again soon.
> A circle round the moon indicates foul weather.

What other weather lore remains with us today?

Not only did the farmer have to contend with the potential weather hazards posed against a successful outcome of his planting, but he also had to face the problem of pest control—household pests as well as those threatening his growing crops and stored grain. Instead of calling in a professional exterminator or choosing one among the possible dozens of brands and varieties of spray guns, bombs, powders, or pastes (as one might do today), the nineteenth-century individual had to fight off his insect, rodent, and other house and garden pests without the aid of professionals or handy commercial insecticides. Reflecting this serious problem, the manual devoted considerable attention to methods for dealing with a variety of undesirables. Pests of particular interest to the farmer considered in the handbook included cabbage worms, "Bugs on vines," caterpillars, crows and blackbirds, and rats. Among the several anti-pest suggestions listed, these three seem especially interesting for their extreme simplicity, if not for their potential efficacy:

> *Bugs on vines,* lay shingles between the hills in the evening, & in the morning raise up a shingle in each hand, & clasp them togather, & you will kill the bugs that have got on the under side during the night for protection.
> *Caterpillers,* place a wollen rag in your bushes at night, and in the morning you will find them adhering to it.
> *Rats,* fry sponge and put in their way.

For eliminating ants the manual proposed two alternative methods: (1) "Crack shag bark walnuts & lay where you wish to collect them, & then wet the cracks whare they come with corrosive sublihate," or (2) "place a small piece of camphine or sprinkle alkihol whare they frequent." In case of a bed bug problem, there were also several methods among which to choose, one being to "rub the bed stids with green tomato vines." Mixtures designed to kill (or at least to ensnare) the cockroach, still a persistent pest in the southern clime, included a compound of meal, red lead, and molasses and one of "strong pink root and molasses." Another prevalent and extremely annoying southern insect pest, the mosquito, could be repelled by one of two ways, depending on the appropriate circumstances: (1) "burn a little brown sugar on a shovel of coals," or (2) "place a piece of flannel or sponge wet with camphorated spirits to a thread fastened across the top of the bed posts."

Insecticides or repellants, however, represent only one item among the dozens of common household necessities now bought in the supermarket (if not completely obsolete), but then made at home. The handbook provided complete instructions for the home manufacture of an amazing number of items, such as boot blacking, boot varnish, bottle stoppers, brass cleaner, furniture polish, waterproof varnish, waterproof paste, glue, cement for mending "Crockreware," cement for glass, and cement for grafting. The finished product in each case was simply a mixture of several basic ingredients. For example, the boot varnish consisted of linseed oil, "muton suet," and beeswax, melted together and applied while still warm to the boots or shoes; the bottle stoppers were fashioned from a compound of wax, lard, and turpentine.

The mid-twentieth-century housewife who does not yet own an automatic washer-dryer and has to take her clothes down the street to the laundromat is likely to consider herself extremely underprivileged. What if she had to make her own soap, boil the water, and scrub by hand? The manuscript contains several recipes detailing the process of making soap, one describing the procedure for what must have been a kind of liquid soap in this manner:

Dissolve 18 lbs of potash, in 3 pailfills of water, than add about 25 lbs of grease, boil it over a slow fire 2 hours, turn it into a barrel and fill it up with water.

Another soap recipe was followed by a bit of labor-saving advice:

Put your cloth[es] in soak them overnight & to every pail of water in which you boil add 1/2 lb of soap they will need no scrubbing merely wrence them out.

On the general subject of washing and cleaning, the handbook listed several suggestions for dealing with specific materials, such as flannel, black veils, and silk. For cleaning silk the following method was recommended:

1/2 lb soft soap 1 tee spoon of brandy, 1 pt gin, spread it on both sides, wash it in several waters, & iron it on the rong side.

To remove grease from silk, the manual advised that one "apply a little magnesia to the rong side." Undoubtedly, the nineteenth-century housewife found the following entry of particular interest and value: "*Set colors*, alum desolved in water will prevent calico from fading." In the event that clothes faded, however, as certainly would have been the result of many hard scrubbings with strong soap, the manuscript provided detailed information on how to dye materials green, red, and black.

Now almost obsolete except for ornamental purposes and special occasions, candles used to fulfill a more vital utilitarian function. Certainly one would never think of making his own candles today—not even for chianti-bottle-lamps in an espresso shop. Nevertheless, the manuscript told how to make them:

How do you account for the revival of interest in crafts today?

2 lb of Allum for every 10 lbs of Tallow desolve it in water before the Tallow is put in & then melt Tallow in the water with frequent stirings & it will clarafy harden the tallow so as to make a most beautiful candle.

In the age before machines and ready-to-wear clothing, women usually ran what amounted to a domestic factory. They would spin the wool or cotton (or, in this case, flax) into yarn, and then weave it into cloth which would be sewn into clothes. Do today's women have anything in common with this woman? Why does she look so sad?

An extremely important area of activity for the farm family involved the preservation of food, and on that subject the home encyclopedia again supplied valuable reference material. In regard to the preservation of fruit, these two suggestions were set forth:

> *Winter fruit.* pack it in dry sand, & it will keep longer than in any other way.
> *Peaches & Plumbs,* preserved ripe through the winter, put them into equal quantities of water and honey.

During the seasons when eggs were plentiful, the housewife did well to preserve the accumulated supply for the times when the chickens were less productive. According to the handbook, eggs could be preserved in this manner:

> *Eggs to preserve;* take 1 qt of salts, & 3 qts of lime, add water untill the whole stired up & disolved is of the consistency of cream; then put in the eggs.

Several entries gave directions for preserving meat, a necessary process in an age without refrigeration and when one did not simply march to the market for the fresh meat which is now always available. The manual proclaimed the following recipe "an excellent method of preserving hams. &c.":

> Cover the bottom of the cask with fine salt; lay on the hams with the skin side down, sprinkle over fine salt; then another layer of hams & so on untill you have disposed of all your hams. Then make a brine in the following proportions: water 6 gal; salt 9 lbs; brown sugar, 4 lbs; salt peter, 3 oz; saleratas, 1 oz; Boil & skum, & when cold pour the brine into the cask until the hams are covered.

Other entries described additional methods for curing hams and pickling beef.

A household item used frequently as an ingredient in the home medical remedies as well as in cooking and preparing various foods, vinegar was an exceedingly useful and versatile liquid. Hence, this manuscript entry would have been of considerable interest and value:

> *Vinegar Preserved for domestic use* cork it up in glass bottles, set them on the fire with cold water, & as much hay or straw as will prevent them from knocking to gather; when the water nearly boils take of[f] the pan, let the bottles remain in the hey 1/4 hour, it will never lose its strength though kept for years.

· · ·

Obviously, the task of preparing and cooking meals kept the housewife of the nineteenth century in her kitchen a much greater portion of the time than does the same task today. Baking one's own wheat bread is rapidly becoming a lost art, and pies and cakes are more and more commonly put together with the aid of packaged ready-mixed ingredients. In previous times, however, it was necessary to begin with the making of the yeast. Here are two of the several methods described in the manuscript:

Are there tasks that the modern homemaker performs that her nineteenth-century counterpart might not have because of lack of knowledge?

> (1) *Yeast,* Boil 1 lb flour 1/2 lb brown sugar, a little salt in two gal water for 1 hour, when milkwarm, bottle & cork it close it will be fit for use in 24 hours, 1 lb will make 16 lb of bread.
> (2) *Yeast.* 1 qt of hops & 7 gal water is boiled about 3 hours, pass it through a cullendar & mix with 3 qts of meal or so much that it will make batter, add 1/2 tea cup of salt, when cooled to milk warm, add 1/2 pt yeast, stir it well, & let it stand 15 or 20 hours then add meal enouf to make it dough, make cakes 3 inches in diameter & 1/2 inch thick, dry it on a board by the fire if not dried in 2 or 3 days it will spoil. they will keep 3 months. 1 soaked 1/2 hour in warm not hot water is enough for a large loaf.

The handbook supplied instructions for making ginger bread, rice cakes, "New Years Cookies," fruit cakes, tea cakes, doughnuts, apple "Dumblings," muffins, chicken pie, lemon pie, bread pudding, citron pudding, wheat bread, "Light Biscuit," and a host of other cakes and pastries. One rather unusual recipe was set forth in verse:

> ### Variety Pudding
>
> Of flour take one half a pound
> Six eggs all very good & sound
> Sugar according to your taste

> Of butter do not make a waste.
> Just as you like you choose your spices
> And when its done tis cut in slices.

To cope with such vague instructions obviously one would have to know something about pudding-making in advance.

In addition to the numerous food recipes, the manuscript also supplied directions for making all sorts of beverages. Aromatic beer, for instance, could be made by pouring two quarts of boiling water into a mixture of oil of spruce, wintergreen, and sassafras, and then adding eight quarts of cold water, one and a half pints of molasses, and one-fourth pint of yeast. After about two hours, it could be bottled. For making ginger beer, the manual prescribed several different techniques, some to be used if the beverage was for immediate consumption and others if one planned to bottle it. To make a drink called "Chery Bounce," one was directed to fill a jug with cherries and to "run it over with aple brandy let it stand a few days, & pore it off, it will keep any length of time." A combination of ten gallons of water, one gallon of molasses, one quart of vinegar, and one-half pound of ginger produced something called "Harvest Drink," apparently a beverage which might be served to a large number of people (perhaps the slaves) to celebrate the harvest. A recipe for making plum wine was the last entry recorded in the manual, an entry added to the reference book some thirty years after it was brought to Arkansas:

Plum Wine

Thoroughly wash the plums, squeeze out the juice and strain through a cloth. To one gallon of juice add three lbs brown sugar. Put in vessels, either bottles or jars and cover with a cloth. Let it stand till the first fermentation ceases, which must be carefully noticed. As soon as fermentation ceases, bottle, cork, and seal air tight.

If bottled before fermentation ceases the bottles will burst. After the 1st fermentation is over a 2nd sets up, which will make vinegar. The wine will be fit for use as soon as sealed, but the older the better. It takes from 4 to 7 weeks for the 1st fermentation to cease. June 20th 1883.

Although busily engaged with cooking, preserving, washing, manufacturing an endless number of necessary articles, and all her other tasks, the housewife was still after all a woman and not just a machine, and it was only natural that she would be interested in certain feminine vanities. One might well wonder when she had time to fit such things as cologne and curling liquid into her tight schedule, especially when even those articles had to be manufactured at home. Nevertheless, the handbook gave directions for making cologne, curling liquid, and "Hare dye" as well:

Cologne, 12 gtts [drops] of bergamot 120 of leavender, 24 of lemon 60 gr musk, 1 pt of purest alkihol.

Curling liquid, for ladies, 5 oz of borax, 1 drachm gum senegal, 1 qt of hot water when desolved, add 2 oz of spts of wine strongly impregnated with campher.

Hare dye, 1 pt pkld herin liquor. 1/2 lb lamp black, 2 oz iron rust boil 2 mts stran it.

As a handy source of information on medicine, animal care, food preservation, cooking, the manufacture of soap, candles, and other necessary household articles, and dozens of other miscellaneous topics, this small volume undoubtedly represented a valuable item in the library of the Alfred H. Carrigan family in southwest Arkansas from the 1850's until sometime in the latter part of the nineteenth century. From the entries in the handbook, one gains an insight into the life of a rural Southern family and a close-up view of the self-sufficiency which circumstances imposed upon them.

What in your opinion might be gained from a close-up view of history of this sort that is lacking in historical overviews usually presented?

U.S. CENSUS
Work In Oswego, New York, c. 1880

One of the most intriguing changes over the past century is in the kind of work that people do. Most of the tasks at which the men and women of the late nineteenth century spent the days of their lives have now disappeared. In traditional land-based cultures, jobs remained the same generation after generation over millennia; today, with the relentless technological innovations in machinery, the old ways of doing things have been destroyed as ever-changing specialized ways of performing industrial and commercial tasks replace them.

Oswego, New York, is a Lake Ontario port city whose population of about 20,000 has remained nearly the same for a century. The 1880 census enumerates the jobs performed by 3,237 of its men, women, and children.

Look closely at the jobs, including those mentioned in the footnote below the table. How many of them are still performed? Also make note of the average annual wage of workers and compare that with the average wage today—about $10,000.

The following is a summary of the statistics of the manufactures of Oswego, New York, for 1880, being taken from tables prepared for the Tenth Census by A. E. Buell, special agent:

Mechanical and Manufacturing Industries	No. of Establish-ments	Capital	AVERAGE NUMBER OF HANDS EMPLOYED Males Above 16 Years	Females Above 15 Years	Children and Youths	Total Amount Paid in Wages During the Year	Value of Materials	Value of Products
All industries	179	$2,611,238	1,754	272	106	$756,435	$3,646,845	$5,619,944
Blacksmithing (see also Wheelwrighting)	11	3,120	10	—	—	2,782	4,275	14,850
Boots and shoes, including custom work and repairing	16	13,750	25	—	—	9,576	21,556	45,983
Bread and other bakery products	7	42,200	23	4	—	10,021	49,651	74,746
Carpentering	11	21,100	61	—	1	21,960	26,323	55,575
Cooperage	12	24,250	47	—	6	12,637	44,595	66,010
Flouring- and grist-mill products	5	465,000	74	—	—	37,102	1,136,974	1,591,759
Foundery and machine-shop products	5	416,818	363	—	2	153,904	258,311	552,780
Furniture	4	19,500	19	1	—	8,902	17,100	37,000
Liquors, malt	3	68,000	12	—	1	6,146	30,970	55,125
Lumber, planed	4	160,500	111	—	—	47,300	163,605	238,932
Marble and stone work	4	11,500	7	—	—	1,875	3,585	11,399
Painting and paperhanging	6	20,300	38	—	2	13,264	20,000	42,350
Photographing	3	10,150	5	1	—	1,732	3,290	7,857
Plumbing and gasfitting	3	12,000	17	—	—	10,100	33,240	55,054
Printing and publishing	3	110,000	70	—	14	27,956	15,401	66,580
Saddlery and harness	4	4,800	8	—	—	2,950	6,600	12,200
Shipbuilding	7	27,500	58	—	—	23,072	22,030	50,563
Tinware, copperware, and sheet-iron ware	15	19,300	34	—	—	15,394	27,700	63,950
Wheelwrighting (see also Blacksmithing)	5	8,600	13	—	—	5,405	5,400	14,900
All other industries (a)	51	1,152,850	759	266	80	344,357	1,756,239	2,562,331

a Embracing baking and yeast powders; baskets, rattan and willow ware; boxes, cigar; boxes, fancy and paper; carriages and wagons; cement; coffins, burial cases, and undertakers' goods; confectionery; cutlery and edge tools; drain and sewer pipe; drugs and chemicals; dyeing and cleaning; gloves and mittens; hats and caps; hosiery and knit goods; instruments, professional and scientific; iron railing, wrought; leather, curried; leather, tanned; lime; lock- and gunsmithing; looking-glass and picture frames; lumber, sawed; malt; mineral and soda waters; mixed textiles; patent medicines and compounds; pumps; sash, doors, and blinds; shirts, soap and candles; sporting goods; starch; tobacco, cigars and cigarettes; upholstering; watch and clock repairing; window blinds and shades; and wood, turned and carved.

From the foregoing table it appears that the average capital of all establishments is $14,587.92; that the average wages of all hands employed is $354.80 per annum; that the average outlay in wages, in materials, and in interest (at 6 per cent.) on capital employed is $25,474.61.

THE HORSE IS KING

Lewis Atherton

The automobile dominates our lives in so many ways today that we find it difficult to imagine a time before the internal-combustion engine changed the world forever. One hundred years ago, however, the horse was almost as important as the auto is today. The amount of change that the "horseless carriage" brought with it is obscured today because we take the invention so much for granted. Certainly, the look of towns is no longer the same. Livery stables, blacksmiths' shops, watering troughs, and hitching posts have now almost disappeared. Even the smell of towns has been transformed. But perhaps most important, the social life of the American people has changed. Dating habits are noticeably different today as is the pace of life. As you read the following article, try to isolate the most significant changes that have occurred since the auto replaced the horse.

Village life moved at the pace of horse-drawn transportation. Tourist homes, tourist courts, garages, filling stations, and stores selling automobile accessories lay in the future. There were no concrete curbs, and parking meters were nonexistent; and small-town workmen would have been baffled at the idea of painting parking lines in streets consisting of dust or mud.

The presence of horses was evident everywhere. Droppings in the streets and town stables attracted swarms of flies, and narrow-rimmed wheels of wagons and buggies cut gaping ruts during rainy seasons. Hitching posts, connected with iron chains, surrounded the village square. Until business growth necessitated removal of hitching lots to the edge of business districts, farmers tied their teams around the courthouse square, let down check reins to ease the tired necks of their horses, and walked across the street to do their trading. Thirsty farm teams quickened their step when they approached town pumps and watering troughs, which also doubled as fire-fighting equipment.

Horses were sentient beings, capable of affection, and an unwritten code censured their abuse. In cold and rainy weather farmers paid the modest fee necessary to stable their teams in commercially operated feed barns and livery stables. The occasional drunk who forgot his team was roughly criticized by the village paper after some citizen had removed them late at night to a livery barn for food and shelter.

Even within the town itself business and social life depended on horse-drawn transportation. Most citizens had horse-and-carriage barns at the rear of their homes to shelter driving equipment. Commercial drays hauled freight to and from the depot, did heavy moving for local citizens, and made daily deliveries for stores unable to afford their own private wagons. Most stores, however, owned single-horse, spring wagons, with business advertisements painted on the sides, which made morning and afternoon

In what other ways did the automobile change the kinds of jobs available?

Horses dominated life up to the middle of the nineteenth century. In many respects, life moved no faster than the horse could move. What difference does the speed of transportation make? What are the advantages and disadvantages of the horse over the automobile? Study the picture of the market square carefully. How would the scene be different today?

deliveries to residential areas. Younger clerks enjoyed driving these conveyances at speeds beyond the limits of safety demanded by elderly residents of the town. Local hotel hacks, pulled sometimes by as many as four horses, rushed back and forth from depots at speeds supposed to impress travellers with their efficiency. By loading sample trunks of travelling salesmen smartly and with dispatch, sounding their horns sharply, and dashing off before a rival hack could clear the depot platform, drivers scored a point in favor of the establishment which they represented. Peddling carts, ice wagons, and sprinkler carts moved more sedately, much to the pleasure of children who begged fruit and small chunks of ice or played in the streams of water being sprayed on dusty streets.

Livery stables served those who could not afford to own rigs or who had temporary and unusual demands. Young people courted and eloped with livery stable teams, and circus agents drove them leisurely round the countryside to post bills. Drummers employed drivers and rigs to haul their sample trunks on two- and three-day side trips to hamlets lacking railroad connections. Picnics, celebrations and fairs in nearby towns,

What kinds of commercial vehicles have replaced those mentioned here?

91

baseball trips, sleighing in winter, funerals—all these and more called for livery-stable teams.

A good bay trotter and a fine buggy appealed to the young man of the 1870's much as the convertible does to his great-grandson. At the peak of its development, a truly fine buggy was an expensive item. Polished and varnished ash shafts, rubber-tired wheels with shiny brass inner rims, brass lamps decorated with large glass rubies, and patent-leather dashboards pleased the eye. Even the harness had its charms—gleaming tan leather with brass fittings, rainbow-colored celluloid baubles, and ruby rosettes. The current generation will never know the thrill of spending $1.75 on a horse and buggy for an afternoon and evening of dating. The carriage with its fast team, yellow fly nets, linen lap robe, and beribboned whip lifted the spirit of the young blade as he drove up and down Main Street with one foot hanging over the body bed and a cigar at an angle in his mouth. Loafers shouted at him and received the expected quip in reply, commented on his extravagance, and wondered at his destination. A touch of the whip and he was on his way. With one horse pacing and the other trotting, he passed the fragrant slaughterhouse at the edge of town and on to the meeting with his best girl.

Is there a contemporary parallel?

. . .

Horses could be a nuisance in many ways. In 1876 the Monroe, Wisconsin, editor warned his readers that city ordinances prohibited the riding of horses on sidewalks, even though it was a temptation to do so in muddy times. When a citizen of Chillicothe, Illinois, in 1875 spoke of Saturday as a lively day, with vacant lots filled with teams, and then added that he thought he was on Broadway in New York City until he saw "George" and his dogs, he expressed in a lighter vein the problem of congestion and the greater danger of accidents on Saturdays. Occasional runaways added zest for spectators if not for the unfortunate individuals involved. A team belonging to a Mr. Bumpus took fright on State Street in Algona, Iowa, in 1877 and dashed around the corner of Thorington Street, breaking the wagon tongue, the whiffletrees, and creating general havoc. Citizens got inside so quickly during the fracas that the town took on a Sunday air of desertion within a matter of seconds.

Constant activity at private and railroad stockyards in country towns also emphasized the importance of horsedrawn transportation. Produce and livestock had to be concentrated at local shipping points because they could not be moved great distances over muddy and unimproved roads in wagons pulled by horses. Small-town elevators and stockyards thus handled an enormous volume of agricultural produce. During 1878, J. J. Wilson's private yards at Algona, Iowa, shipped almost 350 cars of hogs, wheat, and oats, and several more of minor produce. In return, he received 388 carloads of lumber and coal. From the adjoining new depot stockyards 817 cars departed during the same year with wheat, corn, oats, flax, cattle, hogs, butter, and cheese.

Wagons converged on Algona from all directions during weeks when as many as fifty carloads of cattle and hogs left for Milwaukee. Their drivers ate a noon meal at the local hotel and bought family supplies in Algona stores. Livery stables, blacksmith shops, harness shops, and feed barns benefited from their presence. In commenting on business during 1878 the Algona editor said that State Street occasionally had been filled with teams and loaded wagons four and five abreast. At times the line had stretched from the elevator and cattle yards at the depot to the City Hotel, a distance of nearly a mile. Dust and mud, bawling cattle and squealing hogs, horses and men, the plank platform of the Fairbanks scales, loading chutes, and lines of box- and cattle-cars on sidings—all have been challenged by the trucks which now travel midwestern highways. But in the 1870's horses and country towns were equally necessary to assemble agricultural produce for market and to supply country homes with merchandise.

Did the country towns in your area grow or disappear as a result of the introduction of the auto?

As a focal point in the age of horse-drawn transportation, the livery stable had a form, a personality, and an odor as distinctive as that of its twentieth-century successor, the garage and automobile showroom. Brick construction, feed chutes connected directly with the hayloft, and running water in stalls and washrooms marked the more pretentious establishments. Most, however, were large, boxlike structures of graying unpainted wood, with oversized doors to permit carriages to enter the central ramp. A few had signs in front, perhaps a horse's head with crossed whips carved in wood, but, as a rule, the only decorations were tin advertising strips of patent remedies for horseflesh nailed at random to exterior walls. All stables had the same mingled smell of horse urine and manure, harness oil, feed and cured hay.

A small office near the door contained a battered desk, a pot-bellied stove, a few chairs, a cot, and a lantern hanging on a wooden peg for the use of an attendant who was on duty twenty-four hours a day to wait on customers and to guard against the constant threat of fire. A slate on the wall near the office or just within listed the names of horses out on trips and rental charges. So far as possible, customers were held accountable for abusing horses by furious driving, for turning rubber-tired conveyances so short as to fray the rubber against the buggy bed, for failing to feed horses on long trips, and for other injurious acts. Some stables posted slogans to encourage better care of equipment:

> Whip Light,
> Drive Slow.
> Pay Cash
> Before You Go.

and all gave careful instructions to new patrons.

Well-equipped livery stables possessed a surprising variety of vehicles. Fancy buggies and curved sleighs were rented out for single dates; fringed surreys served for double-dating and more prosaic family trips. Carryalls, with seats along the sides and entrance steps in the rear, were used on special occasions—for Sunday School picnics, to carry visiting ball teams to hotel and the playing field, to take elderly ladies to the cemetery on Memorial Day, and in Autumn to taxi passengers to the fair grounds. Light spring wagons hauled drummers and their sample trunks on visits to country stores and hamlets. Of more somber mien were the hearses, with black enclosed sides and oval windows, fringe and plumes, and elaborate box lights. Hearses decorated in white were preferred for children's funerals. Perhaps one or more of the local doctors kept a team and glass-enclosed coupe at the livery stable. Hotel hacks, the town watering cart, and vegetable wagons added to the variety of conveyances parked along the walls.

Who are the modern equivalents of drummers?

Stalls were to the rear, from which horses were led up cleated ramps to the main floor for hitching. A second-floor loft over the stables facilitated the forking down of hay used for feed. Harness for each animal hung on wooden pegs at the front of his stall. Somewhere in the building was the washroom where buggies were washed and wheels were greased. Curry combs, hair clippers, sponges, axle grease, harness soap, and pitchforks were scattered through the building at points most convenient for their use.

• • •

The livery barn was universally condemned by pious mothers who rated it only slightly above the town saloons. Its robust life shocked those refined people who spoke of bulls as "gentleman cows." Unlike twentieth-century automobile dealers, who move in country-club circles, livery stable owners generally ignored high society. Addicted to slouch attire, sometimes noted for profanity, they were numbered among the few local men of property who avoided religious activities and booster movements. Since the usual explanations—stinginess, a choleric disposition, or free-thinking religious principles—did not apply in their case, they puzzled even their own contemporaries. For these mothers, however, it was enough that they were hard to understand and did not practice the finer points of accepted social conduct. The livery stable also served as a loafing place, especially for those most addicted to betting on horse races. Checkers and playing cards were often in evidence, and liquor was tolerated within limits. Most horrible of all, stallions were offered at service as long as public opinion would tolerate it, usually only until mothers of impressionable boys learned of the presence of "gentleman horses" within the city limits.

• • •

Probably no other loafing place in town provided so fine a setting for tall stories, and there the town liars competed for supremacy. They told of working for the contractor who built Niagara Falls, of ice worms ruining a whole summer's supply of ice, and of the half-believable hoop snake. Stories of Civil War exploits appealed to an audience composed in large part of veterans, who could relish the ludicrous overtones:

> Still another told of coming on the battle field of Gettysburg on a gunboat in a driving snow storm. It was the morning of the third day of the battle. He had been drinking gun powder in his whiskey to make him brave, and he performed such feats of daring and valor that General Meade, with tears in his eyes, shook his hand and said, "Abel, I won't forget this."

Youngsters found additional attractions. Horseshoe nails could be bent into rings; old bottles and junk lying around the premises were collected and sold. And when the "Tom shows" *(Uncle Tom's Cabin)* came to town the trained dogs which would chill the local audience by baying on Eliza's trail generally were housed at one of the local livery stables.

Nineteenth-century midwestern civilization was obviously geared to the strength and limitations of horse-drawn transportation. The horse accounted for the carriage sheds and barns in residential sections, for livery and feed barns, for stockyards, harness shops, and blacksmith shops, for the many small carriage factories in country towns, for hitch racks, town pumps, and watering troughs. Cemeteries and schools were laid out with horse-drawn transportation in mind. The horse played a major part in determining trade areas, and his potentialities helped determine nineteenth-century recreational patterns.

How has contemporary architecture become auto-centered?

Other forces began to play an increasingly important part in shaping midwestern life in the years immediately following the Civil War. Technological and managerial revolutions exerted more and more influence. Railroads were already bringing goods from distant points to be exchanged for crops and livestock, and agencies of short-range communication, like the telephone and trolley line, and then the truck and automobile, would soon appear. Tremendous change generated by them would destroy many small-town crafts, and country towns would suffer from wildly fluctuating trade areas. Greater specialization and a higher standard of living would accompany a declining independence from the outside world. But, for the moment, these were the very characteristics —a low standard of living, relative lack of specialization, and freedom from outside control—which set the country town apart from its twentieth-century successor.

People did things for themselves or did without far more than is either possible or necessary today. They lacked hospitals, funeral homes, florist shops, dry-cleaning-and-pressing establishments, beauty shops, country clubs, plumbers, waterworks, telephones, electric lights, ten-cent stores, commercial laundries, radio and television shops.

Small-town business felt little external control. Though manufacturers and wholesalers were beginning to advertise directly to consumers the unique virtues of their own special packaged branded and trade-marked wares, which finally would compel retailers to stock such items, general stores still carried coffee and calico, not a variety of packaged or labelled brands. Storekeepers were relatively free to select their own stock; their customers in turn needed judgment of quality and price in order to spend their money wisely. Officials at the court house were still county and local officials only; and local banks enjoyed a measure of independence unknown in federal reserve and deposit-insurance days.

Even the homes of the period were relatively independent. Storms and blizzards might isolate country towns, and even individual families, without seriously affecting their mode of living. Coal oil lamps, a supply of cordwood in the back yard, meat in the smokehouse, fruits and preserves in the cellar, a cow for milk in the barn—here was food, light and warmth which continued to function when neighbors and the outside world were cut off.

Americans thrill to this saga of independence as their own lives daily become more interdependent. They envy their ancestors, those artisans and storekeepers who rose early in the morning to milk their cows and slop their pigs in order to have their individually owned shops and stores open for early customers. But, as in all Edens, there were serpents. Town ordinances show that conditions were not idyllic. Gallatin, Missouri, in 1873, instructed city authorities to order the removal of "every hog-pen, slaughter house, privy, mud hole, stable . . . in a stinking or unhealthy condition." It was easy to order drastic action, but enforcement in specific cases was another matter because no citizen in a closely-knit community wanted to issue a complaint.

Weigh the health hazards of horses versus automobiles.

Artisans flourished in the relatively isolated and unspecialized economy. Blacksmiths were able and willing to build wagons and plows; harness shops both made and sold harness; shoemakers and tailors turned leather and cloth into finished goods. The revolutions in transportation, manufacturing, and management ruined such business. Gunsmiths, wagon makers, coopers, millers, tanners, and cigarmakers are gone from the country towns where they were well known in the 1870's. Other artisans have survived by changing to new occupations—from tinsmiths to plumbers, for instance, or most commonly by abandoning all manufacturing in favor of service and repair. The shoe repair man on Main Street today is thus a lineal descendant of the craftsman who actually produced shoes in the 1870's.

On balance, has more been lost or gained by the changes in the past century?

PAGES FROM THE SEARS, ROEBUCK CATALOG

Although it is conventional to cite the building of the transcontinental railroad network as an example of the fundamental changes taking place in late-nineteenth-century America, the social effects of those changes are sometimes passed over.

Without an efficient railroad network, Sears, Roebuck, the "cheapest supply house on earth," could not have functioned. From its central loca-tion in Chicago, Sears by the 1890s was able to deliver the items listed in its extraordinary catalog, a publication that was eagerly awaited in isolated farmhouses from Maine to Wyoming.

As its pages clearly indicate, the days of home-made wares were coming to a close as factory-produced and store-bought goods became more common.

OUR $55.00 A GRADE AND $65.00 AA GRADE TOP BUGGY

☞ $55.00 IS THE PRICE OF OUR A GRADE COLUMBUS TOP BUGGY IN LEATHER QUARTER.
$65.00 IS THE PRICE OF OUR AA GRADE COLUMBUS TOP BUGGY IN LEATHER QUARTER.

FOR FULL LEATHER TOP ADD $5.00.

No. 92814. Order by Number.

The above illustration engraved from a photograph will give you some idea of the appearance of our AA and A grades of Top Buggies.

3 feet 2 inch and 3 feet 6 inch, or 3 feet 4 inch and 3 feet 8 inch in height. The material in the wheels is strictly second growth hickory of the very finest quality, and they are put together in the most approved manner possible. Tire is carefully bolted between each spoke. A set of the wheels used in this buggy is worth five sets of the common Special B grade.

SHAFTS. Shafts are all made of selected second growth hickory, of the latest design. They are substantially ironed with heavy irons so that the heels will not straighten out in use.

BODY AND SEAT. WE FURNISH THIS JOB IN EITHER PIANO BOX BODY, as illustrated, or CORNING BODY, and can furnish the body in either 20, 22 or 25 inch width. ALL BODIES are 52 inches long. The CORNING BODY is 23 inches wide and 50 inches long. All bodies and seats are made of the best poplar panels second growth ash sills, are put together in the best manner, screwed and plugged from inside and outside. WIDTH OF SEAT on 20 inch body, measuring over top of cushion, 26 inches; depth, 16 inches; height of back over cushion, 14 inches. WIDTH OF SEAT on 22 inch body, 30 inches; depth, 16 inches; height of back above cushion, 14½ inches. WIDTH OF SEAT on 25 inch, or regular sized body, measuring over top of cushion, 31 ins. Depth, 16 inches; height of back above cushion, 14½ inches. On the Corning body, width of seat measuring over top of cushion, 31 ins.; depth 17 inches; height of back above cushion, 15 inches.

TRIMMINGS. We trim the Seat and back in either the very finest imported all wool English green or blue body cloth, or green genuine machine buffed leather. We use the very best spring back and spring seat cushions. The back of the seat is also wood painted same as body. We use a full length velvet carpet, heavy rubber boot over back of body, and dash frame is made of best steel, covered with the very finest enameled leather.

MOUNTINGS. We furnish this Buggy with silver mountings throughout.

PAINTING. Our AA grade buggies are painted in the very highest style of the art, in 13 coats of paint, the first coats rubbed out with pumice stone. Nothing but the very best grade of paints, oils and varnishes are used, and they are given ample time to dry in a dark, dust proof room, which is kept at an even temperature. Bodies are black, gear dark green with suitable gold stripe.

IN OUR AA GRADE BUGGIES we furnish the very best machine buffed leather quarter top, or at $5.00 extra, full leather top. All tops have machine buffed solid leather valance, front and rear, sewed on. The head lining is of the very best imported all wool English green dyed body cloth.

IN BUYING A TOP BUGGY it will pay you to buy the highest grade COLUMBUS work either at $55.00 or $65.00. You will get such a buggy as you could not buy at retail at less than $150.00, a buggy equal to those which have been retailed at even $200.00 to $250.00. THERE IS NOTHING FINER IN A TOP BUGGY THAN OUR AA GRADE COLUMBUS TOP BUGGY AT $65.00, and it is the cheapest rig you can possibly buy when you consider the quality. Our A and AA grade work is not to be compared with cheap work that is being so extensively advertised and handled through the regular wholesale trade.

$55.00 AND $65.00 ARE OUR REGULAR PRICES when shipped by freight C. O. D. subject to examination on receipt of our required deposit.

A DISCOUNT OF 3% will be allowed if cash in full accompanies your order.

☞ OUR SPECIAL $65.00 TOP BUGGY, is the finest buggy we make and the best buggy turned out by the manufacturer at Columbus, O. YOU WILL GET NOTHING BETTER NO MATTER HOW MUCH YOU MAY PAY.

DESCRIPTION OF OUR AA GRADE $65.00 TOP BUGGIES.

GEAR. We build this job either with a piano box body as shown in the cut, or with a Corning body, as desired. We build it with arch axles and Brewster springs, or with drop axles and elliptic end springs, as desired. The fifth wheel is full wrought, the finest grade; axles all of steel, highest grade; Spindles, steel converted, making them very hard and impervious to wear. Size of axles, ⅞ by 1 inch. All gear wood, such as axle caps, spring bars, side bars and reaches are of the very best, carefully selected second growth Michigan hickory. Reaches are ironed full length with the very best Norway iron. Springs of the best tool steel, oil tempered and tested. All bolts, clips and forgings are of the very best Norway buggy iron.

WHEELS. We use the highest grade wheel we can get in this grade work, either Sarven's patent or compressed band wheel as ordered. The wheels on our A or AA grade work will be as good as new when the cheaper grade of wheel will have long since been worn out. ¾ or ⅞ inch tread, tire is of the very best tire steel, round edge projecting over the felloes just enough to protect the wood from wear. We can furnish wheels for this job either

Be sure to state width of track wanted, 4 feet 8 ins. or 5 feet 2 inches.

No. 92815. Order by Number.

The above illustration engraved from a photograph will give you some idea of the appearance of our AA and A grades of Top Buggies.

━━ The Bows to the Top are Leather Covered, the Top Prop Nuts are Leather Covered, the Seat Handles are Leather Covered, the Steps have Rubber Covered Step Pads. ━━

All these features only to be found on the very finest work. It is not only these little points alone that go to make this Buggy the very best, but the fact that only the most skilled mechanics are allowed to work on the AA grade, nothing but the very finest material enters into every piece and part of the work, and when completed there is nothing finer in appearance, more durable or better made at any price.

AT $65.00 LEATHER QUARTER TOP, OR $70.00 IN FULL LEATHER TOP, we furnish the AA Grade Columbus Top Buggy with full length Velvet Carpet, Toe Carpet, Panel Carpet, Full Length Side and Back Curtains, Storm Apron, Leather Foot Protectors to both sides of box, Anti-Rattlers and Shafts.

FOR POLE WITH NECKYOKE AND WIFFLETREES complete, in place of Shafts, add $3.50.
FOR BOTH POLE AND SHAFTS add $6.00.

OUR A GRADE AT $55.00 IN FULL LEATHER QUARTER TOP, OR $60.00 IN FULL LEATHER TOP is a buggy exactly like the illustration above, and a buggy that will compare in every way with any buggy you can buy elsewhere at from $75.00 to $100.00. It has the highest grade wheel, the very best material in every piece and part. The leather is all genuine machine buffed leather. The difference in price to you is only the difference in cost to us, and that is in trimmings and workmanship. This A Grade Buggy at $55.00 and $60.00 does not have the leather covered bows and leather covered prop nuts, the leather covered seat handles, the rubber covered step pads; it is not painted in 13 coats, nor made and finished by the same class of workmen. It is, however, A STRICTLY HIGH GRADE BUGGY, one that we can recommend in every way, and a buggy we GUARANTEE FOR TWO YEARS, and one that will last a natural life time. We would recommend by all means you buy OUR COLUMBUS, O., A GRADE BUGGY AT $55.00 OR $60.00 if you do not buy our AA GRADE COLUMBUS AT $65.00 OR $70.00.

FOR ADDITIONS TO THE A GRADE COLUMBUS AT $55.00 AND $60.00, add for pole with neckyoke and whiffletrees, in place of shafts, $2.50. For both pole and shafts, $4.50.

THE BUSINESS WE DO IN WATCHES, JEWELRY, ETC., WOULD BE CONSIDERED LARGE FOR THE BIGGEST WHOLESALER IN THE COUNTRY. NO WONDER WHEN YOU SEE OUR PRICES AND LIBERAL TERMS,

MERIT SUNSHINE.

For hard or soft coal or wood, with Reservoir.

The Merit Sunshine is a substantial, well constructed stove of improved design, intended to meet the demand for a well made and attractive stove at a low price. The design is new and neat, and workmanship is equal to the best. The special features of this stove are: Cut top plates with heavy, deep edges; heavy rim covers and centers; heavy grate and fire box lining, dumping and shaking grate; nickel knobs and hinge pins; handsome nickel panel on oven door and on front doors; outside oven shelf; tin lined oven door; improved, nearly square oven, with broad rack.

No. 15826. With hard or soft coal fixtures.
No. 15827. With wood fixtures.
No. 15828. With both fixtures, add $1.25 to prices quoted.

Size.	Covers.	Length of Fire Box.	Size of Oven.	Weight.	Price.
8	8 in.	16 in.	17x19x11½	315 lbs.	$14.40
88	8 in.	18 in.	19x21x12½	350 lbs.	16.80
99	9 in.	18 in.	19x21x12½	355 lbs.	17.40

Merit Sunshine, for hard or soft coal or wood, without Reservoir.

No. 15829. With hard or soft coal fixtures.
No. 15830. With wood fixtures.
No. 15831. With both fixtures, add $1.25 to prices quoted.

Size.	Covers.	Length of Fire Box.	Size of Oven.	Weight.	Price.
8	8 in.	16 in.	17x19x11½	265 lbs.	$10.30
88	8 in.	18 in.	19x21x12½	295 lbs.	12.60
99	9 in.	18 in.	19x21x12½	300 lbs.	13.20

No. 15826.

PRICES ARE FOR STOVE ONLY.

STAR SUNSHINE COOK.

For wood only, with Reservoir.

The Star Sunshine is a beautiful cook stove with all modern improvements. It is heavy and durable. In practical working qualities it is unsurpassed.

The special features are: Handsome skirting, portable outside oven shelf and extended rear shelf, nickeled oven door opener, large nickeled oven door plates, extra heavy covers and centers, tinned lined oven door, top oven plate inlaid with non-conducting plaster composition, nickel tea pot stand and towel rod.

The Star Sunshine is one of the best wood cook stoves in the country. The reservoir has a large capacity and heats water quickly. The Star Sunshine is a first-class stove in every particular. Length of fire box given below is the size when stove is ordered to be used for wood. Has four covers. No. 15832.

Size.	Covers.	L'gth Fire Box.	Size of Oven.	W'ght.	Price.
8	8 in.	20 in.	18x18x11½	240 lbs.	$12.60
88	8 in.	22 in.	20x20x12½	250 lbs.	14.70
9	9 in.	22 in.	20x20x12½	273 lbs.	14.88
888	8 in.	24 in.	22x22x13½	310 lbs.	16.30
19	9 in.	24 in.	22x22x13½	313 lbs.	16.68

No. 15833. The Star Sunshine Cook, without reservoir—otherwise like cut.

Size.	Oven.	Weight.	Price.
8	18x18x11½	195 lbs.	$9.54
88	20x20x12½	225 lbs.	11.28
9	20x20x12½	228 lbs.	11.40
888	22x22x13½	255 lbs.	13.62
19	22x22x13½	260 lbs.	13.80

$3.50 for a set of No. 8 Stove Furniture, to fit any of our cook stoves.

$3.75 for a set of No. 9 Stove Furniture, to fit any of our cook stoves. See Tinware Department.

No. 15832.

Prices named for Stove do not include Pipe or Stove Utensils. Make your own selection from our catalogue.

Assignment 4

DISCOVERING YOUR COMMUNITY'S HISTORY

Even your grandparents and your great-grandparents will not be able to recall firsthand the time before industrialism transformed social patterns, but some material artifacts of that preindustrial culture can no doubt still be found in your own community.

Your assignment is to go into the community in search of traces of the world we have lost. You may want to team up with other members of the class. Bringing along a camera will be useful. Start by familiarizing yourself with the community in which you are living. Either by talking to "old settlers" or by consulting materials in a library, museum, or historical society, provide yourself with clues on the probable location of the early buildings, ruins, artifacts, cemeteries, monuments, statues, and so forth. Then, go out and find physical evidences of the culture of the mid-nineteenth century or before. You are expected to return with at least one piece of tangible evidence—a photograph or drawing you have made, an interview with someone who has at least secondhand recollections of the time, or perhaps a tombstone rubbing (see Appendix, pp. 235–273).

five

Your People and the Great Migrations

America has always been a nation on the move. From the earliest settlers who had the courage and the faith to travel across the ocean to an unknown land, to the modern family that moves to California in search of a better life, Americans have always been restless. Mobility is one of the major themes in American history.

Somewhere in the recent past your family has doubtless participated in one of the great movements of people that created this country. Someone in your family has been a part of the migration from Europe or Asia or Africa to America, the movement from East to West or from South to North, the transplantation from rural to urban living. Do you know whether your grandparents and/or great-grandparents were born in a foreign country, or whether they made any significant moves in this country?

This chapter emphasizes the uprooting of people and their resettlement in places where language, customs, and tradition were often quite different. Although the readings are set in the period between the 1850s and World War I, the range of experiences is timeless. They should give you some sense of those ancestors of yours who underwent this cycle of human drama, punctuated perhaps by the pain of leaving forever ancestral villages and dear friends, perhaps by a joyful sense of release from poverty and oppression.

Travel has become so easy that we sometimes forget how difficult it was for our ancestors to move from one place to another. Americans remain a mobile people: one out of every five of us moves every year. Businessmen and vacationers fly to Europe or across the country without a second thought. Americans have become so accustomed to driving hundreds of miles in their automobiles over weekends that the inconvenience of a gasoline shortage a few years ago took on the proportions of a crisis. And, while surely unusual, the example of a man we know

who lives in New York and works in Chicago is a sign of our times. Yet the lifetime of this country's "senior citizens" reaches back before the jet plane and automobile, when fifteen to twenty-five miles by horse-drawn wagon was an exhausting day's work. America's railroads in 1880 or 1920 may have offered better service than is available today between most cities, but getting across the ocean or across the continent was often a difficult and dangerous experience, especially for immigrants and other travelers with little money.

Yet the immigrants to the United States arrived in overwhelming numbers from around the globe. In 1910 the census takers discovered that there were 92,228,496 people living in the country. Of that number over 10 percent listed as their native tongue a language other than English. Indeed, over 35 million Europeans came to this country between 1815 and 1915, people of widely varying racial and ethnic stock who carried with them the cultural baggage of dozens of societies. The earliest arrivals were English, French, German, Irish, Scotch, and Scandinavian. Later, central, southern, and eastern European nationals predominated—Greeks, Rumanians, Hungarians, Austrians, Italians, Balts, Poles, Russians, and several kinds of Slavs. Indeed, the word "immigrants" almost always brings to mind a picture of people huddled together at Ellis Island in New York harbor shortly after arriving from Italy or eastern Europe. But Europeans were not the only immigrants. The Chinese had come to the West Coast as early as the 1840s, and the Japanese began to arrive in large numbers fifty years later. Mexicans and other Spanish-speaking peoples moved across the Western borderlands. And those Englishmen who came on the *Mayflower,* or the slaves captured and brought against their will from the west coast of Africa, were just as much immigrants as those who later arrived on ocean liners.

So they came, our ancestors, searching for a better life, or merely seeking to survive. While many remained to swell the populations of the coastal cities, millions of newcomers joined in the migration to the frontierlands, or to the cities of the interior. Useful generalizations about such a range of experience are difficult to make. One rather constant phenomenon, however, was discrimination. Long-enduring examples of bias against all nonwhite peoples, including those from Africa, Asia, and Hispanic America, are now fairly well recognized. Intolerance toward Catholics and Jews, the Irish, and southern and eastern Europeans has persisted well into the twentieth century. Legislation that discriminated against specific national groups was passed as early as the 1880s; in subsequent decades an often rabid xenophobia underscored American political life. The culmination of this fear was the passage of a restrictive immigration law in 1924, which limited annual immigration to 2 percent of each national group present in the country in 1890, a clearly discriminatory act against east Europeans and other groups that made up a small proportion of the population in 1890.

One result of racial and ethnic discrimination was the preservation of major elements of old-country cultural patterns, customs, language, and religious practices. (The image of the United States as a great melting pot where different ethnic and racial groups are melded into Americans never had much basis in fact.) This inclination toward preserving racial and ethnic self-consciousness also resulted from failure to achieve the American Dream of security and happiness. First- and second-generation immigrants for the most part entered the social structure at the bottom.

The dream dimmed but persisted. However long the hours and low the wages, the memory of the old country's serfdom was worse. Besides, sons and daughters would inherit the dream, someday. The upward climb on the ladder to success would be long and slow for most members of the ethnic groups, and slower yet for nonwhites. Their persistent attachment to racial and ethnic self-identification seems to be a reflection of this ambivalent search for the American grail.

Before you read this chapter, think a bit about your own immigrant roots. Then, as you read, try to associate these selections with the experiences of your own ancestors, their uprooting and resettling, relative assimilation and survival. Perhaps your family came with hope and had their dreams immediately fulfilled in the new land, much like the English house painters you are about to read of who migrated to Wisconsin. Perhaps your roots go back to the seventeenth or eighteenth centuries, and your ancestors followed the American Dream to the frontier. Possibly your grandmother or great-grandmother came with the same sense of resignation and despair that is described by the immigrant girl Rosa in another essay in this chapter. Whatever your family's particular experiences and expectations, they probably shared the range of hope and despair shown by the Jews of the Lower East Side of New York City and by the blacks seeking salvation in the North related in the final essays of this chapter.

The very first selection invites you to sense the dimensions of what must be the greatest folk migration in all of human history. Your own people are in there somewhere. You might be surprised at the tale your grandparents have to tell.

WORLD MIGRATION IN MODERN TIMES
L. S. Stavrianos

The immigration of millions of people to the United States was part of a mass migration unequaled in human history. Races and cultures that had previously remained segregated over the centuries intermixed after 1500, causing a tremendous impact on world history. What do you think the major results of this mass migration were? How many effects of the greatest movement of people in all of recorded time can you see in American society today? Can you locate the probable movement of your own ancestors in this great human saga?

The European discoveries led not only to new global horizons but also to a new global distribution of races. Prior to 1500 there existed, in effect, worldwide racial segregation. The Negroids were concentrated in sub-Saharan Africa and a few Pacific islands, the Mongoloids in Central Asia, Siberia, East Asia, and the Americas, and the Caucasoids in Europe, North Africa, the Middle East, and India. By 1763 this pattern had been fundamentally altered. In Asia, the Russians were beginning their slow migration across the Urals into Siberia. In Africa the Dutch had established a permanent settlement at the Cape, where the climate was favorable and the natives were too primitive to offer effective resistance. By 1763, 111 years after their landing at Capetown, the Dutch had pushed a considerable distance northward and were beginning to cross the Orange River.

By far the greatest change in racial composition occurred in the Americas. Estimates of the Indian population before 1492 vary tremendously, from 8 million to as high as 100 million. Whatever the figure may have been, there is no disagreement about the catastrophic effect of the European intrusion. Everywhere the Indians were decimated, by varying combinations or physical losses during the process of conquest, disruption of cultural patterns, psychological trauma of subjugation, imposition of forced labor, and introduction of alcohol and of new diseases. Within a century the total indigenous population appears to have declined by 90 to 95 per cent. Most badly hit were the Indians of the Caribbean islands and of the tropical coasts, where they disappeared completely within a generation. More resilient were the natives of the upland tropical regions and of lowland tropical areas such as those of Brazil and Paraguay. Although sustaining very heavy losses, they were able to recover and to constitute the stock from which most of the present-day American Indian population is derived. Only in the twentieth century has this population approached its original numbers in tropical America, while elsewhere it still lags far behind.

The disappearing Indians were replaced by waves of immigrants from Europe and Africa. The resulting settlements were of three varieties. One consisted of the Spanish

Why do you think the initial intermixing of races was destructive rather than assimilative?

and Portuguese colonies in which Iberian settlers constituted a permanent resident aristocracy among subjugated Indians in the highlands and imported Negro slaves in the lowlands. Since there were many more men than women among the European immigrants, they commonly took Indian wives or concubines. A mestizo population grew up, which in many parts of the Americas came to outnumber both Europeans and Indians.

How are the effects of Spanish and Portuguese colonization still apparent?

A second type of settlement developed in the West Indies, where the Europeans— English and French as well as Spanish—again comprised a resident aristocracy, though with an exclusively Negro imported labor force. At first the planters employed indentured servants from Europe to work their tobacco, indigo, and cotton plantations. But with the shift to sugar in the mid-seventeenth century, much more labor was needed, and slaves were brought over from Africa. In the British Barbados, for example, there were only a few hundred Negroes in 1640, but by 1685 they numbered 46,000 as against 20,000 whites. The French islands, likewise, had 44,000 Negroes and 18,000 whites by 1700.

The third type of settlement in the Americas was to be found along the Atlantic seaboard. There the native Indians were too sparse or too intractable to serve as an adequate labor supply, and apart from the southern colonies, the crops did not warrant importing Negro labor. Under these circumstances the English and French settlers cleared the land themselves, lived by their own labors as farmers, fishermen, or traders, and developed communities that were exclusively European in composition.

In conclusion, the mass migrations from Europe and Africa changed the Americas from purely Mongoloid continents to the most racially mixed regions of the globe. Negro immigration continued to the mid-nineteenth century, reaching a total of about fifteen million slaves, while European immigration steadily increased, reaching a high point at the beginning of the twentieth century when nearly one million arrived each year. The net result is that the New World today is peopled by a majority of whites, with substantial minorities of Negroes, Indians, mestizos, and mulattoes, in that order.

The new global racial pattern that resulted from these depopulations and migrations has become so familiar that it is now taken for granted, and its extraordinary significance generally overlooked. What happened in this period to 1763 is that the Europeans staked out claims to vast new regions, and in the following century they peopled those territories—not only the Americas, but also Siberia and Australia. As they expanded territorially so they made possible their own numerical expansion, and they exploited some of the richest resources of the planet. These European Caucasoids came in the eighteenth to the twentieth century to dominate both the areas they populated and much more besides. Taking advantage of the relatively sparse population in the New World, they literally Europeanized North and South America. This could not be done in Asia and Africa, where the indigenous populations were too numerous and highly developed. But in the Americas, and even more in Australia, the Europeans bodily transplanted their civilization in all its aspects—ethnic, economic, and cultural.

How did these migrations change the course of New World history?

The Industrial Revolution was in large degree responsible for this Europeanization. We have seen that increased productivity together with the advances of medical science had led to a sharp increase in Europe's population in the nineteenth century. This created a population pressure that found an outlet in overseas migration. Railways and steamships were available to transport masses of people across oceans and continents, and persecution of one sort or another further stimulated emigration, the chief example of this being the flight of 1 1/2 million Jews from Russia to the United States in the fifteen years preceding World War I. These various factors combined to produce a mass migration unequaled in human history. With every decade the tide of population movement increased in volume. In the 1820's a total of 145,000 left Europe, in the 1850's about 2,600,000, and between 1900 and 1910 the crest was reached with 9 million emigrants, or almost 1 million per year.

Before 1885 most of the emigrants came from northern and western Europe; after that date the majority were from southern and eastern Europe. By and large, the British emigrants went to the Dominions and to the United States, the Italians to the United States and Latin America, the Spaniards and Portuguese to Latin America, and the Germans to the United States and, in smaller numbers, to Argentina and Brazil. From the perspective of world history, the significance of this extraordinary migration is that it was all directed to the New World and Oceania, with the exception of the large flow to Asiatic Russia and the trickle to South Africa. The result has been the almost complete ethnic Europeanization of North America and Australia. The Indian population in South America managed to survive but was left a minority. In other words, the colonial

Uprooting and resettling of large numbers of people brings trouble to indigenous peoples. While the Indian wars in North America date back to the earliest days of European colonization, the last of the bloody struggles was fought only recently, when the pioneers came to the West. The American Indians were in some ways treated like immigrants in their own land. Perhaps Italians and Jews coming to the United States had a better break than most Indians. How do you explain our Indian policy? Do these Indians from Kansas appear "Americanized"? How do you account for their appearance? Is this craftmanship likely to be traditional basketry?

offshoots of the pre-1763 period now, during the course of the nineteenth century, became new Europes alongside the old.

The Americas and Australia were Europeanized economically as well as ethnically. Before 1763 the European settlements in these continents were confined largely to the coasts. But during the following century the interiors of the continents were traversed. The Industrial Revolution made this overland penetration possible by providing the necessary machines and techniques. The wilderness could not have been tamed without the roads leading inward from the coast, the canals connecting riverways, the railroads and telegraphs spanning continents, the steamers plying rivers and coastal waterways, the agricultural machines capable of cutting the prairie sod, and the repeating rifle that subdued the native peoples. These mechanical aids for the conquest of continental expanses were as essential to Latin Americans and Australians as to American frontiersmen. For example, an Argentinian writing in 1878 observed that "the military power of the [Indian] barbarians is wholly destroyed, because the Remington has taught them that an army battalion can cross the whole pampa, leaving the land strewn with the bodies of those who dared to oppose it."

The peopling and economic development of the new continents led automatically to the transplanting of European culture as well. It is true that the culture changed in

Summarize the ways in which the Industrial Revolution aided this mass migration.

PRINCIPAL SOURCES OF EUROPEAN EMIGRATION, 1946–1932

Great Britain and Ireland	18,000,000
Russia	14,250,000*
Italy	10,100,000
Austria-Hungary	5,200,000
Germany	4,900,000
Spain	4,700,000
Portugal	1,800,000
Sweden	1,200,000
Norway	850,000
Poland	640,000†
France	520,000
Denmark	390,000
Finland	370,000
Switzerland	330,000
Holland	220,000
Belgium	190,000
TOTAL	63,660,000

* Consists of 2,250,000 who went overseas, 7,000,000 who migrated to Asiatic Russia by 1914, 3,000,000 who migrated to the Urals, Siberia, and the Far East from 1927 to 1939 and 2,000,000 who migrated to Central Asia from 1927 to 1939. Since 1939, Russian emigration, free and forced, into the trans-Ural areas, has been the greatest single population movement in the world.
† 1920–1932 only.
Source: A. M. Carr-Saunders, *World Population* (Oxford: Clarendon, 1936), pp. 49, 56; and W. S. and E. S. Woytinsky, *World Population and Production* (New York, Twentieth Century Fund, 1953), pp. 69, 93.

transit. It was adapted as well as adopted. Canada and Australia and the United States today are not identical to Great Britain, nor is Latin America an exact reproduction of the Iberian Peninsula. But the fact remains that the languages are essentially the same, even though Englishmen are intrigued by American slang and Frenchmen by the archaic French-Canadian patois. The religions also are the same, despite the campfire revival meetings and the Mormons. The literatures, the schools, the newspapers, the forms of government—all have roots extending back to England and Spain and France and other European countries.

What specific European influences on the major institutions of American society can you name?

There are, of course, certain cultural strains in the Americas and in Australia that are not European. The Negro element in the New World has retained a certain residue of its African background. The surviving native peoples, especially the Indians in Latin America, are responsible for a hybrid culture. Nor should one forget the impact of the wilderness, leaving its indelible imprint on the European immigrants and on their institutions. All these forces explain why New York, Melbourne, and Toronto are very different from London, and why Buenos Aires, Brasilia, and Mexico City differ from Madrid.

What kinds of modifying influences might the author be thinking of?

Yet from a global viewpoint the similarities loom larger than the differences. The Arab peoples, in the course of their expansion from their homeland in the Middle East, spread westward across North Africa to the Atlantic Ocean. Today the culture of Morocco is far more different from that of the Arabian Peninsula than the culture of the United States is from that of Britain, or the culture of Brazil from that of Portugal. Yet Morocco is considered, and certainly considers itself, to be a part of the Arab world. In the same sense, the Americas and Australia today are a part of the European world.

STEERAGE: THE IRISH COME TO AMERICA

Terry Coleman

"Steerage" is defined in the Oxford English Dictionary as "the part of a passenger ship allotted to those passengers who travel at the cheapest rate." This benign definition suggests modest but adequate below-deck accommodations for thrifty travelers. For millions of our immigrant ancestors, however, this experience would haunt the rest of their days.

As diverse as were the immigrant peoples, the horrors of the mid-passage were grimly similar. For up to two weeks on the Atlantic, as many as 900 voyagers were crammed into the steerage, each allotted little more space than their body dimensions. The fetid underdecks of slowly moving ships reduced individuals—whether Russian Jew or Irishman, Greek or German, man, woman, or child—to an undifferentiated suffering mass.

Here and there, a ship's travelers were fortunate enough to have a tolerable passage. Everywhere, moments of youthful hope helped mask the reality. In the years after 1900 steerage conditions tended to improve, and travel time shrank to a more tolerable six or seven days. Yet relative suffering is suffering nonetheless, as the large literature of steerage recollections makes so wrenchingly clear.

'Before the emigrant has been a week at sea he is an altered man. How can it be otherwise? Hundreds of poor people, men, women, and children, of all ages, from the drivelling idiot of ninety to the babe just born, huddled together without light, without air, wallowing in filth and breathing a fetid atmosphere, sick in body, dispirited in heart, the fevered patients lying between the sound, in sleeping places so narrow as almost to deny them the power of indulging, by a change of position, the natural restlessness of the disease; by their agonised ravings disturbing those around, and predisposing them, through the effects of the imagination, to imbibe the contagion; living without food or medecine, except as administered by the hand of casual charity, dying without the voice of spiritual consolation, and buried in the deep without the rites of the church."

These are the words of Stephen de Vere, a landowner and philanthropist from County Limerick, a distant relative of the former Earls of Oxford, a convert to Rome, and a poet who translated Horace's Odes. He saved Irishmen from the gallows, taught in Irish schools, charged his tenants less than a fair rent for his lands, and for more than twenty years abstained from wine to encourage temperance among the poor. In 1847 he went out to America not in the cabin but as a steerage passenger, to see for himself how poor emigrants were treated.

Were these conditions typical for the Irish fleeing the Great Famine?

* * *

The most detailed account of all is by an Irish gentleman, Vere Foster, who was no relation of Stephen de Vere, and must not be confused with him. Foster sailed in the

Washington which left Liverpool for New York in October 1850. This was not a year of great disease. The passage was not stormy, although it was winter. The *Washington* was no hulk, but one of the finest American emigrant ships. She was new, strong, and dry. Her two passenger decks were each over seven feet high, and bulwarks more than six feet high protected the deck from sea spray. She had a crew of thirty-one sailors, three boys, four mates, and a captain. She carried a surgeon. She was a great deal better in all ways than the average run of emigrant ships. She left Liverpool on October 25 with 934 passengers and anchored in the Mersey to take on supplies. Next day Foster went on board to sail as one of the cabin passengers. He was the man who had given away 250,000 copies of his *Emigrants' Guide.* He was a philanthropist, and a relative of Lord Hobart, who was with the Board of Trade in London.

One of the first things Foster saw on board was the doling out of the daily water ration. All 900 or so passengers were called forward at once to receive the water, which was pumped into their cans from barrels on deck. The serving out was twice capriciously stopped by the mates, who cursed, abused, kicked, and cuffed the passengers and their tin cans and, having served about thirty people, said there would be no more water that day. Foster gently remonstrated with one of the mates, observing to him that such treatment was highly improper and unmanly, and that the mate would save himself a great deal of trouble and annoyance and win, instead of alienating, the hearts of the passengers, if he would avoid foul language and brutal treatment: the mate replied that if Foster said another word he would knock him down. By October 30, no food at all had been served to the passengers although the contract tickets stated they were to be fed each day. The poorer steerage passengers had brought nothing with them, and for five days had nothing to eat except what they could beg from their better-off companions. Foster began to write a letter of complaint addressed to the captain on behalf of the steerage passengers. He began "Respected Sir," and had got as far as courteously enquiring when they might expect to be fed, when the first mate knocked him flat on the deck with a blow on the face. "When the mate knocked me down," Foster said, "which he did without the smallest previous intimation or explanation, he also made use of the most blasphemous and abusive language." Foster went to his cabin, the mate remarking that if he found him in the 'tween decks again he would not hit him but throttle him. Next day Foster did manage to get to the captain, Page, to present his letter. The captain told him to read it aloud. Foster had read a third of it, when the captain said that was enough; he knew what Foster was—he was a damned pirate, a damned rascal, and he would put him in chains and on bread and water for the rest of the voyage. The first mate added more foul abuse and blasphemy, and was later found heating a thick bar of iron in the kitchen fire and saying he intended to give Foster a singeing with it.

... The captain never bothered to visit the steerage, and the first and second mates, the cooks, and the surgeon seldom opened their mouths without prefacing what they had to say with, "God damn your soul to hell," or "By Jesus Christ, I'll rope's end you." Those who gave the cooks money or whisky could get five meals cooked a day. Others who had no money to give, or chose not to give, had one meal a day, or one every other day.

... On November 17 the surgeon hurled overboard a great many chamber pots belonging to the women passengers, and told them to come to the privies on deck which were filthy. Foster heard him say: "There are a hundred cases of dysentery on the ship, which will all turn to cholera, and I swear to God that I will not go amongst them; if they want medecines they must come to me." The same morning, the first mate played the hose on the passengers who were in the privies, drenching them. The fourth mate had done the same four days before. One of the passengers who was himself a doctor, went round canvassing for a testimonial to the ship's surgeon, collecting money for a gift to placate him. Nobody wanted to give. The ship's doctor, hearing of this, muttered that the steerage passengers had plenty of money on them, which they would not know what to do with when they got to New York, and that if they would not look after him he would not look after them. Some passengers said they would not mind contributing a shilling each if they thought it might be used to buy a rope to hang him.

The first mate kneed John M'Corcoran, an old man, who afterwards passed blood whenever he went to the privy. The doctor, now he was getting no gift, decided to charge for his services, and extorted half a crown from one passenger and a shilling from another, and charged sixpence for a glass of castor oil. On November 25, a month out, when it had been very cold, another child, making about twelve in all, died of dysentery and from want of proper food. He was thrown into the sea sewn up in a cloth weighted

What permitted the crew to treat the passengers in this inhumane fashion?

The immigrant ships of the late nineteenth century were much larger than, for example, the slave ships that sailed at the beginning of that century. They carried nearly 10 million people from 1880–1900 alone. Were your ancestors part of this wave of migration?

with a stone. No funeral service was conducted: the doctor said the Catholics objected to a layman conducting any such service. The sailors were pulling at a rope, and raising their usual song:

> Haul in the bowling, the Black Star bowling
> Haul in the bowling, the bowling haul—

and the child was thrown overboard at the sound of the last word of the song, which became a funeral dirge.

On November 30, two days off New York, Foster wrote in his diary: "The doctor came down to the second cabin in company with the first mate, and to display his authority, drew himself up and swelled himself up excessively tremendous, roaring out, 'Now then, clean and wash out your rooms every one of you, God damn and blast your souls to hell.'"

• • •

The Atlantic passage in a sailing vessel must by its nature have been an ordeal for most landsmen. Many ships, even the bigger ones, were not dry, particularly when they had a part cargo of iron or railway lines. Captain Schomberg, emigration officer at Liverpool, tried to superintend the loading, not only to make sure the ship was safe but also to look after the passengers' health. "A deep ship will very probably, under ordinary circumstances, be very wet and uncomfortable, and the people will live up to their knees in water . . ." Even the cheerful emigrant from Bristol complained that "two holes, cut for air, often admit water upon us, through the ship's heaving."

The crowding itself made decency and comfort impossible. . . .

On board most ships, men and women were indiscriminately berthed together. Sir George Stephen once asked a ship's mate how he managed with marriages at sea; how did he manage to bed the couple on board? To which the mate replied: "There is no difficulty as to that; there is plenty of that work going on every night to keep them all in countenance." George Saul, passenger broker, said that if people wished to be improperly berthed, he shut his eyes to it, thinking he could not make people virtuous if they were disposed to be immoral. . . .

Sylvester Redmond, journalist, was asked if he thought indiscriminate intercourse took place. He said: "I saw on two occasions, in the daytime, persons in very indelicate positions."

"Of different sexes?—Yes."

This is risible; as it was when a captain in the Royal Navy was solemnly questioned about unmarried men on board being able to "view the married women dressing or undressing, and see what is going on." He had to agree that there was "use given to the eyes." But this berthing together must have been intolerable for a modest woman.

Why were such materials as iron imported from Europe at this time?

Why did conventional standards of privacy not prevail?

106

Sometimes women had to sit up all night on boxes because they could not think of going to bed with strange men, under the same blanket.

• • •

The women got the worst of it in other ways. Those who had no men to look out for them found it difficult to get any food at all. A doctor who had made many voyages from Liverpool to America said that on rough days he had often been obliged to go into the steerage with buckets of water and a bag of biscuits to feed the women to save them from starvation. Women and feeble men went days without a bite. A boarding-house keeper at Liverpool who had made one voyage on a ship with about 400 passengers, said that there was only room for six people to stand and cook at the same time, and there was incessant cooking and fighting from six in the morning till six at night. "The women particularly, who were alone, must have wanted their food."

Why did women not insist on their rights?

. . . On many Irish ships the staple diet was a coarse concoction of wheat, barley, rye, and pease, which became saturated with moisture on board ship, where it fermented and became baked into a solid mass "requiring to be broken down with an axe before using."

Many emigrants would not eat unaccustomed food, though it might have been perfectly good. The Irish, although preferring potatoes, which they never got, would eat oatmeal. The English, thinking it food for horses, would not. One passenger said he had seen it thrown into the St. Lawrence. He had seen the river covered with oatmeal. Many emigrants were too poor and ignorant to know what to do with the food they were given. One captain said a third of them did not know what tea was. "It is no uncommon thing to see an Irishman survey his allowance of tea for a while, and then fill his pipe with a portion, and smoke it with evident satisfaction."

How could it be that so many Irish knew nothing about tea?

• • •

On September 3, 1853, Delaney Finch, a farmer, sailed from Liverpool to Quebec in the *Fingal,* with 200 other passengers and 1,100 tons of railroad iron. She was lost on the return voyage. Finch said she was a good ship, though the berths broke down. On the voyage of seven weeks, thirty-seven or forty-one passengers died: he could not remember which. Later he was asked what happened. He said: "I should not like to give an opinion, but my impression is, that Epsom salts and castor oil are very improper medecines to administer to persons labouring under the cholera."

How do you explain the callous disregard for the lives of the Irish immigrants?

"Is that what they gave?—Yes."

"Epsom salts and castor oil?—Yes, and thirty-five drops of laudanum, and then rubbing a man's face with vinegar."

He was asked if any record was kept of the deaths: "When we got to Quebec, I and Mr. Liefchild, a gentleman who was in the second cabin, had to put down the names of the parties who died on the voyage, but it was more guess-work than certainty."

Then he was asked how the burials were carried out, and he said the bodies were thrown overboard, not covered up or anything.

"Did he [the captain] give directions to have the corpse sewn up in canvas, and thrown over?—No, he did not use his jurisdiction in that matter, because he said in the cabin, 'We are not bound to do it; it is only according to courtesy.' "

From England to Wisconsin

We usually think of nineteenth-century immigrants to the United States as a mass of people speaking one or another foreign language, and faced with a difficult adjustment to their new land. Many immigrants, however, came from the British Isles and had no language problems, though in other ways they faced the same trials as all of the other newcomers. The stream of immigrants from Britain continued long after the colonies declared their independence. In fact, the number of immigrants from Britain in the late 1840s increased greatly, possibly even exceeding the number from Ireland that reached a peak about the same time. Among the migrants from the British Isles were two house painters, Fred Chaney and Frank Johnson. Each left behind a wife and children, who would follow later.

Chaney and Johnson traveled all the way to Fond du Lac, Wisconsin, before they found work. They achieved a measure of success and, following the common immigrant custom, sent for their families. More fortunate probably than most, the Chaneys and Johnsons had been separated for only about eighteen months before the women and children crossed the ocean. The Johnsons were reunited in New York City and remained there. The Chaneys settled in Fond du Lac.

Their letters back and forth during this time provide us with interesting descriptions of the passage across the Atlantic at mid-century as well as the trip to Wisconsin. The route these two immigrants took was similar to the one taken by a great many residents of New England and the Middle Atlantic states as they sought opportunity in the Middle West. The letters even mention "Oregon Fever," the urge to continue the quest for fame and fortune all the way to the West Coast—an urge that these settlers resisted.

For these British immigrants the American Dream seems to have come true. Although they did not make a fortune, they saw America as a land of opportunity where jobs were plentiful, investment opportunities were everywhere, and the cost of living only half what it had been in Britain. Yet even for the successful immigrants there were many trials and many difficulties to overcome.

[Autumn], 1849

Dear Ann and Dear Betsey,
We started from London on 24th Augt and sailed from Portsmouth on 1 Sept, and was 5 Weeks on our Passage. We had a Pleasant Voyage, came to New York and had a look around. We had the promises of 3 or 4 Houses in a fortnights time. It would not do to wait. We went from New York to Albany 150 miles. We had no Luck and went on to Utica 110 Miles further where we now write from. We are rather to late for Business here. We are now starting for Buffalow.

Was anxious to let you now our affairs as soon as possible to comfort you a little, and anxious are we to hear how you are in health and circumstances. We feel great concern for you, and believe you do the same for us. I am sorry I could not send better News, but we would not wait any longer writing to you.

America is a fine Country. No man in Existence can truly describe its beauties. We wish we were all settled here together, it would be the greatest happiness we could Experience. God alone knows what he intends to do with us. May we have Grace and Faith to leave all things in his hands.

We wish you to get all the News ready for our Next Letter which we hope to send in a few Days with Directions where to write to us. Remember us to all the Dear Children, give them a kiss apiece for us. Keep up your Spirits and we will do the same. It may be like Old Jacob coming down to Egypt to live.

Give our kind Love to your Mother, John, Henry in particular. Tell him I shall write a long letter to him as soon as we get settled. Richard, Wife and Betsy, Charles, Sarah, not forgetting above all Mr. and Mrs. Farrow, Hugh, William, Wife and Child.

Yours affectionately,

No more at present from Fred and Frank Dear Betsy, give the babe a kiss for me, Frank. I have been to see a Baptiss Member who is the largest Painter in this town who came here very low and is now a great Man. He Encouraged us very much by saying when we once got into Work we should sure to do well as we can keep a Famely at half the price of beggerly England.

What does this letter reveal about the writer's intention in coming to America?

An immigrant group probably consisting of several families photographed at Ellis Island. Do thay have hope or fear in their faces? Why was so much immigration encouraged by America in the late nineteenth and early twentieth centuries? Will the process of Americanization be easier for the men, the women, or the children? They even look "foreign," do they not? Will that look change in a few years? Perhaps you can imagine one of your ancestors in a group like this, just off the boat.

[*Autumn*], 1849

Dearest Ann, Betsey, Clara and all young ones,
We think by this time you [are] anxiously waiting to hear from us, we are also anxious to hear from you without one moments delay. Our last letter we sent did not hold out much comfort for you or us either, but by the Blessing of a Merciful God we can give you some Good News. We think we have found the Land of Promise at last, and the God of Promises is with us.

I have not room to give any account at present of our travels but suffice it to say we have settled at Fond de Lack, Wisconsin, United States America. We came here heavy hearted after failing all our journey on account for being to late for the season here. God raised us up Good Friends. Arrived here on Saturday Night, went to work on Monday, and earned 6£ in American Money in 5 days at painting, equal to 3£ in English Money. This is a New and Flourishing Town only a few Months started. We have plenty of Work and likely to continue for Years, but the thing is this, in all New Places we are forced to work for Barter so we are now working out 50 Dollars for a Town Lot of Ground that will Build 6 or 8 Houses. We are also working for another Man for Timber to Build your Houses. We are now working for Mr. Edwards who is Building a large House for Shop. Tell Mr. Vinters he knows him well. He kept the Bakhouse that Child [h]as got on the Highway. He was Sectary to the Bakers Society. Desire to be remembered to him, tho 5 Thousand Miles of[f].

We have plenty of London cockneys here and plenty coming every day. This will be a fine place for Business soon, so you see we cannot help you to come out. You must directly think about it as it will take some time to arrange with the Parishes. You must come out about the 1st of March as the lakes are frosen over in Winter.

Ann and Betsey, you must exert yourselves with all your Might, you must throw yourself on the Parish or they will not do anything for you, and that for some time before they will do any thing for you. If it is St. Lukes Parish go to Mr. Smith, he knows me well, and see what he can do. If St. Georges go and see Mr. Knight the Rope Maker, he knows me well, he is [a] very kind and liberal Man, he is the first Man in the Parish, and is sure to do what he can. Do not let the parish know that you can work at the Needle, as they would say you could earn your own living. You must push it with all your strength. When you arrive here you will find every thing heart can wish, house of your own, no Rent to pay. We shall be able no doubt to work out a good Cow, and to have a Barrell of Flour by that time.

Everything here is very Cheap, 2 days work will keep a Man for a Week. . . . We have heard a Good deal about America, but never thought it was like this. We can look out from our Window over 50 Miles of Beautiful country, no place in the world to equal America. Plenty work for Dress Makers, first rate pay to.

Tell Betsey Frank wants her to go to Bunyan and ask him to send on a slip of paper the different Colors for Graining. Tell him to send the Names of Colors how to Mix them and for Graining, and Receipts for all Woods. Give Frank['s] kind respects to him.

Now Ann I wish you to be sure to enquire the prices of the Plush, different sorts and colors for making Mens Caps, also the prices of the Peaks per Dozen of the same, also prices of Threads, Cottons, pins, Needles, etc., which are very dear here. Our Landlady Makes Caps, and she will send money over by the time you come to bring her some. She and her Husband are the best Creatures in the world. All our prospects, Work and everything is oweing to them, they long to see you all over safe, tho never seen you. Dont forget to send particulars upon any account. If you could get plenty of Beads to bring you would get a capital price for them here. Clara is sure to make Money here.

[*Unsigned, but probably also from Fred and Frank*]

Why do you think exchange was by barter rather than by currency?

What does the fact that foodstuffs were cheap, but fabrics and beads could be sold dearly indicate about the economy of Wisconsin then?

[Autumn], 1849

Dear Betsey,

You can tell Mr. Powell that there is a good prospect here for a man who has got 2 or 3 Hundred Pounds as he could double it in about 12 Months in Buying Land and Building, as the Houses are let or sold before finished, and will be so for some time to come, as this is a thriving town, as a New Canal is cut from this Town to run into the Main Rivers to convey goods to all parts. We have 2 steamers already running on it. Land very cheap here, but will soon rise high. Last spring there was only 3 Houses in this place, now there is 3 or 4 Hundred, and next year will be Treble that.

Betsey, you can tell Mr. Powell that had I a few Pounds it would be of infinite Value to me at this time. I am sure I could more than double it in a few Months.

Give my kind respects to Mrs. Powell and Mr. Powell, hope they are quite well. Give a kiss to all the young ones for me, and when you come over I will pay you back again.

Your affecly
F[rank] Johnson

What part did speculation in land play in the settlement of the West?

Decr. 16, 1849

Dearest Betsey & Dearest Children,

I Received you Letter of 12th Decr., it came from England to New York in 13 days and from New York to me in 11 days more, being only 24 in all, this is quick travelling. I was most happy to hear that you and the dear Children are all well in health. I hope when you receive this you will not lose a day without sending an answer, it is very uncertain that I shall be able to send another Letter, for at this time of Year the Lakes are frose over and the Mail has to travel some Hundred[s] of Miles on Sledges through the snow, and by the time my Letter came to England you, I hope, will have started, so write immediately and send all the News you can.

You wish me to give you a true account [of] how I am getting on. When I came here I found plenty of Work but no Money, it was all done in Barter. I have bought a plot of Ground and Built a cottage on it. I have paid part of the Money in Labour, and have to pay the rest in Labour. I have been very fortunate since I have been here in getting Work, especially as I came just before the Winter set in. Of course I do not care what I do if I dont get work at my own trade. I go to Labouring work, I have now 3 Jobs in hand, and one is to Work out 2 Waggon Loads of Fire Wood, another for a Hundred and Half of Flour, another for Wearing Apparel. There is plenty of Work, but all must be taken out in Goods, so you see I can keep 2 Familys here better than I could keep one in England. Good Flour is only 5s English money, pr Hundred Weight, Prime Beef 2 pence pr pound, and every thing else equally low, and no Rent to pay.

Dear Betsey, I feel very anxious to see you come out and hope the Parish Authority will be kind enough to help you and the Children for to come. I feel very thankful to hear they have acted so kind towards you, and that you have been so comfortable and also that the children are with you. Should be very Glad to hear if your Confinement was over. I feel very anxious about you. Do not fail to send all particulars as to the time of coming out. I would advise you by all means to come out in the Middle of March. The ship will not be so crowded. There will not be any sickness or fever that is some times the case through the Hot Weather.

Dear Betsey save all the Means you are able as it will cost a good bit to bring you from New York to me. You had better bring all the Bed and Bedding you can, as Blankets are very dear here, and any other things that are not to heavy or cumbersome. You wished me to write about the disturbance with the Indians. We have not heard a word about it. We seldom see any of them, but they are very sociable and Quiet People.

We have fine weather here, tho in the Middle of Winter we have always a clear Sky, Warm Sun, no fogs, and from what I have seen not so severe as our winters. Nearly all our Neibours are English People.

I Remain your Affec. Husband,
F. Johnson

What indications are there in this letter that the country was still primitive?

Apparently Betsey Johnson obtained the coveted parish aid, for some time in 1850 she arrived in New York where Frank joined her and where they remained. In the summer of the same year Ann Chaney and her daughters Clara, Eliza, Emma, and Jane, also with parish assistance, sailed for Canada en route to join Fred Chaney in Wisconsin. In her first letters to her family in England Ann gives a vivid account of life aboard an immigrant ship and records her first ebullient impressions of the strange new world. Clara's first letter to her grandmother is interesting for its contrast of English and American ways and for its evidence of the adaptability of a sixteen-year-old London girl to frontier conditions.

My dear Mother, Brother and Sister,

I know you are very anxious to hear from me, as I expect you have not herd of the vessel. We left Hatton Garden at ten o'clock on the 3rd August for the Railway Station, and left there at twelve for Blackwall where [we were met by] some of the Ladies and Gents, and a widow as sub-Matron. She was not with them. She had aplied for her passage within the last two days of leaving London. All eyes was upon her. She was a respectable looking person, but disguised by licour. All the Girls took a dislike to her.* She was very bussy telling them she would see them done well by, and asking the Gentlemen for instructions. They treated her very cool, and told her I would give them her. Mr. Quickett, after paying for the Children to Toronto, paid me over eight pounds. We joined the Ship at Gravesend, and the Gentry left us there. The Government Oficer ordered the Steward to cook us some beef steaks and Mr. Blackey looked dagers at him. Last fresh meat we had.

We sailed from Gravesend at 4 on Sunday morning. I went on deck and enjoid an hour there, being a delightful morning. At 6 the provisionry was given out for the week for the whole party—biscuits, rice, peas, tea, sugar, pork, beef, plumbs and [?] soup, cheese and butter. Fancy all this stuff in my little Cobard with the addition of this troblesome nuisance. I get Dinner in the best way we could, being very troblesome to get it cooked.

The pilot left us on Sunday evening at the Downs, the weather being rough, cast anchor and sailed earley on Monday morning. We was all getting very sick while the vessel is getting out of the Chanel, it is fact about the sails being shipt very often, the sailors shouting and tossing about the Deck. The Carpenter came to make the boxes fast, the water cans tied.

I appointed two Cooks, but the convenience was very bad. A bad Cook, a littel Black man. We have biscuit eat like baked sawdust, fresh water stinking, pudding boiled in salt water and not half done, peas and rice the same, and hard salt beef. The Girls get disatisfied with their food. Some of them are bold low creatures, and to get order is quite impossible. My cooks very ill. The Doctor divided the party into four meses, each cook for themself. This relieved me very much. I was very sick and low part of the time, but I think if I could have enjoid my food I should have been very well. I am very well now. The Children are all very well. Littel Jean ha[s] been the best Sailour and a general Favourite in particular with the Black Steward.

Now my dear Mother, we are getting very tired of the sea, the wether very rough and contrary winds. I lay in my birth and listen, try to listen, but I cannot distinguish such a confusion of noises. The sea roars, the waves dash against the vesel with such force you would think it had struck against a rock. Then it would heave from one side to the other. Boxes slip, tins and sugar, treacle, rice, cheese, plumbs and everything we had dashed about, the vesel cracking and groaning you would think it must devide or sway under the water.

We had several squals. The men said our ship is the dryest they have sailed in, and she rode through the squals bravely. We had two or three nights and days of this sort, and a day or so quit calm. You can have no idea of the beauty of the sea when the sun sets. I [never?] saw anything so beautifull, the sea deep blue, and sometimes on looking over the side of the vesel can see very curious fish, some like a flat round with a bright cross up them, and other different forms, and when the sea is rough great monsters seem to play in the waves.

Now we are about to enter the Gulf. This night was awful, the rain poured in to torrents, and the wind blew huricans. The water, all thoe the [h]atch was on which all most stifold us, was pouring down. I herd the Cheif Mait tell the people in the sterage that he did not think one of us could see the morning, but thank God mercies came, but the hurican continued. The vesel was on its side. The sailors [said?] had that occured in the night we must have been lost. In the afternoon the storm seased to a calm. Now the pilot came on board, this caused much excitement, but he had joined us two hundred miles beyond his station. He had been out some time looking for us.

We enter the river St. Lorance, here we wait for the tide. The senery is delightfull. At last disernible the numerus little hills scatered at the slopes near the water by milk white houses, and the boats come along side. Now we are at dock near the quarintine ground, and if we was not in [h]e[a]lth we should have to stop some time there. Mrs. Sidney Herbert's Brother had been there, we had been expected these three weeks. I would not have sent [this letter?] till we got to Toronto, but I know you are anxious. I shall long to hear from you. We are near Quebec.

I have just been on deck and the sight very impresing. We seam encircled by land and the slopes up from the water, and laid out butifuly, houses with slated roofs, and we see a great water fall.

[Unsigned, but probably from Ann Chaney]

Summarize the hardships that the immigrants endured on the transatlantic journey.

*Apparently Ann Chaney was in charge of a party of young women being assisted by the parishes to emigrate to Canada to seek employment, probably as domestics. From the context it would appear that the woman "disguised by licour" was either to serve as Ann's subordinate or was in charge of a similar group of female emigrants.

My very dear Mother,

I know you are very anxious to hear of me, and I am also very anxious to let you know I am very greived to hear how you was moved.

Well, I will give a sketch from Quebec. We met Mr. a'Court [Harcourt?] there and he accompanyed us, providing cabin fair to Toronto. The weather was very [good?] and the views along very beautiful. In two or three days the Girls was provided with places. I wrote to Fredrick the day I arrived there, and waited three weeks and no answer.

I was treated with great kindness, but still I could not stop any longer, so I packed up and started at a venture at two o'clock in the afternoon, and passed Niagra Fawls that night. We had left the boat and was in horse cars. The night was dark and we could but hear the tremendous roar of the waters and see the white foam to a Great Hight. We stopt [at?] Keep Chipawea [?] 7 miles from there, from there to Buffalo by steam boat, from there to Detroit. Stopt at a Dashing Hotel till morning, then by rail to New Buffalo. Waited till three in the morning, the boat being full, was thought I should not go, but the lugage was at the last minute put on board. I had left the Children with a woman on the warf who had promised to not to leave them, and Clara and me sought the goods. The boat pushed into the lake and I thought all was wright but presently found the Children was left on the warf and ran about like one mad to find the Captain. He was on the second deck. He said they would be sent to me. He tried to get from me, and went down the roaps, I went down the roaps as well as he, and I was left there with the Children, and Clara and the lugage went on to Chicago. I went by the next boat, and found Clara at a respectable hotel, where we all stopt that night, then we left there for Milwacke late at night, and was to go the next morning. We went to the warf, the boat was to full and we could not go that day.

The next morning we went on board and the boat put out into the lake but the weather was to rough to procede. The third morning we left Milwake for Sheboggan. There we stopt one night, then toke a team to go to Fondulake which was forty five miles.

We started this distance, was all through a wood. The trees have been cut down to make a road, and a queer road it was, over stumps of trees and stones, down steaps, up hills, mud, and then you come to a hole partly piled up with sticks, then to a great swamp and bodys of trees put cross to form a road. So you may think this was very rough riding, but thoe the morning was frosty we was not the least cold, the sun out and the weather bright and pleasant, and plenty of Buffalo skins to rap our feet in. These woods are not drery as you would think—hear and there is a open space, been cleared, and a few cottages. A few miles further and another or two. There are several taverns in this wood. We stopt one night at a log tavern, you cannot get through in one day.

I met with a young man in Milwake who knew Fredrick and directed me to the spot. It is in the lower vilage. On a prary ground, there is no trees close, but at a littel distance there is plenty of woods. Well, we was directed over the Bridge, then we was shone his Shanty. We drove to the door of this most splend[id] cottage. It was a wooden house with two windows in it, and one good sized room and one small with two bed steds the old Chap manufactured himself. He was not at home. His nearest neighbour came and insisted on us going to her house to dinner, and sent for him. He was expecting us. He had received and answered my letter but I had not received it. Frederick toke me to see several people all who was very glad to see me, and are very friendly, and we have several visits.

There is very little money here, but traid one with the other. There are stores and they [have] every thing, and you have bills on these stores and take what you want. I have been to one of the largest stores who deal largely in Close, and has promised me work, and we I do think may be comfortable. Fredrick has agreed part material for a better house wich is to be done in the Spring.

My dear Mother, only for the thort that we are so far apart I am very comfortable and my helth is much improved. We are all in good helth.

I have been here five days before I sent this, that I might send you all the news I could. I gave Mr. a'Court your address. He assured me he would call on you. He is Sir Sidney Herbert Wifes Brother. He expected to be in England in three months.

Fredrick had a letter from Frank a few days ago. He has some work at New York and he thinks to come to Fondulack next Spring. They are all well.

Now my dear Mother and Brothers and Sister except our sesear [sincere?] love from your affectionate Daughter and family. Love to John, hope him and his mother is comfortable.

A. F. and C. Chaney

We have a pig near ready to kill and three others not quite ready. I was in Milwakey three days and nights. I received five pounds of Mr. a'Court and spent all I had in travelling. Please to remember me to Mr. and Mrs. Venters and Helen and [H?]inton. I could have called on Mr. [H?]intons famely if I had known there adress.

How many different means of transportation did the writer use to reach Wisconsin? How do you account for so many changes?

December, 1850

Dear Grandmother,

Thinking by this time that you and Uncle John will be saying Ah Clara is gone and forgot all about us, but I hope not to deserve this acuseasation, but I thourt it better to defer writing a few weeks after Mother's letter....

... A dollar goes much further here than it would in England. Harricot beans a dollar a Bushel. Father brought home for half dollar 2 pounds of sugar, quarter of a pound of tea, a pound and 1/2 of coffee, this seemed a good deal to us for 2 english shillings. We have to roast and grind our own coffee, bake our own Bread. We mostly have meat for Breakfast. The Yankees generally live well, we have three meals a day, they [call?] the third Supper. They do not have 3 trays like they do in england, they have apple sauce, preserves, meat and several kinds of cakes on the Table at one time. At every meal they have tea or coffee. Dear Grandmother, I think you may see it is much easier to get on here than in england. We are in expectation of a rail road coming near us in the spring, which will make the place very Flourishing and money more plentiful. We are invited to dinner Christmas day by that mans brother that mother took the letter for. Mother and I went with a person from England who are Cabinet makers in the Town to see Mrs. Smiths farm who are also english. These Smiths have not been here two years, they came without a penny but now they are in a Flourishing condition. They rent the farm at 2 hundred dollars a year, but there corn that they grow pays there rent and a hundred dollars over. They have 14 cows, 10 calves, and 2 sheep, 23 pigs, 20 fowls. They have 100 acres of land, 50 in cultivation and the rest in pasture. They made us very welcome. I made a Chrochet cap for which we take out in butter. We have several invitations to different farmers when it is good sleaighing, that will be when the snow gets a little deeper on the ground.

The frost set in about the begining of December, it was very severe for a few days, and frose the lakes and rivers up. The weather is dry and clear and fine sunshiny weather. Teams which are drawn by oxen and mools, sleaighs, cutters, all cross the river and lakes on the ice. The inhabitants look forword with pleasure to deep snow and kalaclate on many pleasant visits. The winter last about six months, snowing and freeseing, snowing and freeseing all the winter.

Dear grandmother, the stoves are very different here to what they are at home, they are in sort of iron box with oven and a pipe going up through the ceiling. They mostly stand in the middle of the room and throw out a great heat. There is no coals burnt here, all wood. The men go up in the woods to get it, and chop or saw it at there own place.

We killed the sow and salted it down, now we have three young ones left which Father means to keep. We give them very little food. They run about the prairies and pick up anything they can eat. Sometimes they will go away for days together.

Dear Grandmother, when you write again please to put James Fredrick instead of Mr. Chaney as the letters stop at the post office until called for, and they make a peice of work if they are not directed so.

Dear Grandmother, I have not room for any more, but hope you will write directly you receive this, and I will write directly I receive your answer. We are all in good health, as we hope you are also. Mother and Father send their love to you and Uncle John, Uncle Charles, Aunt Sarah, Phil, Sally and the baby and all inquiring frends. The children send their love.

I am your ever affectionate [grand] daughter Clara Chaney.

What kinds of adjustments did the woman who wrote this letter have to make?

March 1st, 1851

Dear Mother and Charles,

We received your last letter and was very sorry to hear you was so poorly, we hope you are better. We should be glad to have a long letter from you. If you cannot write it, ask Charles to send us a long letter.

We thought you would like to know how we are getting on. We are all in good health, thank the Lord, Ann, Emma and Clara are getting fatter than my Pigs, and no wonder if you could see how they go into it. Plenty to Eat and plenty fine fresh Air. Eliza and Jane are growing very fast and in good health. We have just agreed with a Carpenter to put our House up, we have got the principle of the Materials and expect to have it up very shortly. We are going to have the Ground plowed up and sown with Potatoes, Greens, etc., which will supply us through the Season. We have 3 Pigs and all in thriving condition, expecting every day to be confined. I hope we shall have a Score of Young ones. We have been pretty well off for Work, the Weather is now very fine and we expect to be very Busy this summer. We have had a very fine Winter, not too Cold, we all stood it like trumps.

We have just received a letter from Frank and was very glad to hear he was doing very Comfortable, and expects this summer to do better still. He has written to us to say if we was not doing well where we are to go up to New York, he believes we should do well there. But as a rolling stone gathers no moss we think we can do better hear at least we intend giving it a fair trial. We shall have no Rent to pay here, can grow all our own vegetables, and fatten the principle of our Meat. All this we must pay for at New York. We have several good Ministers here and several Chapels, they are now Building one within a quarter of a Mile of us, Congregationist. Our Neighbours are all very kind and we [get] many invitations. . . .

We have heard and read a good deal about the Worlds Fair, we have just seen a Hansome En-graving of it Gilt in Gold. Suppose it will be a spendid Affair.

Frank says he has written two Letters to England and received no answer. He has lost his last young one 11 months old. I think the California Mania is now at an end. We hear of Numbers that have starved to Death there, and Numbers that have perished in coming home. The Oregon Fever [h]as now started and Numbers are going from this part of America, there. They are giving 320 acres of Land to all that go there. It is 6 Months travelling across the Land about Two Thousand Miles from this part of America. By Sea it is Nineteen Thousand Miles. I do not think I shall ever go there.

We have nearly got rid of the Indians, they will receive their last payment from the Government the latter end of this Year, as the Government Bought them out. They will have to go a Hundred Miles further west, but they are very Quiet peaceable and Good Natured, we never hear any bad accounts of them. They are what are called Civilised, but further West and South they are Savage, Murderous and Cruel. They bring into the Town a good deal of Venison, Sugar, Honey, Fish, etc., etc. We expect we shall have a Railway running through our Town this Summer, if so it will be a busy place. We all like the Country well, we have no wish to return to Old England again, altho some say with all her faults they love her still—Trash—Trash—certainly we should like to see Old Friends and Old Faces, but as that cannot be, God grant we may all Meet together in Heaven.

It is a Beautiful Country, I have travelled about 16 Hundred Miles from East to West, and Ann has travelled about the same distance from North to West. We have seen some fine Citys and Towns, and as to the Views of Scenery it cannot be surpassed, if it can be equalled anywhere.

We all join in our best love and Esteem to you and all Friends and Remain

Yours Affectly
J. F. Chaney

What indications are there that the country was becoming more civilized within two years of initial settlement?

114

ROSA

Marie Hall Ets

In many ways the immigrant experience was more difficult for women than for men. Often, as the previous selection pointed out, women came along to join husbands or lovers who had gone ahead. Sometimes, through arrangements, they came to meet men whom they had never seen before, and married in this new and strange land.

Men usually found it easier to learn English and adapt to American ways than women because often women were forced to remain at home, thus missing the same opportunities to become Americanized. But social patterns varied. Many immigrant women were compelled to work long hours in factories or as domestic servants.

Below is a selection from a remarkable autobiography of an Italian woman, told to and written down by a social worker who had befriended her.

Rosa is one of those ordinary people who made up the bulk of immigrants from all countries. She grew up in Italian Lombardy, in a silk-making village. There she lived with a foster mother, Mamma Lena, and went to work at an early age. She was attractive and physically mature, and her foster mother feared that she would "get into trouble" with the men. Consequently, when she was fifteen a marriage was arranged between her and a man she did not love, a man, as it turns out, who treated her badly. Her new husband left for America, and after a time, Rosa reluctantly joined him in a Missouri mining village. The year was 1884. Her hopes and dreams and fears, while perhaps not typical, are representative of the experiences of many millions of immigrants who came to America.

So then the time came. I was in church waiting to be married with Santino. The priest was there in front and he was asking me the question. But I couldn't answer. I *couldn't!* I couldn't say yes! I was just there, that was all. I couldn't say anything. But Father Pietro didn't know I didn't answer and he didn't make me. He married me with Santino anyway. But the people all knew. When the people came home to Mamma Lena's for the wedding dinner all the women were saying, "Rosa didn't say yes!"

"Why didn't you say yes, Rosa?"

"You're not married when you don't say yes!"

"Rosa didn't say yes!"

I can't stand it to tell about that marriage and about Santino! I have to leave them out of my story, that's all. I can't tell about them!

The next day I was back at work in the silk mill of Signor Rossi and bringing my wages to Mamma Lena like before.

One night a few months after the marriage when I came from my work Santino said we were going to the dance hall. I was tired and kind of sick. "Why do you want to go when you don't know to dance?" I asked him. He didn't like it that I asked him why and

What does this sentence say about conditions in the old country that may have fostered emigration?

115

he didn't answer. Mamma Lena was brushing crumbs from the table to the chickens. She was listening but she said nothing either. So I knew I would have to go. I ate the black bread and cabbage soup that Mamma Lena gave me for my supper, then I washed, put on my sailor dress and leather shoes, and we went.

Santino didn't try dancing himself—he knew he couldn't. But he told me to dance with his friends—a lot of men that were there. He wanted to show them how I could dance. I didn't know those men, but I did like he said—I tried to dance with them. But those men didn't know how at all. It was impossible to dance with them! So I sat down at the side and Santino and his friends sat at the table drinking.

After a little while Pio, the son of the *portinaia* at the mill, came in. I knew Pio when he was a little boy. He was an old friend to me and he was a wonderful dancer. So when Pio asked me to dance with him I was glad. And we danced the whole evening. Then because I was feeling so sick and tired I went home by myself and went to bed. When Santino came home he was drunk and so mad that I had danced with Pio that he said he would kill me. He pulled me out of the bed and threw me on the floor.

Other nights when Santino was drunk and beating me Mamma Lena had sat up in her bed and watched, but she had said nothing. This night—I guess she could see it that he wanted to kill me for sure—she jumped up and came over and stopped him. She pulled him away so he couldn't reach to kick me. When she did that he started fighting with her. He should have known better than to try to fight Mamma Lena! Mamma Lena was so mad she didn't care what she did. She wasn't afraid of hurting him or anything. And in the end she put him out the door and he went rolling down the steps. "And don't ever come back to this house!" she yelled after him. "Don't ever come back! I never want to see you again!"

Before he married me that man was always sweet to Mamma Lena to make her like him. But after the marriage she could see it herself—how bad he was. He was all the time drunk and beating me, and she didn't like him herself.

A few weeks after the fight—Santino was not living in Mamma Lena's—one of those agents from the big bosses in America came to Bugiarno to get men for some iron mines in Missouri. The company paid for the tickets, but the men had to work for about a year to pay them back, and they had to work another year before they could send for their wives and families. So this time when that agent came Santino and some of his friends joined the gang and went off to America. He didn't even come back to the *osteria* [boarding house] to get his clothes.

How did your ancestors secure the money to make the trip?

When I heard that Santino was gone, oh, I was happy! I was thinking that probably I would never see that man again. America was a long way off.

Mamma Lena was better to me now and gave me more to eat. And I kept getting bigger and bigger. And then one day I felt kicking inside of me and I knew it was a baby. How that baby got in there I couldn't understand. But the thing that worried me most was how it was going to get out! A baby couldn't make a hole and come out like the moth in a cocoon. Probably the doctor would have to cut me. I didn't want to ask Mamma Lena, but what was I going to do? That baby was kicking to get out—I would have to ask someone. So I told her.

"Well," said Mamma Lena. "You'll have to pray the Madonna. If you pray the Madonna with all your heart maybe the Madonna will make a miracle for you and let the baby come out without the doctor cutting you."

Was religion as important to your ancestors? Is it as important to you?

And so I started to pray for that miracle. I prayed to the little statue Madonna over the chicken coop and I prayed to the big Madonna in the church. And every night I gave myself more Ave Marias to say, so that when I woke up in the morning I would find the baby there in the bed beside me. But it never was. It was still inside and kicking.

At last there came a day when I had to leave my work and go home. After that I didn't know what happened. I was three days without my senses. Mamma Lena got two doctors —she got the village doctor, then she got the doctor she had to pay. But both doctors said the same. They said the baby could not be born—that they would have to take it in pieces. And they were even scolding her. They said, "How can a girl make new bones when her own bones are not finished growing? The girl is too young!" Mamma Lena was in despair. She wanted that baby. So she told the doctors to go and she ran to the church and prayed to the big Madonna. She told the Madonna that if She would let the baby be born alive she would give Her that beautiful shawl that Remo and me won in the dance. (As soon as Mamma Lena had found out about the prize shawl she had made Zia Teresa bring it to her. And she would not speak to Zia Teresa for about three weeks because she said Zia Teresa had helped me deceive her.)

Immigrants trained in one occupation often found their training useless in America. Few silkworms, for example, were raised in the United States. Do immigrants even today need retraining when they arrive? How does this photograph suggest traditional work roles? Is this a common variety of "women's work"?

And right then when she was praying, my baby was born—a nice little boy. She came home and she could hear it crying. Think what a miracle! Two doctors said that baby couldn't be born! For a long time she didn't know whether I was going to live or not, but she was so happy to have that baby that she was thanking the Madonna. She took the shawl to the priest the next day. And that shawl made so much money in the raffle that the Madonna got all new paint and a new sky and new stars behind Her.

In the fever that followed the birth of my baby I lost my hair and my voice. Little by little my hair came back, and my voice to speak came back too, but I could never sing like before. And as soon as I could walk again I went back to my work in the mill. They had a special room in the mill just for nursing the babies. So Mamma Lena would bring the baby to me and I would stop work and go in there and nurse him. And I nursed him at lunchtime too.

Not long after the baby was born Mamma Lena got five little coral horns one day from another lady and tied them on a string around his neck. She said she didn't want anyone to witch that baby with the evil eye and make him sick. I told her I didn't believe in those things. I said, "Only God and the Madonna make you sick and make you well. How can people make you sick!" She didn't scold. She said it was good that I believed only in God and the Madonna. But she kept those horns around the baby's neck anyway. How could anyone witch that baby with the evil eye when the Madonna made a miracle to let him be born? I guess Mamma Lena remembered Braco and she didn't want to take any chance.

There used to be a lot of men, and women too, in the villages of Lombardy that the people called witches—*maliardi.* The people thought those men and women had the evil eye. In this country too some of the old people believe in the evil eye. When my Visella got the heart trouble and died some of the women were saying it was the evil eye. I said no. I said God wanted her, that was all. But that Braco, I remember him

Were the working conditions of women in America much different from those in Italy?

117

myself. He was all the time singing. But then one day someone witched him and he couldn't talk and he couldn't sing. He was *muto*. Three years he couldn't talk and he couldn't sing. After three years a man appeared and said, "Braco, you're going to sing and you're going to talk again." And when Braco tried, he could! He could sing and he could talk! As quick as he could Braco grabbed a big knife and started after that man to catch him. Braco ran all through the town trying to catch that *maliardo* to kill him. But he never saw him again. That man disappeared entirely. No one knew where he came from or where he went. (Nobody can witch me, though. I'm too strong in believing in God and the Madonna.)

So I was around fifteen years old and I had to be like an old woman. I was not allowed to walk with the young people when they went to the square on Christmas Eve or dance with the masks when they came to the stables in the time of the carnival. I couldn't even sit with the other young girls at lunchtime at the mill. But as I got strong again I began imitating funny people and telling stories again to make the women and girls all laugh. And nighttimes and Sundays I had my baby, my Francesco, to give me joy and make me laugh. And now that I was married Mamma Lena no longer scolded or beat me like before.

"But you did wrong to make that beautiful young girl marry a man like Santino!" Zia Teresa would say.

"Yes, I made a mistake," Mamma Lena would say. "But it was not my fault. I didn't know before how bad he was. And now Rosa is married and has her baby and I don't have to worry anymore."

My Francesco had learned to walk and was learning to talk when here, coming into the *osteria* one Sunday, were some of those men who had gone to America with Santino. I stopped playing with my baby and went and called Mamma Lena from the wine cellar.

"Those men in the iron mines in Missouri need women to do the cooking and washing," said one of the men. "Three men have sent back for their wives, and two for some girls to marry. Santino says for you to send Rosa. He sent the money and the ticket." And the man pulled them from an inside pocket and laid them on the table. Then all four sat down and ordered wine and polenta. Mamma Lena took the ticket and the money and put them in the pocket of her underskirt, and without a word started serving them.

Why did the custom of mail-order brides from the Old World grow?

When the men were ready to leave the one who had brought the message spoke again. "In two weeks another gang of men from the villages is leaving for the iron mines in Missouri. Your daughter and the other wives and girls can go with them." But still Mamma Lena didn't tell him if I was going or not going.

After they were gone I helped her clear the table and wash the dishes. Then I took Francesco in my arms and waited for her to speak. She took her rag and started to wipe the table, but instead of wiping it she sat down on the bench beside it.

"Yes, Rosa," she said. "You must go. However bad that man is, he is your husband—he has the right to command you. It would be a sin against God not to obey. You must go. But not Francesco. He didn't ask for Francesco and I would be too lonesome without him."

What attitudes toward marriage and the family does this reveal?

Me, I was even wanting to sin against God and the Madonna before I would leave my baby and go off to Santino in America! But Mamma Lena said I must go. There was nothing I could do.

Mamma Lena was good to me though. She thought I would be not so lonesome—not so homesick in America—if I had the oil like the poor always had in Bugiarno. So she made me three bottles full and sealed it up so it looked like wine. That oil is made from the seed of the mustard plant—mustard or turnip?—I don't know what it's called in English. You eat the part underground but it's not pinchy like radishes. Only the rich people in the cities in Italy can have the olive oil. We poor people used that oil that the women made themselves.

And so I had to leave Mamma Lena and my baby and go off with that gang of men and one or two women to America.

The day came when we had to go and everyone was in the square saying good-bye. I had my Francesco in my arms. I was kissing his lips and kissing his cheeks and kissing his eyes. Maybe I would never see him again! It wasn't fair! He was *my* baby! Why should Mamma Lena keep him? But then Pep was calling and Mamma Lena took Francesco away and Zia Teresa was helping me onto the bus and handing up the bundles.

"But Rosa, don't be so sad!" It was the other Rosa and Zia Maria in the station in Milan, kissing me good-bye and patting my shoulder. "It is wonderful to go to America even if you don't want to go to Santino. You will get smart in America. And in America you will not be so poor."

Then Paris and we were being crowded into a train for Havre. We were so crowded we couldn't move, but my *paesani* [friends] were just laughing. "Who cares?" they laughed. "On our way to America! On our way to be millionaires!"

Day after day in Havre we were leaving the lodging house and standing down on the docks waiting for a ship to take us. But always the ship was full before it came our turn. "O Madonna!" I prayed. "Don't ever let there be room! Don't ever let there be room!"

But here, on the sixth day we came on. We were almost the last ones. There was just one young French girl after us. She was with her mother and her sister, but when the mother and sister tried to follow, that *marinaro* [sailor] at the gate said, "No more! Come on the next boat!" And that poor family was screaming and crying. But the *marinaro* wouldn't let the girl off and wouldn't let the mother and sister on. He said, "You'll meet in New York. Meet in New York."

All us poor people had to go down through a hole to the bottom of the ship. There was a big dark room down there with rows of wooden shelves all around where we were going to sleep—the Italian, the German, the Polish, the Swede, the French—every kind. And in that time the third class on the boat was not like now. The girls and women and the men had to sleep all together in the same room. The men and girls had to sleep even in the same bed with only those little half-boards up between to keep us from rolling together. But I was lucky. I had two girls sleeping next to me. When the dinner bell rang we were all standing in line holding the tin plates we had to buy in Havre, waiting for soup and bread.

"Oh, I'm so scared!" Emilia kept saying and she kept looking at the little picture she carried in her blouse. "I'm so scared!"

"Don't be scared, Emilia," I told her. "That young man looks nice in his picture."

"But I don't know him," she said. "I was only seven years old when he went away."

"Look at *me*, said the comical Francesca with her crooked teeth. "I'm going to marry a man I've never seen in my life. And he's not *Lombardo*—he's *Toscano*. But I'm not afraid."

Of course Francesca was not afraid. "Crazy Francesca" they called her at the silk mill. She was so happy she was going to America and going to get married that she didn't care who the man was.

On the fourth day a terrible storm came. The sky grew black and the ocean came over the deck. Sailors started running everywhere, fastening this and fastening that and giving orders. Us poor people had to go below and that little door to the deck was fastened down. We had no light and no air and everyone got sick where we were. We were like rats trapped in a hole, holding onto the posts and onto the iron frames to keep from rolling around. Why had I worried about Santino? We were never going to come to America after all! We were going to the bottom of the sea!

But after three days the ship stopped rolling. That door to the deck was opened and some sailors came down and carried out two who had died and others too sick to walk. Me and all my *paesani* climbed out without help and stood in line at the wash-house, breathing fresh air and filling our basins with water. Then we were out on the narrow deck washing ourselves and our clothes—some of us women and girls standing like a wall around the others so the men couldn't see us.

Another time there was fog—so much fog that we couldn't see the masts and we couldn't see the ocean. The engine stopped and the sails were tied down and a horn that shook the whole boat started blowing. All day and all night that horn was blowing. No one could sleep so no one went to bed. One man had a concertina and the ones who knew how to dance were dancing to entertain the others. Me, I was the best one. There was no one there to scold me and tell me what to do so I danced with all my *paesani* who knew how. Then I even danced with some of the Polish and the French. We were like floating on a cloud in the middle of nowhere and when I was dancing I forgot for a little while that I was the wife of Santino going to him in America. But on the third day the fog left, the sails came out, the engine started, and the ship was going again.

Sometimes when I was walking on the steerage deck with Giorgio—the little boy of one woman from Bugiarno who was all-the-way seasick—I would look back and see the rich people sitting on the higher decks with nice awnings to protect them from the cinders and the sun, and I would listen to their strange languages and their laughing. The rich always knew where they were going and what they were going to do. The rich didn't have to be afraid like us poor.

Where did immigrants derive their exaggerated ideas of opportunities available in America?

Compare conditions on an immigrant ship and on a slave ship.

Then one day we could see land! Me and my *paesani* stood and watched the hills and the land come nearer. Other poor people, dressed in their best clothes and loaded down with bundles, crowded around. *America!* The country where everyone could find work! Where wages were so high no one had to go hungry! Where all men were free and equal and where even the poor could own land! But now we were so near it seemed too much to believe. Everyone stood silent—like in prayer. Big sea gulls landed on the deck and screamed and flew away.

Then we were entering the harbor. The land came so near we could almost reach out and touch it. "Look!" said one of the *paesani.* "Green grass and green trees and white sand—just like in the old country!" The others all laughed—loud, not regular laughs—so that Pep wouldn't know that they too had expected things to be different. When we came through that narrow place and into the real harbor everyone was holding their breath. Me too. There were boats going everywhere—all sizes and all kinds. There were smoke chimneys smoking and white sails and flags waving and new paint shining. Some boats had bands playing on their decks and all of them were tooting their horns to us and leaving white trails in the water behind them.

"There!" said Pep, raising his hand in a greeting. "There it is! *New York!*"

The tall buildings crowding down to the water looked like the cardboard scenery we had in our plays at the *istituto* [institute].

"Oh I'm so scared!" said Emilia again. "How can I know that man I am going to marry? And what if he doesn't meet me?"

Us other women and girls were going to meet our husbands, or the men to marry, in the iron mine in Missouri. Only the man to marry Emilia lived in New York and was meeting her here. He didn't work in the mines. He played a trumpet and had his own band.

"Look," said Pep. "Brooklyn Bridge! Just opened this year with fireworks and everything."

"And there's Castle Garden."

"Castle Garden! Which? Which is Castle Garden?"

Castle Garden! Castle Garden was the gate to the new land. Everyone wanted to see. But the ship was being pulled off to one side—away from the strange round building.

"Don't get scared," said Pep. "We go just to the pier up the river. Then a government boat brings us back."

Doctors had come on the ship and ordered us inside to examine our eyes and our vaccinations. One old man who couldn't talk and two girls with sore eyes were being sent back to the old country. "O Madonna, make them send me back too!" I prayed. "Don't make me go to Santino!"

About two hours later me and my *paesani* were back at Castle Garden on a government boat, bumping the dock and following Pep across a boardwalk and leaving our bundles with some officers. I wanted to hold onto my bottles of oil—they might get broken—but the officers made me leave those too. Then one by one we went through a narrow door into Castle Garden. The inside was a big, dark room full of dust, with fingers of light coming down from the ceiling. That room was already crowded with poor people from earlier boats sitting on benches and on railings and on the floor. And to one side were a few old tables where food was being sold. Down the center between two railings high-up men were sitting on stools at high desks. And we had to walk in line between those two railings and pass them.

"What is your name? Where do you come from? Where are you going?"

Those men knew all the languages and could tell just by looking what country we came from.

After Pep, it was my turn.

"Cristoforo, Rosa. From Lombardy. To the iron mine in Missouri."

Emilia was holding me by the skirt, so I stayed a little behind to help her. "Gruffiano, Emilia. From San Paola. What, *signore?* You don't know San Paola?"

"She's from Lombardy too," I said. "But she's going to stay in New York."

"And do you know the man I am going to marry, *signore?*" asked Emilia. "See, here's his picture. He has to meet me in Castle Garden. But how can I know him? He plays the *tromba* and owns his own band."

"Get your baggage and come back. Wait by the visitors' door—there at the left. Your name will be called. All right. Move on!"

There were two other desks—one for railroad tickets and one for American money —but we *Lombardi* had ours already so we went back for our bundles. But I couldn't find my straw-covered bottles. Everybody was trying to help me find them. Then an

Given these social inequalities on board ship, why were immigrants not more skeptical about the country they would soon enter?

Through what port of entry did your ancestors come?

Misunderstandings or simple misspellings caused many immigrants to enter the new country with a new name. Was your family name changed?

120

inspector man came. "What's all the commotion?" he asked. "Oh, so those bottles belonged to her? Well ask her," he said to the interpreter. "Ask her what that stuff was? Was it poison?"

When Pep told him he said, "Well tell her her bottles are in the bottom of the ocean! Tell her that's what she gets for bringing such nasty stuff into America! It made us all sick!"

My *paesani* looked at their feet or at the ground and hurried back into the building. Then they busted out laughing. That was a good one! That was really a good one! And even I had to laugh. I was brokenhearted to lose my good oil but it was funny anyway —how Mamma Lena's nice wine bottles had fooled those men in gold braid.

We *Lombardi* put down our bundles and sat on the floor near the visitors' door. At last after all the new immigrants had been checked, an officer at the door started calling the names. "Gruffiano, Emilia" was the first one.

"Presente! Presente!" shouted Pep jumping to his feet and waving his hands. But Emilia was so scared I had to pull her up and drag her along after him.

At the door the officer called the name again and let us pass. Then here came up a young man. He was dressed—O Madonna!—like the president of the United States! White gloves and a cane and a diamond pin in his tie. Emilia tried to run away but Pep pulled her back. *"Non è vero! Non è vero!* It's not true!" she kept saying.

"But it *is* true!" the young man laughed. "Look at me, Emilia! Don't you remember Carlo who used to play the *tromba* in San Paola when you were a little girl?" And he pulled her out from behind us and took her in his arms and kissed her. (In America a man can kiss the girl he is going to marry!) "But I never thought you would come like this," he said, holding her off a little and looking at her headkerchief and full skirt. "I'm afraid to look. Did you come in the wooden soles too?"

"No," said Emilia, speaking to him for the first time. "My mother bought me real shoes to come to America!" And she was lifting her feet to show him.

"She looks just the same as when she was seven years old," the young man said to Pep, and he was happy and laughing. "But I'm going to take her up Broad Street and buy her some American clothes before I take her home."

I was glad for Emilia that she was going to marry that nice young man, but why couldn't something like this ever happen to me?

Did most immigrants accept "Americanization" without reservation, or was there some resistance?

Other visitors were called. Some families separated at Havre found each other again and were happy. But that nice young French girl, she was there all alone—nobody could find her mother and her sister. I don't think they ever found each other again.

When the gate was opened men wearing badges came running in, going to the different people. One dressed-up man with a cane and waxed mustache came to us. *"Buon giorno, paesani! Benvenuto!* Welcome to America! Welcome to the new country!" He was speaking Italian and English too and putting out his hand to shake hands with Pep. The other *paesani* looked on in wonder. A high man like that shaking hands with the poor! This was America for sure!

"I heard your talk and knew you were my *paesani.* I came to help you. You have the railroad tickets and the American money?"

"Sì, signore," said Pep and we all showed our tickets and our money.

Then Pep asked about the women's chests that had come on an earlier ship. "Leave it to me," said our new friend. "Leave it to me, your *paesano,* Bartini. I will find them and send them to Union. And in three days when your train goes I will put you on myself so you won't go wrong."

"Three days! But no, *signore!* We want to go today."

"My dear man," laughed Bartini, "you're lucky I found you. There's no train to Missouri for three days. But don't worry! Bartini will take care of everything. You can come and eat and sleep in my hotel, comfortable and nice, and in three days I will take you and put you on the right train."

And in three days he did put us on the train but he took all our money first, about thirteen dollars each one. He left us not even a crust of bread for our journey. And we didn't even guess that he was fooling us.

The American people on the train were sorry when they saw we had nothing to eat and they were trying to give us some of their food. But Pep said no. He was too proud to take it. Me, I would have taken it quick enough. But I couldn't after Pep said no— even with that little Giorgio crying with his face in my lap. Those American people were dressed up nice—the ladies had hats and everything—but they were riding the same class with us poor—all equal and free together.

"Look, Giorgio," I said, to make him forget his pains. "Horses and cows just like in

Would you describe America as a class-free society?

121

Italia. But here there are no shepherds to watch every blade of grass they eat. Here they can go all around and eat what they want."

At last we were in the station in St. Louis changing trains for Union. We were sick for food but everyone was awake now—everyone excited. Domiana could scarcely wait to see her husband, Masino. And Francesca—"Crazy Francesca"—was trying to find out from Pep what kind of a man was waiting to marry her. All the *paesani* were laughing, but not me. Me, I was hiding my rosary in my hand and kissing the cross and trembling inside. "O Madonna," I prayed, "You've got to help me! That man is my husband—I must do what he wants, to not offend God and offend You! But You've got to help me!"

Then the conductor was calling, "Union! Union!" And everybody was picking up bundles and pushing to the windows. There was a little wooden station ahead and beside it were all our *paesani* from the iron mine with two wagons with horses to meet us.

"Look, Rosa, the one with white teeth and black mustache, he's my cousin, Gionin. I think the young man beside him is the one I'm going to marry!"

"He looks nice, Francesca," I said.

I thought maybe Santino didn't come, or maybe I'd forgotten what he looked like. But then I saw him—a little back from the others—just as I remembered him.

Pep, a bundle on his back, was getting off first—laughing and excited—proud that he had brought us new *paesani* all the way from the old country.

"*Benvenuto*, Pep! *Benvenuto, paesani! Benvenuto!* But *Gesu Maria!* Why those three days doing nothing in New York?"

"Bartini said there were no trains for three days."

"No trains for three days! There come two trains every day to Missouri. Wait till we can get our hands on Bartini! But forget it now. Now we are all together. Just a little ride through the woods and you are in your new home. And in camp there is plenty to eat. Can a girl as beautiful as Rosa help cook it?"

It was like a *festa.* Everybody in their best clothes and everybody talking and laughing.

Francesca's cousin Gionin was introducing Francesca to the man she was going to marry, but they didn't know what to say. They just stood there getting red and red. Masino, the husband of Domiana, was laughing and crying at the same time, hugging Domiana, then taking Giorgio in his arms and kissing him. Without looking I could see Santino still back at one side eying me with his half-closed eyes. He did not come to me and I did not go to him. Instead I stood there talking and laughing with the *paesani* who had come to meet us—mostly young men I had known in Bugiarno. Twelve of them were going to eat in my house. I was to cook for them. "But I don't know how to cook!"

"*Per l'amore di Dio* [For the love of God], don't worry about that. We will teach you!"

"Watch close the way we are going, Rosa." It was Gionin, the cousin of Francesca. He was sitting next to me on the wagon. "You will be walking back here every two or three days to get groceries and ask for mail." He was not *Lombardo* like the others—he and his friend were *Toscani.* I had to listen careful to understand his words. But his talk sounded nice and so respectful. "Here in America they have the courthouse and the jail on the square, in place of a church."

What statement does this make about the differences between the two cultures?

The old *paesani* were all asking questions at once of the new ones. They wanted to know about this one and that one and all that had happened in Bugiarno since they went away. Only Santino said nothing. I could see him out of the corner of my eye sitting up near the driver watching me. But somehow I was not so afraid with Gionin beside me. And Gionin was one of the twelve going to eat in my house.

After two or three miles the wagons came out from the woods and there, below, was the iron mine and the camp. Down there there were no trees and no grass—just some shacks made of boards and some railroad tracks. The sun was going down behind the hills and a few miners with picks and sledgehammers were coming out from a tunnel. Other men down in an open place were wheeling away their tools in wheelbarrows. The new *paesani* grew silent—as if they had expected something else—as if they were no longer sure they were going to be millionaires. And me, looking up to see which shack Gionin was pointing to, met the eyes of Santino.

Contrast this attitude with the one expressed by the English settlers in the last selection. How do you account for the difference?

I had never seen houses like these before—nothing but boards. The one where we stopped was larger than the others and had two doors to go in. Me and Santino were going to live in the side we were going in, and Domiana and Masino in the other. There was one large room with a long table and benches and a big cook stove and some shelves with pans and things. Then behind was a little room with an iron-frame bed and straw mattress. Gionin and some of the other men carried in my two chests. Then they came back and put food on the table.

Bread! White bread! Enough for a whole village! And butter to go on it! I ate until I no longer had any pains in my stomach. Then I went back by the stove to watch Gionin. He had built a fire and was making coffee. Never in my life had I made coffee and I would have to learn if I was going to cook for these men in America.

• • •

As the weeks went by I grew friendly with other Americans too—with old Mr. Miller and his daughter, Miss Mabel, in the store at Union. They were the boss of the store and of the post office, but they were treating me like I was as good as them. "Here's Rosa!" they would say when they saw me come in. "Hello, Rosa! Come in!" And when they saw how much I wanted to speak English they were helping me. And as it grew cold with the winter they made me come in to dry my feet and get warm. And they gave me coffee.

But those saloons in Union were bad. I didn't even want to walk past. Freddy's saloon was the worst. Some of those bad women who lived upstairs were always standing in the window looking out over the half curtain. And Annie, the friend of Santino, always thumbed her nose at me and made faces. She didn't know that I was more happy when he stayed with her than when he came home. Probably she didn't like it that Santino left most of his pay in the pocket of my underskirt so she and his other friends in Freddy's saloon couldn't get it when he was drunk.

Santino had started getting whiskey from some American men who brought it to the camp. More and more he would come home drunk and start beating me. Probably he would like it better if I was not so meek—if I fought with him. But I didn't want to offend God and the Madonna. Gionin couldn't stand it. He would put his head in his hands. Or he would get up and go out. Gionin really loved me—that I knew. And that made me feel not so lonesome. But Gionin couldn't do anything—Santino was my husband.

Why were new arrivals to this country more generally feared and avoided than welcomed?

Jews Without Money
MICHAEL GOLD

Arriving safely in America was only the first step in an extensive process of adjustment for the immigrant. There was usually a long wait at the port of debarkation, embarrassing questions to answer, forms to fill out, a complicated bureaucracy to get past. Then there was a job to find, housing to locate, a new language to learn. The land was strange, and the customs different. In facing this alien and sometimes hostile environment, most immigrants sought out others from their own country, perhaps from their own village. In the Eastern port cities they formed ghettos that were often isolated from the rest of the city yet dependent on its larger political and economic structures. The new land and the new customs put unusual pressure on the immigrant families and often drove a wedge between husband and wife, parents and children.

In what follows, Michael Gold details a remarkable range of immigrant expectation and reality in New York City at the turn of the century. The tension, pathos, and despair that beset his own family, Jews from eastern Europe, are typical of the reactions of many other immigrants. Did your ancestors come to this country with the same illusions as Gold's? How did they react to the steady erosion of these dreams? Would you have had the courage to persevere?

SAM KRAVITZ, THAT THIEF

"Why did I choose to come to America?" asked my father of himself gravely, as he twisted and untwisted his mustache in the darkness. "I will tell you why: it was because of envy of my dirty thief of a cousin, that Sam Kravitz, may his nose be eaten by the pox.

"All this time, while I was disgracing my family, Sam had gone to America, and was making his fortune. Letters came from him, and were read throughout our village. Sam, in two short years, already owned his own factory for making suspenders. He sent us his picture. It was marveled at by everyone. Our Sam no longer wore a fur cap, a long Jewish coat and peasant boots. No. He wore a fine gentleman's suit, a white collar like a doctor, store shoes and a beautiful round fun-hat called a derby.

"He suddenly looked so fat and rich, this beggarly cobbler's son! I tell you, my liver burned with envy when I heard my father and mother praise my cousin Sam. I knew I was better than him in every way, and it hurt me. I said to my father, 'Give me money. Let me go at once to America to redeem myself. I will make more money than Sam, I am smarter than he is. You will see!'

"My mother did not want me to go. But my father was weary of my many misfortunes, and he gave me the money for the trip. So I came to America. It was the greatest mistake in my life.

What were your ancestors' reasons for coming to America?

Have you ever heard anyone express regrets for emigrating?

124

"I am not discouraged, children. I will make a great deal of money some day. I am a serious married man now and no greenhorn. But then I was still a foolish boy, and though I left Roumania with great plans in my head, in my heart a foolish voice was saying: 'America is a land of fun.'

"How full I was of all the *Baba* stories that were told in my village about America! In America, we believed, people dug under the streets and found gold anywhere. In America, the poorest ragpicker lived better than a Roumanian millionaire. In America, people did little work, but had fun all day.

"I had seen two pictures of America. They were shown in the window of a store that sold Singer Sewing Machines in our village. One picture had in it the tallest building I had ever seen. It was called a skyscraper. At the bottom of it walked the proud Americans. The men wore derby hats and had fine mustaches and gold watch chains. The women wore silks and satins, and had proud faces like queens. Not a single poor man or woman was there; every one was rich.

"The other picture was of Niagara Falls. You have seen the picture on postcards; with Indians and cowboys on horses, who look at a rainbow shining over the water.

Why were people so willing to believe these images?

"I tell you, I wanted to get to America as fast as I could, so that I might look at the skyscrapers and at the Niagara Falls rainbow, and wear a derby hat.

"In my family were about seventy-five relatives. All came to see me leave Roumania. There was much crying. But I was happy, because I thought I was going to a land of fun.

Lack of space and inadequate facilities were common conditions aboard immigrant ships. Since ships often stopped at many ports on the way, people from widely different backgrounds had to adjust to one another's habits under these trying circumstances. What do you know of your family's experiences in reaching this country?

"The last thing my mother did, was to give me my cousin's address in New York, and say: 'Go to Sam. He will help you in the strange land.'

"But I made up my mind I would die first rather than ask Sam for help.

. . .

"*Nu,* I will not mention how bad I felt when I saw the cigarmaker uncle's home. It was just a big dirty dark room in the back of the cigar store where he made and sold cigars. He, his wife and four children lived in that one room.

"He was not glad to have me there, but he spread newspapers on the floor, and Yossel and I slept on them.

Why did he refuse to accept the reality before him?

"What does it matter, I thought, this is not America. To-morrow morning I will go out in the streets, and see the real American fun.

"The next morning [my friend] Yossel and I took a long walk. That we might not be lost, we fixed in our minds the big gold tooth of a dentist that hung near the cigar shop.

"We walked and walked. I will not tell you what we saw, because you see it every day. We saw the East Side. To me it was a strange sight. I could not help wondering, where are all the people running? What is happening? And why are they so serious? When does the fun start?

Did your relatives settle in a large city? Did they ever give you their impressions?

"We came to Allen Street, under the elevated. To show you what a greenhorn I was, I fell in love with the elevated train. I had never seen anything like it in Roumania.

"I was such a greenhorn I believed the elevated train traveled all over America, to Niagara Falls and other places. We rode up and down on it all day. I paid the fare.

"I had some money left. I also bought two fine derby hats from a pushcart; one for Yossel, and one for me. They were a little big, but how proud we felt in these American fun-hats.

"No one wears such hats in Roumania. Both of us had pictures taken in the American fun-hats to send to our parents.

"This foolishness went on for two weeks. Then all my money was gone. So the cigar-maker told me I should find a job and move out from his home. So I found a job for seven dollars a month in a grocery store. I lived over the store, I rose at five o'clock, and went to bed at twelve in the night. My feet became large and red with standing all day. The grocerman, may the worms find him, gave me nothing to eat but dry bread, old cheese, pickles and other stale groceries. I soon became sick and left that job.

Why were immigrants generally so easily exploited?

"For a week I sat in Hester Park without a bite of food. And I looked around me, but was not unhappy. Because I tell you, I was such a greenhorn, that I still thought fun would start and I was waiting for it.

"One night, after sleeping on the bench, I was very hungry in the morning and decided to look up my rich cousin, Sam Kravitz. I hated to do this, but was weak with fasting. So I came into my cousin's shop. To hide my shame I laughed out loud.

"'Look, Sam, I am here,' I laughed. 'I have just come off the boat, and am ready to make my fortune.'

"So my cousin Sam gave me a job in his factory. He paid me twenty-five cents a day.

"He had three other men working for him. He worked himself. He looked sick and sharp and poor and not at all like the picture of him in the fun-hat he had sent to Roumania.

"*Nu,* so your father worked. I got over my greenhorn idea that there was nothing but fun in America. I learned to work like every one else. I grew thin as my cousin.

"Soon I came to understand it was not a land of fun. It was a Land of Hurry-Up. There was no gold to be dug in the streets here. Derbies were not fun-hats for holidays. They were work-hats. *Nu,* so I worked! With my hands, my liver and sides! I worked!

"My cousin Sam had fallen into a good trade. With his machines he manufactured the cotton ends of suspenders. These ends are made of cotton, and are very important to a suspender. It is these ends that fasten to the buttons, and hold up the pants. This is important to the pants, as you know.

"Yes, it was a good trade, and a necessary one. There was much money to be made, I saw that at once.

"But my cousin Sam was not a good business man. He had no head for figures and his face was like vinegar. None of his customers liked him.

"Gradually, he let me go out and find business for him. I was very good for this. Most of the big suspender shops were owned by Roumanians who had known my father. They greeted me like a relative. I drank wine with them, and passed jokes. So they gave me their orders for suspender ends.

"So one day, seeing how I built up the business, Sam said: 'You shall be my partner. We are making a great deal of money. Leave the machine, Herman. I will take care of the inside shop work. You go out every day, and joke with our customers and bring in the orders.'

"So I was partners with my cousin Sam. So I was very happy. I earned as much as thirty dollars a week; I was at last a success.

"So a matchmaker came, and said I ought to marry. So he brought me to your momma and I saw at once that she was a kind and hard-working woman. So I decided to marry her and have children.

"So this was done.

"It was then I made the greatest mistake of my life.

"Always I had wanted to see that big water with the rainbow and Indians called Niagara Falls.

"So I took your momma there when we married. I spent a month's wages on the trip. I showed America to your momma. We enjoyed ourselves.

"In a week we came back. I went to the shop the next morning to work again. I could not find the shop. It had vanished. I could not find Sam. He had stolen the shop.

"I searched and searched for Sam and the shop. My heart was swollen like a sponge with hate. I was ready to kill my cousin Sam.

"So one day I found him and the shop. I shouted at him, 'Thief, what have you done?' He laughed. He showed me a paper from a lawyer proving that the shop was his. All my work had been for nothing. It had only made Sam rich.

"What could I do? So in my hate I hit him with my fist, and made his nose bleed. He ran into the street yelling for a policeman. I ran after him with a stick, and beat him some more. But what good could it do? The shop was really his, and I was left a pauper."

Why was a matchmaker considered necessary?

· · ·

BANANAS

My proud father. He raved, cursed, worried, he held long passionate conversations with my mother.

"Must I peddle bananas, Katie? I can't do it; the disgrace would kill me!"

"Don't do it," my mother would say gently. "We can live without it."

This woman is one of "1,000 marriageable girls" brought over on one ship from eastern Europe in the late nineteenth century. Marriage was thought of as both a religious obligation and a rational decision in eastern European Jewish culture, so that arranged marriages were common. Why has this idea largely been replaced among second- and third-generation Jewish-Americans?

"But where will I find work?" he would cry. "The city is locked against me! I am a man in a trap!"

"Something will happen. God has not forgotten us," said my mother.

"I will kill myself! I can't stand it! I will take the gas pipe to my nose! I refuse to be a peddler!"

"Hush, the children will hear you," said my mother.

I could hear them thrashing it out at night in the bedroom. They talked about it at the supper table, or sat by the stove in the gloomy winter afternoons, talking, talking. My father was obsessed with the thought of bananas. They became a symbol to him of defeat, of utter hopelessness. And when my mother assured him he need not become a peddler, he would turn on her and argue that it was the one way out. He was in a curious fever of mixed emotions.

Two weeks [later] . . . he was in the street with a pushcart, peddling the accursed bananas.

He came back the first night, and gave my mother a dollar bill and some silver. His face was gray; he looked older by ten years; a man who had touched bottom. My mother tried to comfort him, but for days he was silent as one who has been crushed by a calamity. Hope died in him; months passed, a year passed, he was still peddling bananas.

I remember meeting him one evening with his pushcart. I had managed to sell all my papers and was coming home in the snow. It was that strange, portentous hour in downtown New York when the workers are pouring homeward in the twilight. I marched among thousands of tired men and women whom the factory whistles had

What was the "trap"?

From what you have read so far, what kind of man was the author's father? Why would this job depress him so?

Having survived the sea voyage in crowded, unsanitary ships, immigrants who settled in cities often faced a similar situation in their living quarters. The one-room flats that families generally occupied (below) were microcosms of the ghetto streets (right) where they were located—both teemed with too much life, both harbored conditions inimical to that life. What perils might these people have faced and, in spite of such dangers, what would have kept them there?

128

unyoked. They flowed in rivers through the clothing factory districts, then down along the avenues to the East Side.

I met my father near Cooper Union. I recognized him, a hunched, frozen figure in an old overcoat standing by a banana cart. He looked so lonely, the tears came to my eyes. Then he saw me, and his face lit with his sad, beautiful smile—Charlie Chaplin's smile.

"Ach, it's Mikey," he said. "So you have sold your papers! Come and eat a banana."

He offered me one. I refused it. I was eleven years old, but poisoned with a morbid proletarian sense of responsibility. I felt it crucial that my father *sell* his bananas, not give them away. He thought I was shy, and coaxed and joked with me, and made me eat the banana. It smelled of wet straw and snow.

"You haven't sold many bananas to-day, pop," I said anxiously.

He shrugged his shoulders.

"What can I do? No one seems to want them."

It was true. The work crowds pushed home morosely over the pavements. The rusty sky darkened over New York buildings, the tall street lamps were lit, innumerable trucks, street cars and elevated trains clattered by. Nobody and nothing in the great city stopped for my father's bananas.

"I ought to yell," said my father dolefully. "I ought to make a big noise like other peddlers, but it makes my throat sore. Anyway, I'm ashamed of yelling, it makes me feel like a fool."

I had eaten one of his bananas. My sick conscience told me that I ought to pay for it somehow. I must remain here and help my father.

"I'll yell for you, pop," I volunteered.

"Ach, no," he said, "go home; you have worked enough to-day. Just tell momma I'll be late."

Textbooks usually note that immigrant labor was hard. In what sense is that true here?

But I yelled and yelled. My father, standing by, spoke occasional words of praise, and said I was a wonderful yeller. Nobody else paid attention. The workers drifted past us wearily, endlessly; a defeated army wrapped in dreams of home. Elevated trains crashed; the Cooper Union clock burned above us; the sky grew black, the wind poured, the slush burned through our shoes. There were thousands of strange, silent figures pouring over the sidewalks in snow. None of them stopped to buy bananas. I yelled and yelled, nobody listened.

My father tried to stop me at last. "*Nu,*" he said smiling to console me, "that was wonderful yelling, Mikey. But it's plain we are unlucky to-day! Let's go home."

I was frantic, and almost in tears. I insisted on keeping up my desperate yells. But at last my father persuaded me to leave with him. It was after nightfall. We covered the bananas with an oilcloth and started for the pushcart stable. Down Second Avenue we plodded side by side. For many blocks my father was thoughtful. Then he shook his head and sighed:

"So you see how it is, Mikey. Even at banana peddling I am a failure. What can be wrong? The bananas are good, your yelling was good, the prices are good. Yes, it is plain; I am a man without luck."

• • •

"Ach, Gott, what a rich country America is! What an easy place to make one's fortune! Look at all the rich Jews! Why has it been so easy for them, so hard for me? I am just a poor little Jew without money."

"Poppa, lots of Jews have no money," I said to comfort him.

"I know it, my son," he said, "but don't be one of them. It's better to be dead in this country than not to have money. Promise me you'll be rich when you grow up, Mikey!"

"Yes, poppa."

Do you agree?

"Ach," he said fondly, "this is my one hope now! This is all that makes me happy! I am a greenhorn, but you are an American! You will have it easier than I; you will have luck in America!"

"Yes, poppa," I said, trying to smile with him. But I felt older than he; I could not share his naïve optimism; my heart sank as I remembered the past and thought of the future. At the age of twelve I carried in my mind a morbid load of responsibility.

I had been a precocious pupil in the public school, winning honors not by study, but by a kind of intuition. I graduated a year sooner than most boys. At the exercises I was valedictory orator.

My parents were proud, of course. They wanted me to go on to high school, like other "smart" boys. They still believed I would be a doctor.

But I was morbid enough to be wiser than my parents. Even then I could sense that education is a luxury reserved for the well-to-do. I refused to go to high school. More than half the boys in my graduating class were going to work; I chose to be one of them.

What kind of educational opportunities did your grandparents or parents have?

It was where I belonged. I figured it out on paper for my parents. Four years of high school, then six years of college before one could be a doctor. Ten years of study in all, with thousands of dollars needed for books, tuition, and the rest.

There were four of us in my family. My mother seemed unable to work. Would my father's banana peddling keep us alive during those ten years while I was studying?

Of course not. I was obstinate and bitter; my parents wept, and tried to persuade me, but I refused to go to high school.

Miss Barry, the English teacher, tried to persuade me, too. She was fond of me. She stared at me out of wistful blue eyes, with her old maid's earnestness, and said:

"It would be a pity for you to go into a factory. I have never seen better English compositions than yours, Michael."

"I must work, Miss Barry," I said. I started to leave. She took my hand. I could smell the fresh spring lilacs in the brass bowl on her desk.

"Wait," she said earnestly, "I want you to promise me to study at night. I will give you a list of the required high school reading; you can make up your Regents' counts that way. Will you do it?"

Was self-education a real option? What kind of obstacles would he face if he tried?

"Yes, Miss Barry," I lied to her sullenly.

I was trying to be hard. For years my ego had been fed by every one's praise of my precocity. I had always loved books; I was mad about books; I wanted passionately to go to high school and college. Since I couldn't, I meant to despise all that nonsense.

"It will be difficult to study at night," said Miss Barry in her trembly voice, "but Abraham Lincoln did it, and other great Americans."

"Yes, Miss Barry," I muttered.

130

She presented me with a parting gift. It was a volume of Emerson's Essays, with her name and my name and the date written on the flyleaf.

I thanked her for the book, and threw it under the bed when I got home. I never read a page in it, or in any book for the next five years. I hated books; they were lies, they had nothing to do with life and work.

It was not easy to find my first job. I hunted for months, in a New York summer of furnace skies and fogs of humidity. I bought the *World* each morning, and ran through the want ads:

Agents Wanted—Addressers Wanted—Barbers Wanted—Bushelmen Wanted—Butchers Wanted—Boys Wanted—

That fateful ad page bringing news of life and death each morning to hundreds of thousands. How often have I read it with gloomy heart. Even to-day the sight of it brings back the ache and hopelessness of my youth.

There was a swarm of boys pushing and yapping like homeless curs at the door of each job. I competed with them. We scrambled, flunkeyed and stood at servile attention under the boss's eye, little slaves on the block.

No one can go through the shame and humiliation of the job-hunt without being marked for life. I hated my first experience at it, and have hated every other since. There can be no freedom in the world while men must beg for jobs.

Have you ever experienced this?

I rose at six-thirty each morning, and was out tramping the streets at seven. There were always hundreds of jobs, but thousands of boys clutching after them. The city was swarming with these boys, aimless, bewildered and as hungry for work as I was.

I found a job as errand boy in a silk house. But it was temporary. The very first morning the shipping clerk, a refined Nordic, suddenly realized I was a Jew. He politely fired me. They wanted no Jews. In this city of a million Jews, there was much anti-Semitism among business firms. Many of the ads would read: Gentile Only. Even Jewish business houses discriminated against Jews. How often did I slink out of factory or office where a foreman said Jews were not wanted. How often was I made to remember I belonged to the accursed race, the race whose chief misfortune it is to have produced a Christ.

Have you or members of your family ever felt prejudice?

At last I found a job. It was in a factory where incandescent gas mantles were made, a dark loft under the elevated trains on the Bowery near Chatham Square.

This was a spectral place, a chamber of hell, hot and poisoned by hundreds of gas flames. It was suffocating with the stink of chemicals.

I began to sweat immediately. What was worse, I could not breathe. The place terrified me. The boss came up and told me to take off my coat. He was a grim little man, thick as a cask about the middle, and dressed in a gaudy pink silk shirt. He chewed a cigar. His face was morbid and hard like a Jewish gangster's.

"Monkey Face," he called, "show this new kid what to do."

An overgrown Italian boy approached, in pants and undershirt streaked with sweat. His slit nose, ape muzzle, and tiny malicious eyes had earned him his appropriate nickname.

"Come here, kid," he said. I followed him down the loft. There were thirty unfortunate human beings at work. Men sat at a long table testing mantles. Their faces were death masks, fixed and white. Great blue spectacles shielded their eyes.

Little Jewish and Italian girls dipped racks of mantles in chemical tanks. Boys stood before a series of ovens in which sixty gas jets blazed. They passed in the racks for the chemicals to burn off. Every one dripped with sweat; every one was haggard, as though in pain.

"Where did yuh work last?" growled Monkey Face.

"It's my first job. I'm just out of school."

"Yeh?" he snickered. "Just out of school, huh? Well, yuh struck a good job, kid; it'll put hair on your chest. Here, take dis."

I took the iron rack he gave me, and dropped it at once. It scorched my hand. Monkey Face laughed at the joke.

"You son-of-a-bitch!" I said, "it's hot."

He pushed his apish face close to mine.

"Yuh little kike, I'll bite your nose off if yuh get fresh wit' me! I'm your boss around here."

He went away. I worked. Racks of mantles were brought me, and I burned them off. Hell flamed and stank around me. At noon the boss blew a whistle. We sat on benches for our half-hour lunch. I could not eat for nausea. I wanted air, air, but there was no time for air.

There was no time for anything but work in that evil hell-hole. I sweated there for

Child labor was common in your grandparents' or great-grandparents' generation. Cigars, requiring unskilled drudgery for their manufacture, were often produced by family groups in their tenement flats. Even outside larger urban areas, children (like the young spinner in a Carolina cotton mill pictured on the facing page) were hired to run dangerous machinery for up to sixteen hours a shift. What effect might child labor have had on the family as a social unit? How is the family affected today when few young people need to work?

six months. Monkey Face tortured me. I lost fifteen pounds in weight. I raged in nightmares in my sleep. I forgot my college dreams; I forgot everything, but the gas mantles.

My mother saw how thin I was becoming. She forced me to quit that job. I was too stupefied to have done this myself. Then I read the Want Ads for another month. I found a job in a dark Second Avenue rat-hole, a little printing shop. Here I worked for another five months until I injured my hand in a press.

Another spell of job-hunting. Then a brief interval in a matzoth bakery. Job in an express company. Job in a mail order house. Job in a dry goods store.

Jobs, jobs. I drifted from one to the other, without plan, without hope. I was one of the many. I was caught like my father in poverty's trap. I was nothing, bound for nowhere.

At times I seriously thought of cutting my throat. At other times I dreamed of running away to the far west. Sex began to torture me. I developed a crazy religious streak. I prayed on the tenement roof in moonlight to the Jewish Messiah who would redeem the world. . . . I spent my nights in a tough poolroom. I needed desperate stimulants; I was ready for anything. At the age of fifteen I began drinking and whoring . . .

And I worked. And my father and mother grew sadder and older. It went on for years. I don't want to remember it all; the years of my adolescence. Yet I was only one among a million others.

Is it easier to escape the trap of poverty now?

A man on an East Side soap-box, one night, proclaimed that out of the despair, melancholy and helpless rage of millions, a world movement had been born to abolish poverty.

I listened to him.

O workers' Revolution, you brought hope to me, a lonely, suicidal boy. You are the true Messiah. You will destroy the East Side when you come, and build there a garden for the human spirit.

O Revolution, that forced me to think, to struggle and to live.

O great Beginning!

Why did radicalism have such appeal?

LETTERS FROM BLACK MIGRANTS *

Among the paradoxes that abound in history is the equivocal effect of war. World War I, occasion of hideous carnage on the battlefields of Europe, provided unprecedented opportunity for black people in America. Brutalized by Jim Crow segregationist rule throughout the South, blacks sought salvation in Northern cities, where a combination of full war production and labor shortages meant steady work at decent pay. One indication of this mass movement is revealed in census records, which show staggering net population losses of blacks in the Deep South between 1910 and 1920: 130,000 from Mississippi, 70,000 from Alabama, 74,000 from South Carolina, 75,000 from Georgia. Where did they go? To New York City and Philadelphia, to Cleveland and the other industrial cities of Ohio, to Chicago, Detroit, and St. Louis. This was the beginning of a major demographic movement that has continued into the 1970s, a movement with profound implications in twentieth-century American history. Although the statistical data are sterile, the letters that follow, written to *The Defender*, a Chicago black newspaper, indicate the full range of human emotions accompanying this extraordinary uprooting.

WHO CAME

Dallas, Tex., April 23, 1917.

Dear Sir: Having been informed through the Chicago Defender paper that I can secure information from you. I am a constant reader of the Defender and am contemplating on leaving here for some point north. Having your city in view I thought to inquire of you about conditions for work, housing, wages and everything necessary. I am now employed as a laborer in a structural shop, having worked for the firm five years. I stored cars for Armour packing co. 3 years, I also claims to know something about candy making, am handy at most anything for an honest living. I am 31 yrs. old, have a very industrious wife, no children. If chances are available for work of any kind let me know. Any information you can give me will be highly appreciated.

What was happening in 1917 to open up industrial jobs in the North for blacks?

Memphis, Tenn., May 22nd, 1917.

Sir: As you will see from the above that I am working in an office somewhat similar to the one I am addressing, but that is not the purpose with which I sat out to write.

What I would like best to know is can you secure me a position there? I will not say that I am capable of doing any kind of labor as I am not. Have had an accidental injury to my right foot; hence I am incapable of running up and down stairs, but can go up and down by taking my time. I can perform janitors duties, tend bar, or grocery store, as clerk. I am also a graduate of the Law Department, Howard University, Washington, D. C. Class of '85 but this fact has not swelled my head. I am willing to do almost anything that I can do that there is a dollar to it.

I am a man of 63 years of age. Lived here all of my life, barring 5 or 6 years spent in Washington and the East. Am a christian, Baptist by affiliation.

Have been a teacher, clerk in the government department, Law and Pension offices, for 5 years, also a watchman in the War Dept., also collector and rental agent for the late R. R. Church, Esq. Member of Canaan Baptist Church, Covington, Tenn. Now this is the indictment I plead to.

Sir, If you can place me I will be willing to pay anything in reason for the service. I have selected a place to stop with a friend of earlier days at——, whenever I can get placed there. An early reply will be appreciated by yours respectfully.

What does this tell you about the situation of blacks in the South's economy?

*Arrangement of letters and headings is supplied by the editors.

Palestine, Tex., Mar. 11th, 1917.

Sirs: this is somewhat a letter of information I am a colored Boy aged 15 years old and I am talented for an artist and I am in search of some one will Cultivate my talent I have studied Cartooning therefore I am a Cartoonist and I intend to visit Chicago this summer and I want to keep in touch with your association and too from you knowledge can a Colored boy be an artist and make a white man's salary up there I will tell you more and also send a fiew samples of my work when I rec an answer from you.

Would you say he has faith in himself?

Alexandria, La., June 6, 1917.

Dear Sirs: I am writeing to you all asking a favor of you all. I am a girl of seventeen. School has just closed I have been going to school for nine months and I now feel like I aught to go to work. And I would like very very well for you all to please forward me to a good job. but there isnt a thing here for me to do, the wages here is from a dollar and a half a week. What could I earn Nothing. I have a mother and father my father do all he can for me but it is so hard. A child with any respect about her self or his self wouldnt like to see there mother and father work so hard and earn nothing I feel it my duty to help. I would like for you all to get me a good job and as I havent any money to come on please send me a pass and I would work and pay every cent of it back and get me a good quite place to stay. My father have been getting the defender for three or four months but for the last two weeks we have failed to get it. I dont know why. I am tired of down hear in this——/ I am afraid to say. Father seem to care and then again dont seem to but Mother and I am tired tired of all of this I wrote to you all because I believe you will help I need your help hopeing to here from you all very soon.

From her letter, what do you think her chances are of finding a good job?

New Orleans, La., June 10, 1917.

Kind Sir: I read and hear daly of the great chance that a colored parson has in Chicago of making a living with all the priveleg that the whites have and it mak me the most ankious to want to go where I may be able to make a liveing for my self. When you read this you will think it bery strange that being only my self to support that it is so hard, but it is so. everything is gone up but the poor colerd peple wages. I have made sevle afford to leave and come to Chicago where I hear that times is good for us but owing to femail wekness has made it a perfect failure. I am a widow for 9 years. I have very pore learning altho it would not make much diffrent if I would be throughly edacated for I could not get any better work to do, such as house work, washing and ironing and all such work that are injering to a woman with femail wekness and they pay so little for so hard work that it is just enough to pay room rent and a little some thing to eat. I have found a very good remady that I really feeling to belive would cure me if I only could make enough money to keep up my madison and I dont think that I will ever be able to do that down hear for the time is getting worse evry day. I am going to ask if you peple hear could aid me in geting over her in Chicago and seeking out a position of some kind. I can also do plain sewing. Please good peple dont refuse to help me out in my trouble for I am in gret need of help God will bless you. I am going to do my very best after I get over here if God spair me to get work I will pay the expance back. Do try to do the best you can for me, with many thanks for so doing I will remain as ever,
Yours truly.

Do you think she will be better or worse off in the city?

These cotton pickers faced economic hardship in the South in the war years because of widespread crop failures, brought on by a boll weevil plague and extensive flooding. Given the conditions of industrial labor described in this chapter, why did they look upon the North as a land of promise?

WHY THEY CAME

Mobile, Ala., April 25, 1917.

Sir: I was reading in theat paper about the Colored race and while reading it I seen in it where cars would be here for the 15 of May which is one month from to day. Will you be so kind as to let me know where they are coming to and I will be glad to know because I am a poor woman and have a husband and five children living and three dead one single and two twin girls six months old today and my husband can hardly make bread for them in Mobile. This is my native home but it is not fit to live in just as the Chicago Defender say it says the truth and my husband only get $1.50 a day and pays $7.50 a month for house rent and can hardly feed me and his self and children. I am the mother of 8 children 25 years old and I want to get out of this dog hold because I dont know what I am raising them up for in this place and I want to get to Chicago where I know they will be raised and my husband crazy to get there because he know he can get more to raise his children and will you please let me know where the cars is going to stop to so that he can come where he can take care of me and my children. He get there a while and then he can send for me. . . .

How much per month this leave for food for ten people?

Houston, Texas, April 20, 1917.

Dear Sir: . . . I am 30 years old and have Good Experience in Freight Handler and Can fill Position from Truck to Agt. would like Chicago or Philadelphia But I dont Care where so long as I Go where a man is a man. . . .

How does his motive differ from that of the previous writer?

It has been estimated that by the end of 1918 more than 1 million blacks had left the South. Why did Southern whites react with alarm to this mass migration?

Troy, Ala., Oct. 17, 1916.

Dear Sirs: I am enclosing a clipping of a lynching again which speaks for itself. I do wish there could be sufficient presure brought about to have federal investigation of such work. I wrote you a few days ago if you could furnish me with the addresses of some firms or co-opporations that needed common labor. So many of our people here are almost starving. The government is feeding quite a number here would go any where to better their conditions. If you can do any thing for us write me as early as posible.

How common were lynchings? What purpose did they serve?

Brookhaven, Miss., April 24, 1917.

Gents: The cane growers of Louisiana have stopped the exodus from New Orleans, claiming shortage of labor which will result in a sugar famine.

Now these laborers thus employed receive only 85 cents a day and the high cost of living makes it a serious question to live.

. . . Please dont publish this letter but do what you can towards helping them to get away. If the R. R. Co. would run a low rate excursion they could leave that way. Please ans.

What does this indicate about the political and legal structure of the South?

Memphis, Tenn., 4–23–17.

Gentlemen: I want to get in tuch with you in regard of a good location & a job I am for race elevation every way. I want a job in a small town some where in the north where I can receive verry good wages and where I can educate my 3 little girls and demand respect of intelegence. I prefer a job as cabinet maker or any kind of furniture mfg. if possible.

Let me hear from you all at once please. State minimum wages and kind of work.

In sum, why did black leave the South?

WHAT THEY FOUN

Macon, Ga., May 27, 1917.

Dear Mary: . . . I got a card from Mrs. Addie S —— yesterday she is well and say washington D.C. is a pretty place but wages is not good say it better forther on Cliford B—— an his wife is back an give the North a bad name Old lady C—— is in Cleavon an wonte to come home mighty bad so Cliford say. I got a hering from Vick C—— tell me to come on she living better than she ever did in her life Charlie J—— is in Detroit he got there last weak Hattie J—— lef Friday Oh I can call all has left here Leala J—— is speaking of leaving soon There were more people left last week then ever 2 hundred left at once the whites an colored people had a meeting Thursday an Friday telling the people if they stay here they will treat them better an pay better. Huney they are hurted but the haven stop yet. The colored people say they are too late now George B—— is on his head to go to Detroit Mrs. Anna W—— is just like you left her she is urgin everybody to go on an she not getting ready May you dont no how I mis you I hate to pass your house Everybody is well as far as I no Will J—— is on the gang for that same thing hapen about the eggs on Houston road. His wife tried to get him to leave here but he woulden Isiah j—— is going to send for Hattie. In short Charles S—— wife quit him last week he aint doin no better. . . . I received the paper you sent me an I see there or pleanty of work I can do I will let you no in my next lettr what I am going to do but I cant get my mind settle to save my life. Love to Mr. A——. . . .

On the basis of what she knows of conditio in the North and South would you advise Mary B. to migrate?

Chicago, Illinois.

My dear Sister: I was agreeably surprised to hear from you and to hear from home. I am well and thankful to say I am doing well. . . . Please remember me kindly to any who ask of me. The people are rushing here by the thousands and I know if you come and rent a big house you can get all the roomers you want. You write me exactly when you are coming. I am not keeping house yet I am living with my brother and his wife. My sone is in California but will be home soon. He spends his winter in California. I can get a nice place for you to stop until you can look around and see what you want. I am quite busy. I work in Swifts packing Co. in the sausage department. My daughter and I work for the same company—We get $1.50 a day and we pack so many sausages we dont have much time to play but it is a matter of a dollar with me and I feel that God made the path and I am walking therein.

Tell your husband work is plentiful here and he wont have to loaf if he want to work. . . .

Has she improved her condition? Why would she recommend that others come?

Blacks found employment throughout the North, especially in war-related industries. Despite their contribution to the war effort, after the war they were often the victims of the last-hired, first-fired principle. Has this practice changed over the years?

Pittsburg, Pa., May 11, 1917.

My dear Pastor and wife: . . . I am in this great city & you no it cool here right now the trees are just peeping out. fruit trees are now in full bloom but its cool yet we set by big fire over night. I like the money O. K. but I like the South betterm for my Pleasure this city is too fast for me they give you big money for what you do but they charge you big things for what you get and the people are coming by cal Loads every day its just pack out the people are Begging for some whears to sta If you have a family of children & come here you can buy a house easier than you cant rent one if you rent one you have to sign up for 6 months or 12 month so you see if you dont like it you have to stay you no they pass that law becaus the People move about so much. . . .

What similarities are there to what earlier immigrants found upon arriving in the city?

Hattiesburg, Miss. Chicago, Illinois, 11/13/17.

Dear M——: . . . M——, old boy, I was promoted on the first of the month I was made first assistant to the head carpenter when he is out of the place I take everything in charge and was raised to $95. a month. You know I know my stuff.

Whats the news generally around H'burg? I should have been here 20 years ago. I just begin to feel like a man. It's a great deal of pleasure in knowing that you have got some privilege My children are going to the same school with the whites and I dont have to umble to no one. I have registered—Will vote the next election and there isnt any "yes sir" and "no sir"—its all yes and no and Sam and Bill.

Florine says hello and would like very much to see you.

All joins me in sending love to you and family. How is times there now? Answer soon, from your friend and bro.

Which of the migrants' hopes for coming North has the writer realized? Do you think he is typical?

139

AN ESSAY ON THE MIGRATION OF YOUR PEOPLE

In this assignment you will work with your instructor and librarian to locate your ancestors in the stream of the great migrations. Your emphasis will be on history rather than on biography, however, as you study the uprooting and movement of the group to which your ancestors belonged.

To begin, ask yourself where any one of your ancestors lived one hundred years ago today. Locate that place on a map. Gather some basic information on that country and/or locality from your library. Check pages 250–253 in the Appendix for a list of books on immigration and on specific ethnic groups. What were the patterns of family life, the religious beliefs, distribution of land, foods, value systems, educational and social facilities, male-female relationships, songs, legends, celebrations, etc., in the place your ancestors lived?

You should also look for statistics on the migration patterns of members of your ancestor's ethnic or racial group, where they tended to go, when, and in what numbers. You might construct a line or bar graph that illustrates the movement of that people over time to the United States. In some cases longstanding patterns of settlement would later change dramatically. This is particularly true of the Afro-American experience. After forced migration on slave ships, many generations of blacks resided in the South during the slave period and for two or three generations thereafter. The movement of the majority of black Americans from the rural South to the urban North constitutes a second major migration, a pattern that has also been followed by other American immigrant groups to a lesser extent. On the other hand, you may be a representative of a family that is unusual by American standards of mobility in that it has remained rooted for a century or more. If so, ample family records should be close at hand. Most Americans, however, must look to an "Old Place" to find their past.

You might use your historical studies to construct a theory explaining why so many of your ancestor's people were forced to leave home and find a new life elsewhere. After doing this, try to locate some materials that describe the "mid-passage" of people like your ancestor. How did they travel across seas or on land, and under what conditions?

This assignment is based on the assumption, in Alex Haley's words, that "Any individual's past is the essence of the millions." Although you may not have the factual data at hand to write specifically of your own ancestor, enough secondary sources exist to permit you to reconstruct both the causes and effects of a move like the one your ancestor made a century ago.

After finishing your research, write an essay based on your theory about why your ancestor left. Describe conditions in the Old Place (either here or in another country), including prevailing cultural patterns, social and economic class structure, migration trends, and so on. Also, if possible, tell of the typical mid-passage experience of the emigrant group to which your ancestor belonged.

six

The Depression

Some events are so important that their influence cuts across class lines, affects all races and ethnic groups, and leaves no region untouched. The depression of the 1930s was such an event. No one who lived through those years in the United States could ever completely forget the bread lines, the millions of unemployed, or the forlorn and discouraged men and women who saw their mortgages foreclosed, their dreams shattered, their children hungry and afraid.

The depression was precipitated by the stock market crash in October 1929, but the actual cause of the collapse was an unhealthy economy. While the ability of the manufacturing industry to produce consumer goods had increased rapidly, mass purchasing power had remained relatively static. Most laborers, farmers, and white-collar workers, therefore, could not afford to buy the automobiles and refrigerators turned out by factories in the 1920s, because their incomes were too low. At the same time, the federal government increased the problem through economic policies that tended to encourage the very rich to oversave.

Herbert Hoover, a sensitive and humane engineer, had the misfortune of being President when the depression began. Even though he broke with the past and used the power of the federal government to stem the tide of depression, especially through loans to businesses and banks, his efforts proved to be too little and too late. Somewhat unfairly his name became synonymous with failure and despair. As a result, Hoover was defeated by Franklin Roosevelt, who took office in March 1933 with the country in a state of crisis. Many banks had failed, millions were unemployed, and in the Middle West thousands of farmers seemed ready to use violence to protest their hopeless situation.

Roosevelt had a sense of confidence that was contagious. In his inaugural address he announced, "We have nothing to fear except fear itself," which was, of course, not exactly true. But he acted swiftly and decisively, if not always consistently, to right the economy. He closed all the banks and then gradually reopened those that were sound. He rushed through Congress a series of acts ranging from attempts to aid business and agriculture to emergency banking legislation and to the legalization of the sale of beer and wine for the first time in thirteen years. Very few people who lived through the 1930s were neutral about Roosevelt. He came to be hated by many businessmen, who called him a socialist or simply "that man in the White House." Others, more radical than the President, attacked him for not going far enough in his reforms, for trying to patch up the American free enterprise system rather than replacing it with some form of socialism. More important, however, he was loved and admired by the great mass of ordinary Americans, who crowded around the radio to listen to his comforting voice in "fireside chats" that explained the complex government programs.

Many of his New Deal measures, such as the Social Security Act and the Wagner Act (aiding the cause of unionism), had far-reaching influence. None, however, solved the massive social and economic problems facing the country. The long list of agencies and administrations, popularly known by their initials—from the AAA that aided farmers to the WPA that provided jobs for the unemployed—succeeded only to the extent of restoring a measure of self-respect and hope to some hard-hit by the depression. Financially, the country remained in a slump. It was not until the 1940s, when defense spending stimulated the economy, that the nation finally emerged from its worst economic crisis.

To many, the fact that the nation could go into such a deep slough was puzzling. The early and middle twenties, in which people became fully conscious of being part of the age of the machine, seemed to auger unending economic expansion. Two years before the stock market crash, in 1927, Henry Ford produced his fifteen-millionth automobile and then promptly switched from his all-black Model T to the more colorful and modern Model A. In the same year, the world "shrank" considerably when radio-telephone service was established between New York, London, San Francisco, and Manila, and Charles Lindbergh opened the way for rapid transatlantic travel by his solo flight from New York to Paris. The year 1927 also foreshadowed the great media explosion with the establishment of the first national radio network and the release of the first feature-length film with spoken dialogue. Within a few years, millions would be listening to radio shows like "The Shadow" and "The Lone Ranger" and flocking to their neighborhood theaters to live vicariously with their movie-star heroes and heroines—Clark Gable, Greta Garbo, Gary Cooper, Bette Davis. Technology, with its many facets, seemed to be widening horizons.

This promise of prosperity through technology was deceptive, though. For one thing, although radios and electric refrigerators and flush toilets were being produced by the millions, millions of Americans outside the middle and upper classes still had to use iceboxes and outhouses and live much the same way their ancestors had. Furthermore, as already noted, the prosperity of the middle class was itself based on an economic lie. The depression punctured its inflated dreams. The great majority of Americans suffered, therefore, from the economic collapse whether they were business executives, farmers, workingmen, housewives, or secretaries. In a sense, the depression was not as devastating for the lower classes as it was for the upper and middle classes. The sharecropper in Mississippi, the unemployed black in Chicago, probably did not notice the depression as much because his life was already depressed.

There are many ways to chart the impact of the depression on the lives of Americans. One can mention the $26 billion wiped out by the stock market crash or the millions who lost their savings when the banks failed. The total industrial production in 1932 was half of what it had been in 1929. No one knows how many men and women lost their jobs; estimates of those out of work range from 12 million to 16 million at the peak of the depression, and in some cities the unemployment rate was more than 50 percent. For those who did work, the average pay ranged from twenty to thirty cents an hour in 1932 in heavy industry. In addition, one out of every four farmers lost his farm, and millions were evicted from their homes because they could not pay the rent. (There were 200,000 evictions in New York City alone in 1931.)

But none of these statistics really communicates the hopelessness and the despair of the depression years. In Chicago men and women fought with children over the garbage dumped by trucks. A social worker noticed that the children in one city were playing a game called Eviction. "Sometimes they play 'Relief,' " she remarked, "but 'Eviction' has more action and all of them know how to play." In Philadelphia a store owner told of one family he was keeping on credit. "Eleven children in that house," he reported. "They've got no shoes, no pants. In the house, no chairs. My God, you go in there, you cry that's all."

The search for a secure job, the fear of failure, the worry about vanished savings, lost hope and shattered dreams, and the nagging worry that it would all happen over again separated those who lived through the depression from those who were born in the 1940s and after. Parents who experienced the depression urged their children to train for a good job, to get married and settle down. But often their children, products of an age of affluence, cared little about security and sometimes rejected the material objects, the signs of success, that took on such importance for parents. Studs Terkel of Chicago, who has made an art of talking to people and arranging their thoughts into books, spoke to a young woman who remarked:

Everytime I've encountered the Depression, it has been used as a barrier and a club, it's been a counter-communication. Older people use it to explain to me that I can't understand *anything:* I didn't live through the Depression. They never say to me: "We can't understand you because we didn't live through the leisure society." All attempts at communication are totally blocked.*

Are your feelings the same as this woman's, or do you think it is possible to bridge the gap between the depression generation and those who came after? The following selections, most of which are autobiographical accounts and recollections of the 1930s, should help you begin to understand the experience and effects of that era. After you have read them, we will ask you to go out on your own to talk to someone who remembers the depression.

---

*Studs Terkel. *Hard Times: An Oral History of the Great Depression* (New York: Pantheon, 1970), p. 39.

BREAKDOWN:
Two Reactions to the Depression
Louis Adamic

There was no typical response to the tragedy of the depression, but almost everyone suffered. Although statistics are often used to document just how widespread that suffering was, unemployment figures do not adequately convey the despair and degradation that financial loss exacts. The following accounts tell the pathetic story of two families in differing economic and social circumstances that collapsed because of the economic disaster. Both shared in suffering that went beyond physical deprivations, yet there were some subtle differences in their reactions. As you read the following accounts, try to imagine what your own response might have been.

JIM F——

Jim F—— had worked as a truck-driver for the same concern for five years, making forty-five dollars a week. He and Mrs. F—— were a happy, respectable couple. They had four children, all of them fairly normal. In April, 1930, when he was thirty-six years old, Jim lost his job when the firm went bankrupt. For six months he had no work at all. In September he drove a truck for another concern for two weeks, making only twenty-three dollars a week. It was his last job. In December he lost all his savings—$350—in a bank failure. Then two of the children became ill. He had a hard time in borrowing money to pay the doctor and the druggist. They began to pawn things; finally, Mrs. F—— was forced to pawn her wedding ring. In September, 1931, the rent was three months in arrears. The landlord threatened eviction. Then Jim "got out of his mind," as Mrs. F—— put it to me, and joined two other men (also married men and fathers of children, living in the same apartment-house) in a robbery. They got thirty-three dollars and were arrested almost at once. The family situation was explained to the district attorney and reputable persons testified as to Jim's pre-Depression character, but in vain. Jim was sentenced to five years in Sing Sing. In October, when Jim was being tried, Mrs. F——, not knowing what else to do, appealed to organized charity for the first time and now, living in a single-room flat with her children, she managed to keep them and herself alive on the few dollars she received as relief. She felt disgraced. None of her relatives and former friends knew where she was. Jim himself was a hopeless man in Sing Sing. He felt that when he got out of prison, even should the conditions improve, his chances of employment would be slim because of his criminal record. Mrs. F—— visited him in prison just before Christmas (the fare was paid by the charity organization). His forehead, when she saw him, was scarred and blue, because every now and then he went "crazy" and banged his head against the walls of his cell. But the worst phase of the situation was that the children were being seriously affected. Unable to restrain herself, Mrs. F—— wept a great deal, and the children bawled with her. There were nights when

Are crime and poverty related? Is the solution to crime toughter law enforcement or economic reform?

Why was accepting relief looked upon as a disgrace? Is this still the case?

143

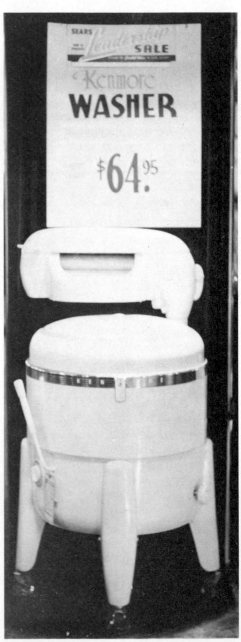

Although everyone was hit to some extent by the depression, the differences between the middle-class and lower- or working-class modes of living can still be detected in photographs of this period. The difference is obvious in these pictures of how clothes might have been washed in a farmer's family and in a white-collar family. Subtler differences can be detected by examining the two views of a family meal on the next page. What differences can you find? With which pattern would your parents have been more familiar?

all five of them cried for hours. They all slept in the same room, except the oldest boy, whose bed was the tub in the windowless bathroom. All four children, two of them of school age, were underweight, suffering with frequent ailments due to poor resistance. When I visited the family one child was in bed with a cold; two other children were in the same bed—the only one—"to keep warm." There was no heat in the dwelling. Mrs. F—— said to me, "We'd all be better off dead."

What did the depression do to the American Dream?

MR. D——

In 1929 Mr. D—— was worth over $200,000. He was a retired business man, playing the market "a little." He had a fine home in a New York suburb. His oldest son was at Harvard. Two daughters were in private schools. Mr. and Mrs. D—— had just booked a 'round-the-world passage when the Crash came. Of a sudden the world tumbled down about their heads. Hoping to save at least a part of his fortune, Mr. D—— mortgaged his home, but he no sooner got the mortgage money than it was "swallowed up by Wall Street." He was too proud to appeal to people he knew who were still wealthy. For two years the whole family struggled to save the home. During 1931 they actually starved. They sold their expensive furniture, piece by piece. The girls had to be recalled from their schools. The son quit Harvard. But it was no use. Gradually the family broke up even before the foreclosure on the home, late in 1931. The children now were scattered all over the country. One of the girls sang in a night club in Chicago. The son was a Communist who swore he would never marry or have children under the "present system." After the foreclosure Mr. and Mrs. D—— moved into a furnished room in New York City. He could get nothing to do. His mind was being affected by his plight. Finally, Mrs. D—— appealed to the charity organization they had supported in a small way for years before the Crash.

Was the depression worse for someone like Mr. D—— or for someone like Mr. F——?

HOW THE E. FAMILY LIVES
Eli Ginzberg and Hyman Berman

The following is the story of "commonplace people" with few ambitions who seem never to have been influenced by the American Dream. They were working-class people who barely survived before the depression; after the crash, they faced an even tighter budget. The budgets included here indicate how inexpensive most things were in the 1930s, and how it was possible to survive, and for a time even live comfortably, on a small income. But for many even a small income was difficult to achieve, as this family found out. Could you live on their "ideal budget"? Why didn't a family like this collapse like those of Jim F—— and Mr. D——?

Mr. E., age thirty-six, is a mechanic in a large factory on the "west side" of Chicago. He is married to a childhood playmate now aged thirty-three, and has three children—Helen, aged seven, Robert, aged five, and Julia, aged 15 months. Mr. E. and his wife have had a common school education and are commonplace people who have no particular abilities or disabilities, but are fairly energetic and thrifty. Until recently they have managed to make a fairly comfortable living. About two years ago they had a fund of several hundred dollars saved up and were hoping to make a first payment on a home in one of the outlying neighborhoods. At that time Mr. E.'s health began to fail, and in a short time he was compelled to quit work. A local physician told him he had "consumption," and Mr. E. began to treat his cough with home remedies and patent medicines. Meantime there was no income, and in about five months every resource was exhausted; savings were spent, cheaper quarters found, superfluous furniture sold, credit at neighborhood stores exhausted, sick benefits from the lodge were withdrawn, and expenses trimmed at every point, even to dropping payments on life insurance. In short there was nothing to do but follow the suggestions of an interested neighbor and "appeal to the charities." They were then about $250 in debt....

... An estimate of the family's original average of expenditures follows:

Rent (four rooms, stove heat)	$35.00
Fuel and light (coal and gas)	7.50
Food	62.25
Clothing	24.00
Household expenses (including upkeep on furniture)	8.20
Carfare	5.00
Health	5.00
Insurance	1.15
Spending money and recreation	4.00
Savings	8.50
Average monthly total expense	$160.60

Is health care better provided for today? Can families still be wiped out financially by illness?

Compare this total with your family's present monthly expenditures.

147

Mr. E.'s earnings at 72 cents an hour, including a little extra money he earned at overtime work, had enabled him to meet this budget very easily. During his illness, of course, the standard of living rapidly fell and no organized scheme of expenditures could be found from the household account book. During the last month before they appealed to the charities, the E.'s had pared their expenses down to absolute necessities: "We barely lived," as Mrs. E. expressed it.

Their expenditures, when classified as above, were as follows:

How many hours would Mr. E. have had to work to meet his budget? Have unions made a difference in this respect?

Rent	$23.00
Fuel and light	4.50
Food	47.88
Clothing	8.00
Household expenses	3.16
Carfare	.85
Health	12.00
Insurance	0.00
Spending money and recreation	.36
Savings	0.00
Total	$99.75

Value of articles given by neighbors, friends, relatives:

Food	$10.00
Clothing	3.00
Fuel	2.00
Total	$114.75

When Mr. E. came home from the sanitarium some eight months later and went back to his work, the worker made a similar estimate to determine whether the family would be fully self-supporting, or would need further assistance. Her figures were approximately those shown in the table, but when the social worker talked over the budget problem in a friendly way with Mrs. E., the worker pointed out several changes that she proposed should be made. Among these were:

ITEM	TOTAL	GENERAL FAMILY EXPENSE	MR. E.	MRS. E.	HELEN	ROBERT	JULIA
Housing	$ 35.00	$35.00					
Food	59.81		$17.77	$14.30	$10.40	$ 8.67	$ 8.67
Clothing	29.00		9.00	7.50	5.00	3.75	3.75
Fuel and light	8.50	8.50					
Household expenses	5.00	5.00					
Carfare	5.04		3.64	1.40			
Spending money and recreation	2.50		1.00	1.00	.25	.25	
Health	7.00	7.00					
Education	.90	.75			.15		
Insurance	6.25		5.00	1.25			
Savings	10.00	10.00					
Total	$169.00	$66.25	$36.41	$25.45	$15.80	$12.67	$12.42

(1) A better grade of food could be secured with perhaps a slight decrease in cost by purchasing in larger quantities rather than from day to day, and by patronizing "cash-and-carry" shops; (2) household expenses could be materially reduced by the same plan and by purchasing furniture, when needed, for cash rather than on installments; (3) the worker believed that the family should have a daily and Sunday paper or some good popular magazine; (4) the expenditures for health had been too low previously, dental care in particular being badly needed; (5) the family had too little insurance for safety; (6) some economies should be effected in spending money; and (7) it ought to be possible to increase the savings item a little. The total budget was a little larger than formerly, but Mr. E. had had a slight increase in wages and could meet it easily. . . .

Mrs. E. confided to the worker that their income had never been large enough to meet

Would your family be satisfied with these expectations today? Would you?

148

their real needs though they had succeeded in living within it and saving a little. Neither she nor Mr. E. had "aspirations beyond their station in life," but they both thought that their present living quarters were inadequate, that they needed several new pieces of parlor furniture and some really nice clothing. They would like to go to church more often and to make friends and also to join one or two neighborhood organizations. Mr. E. in particular was anxious to join a popular fraternal order to which many of the men at the shop belonged. They felt debarred from these relations now because they could not afford suitable clothing and proper home furnishings. For her part she had always wanted to go to the opera and see what it was like, and she wanted to send her washing to the "wet wash." Mr. E. had had the promise of a foreman's job before he became ill, with an increase of pay. He and his wife had thought then that they would be able to have everything they wished. In fact they had worked out a tentative monthly budget. Mrs. E. was reluctant to show this "ideal" budget since they "weren't in the habit of counting too much on the future." The estimate was:

Rent (5 rooms, steam heat)	$60.00
Fuel and light (gas and electricity)	5.00
Food	65.00
Clothing	32.00
Household expenses	12.00
Carfare	6.00
Health	5.00
Insurance	3.00
Organization and church dues	5.00
Spending money and recreation	15.00
Savings (including $30 monthly to buy a home)	42.00
Total	$250.00

What would a comfortable monthly budget for a family of four total today?

As the budget of the E. family indicated, little money was available for entertainment in the 1930s. Reading was a popular family pastime, as the increase in library circulation throughout the country in these years shows. The most popular at-home entertainment by far, however, was listening to the radio. Away from home, people liked to gather at a familiar meeting place to discuss the hard times. And, because movie tickets were relatively inexpensive—as little as fifteen cents—an evening at the movies was a popular entertainment, especially when escapist themes were dramatized. What effect has television had on changing the way Americans spend their leisure time in the 1970s?

I'd Rather Die

Eli Ginzberg and Hyman Berman

One of the hardest things for many people to get used to in the 1930s was the idea of being poor, for somehow Americans were not supposed to be poor. If one worked hard, got good grades, one ought to be a success. The following is the account of a father and son and how they dealt with poverty and failure. Neither seems to have been radicalized by his experience of poverty, as might have been expected. In fact, both tried to adjust themselves to the system that had failed them. Perhaps it was easier to be poor when most of those around you were also poor. But there was a toll to be paid for that adjustment. As you read their story, try to determine what effect the depression had on their willingness to accept the American Dream.

I went to work for Travis and Son a few weeks after Dad died. It's an overall factory—run by old Dave MacGonnigal and his four boys.

Dad was a pattern-maker there and worked for Old Dave over forty-five years. If things hadn't gone the way they did, I'd never known what he went through to keep us alive all those years. After Dad's death when the bottom dropped out from under the family I couldn't find a job anywhere. Finally I applied to Old Dave MacGonnigal.

"... Well," he said to me, "you needn't think that because you've got that high school diploma you can sit around on your tail here and talk Latin. We work here, boy. I put on overalls and work like the rest. You soldier on me and I'll fire you like a shot—understand?"

Seemed to me at the time that the job was something handed down out of heaven. I was so happy and relieved I didn't even ask the old man how much he was going to pay me. Rushed on home as fast as I could go to tell Mom.

I can tell you I didn't feel that way when the end of the first week came around. I drew six dollars and fifty cents.

I don't ever remember want or any feeling of insecurity when I was little. Dad made good money in those days—say, about $50 or $60 a week. You know, a pattern-maker has a pretty important job in an overall factory. If the patterns he lays out aren't right to the fraction of an inch the cutters will ruin a lot of goods. There's a good deal of figuring to it, complicated figuring, and he can't make mistakes. Dad never learned mathematics because he hadn't a chance to go to high school. But he'd worked out a system of his own with all sorts of funny little signs and symbols. Nobody else understood it. He could take a problem of figuring up goods and have it done in a minute where some of the efficiency experts Old Dave had in from time to time would take an hour to work it. And Dad's would be nearer the right answer than the experts'. The boys in the cutting room told me all about it when I came there to work. So they paid Dad a pretty good salary, though not what he was worth.

Why didn't a young man like this become a radical and try to change the system?

152

We had our own home ... and we had a car. My two older brothers and my sister finished high school. My oldest brother, after being a salesman for a few years ... worked his way through Columbia University. I don't guess he could have done it by work alone. But he won one scholarship after another and finally a travelling fellowship that gave him a year in Europe....

The first hard times I remember came in 1933, when I was in the eighth grade. Travis and Son shut down and for six months Dad didn't draw a penny. Things must have been pinching for two or three years before that because by that time the house was mortgaged and the money spent. I don't know much about the details. Anyhow, my brother ... couldn't help much.

Then we were really up against it. For a whole week one time we didn't have anything to eat but potatoes. Another time my brother went around to the grocery stores and got them to give him meat for his dog—only he didn't have any dog. We ate that dog meat with the potatoes. I went to school hungry and came home to a house where there wasn't any fire. The lights were cut off. They came out and cut off the water. But each time, as soon as they left, my brother went out and cut it on again with a wrench.

I remember lying in bed one night and thinking. All at once I realized something. We were poor. Lord! It was weeks before I could get over that....

Why are people ashamed to be poor in America?

... We lost our car and house and kept moving from one house to another. Bill collectors hunted us down and came in droves. Every now and then my brother or Dad would find some sort of odd job to do, or the other brother in Chicago would send us a little something. Then we'd go wild. I mean we'd go wild over food. We'd eat until we were sick. We'd eat four times a day and between meals. We just couldn't help ourselves. The sight and smell of food sort of made us crazy, I guess.

The winter of 1934 was the hardest time of all.... We were completely out of coal one time when we were living away out at the edge of town. The weather was freezing bitter then, so at night my brother and I would bundle up and go about a quarter of a mile away to a big estate on the Tennessee River. We made a hole in the fence and stole some of the wood that was piled a good distance from the house. We just walked in and got it. I don't remember that we tried to be quiet about it in particular.

After awhile things got some better. My brother in Chicago got so he could send money home and my other brother got another newspaper job. Dad went back to regular work at Travis and Son, though he only got about $20 a week....

I went on through high school and made good marks. In my senior year I had an average of 98 and was elected class president and was valedictorian at graduation. I expected to go to college the next fall. Now, I can't see how on earth I could have expected to. I knew that there was no money for it. But somehow or other it just seemed to me that a way would turn up.

Do good marks in school assure you of a better job or success in life?

Mother felt the same about it. She'd say, "If you want a college education badly enough you will get it. Any boy who is determined can work his way through."

That summer we had a scare. There was some sort of strike at Travis and Son. Seems that after the NRA blew up, Old Dave put the girls in the sewing room on piecework and some of them just couldn't make a living. They protested but it didn't do no good.... Then some organizer came and got them to go out on strike. The men went out too, and they ganged around the entrance blocking off part of the street.

What was the NRA?

Dad didn't know what to do. He walked the floor at home. He said that the girls were right, but he didn't believe they could win out because the mayor had said he'd back Old Dave to the limit. I remember Mama telling Dad, "Oh, Bob, please don't do anything foolish—! We've been through such a hard time. What on earth would we do if we had to face it again? I couldn't bear it!"

So Dad went to work the next morning. I had some errands to do for Mama so I went to town with him. Old Dave had called up and said he'd have policemen to carry Dad through the strikers. When we got there the policemen were ready all right. They told Dad they'd rush him through. He started out, with me tagging behind. Then he made me go back to the corner and started again. The strikers were bunched up at the door of the factory. They weren't saying a thing or making a move. Just men and women standing there watching.

Do you think the depression made people more or less willing to go on strike?

I saw Dad stop again. He had an argument with the police. I heard him say pretty loud, "No, I'll go by myself or I won't go at all." He said it two or three times.

The policemen were mad. "Okay, Cap," I heard one of them say. "It's your look-after, not mine."

Dad walked on without them, but they sort of edged along some way behind.

153

All at once the strikers began yelling and meeowing. Dad walked on. When he was right at them, about a dozen men and women grabbed at him and started tearing his coat and shirt.

I started running down there and so did the police. . . . But right then the strikers got into a free-for-all fight among themselves. Dad had a lot of good friends among them and these friends jumped on the ones who'd grabbed him. They pulled them off and Dad walked on through and went into the factory. He never was bothered again. Old Dave and the others had to have the police to get in and out. Dad came and went without anybody trying to stop him.

So the strike petered out and the strikers were out of jobs. Some of them came to Dad and he tried to get them back on. But Old Dave said he wouldn't touch a one of them with a ten-foot pole.

One night late in July Dad didn't come home at his usual time. . . . The doctors never did know what was wrong with Dad. He was sixty, but there wasn't anything like cancer or tuberculosis. One of the doctors at the hospital told me he was really just worn out completely. I guess he was right.

HARD TIMES
Studs Terkel

The depression meant different things to different people. For a wealthy young Southern belle it was a disconnected telephone that symbolized a changed role. For a farmer from South Dakota it was surpluses amid starvation and using old automobile seat covers for clothing.

The following two interviews were done by Studs Terkel, a historian and writer who uses a tape recorder to discover the past as ordinary people remember it. His technique is as interesting as the stories he uncovers. Perhaps you too can learn something about the impact of the depression on your family and your neighborhood by asking questions and listening.

DIANA MORGAN

She was a "southern belle" in a small North Carolina town. "I was taught that no prince of royal blood was too good for me." (Laughs.) Her father had been a prosperous cotton merchant and owner of a general store. "It's the kind of town you became familiar with in Thornton Wilder's Our Town. *You knew everybody. We were the only people in town who had a library."*

Her father's recurring illness, together with the oncoming of hard times—the farmers and the townspeople unable to pay their bills—caused the loss of the store. He went into bankruptcy.

The banks failed about the time I was getting ready to go to college. My family thought of my going to Wellesley, Vassar, Smith—but we had so little money, we thought of a school in North Carolina. It wasn't so expensive.

It was in my junior year, and I came home for Christmas. . . . I found the telephone disconnected. And this was when I realized that the world was falling apart. Imagine us without a telephone! When I finished school, I couldn't avoid facing the fact that we didn't have a cook any more, we didn't have a cleaning woman any more. I'd see dust under the beds, which is something I'd never seen before. I knew the curtains weren't as clean as they used to be. Things were beginning to look a little shabby. . . .

The first thing I noticed about the Depression was that my great-grandfather's house was lost, about to be sold for taxes. Our own house was sold. It was considered the most attractive house in town, about a hundred and fifty years old. We even had a music library. Imagine my shock when it was sold for $5,000 in back taxes. I was born in that house.

I never felt so old in my life as I felt the first two years out of college. 'Cause I hadn't found a new life for myself, and the other one was finished.

I remember how embarrassed I was when friends from out of town came to see me, because sometimes they'd say they want a drink of water, and we didn't have any ice.

Compare Diana Morgan's reaction to the depression with that of the boy in the previous article.

Why did so many people lose their homes during the depression? Did anyone in your family suffer such a loss?

155

(Laughs.) We didn't have an electric refrigerator and couldn't afford to buy ice. There were those frantic arrangements of running out to the drugstore to get Coca-Cola with crushed ice, and there'd be this embarrassing delay, and I can remember how hot my face was.

All this time, I wasn't thinking much about what was going on in this country.... I was still leading some kind of social life. Though some of us had read books and discussed them, there wasn't much awareness.... Oh, we deplored the fact that so many of our young men friends couldn't find suitable things to do....

One day a friend of my father stopped me on the street and said, "Would you like a job? A friend of mine is director of one of those New Deal programs. She'll tell you about it."

Oh, I was so excited, I didn't know what to do—the thought of having a job. I was very nervous, but very hopeful. Miss Ward came. She looked like a Helen Hokinson woman, very forbidding, formal. She must have been all of forty-five, but to me she looked like some ancient and very frightening person from another world.

She said to me, "It's not a job for a butterfly." She could just look at me and tell that I was just totally unsuitable. I said I was young and conscientious and if I were told what I was supposed to do, I would certainly try to the best of my ability.... She didn't give me any encouragement at all.

When she left, I cried for about an hour. I was really a wreck. I sobbed and sobbed and thought how unfair she was. So I was very much amazed to receive a telegram the next day summoning me to a meeting in Raleigh—for the directors of women's work.

What was the purpose of such projects?

There were dozens of women there, from all over the state, of all ages. It seemed to me very chaotic. Everyone was milling around, talking about weaving projects, canning, bookbinding.... Everyone there seemed very knowledgeable. I really didn't know what they were talking about. And nobody really told me what I was supposed to do. It just seemed that people were busy, and I somehow gathered that I was in.

So I went back home. I went to the county relief offices at the courthouse. There were people sitting on the floor of a long hallway, mostly black people, looking very depressed, sad. Some of them had children with them, some of them were very old. Just endless rows of them, sitting there, waiting....

My first impression was: Oh, those poor devils, just sitting there, and nobody even saying, "We'll get to you as soon as we can." Though I didn't know a thing about social work, what was good and what wasn't good, my first impulse was that those people should be made to feel somebody was interested in them. Without asking anybody, I just went around and said, "Have you been waiting long? We'll get to you just as soon as we can."

I got the feeling the girls in the office looked very stern, and that they had a punitive attitude: that the women just had to wait, as long as they were there and that you had to find out and be sure they were entitled to it before they got anything.

I didn't know a thing about sewing, bookbinding, canning ... the approved projects. I'd never boiled an egg or sewed a stitch. But I knew seamstresses, who used to make clothes for us when we were children. I went to see them and got them to help me. I sought help from everybody who knew how to do things.

Is the process of securing relief still the same?

In the meantime, I would work in the relief office and I began interviewing people ... and found out how everybody, in order to be eligible for relief, had to have reached absolute bottom. You didn't have to have a lot of brains to realize that once they reached that stage and you put them on an allowance of a dollar a day for food—how could they ever pull out of it?

Caroline, who used to cook for us, came in. I was so shocked to see her in a position where she had to go to the agency and ask for food. I was embarrassed for her to see me when she was in that state. She was a wonderful woman, with a big heart. Here she was, elderly by now, and her health wasn't good at all. And she said, "Oh the Lord's done sent you down from heaven to save me. I've fallen on hard times. How beautiful you are. You look like an angel to me." In the typical southern Negro way of surviving, she was flattering me. I was humiliated by her putting herself in that position, and by my having to see her go through this. (Weeps softly; continues with difficulty.)

For years, I never questioned the fact that Caroline's house was papered with newspapers. She was our laundress for a while, and I remember going to her house several times. Caroline was out in the yard, just a hard patch of dirt yard. With a big iron pot, with fire under it, stirring, boiling the white clothes....

She was always gracious and would invite me in. She never apologized for the way anything looked. I thought to myself at the time: How odd that Caroline uses newspapers to paper walls. I didn't have any brains at eleven or twelve or whatever to think: what kind of country is this that lets people live in houses like this and necessitates their using the Sunday paper for wallpaper. I'm shocked that I can't say to you: "When I was twelve, I was horrified when I first went into this house." I was surprised, but I wasn't horrified.

The girls at the office—when the clients had all gone—it's funny you treat them this way, and you still call them clients—when they had all gone, the girls would be very friendly with me. They would ask what I wanted to know and would show me the files. I was quite impressed with their efficiency. But when they were dealing with clients, they were much more loose. I didn't see why they had to be this way. Perhaps they were afraid the people in town would think they were too easy with the welfare people.

Because even then, people were saying that these people are no good, they didn't really want to work. Oftentimes, there were telephone calls, saying so-and-so Joe Jones got a bag of food from Welfare, he got an automobile, or his wife's working or something like that. I spent my time away from the job talking to my old friends, defending the program, saying: You don't know about the situation. They would tell me I was terribly sentimental and that I had lost my perspective. That was when I first heard the old expression: If you give them coal, they'd put it in the bathtub. They didn't even have bathtubs to put coal in. So how did anybody know that's what they'd do with coal if they had it?

How do you react to poverty?

We were threatened the whole time, because funds were constantly being questioned by the legislators. After I'd been there three months, the program *was* discontinued. By this time, I was absolutely hooked. I could almost weep thinking about it. I told Miss Ward, who had by now become my staunch friend, that this is what I want to do with myself: I want to do something to change things.

Do you know what your parents thought about the idea of relief in the 1930s?

By this time, the girls in the office—Ella Mae was the one I liked best—were perfectly willing to let me interview people, because they had more than they could do. Something like 150 cases each. In two months, I was employed as a case worker.

As I recall, when a person came into the office and applied for help, you filled out a form, asked all those humiliating questions: Does anybody work? Do you own your own house? Do you have a car? You just established the fact they had nothing. Nothing to eat, and children. So you give them one food order. You couldn't give them shoes, or money for medicine—without visiting and corroborating the fact that they were destitute.

Who applied for relief in the 1930s?

So, of course, you get out as fast as possible to see those people before the $4 grocery order ran out. You know, the day after tomorrow, I used to drive out to make house calls. It was the first I'd been off Main Street. I'd never been out in the rural area, and I was absolutely aghast at the conditions in the country.

I discovered, the first time in my life, in the county, there was a place called the Islands. The land was very low and if it rained, you practically had to take a boat to get over where Ezekiel Jones or whoever lived. I remember a time when I got stuck in this rented Ford, and broke down little trees, and lay them across the road to create traction, so you could get out. Now I regard that as one of my best experiences. If somebody said to you: What would you do, having been brought up the way you were, if you found yourself at seven o'clock at night, out in the wilderness, with your car stuck and the water up to your hubcaps or something like that? Wouldn't you worry? What would you do? I could get out of there: I could break down a tree or something. It helps make you free.

How did the depression change woman's role?

I would find maybe two rooms, a dilapidated wooden place, dirty, an almost paralyzed-looking mother, as if she didn't function at all. Father unshaven, drunk. Children of all ages around the house, and nothing to eat. You thought you could do just absolutely nothing. Maybe you'd write a food order. . . .

• • •

This family . . . the Rural Rehabilitation program came along, the RRA. I had the joy of certifying certain families from the relief rolls to go to the land bought by the government. To have better houses, to have equipment. And I saw this family move to a different house. Saw that woman's face come alive—the one who'd been in that stupor —her children clean, her house scrubbed—I saw this family moved from a hopeless situation. . . . The man had been a sharecropper. Apparently, he had once been a very good worker. There he was with nothing, till . . . I could go on about that. . . .

I had twelve families in this program. And Ella Mae had twelve. It was a beautiful

Are rehabilitation programs superior to relief programs?

farm, maybe two, three hundred acres. With houses, not two-room shacks. Ella Mae and I were involved in the thrilling task of selecting the families. Ella Mae would say, "I think Jess Clark would be good." And Davis, the man in charge of the program, would say, "That old, lazy bum? He's not gonna be able to do nothin'. You're just romantic." So we became personally involved in seeing these people prove their own worth. . . .

Every month the program was threatened with lack of funds. We didn't know if Congress was gonna discontinue it. A lot of the public thought the money was being spent foolishly.

With the program in danger of being killed from month to month, the state administrator suggested she accept other job offers. She attended the New York School of Social Work, under federal auspices; she married; there was an absence of six months from the county.

The first thing I did when I got back, I got out of the car and rushed over to the courthouse—to know how did those people perform. Did they make it?

I talked about this one white family. There was a Negro family, nine of them living in one room. The man was not young; he was in his sixties. But he impressed me as being a strong person—who would really make it, if he had a chance. Every one of the people we had certified had done well and had begun to pay back the loans. Not one of them had been lazy and done a bad job. They were absolutely vindicated. The people were vindicated, not us.

OSCAR HELINE

For all his seventy-eight years, he has lived on this Iowa farm, which his father had cultivated almost a century ago. It is in the northwestern part of the state, near the South Dakota border. Marcus has a population of 1,263.

On this drizzly October Sunday afternoon, the main street is deserted. Not a window is open, nor a sound heard. Suddenly, rock music shatters the silence. From what appeared to be a years-long vacant store, two girls and a boy emerge. They are about thirteen, fourteen.

I ask directions. They are friendly, though somewhat bewildered. "An old man?" They are eager to help. One points north; another, south; the third, west. Each is certain "an old man" lives somewhere in the vicinity.

Along the gravel road, with a stop at each of three farmhouses: no sign, no knowledge of "an old man," nor awareness of his name. At each is a tree bearing the identical sticker: "Beware The Dog." One trots forth, pauses warily and eyes the stranger in the manner of Bull Connor and a black militant. The young farmers are friendly enough, but innocent of Oscar Heline's existence.

At the fourth farm, an elderly woman, taken away from the telecast of the Tigers—Cardinals World Series game, knows. . . . Several gravel roads back I find him.

The struggles people had to go through are almost unbelievable. A man lived all his life on a given farm, it was taken away from him. One after the other. After the foreclosure, they got a deficiency judgment. Not only did he lose the farm, but it was impossible for him to get out of debt.

He recounts the first farm depression of the Twenties: "We give the land back to the mortgage holder and then we're sued for the remainder—the deficiency judgment—which we have to pay." After the land boom of the early Twenties, the values declined constantly, until the last years of the decade. "In '28, '29, when it looked like we could see a little blue sky again, we're just getting caught up with the back interest, the Thirties Depression hit. . . ."

Why did the depression hit farmers particularly hard?

The farmers became desperate. It got so a neighbor wouldn't buy from a neighbor, because the farmer didn't get any of it. It went to the creditors. And it wasn't enough to satisfy them. What's the use of having a farm sale? Why do we permit them to go on? It doesn't cover the debts, it doesn't liquidate the obligation. He's out of business, and it's still hung over him. First, they'd take your farm, then they took your livestock, then your farm machinery. Even your household goods. And they'd move you off. The farm-

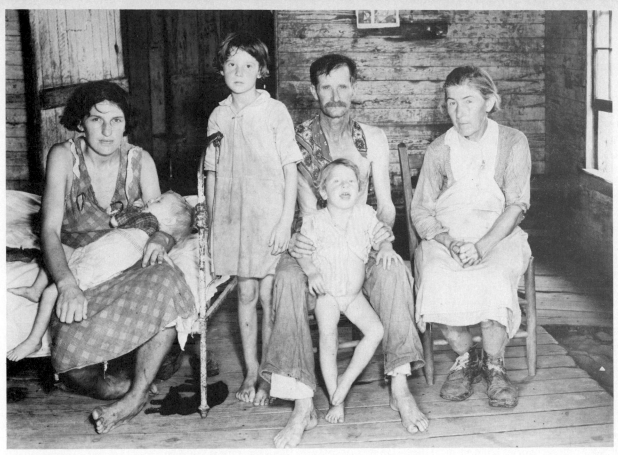

Rural areas in the South, farmed mostly by poor black and white tenants and sharecroppers, were hardest hit by the depression: for more than 1 million farmers, annual income was no more than $300 to $400. Many—facing conditions of miserable housing, shoddy clothing, and inadequate diet—took to the road, often settling into already crowded city slums in order to become eligible for local relief funds. Why did social workers react as they did to the migrants' plight?

ers were almost united. We had penny auction sales. Some neighbor would bid a penny and give it back to the owner.

Grain was being burned. It was cheaper than coal. Corn was being burned. A county just east of here, they burned corn in their courthouse all winter, '32, '33. You couldn't hardly buy groceries for corn. It couldn't pay the transportation. In South Dakota, the county elevator listed corn as minus three cents. *Minus* three cents a bushel. If you wanted to sell 'em a bushel of corn, you had to bring in three cents. They couldn't afford to handle it. Just think what happens when you can't get out from under. . . .

We had lots of trouble on the highway. People were determined to withhold produce from the market—livestock, cream, butter, eggs, what not. If they would dump the produce, they would force the market to a higher level. The farmers would man the highways, and cream cans were emptied in ditches and eggs dumped out. They burned the trestle bridge, so the trains wouldn't be able to haul grain. Conservatives don't like this kind of rebel attitude and aren't very sympathetic. But something had to be done.

I spent most of my time in Des Moines as a lobbyist for the state cooperatives. Trying to get some legislation. I wasn't out on the highway fighting this battle. Some of the farmers probably didn't think I was friendly to their cause. They were so desperate. If you weren't out there with them, you weren't a friend, you must be a foe. I didn't know from day to day whether somebody might come along and cause harm to my family. When you have bridges burned, accidents, violence, there may have been killings, I don't know.

There were some pretty conservative ones, wouldn't join this group. I didn't want to particularly, because it wasn't the answer. It took that kind of action, but what I mean is it took more than that to solve it. You had to do constructive things at the same time. But I never spoke harshly about those who were on the highway.

Some of the farmers with teams of horses, sometimes in trucks, tried to get through. He was trying to feed his family, trying to trade a few dozen eggs and a few pounds of cream for some groceries to feed his babies. He was desperate, too. One group tried to sell so they could live and the other group tried to keep you from selling so they could live.

The farmer is a pretty independent individual. He wants to be a conservative individual. He wants to be an honorable individual. He wants to pay his debts. But it was hard. The rank-and-file people of this state—who were brought up as conservatives, which most of us were—would never act like this. Except in desperation.

There were a few who had a little more credit than the others. They were willing to go on as usual. They were mostly the ones who tried to break the picket lines. They were the ones who gained at the expense of the poor. They had the money to buy when things were cheap. There are always a few who make money out of other people's poverty. This was a struggle between the haves and the have-nots.

The original bankers who came to this state, for instance. When my father would borrow $100, he'd get $80. And when it was due, he'd pay back the $100 and a premium besides that. Most of his early borrowings were on this basis. That's where we made some wealthy families in this country.

We did pass some legislation. The first thing we did was stop the power of the judges to issue deficiency judgments. The theory was: the property would come back to you someday.

The next law we passed provided for committees in every county: adjudication committees. They'd get the person's debts all together and sit down with his creditors. They gave people a chance. People got time. The land banks and insurance companies started out hard-boiled. They got the farm, they got the judgment and then found out it didn't do them any good. They had to have somebody to run it. So they'd turn around and rent it to the fella who lost it. He wasn't a good renter. The poor fella lost all his capacity for fairness, because he couldn't be fair. He had to live. All the renters would go in cahoots. So the banks and companies got smart and stopped foreclosing.

Through a federal program we got a farm loan. A committee of twenty-five of us drafted the farm legislation of this kind thirty-five years ago. We drew it up with Henry Wallace. New money was put in the farmers' hands. The Federal Government changed the whole marketing program from burning 10-cent corn to 45-cent corn. People could now see daylight and hope. It was a whole transformation of attitude. You can just imagine . . . *(He weeps.)*

It was Wallace who saved us, put us back on our feet. He understood our problems.

Why couldn't farmers sell their goods if there was so much hunger in the land?

How is the farmer's situation different today?

Are farmers still rugged individualists?

Who was Henry Wallace? What did he accomplish?

160

When we went to visit him, after he was appointed Secretary, he made it clear to us he didn't want to write the law. He wanted the farmers themselves to write it. "I will work with you," he said, "but you're the people who are suffering. It must be your program." He would always give his counsel, but he never directed us. The program came from the farmers themselves, you betcha.

Another thing happened: we had twice too many hogs because corn'd been so cheap. And we set up what people called Wallace's Folly: killing the little pigs. Another farmer and I helped develop this. We couldn't afford to feed 45-cent corn to a $3 hog. So we had to figure a way of getting rid of the surplus pigs. We went out and bought 'em and killed 'em. This is how desperate it was. It was the only way to raise the price of pigs. Most of 'em were dumped down the river.

The hard times put farmers' families closer together. My wife was working for the country Farm Bureau. We had lessons in home economics, how to make underwear out of gunny sacks, out of flour sacks. It was cooperative labor. So some good things came out of this. Sympathy toward one another was manifest. There were personal values as well as terrible hardships.

Mrs. Heline interjects: "They even took seat covers out of automobiles and re-used them for clothing or old chairs. We taught them how to make mattresses from surplus cotton. We had our freedom gardens and did much canning. We canned our own meat or cured it in some way. There was work to do and busy people are happy people."

Have you ever heard anyone say he profited from the experience of the depression?

Franklin Roosevelt drew much of his support from the working class—farmers and industrial laborers. In return for their confidence, he initiated a wide-based program of relief and reform that, nevertheless, failed to lift the country out of the depression. Why, in light of his failures, did he continue to largely receive their support?

The real boost came when we got into the Second World War. Everybody was paying on old debts and mortgages, but the land values were going down. It's gone up now more than ever in the history of the country. The war. . . . (A long pause.)

It does something to your country. It's what's making employment. It does something to the individual. I had a neighbor just as the war was beginning. We had a boy ready to go to service. This neighbor one day told me what we needed was a damn good war, and we'd solve our agricultural problems. And I said, "Yes, but I'd hate to pay with the price of my son." Which we did. (He weeps.) It's too much of a price to pay. . . .

What do you think about this economic justification for war?

In '28 I was chairman of the farm delegation which met with Hoover. My family had always been Republican, and I supported him. To my disappointment. I don't think the Depression was all his fault. He tried. But all his plans failed, because he didn't have the Government involved. He depended on individual organizations.

It's a strange thing. This is only thirty-five years ago—Roosevelt, Wallace. We have a new generation in business today. Successful. It's surprising how quickly they forget the assistance their fathers got from the Government. The Farm Bureau, which I helped organize in this state, didn't help us in '35. They take the same position today: we don't need the Government. I'm just as sure as I'm sitting here, we can't do it ourselves. Individuals have too many different interests. Who baled out the land banks when they were busted in the Thirties? It was the Federal Government.

In what sense are people today—rich and poor—dependent on federal aid? Is this a healthy trend?

What I remember most of those times is that poverty creates desperation, and desperation creates violence. In Plymouth County—Le Mars—just west of us, a group met one morning and decided they were going to stop the judge from issuing any more deficiency judgments. This judge had a habit of very quickly O.K.'ing foreclosure sales. These farmers couldn't stand it any more. They'd seen their neighbors sold out.

Is this equally applicable today?

There were a few judges who would refuse to take the cases. They'd postpone it or turn it over to somebody else. But this one was pretty gruff and arrogant: "You do this, you do that, it's my court." When a bunch of farmers are going broke every day and the judge sits there very proudly and says: "This is my court . . ."; they say: "Who the hell are you?" He was just a fellow human being, same as they were.

These farmers gathered this one particular day. I suppose some of 'em decided to have a little drink, and so they developed a little courage. They decided: we'll go down and teach that judge a lesson. They marched into the courtroom, hats on, demanded to visit with him. *He* decided he would teach *them* a lesson. So he says: "Gentlemen, this is my court. Remove your hats and address the court properly."

They just laughed at him. They said, "We're not concerned whose court this is. We came here to get redress from your actions. The things you're doing, we can't stand to have done to us any more." The argument kept on, and got rougher. He wouldn't listen. He threatened them. So they drug him from his chair, pulled him down the steps of the courthouse, and shook a rope in front of his face. Then, tarred and feathered him.

The Governor called out the National Guard. And put these farmers behind barbed wire. Just imagine . . . (he weeps) . . . in this state. You don't forget these things.

How might this incident have shaken his faith in the American Dream?

Assignment 6

A PROJECT IN ORAL HISTORY: IMPACT OF THE DEPRESSION

This project in oral history has several objectives. First, you should utilize your interviewing techniques by talking to a resident of the community in which you are living. Select a person, aged fifty to sixty or older, and attempt to recover some of the history of the depression years.

You might follow a line of questioning similar to this: Do you remember the stock market crash? What did you think of Herbert Hoover? Did you or your family lose any money in the market or in bank failures? What was your attitude toward Franklin Roosevelt? Did you ever listen to him on the radio? What else did you listen to on the radio?

Were you or someone in your family unemployed? Do you know anyone who worked for the CCC or WPA? What kinds of experiences did he or she have? Did you move from one house to another? What did you do for fun? Did people have more fun in those days? Were the movies important in any way? What about the importance of the automobile? What did economic hardship do to family life? Did anyone you knew lose faith in the American system? Does the fact that you lived through the depression influence your ideas and attitudes today?

Try not to let a preconceived idea of how the

discussion should flow interfere with the direction the conversation will spontaneously take. Use your common sense and be flexible. Interrupt as little as possible, except when you have to jog the interviewee's memory. Your role is to listen.

Use the same techniques and questions when you interview members of your own family on their depression experiences. Then, write a preliminary report on your findings, to be incorporated later in your research paper.

BIBLIOGRAPHIC NOTE

For a lively introduction to the depression era, see W. E. Leuchtenburg, *Franklin D. Roosevelt and the New Deal, 1932–1940* (1963). Enormous detail and texture emerges from the continuing biographical studies on Roosevelt and his times by Frank Freidel and Arthur Schlesinger, Jr. For specific information on aspects of life then, you should consult David Shannon, ed., *The Great Depression* (1960), a collection of contemporary bits and pieces, and the very graphic book by Dorothea Lange and P. S. Taylor, *An American Exodus: A Record of Human Erosion in the Thirties* (1969). Studs Terkel's *Hard Times* (1970), a selection from which has been included in this chapter, provides not only excellent firsthand accounts of life in the thirties but a model of the techniques used in oral history as well.

seven

World War II

Strange as it must seem to a generation of Americans accustomed to an overwhelming American presence throughout the world, the United States sat on the sidelines as World War II approached. Although the likelihood of a second world war increased throughout the 1930s, not many Americans appeared to notice. The armed struggle between Japan and China seemed far away to an American middle class that was preoccupied with preserving itself amid a severe economic depression. Even the ominous regime that Adolf Hitler led to power in Germany in 1933 could parade its barbarism throughout the decade without arousing much American censure. Germany abandoned the League of Nations in 1933, and by 1935, in flagrant scorn of the armaments provisions of the Treaty of Versailles, had rebuilt a vast army and air force. Then in March 1936 it flouted international opinion by forcibly reoccupying the Rhineland. Yet just six months later a team of Americans participated with athletes from around the world in the Berlin Olympics, thus tacitly acknowledging Hitler's international respectability. Popular American myopia continued from 1936 to 1939 as the German *Luftwaffe* enjoyed a dress rehearsal for World War II in the service of Francisco Franco's Fascists in the Spanish Civil War. Even the 1938 German seizure of Austria passed without effective objection. President Franklin D. Roosevelt joined most other world leaders in praising the Munich Pact, the high point of appeasement.

From the American perspective these were matters for the Europeans to settle. In effect, the United States government played the role of a minor power throughout the 1930s, neither participating in the recurring European diplomatic crises nor seeking to generate popular support for international collaboration. Many American political leaders reflected the popular belief that American involvement in World War I had been a mistake, that Europeans, insufficiently grateful for American aid in the earlier war, were about to battle again and were trying to maneuver the United States into another of their seemingly endless conflicts.

On September 1, 1939, the war began in earnest when Germany invaded Poland, and England and France kept their alliance with Poland by declaring war on Germany. Americans worried and wondered; still, most thought that the United States was safe and could stay out of war. Then Hitler's *Blitzkrieg* of the spring of 1940 shattered the western front: Norway, Denmark, and the Low Countries fell; France was taken with astonishing ease; now England stood alone against the Nazi war machine. Although most Americans clearly sympathized with Britain and the Allied powers, the strong public opposition during 1940 and 1941 to full belligerency limited the role of the United States. It did send arms and supplies to England, and the navy expanded the scope of its activities in Atlantic and Caribbean waters. Yet most Americans still hoped that the United States could avoid joining the fight.

These hopes were destroyed on December 7, 1941, the day of the surprise Japanese attack on Pearl Harbor that quickly brought the United States into war against the Axis powers of Germany, Italy, and Japan. Although the careful observer of the long-deteriorating relationship between Japan and the United States might have predicted the outbreak of hostilities, the attack on Pearl Harbor shocked all Americans. To this day millions of people can recall exactly what they were doing when the news flashed over the radio. Pearl Harbor united and activated the people of this country in a way seldom experienced, before or since. Patriotism ran high as the nation prepared to defeat the Axis. All of the debates about intervention or isolation were swept away: innocent and peace-loving America had been attacked by the forces of evil.

World War II, like the depression, was a transcendent event that affected all Americans and their families. Over 400,000 Americans lost their lives in the war and more than 670,000 were wounded. For many families the war meant utter tragedy—the death in faraway places of sons, husbands, fathers, brothers, and other loved ones. Even many of the military men who survived would be haunted all their lives by the memory of the terror and slaughter and the untimely deaths of comrades and friends.

Paradoxically, many men and women found military service the high point of their lives. The terror faded with time and only the memory of adventure, comradeship, and the glory of being involved in an epic common cause remained. Strange names like Truk, Leyte, Anzio, El Alamein, and Midway assumed permanent, almost fond memories for those who were there. Catapulted out of small-town lives and mundane jobs into exotic places, many men and women in the armed services felt released from the normal restraints and responsibilities of marriage, family, and work. Despite occasional or frequent danger, many had the time of their lives, whether in the Moroccan desert or on shore patrol duty at Atlantic City, New Jersey.

An even more common shared experience—of soldier and civilian alike—was uprooting. Although Americans have historically been a mobile people, the impact of World War II on mobility was extraordinary. Military service naturally relocated millions. All men between the ages of eighteen and forty-five had to register for the draft; many others enlisted. There were 500,000 in the armed forces by 1940; 3,800,000 by 1942; and over 12 million by 1945. By the end of the war one out of every five American males between the ages of eighteen and forty-five had served in the armed forces. Many of those not in the services found work in war industries, jobs that frequently meant having to move. Statistics indicate a substantial migration away from New England and the upper Plains states; in another exodus hundreds of thousands left the South, from all along the arc stretching from West Virginia toward Mississippi and Oklahoma. Across the nation nearly 10 million people left farms during the decade of the 1940s. Increasing numbers crowded into the major cities of New York and northern New Jersey, and into Chicago, Cleveland, Detroit, Baltimore, and Miami. In particular, people sought the sun-drenched new world of California.

Millions of these Americans moved eagerly into a war-based economy, and the nation's policy-makers discovered a hedge against another major economic disaster. Gone finally was the depression of the 1930s, with full employment returning for the first time since the 1920s. The American economy, fed by public and private capital, thus entered its still-continuing dependence on the production of war or war-related materials. For unemployed workers the return to full production was a great opportunity after the lean thirties and surely sufficient reason to uproot a family. Employment in major industries, which had dropped to 23 million in the depths of the depression, ballooned to over 42 million in 1943. Unemployment, near 13 million in 1933, fell to 670,000 in 1944. Spending for national defense became a way of life for the American government. For working people, war jobs suggested the possibility that good wages and steady work would mean a decent home and a better education for their children.

Among the beneficiaries of the wartime demand for labor were black Americans. Repeating a pattern established during World War I, a mass of black Americans streamed out of the rural South to the urban North to find steady jobs at decent wages. The war did not end racial tension and violence, but it did raise hopes for justice and equal opportunity. Many of the black American servicemen sent abroad, even while relegated to units racially segregated by American military precedent, found psychological release from the oppression of racism for the first time.

Yet the opportunities that the war provided for American blacks were severely circumscribed. Jammed into the black ghettos of central cities, which rarely provided adequate housing, transportation, education, or cleanliness, many black families became trapped. At the war's end black men and women fell victim in large numbers to the "last hired, first fired" principle of black employment. And returning black servicemen found that the high democratic idealism of wartime struggle had little relevance to postwar life in the slums of Northern cities or the dusty towns of the rural South.

Racism's twisted cruelty was more overtly expressed when the government of the United States arbitrarily incarcerated most Americans of Japanese descent. Soon after Pearl Harbor, about 125,000 Japanese-Americans (over 70 percent of them American citizens) were forcibly removed from their West Coast homes and imprisoned in concentration camps in the interior. Their property was seized with little or no compensation, and the process was upheld by the Supreme Court. No similar treatment was considered necessary either for German-Americans or Italian-Americans. The objectives of total victory justified all expedients, notwithstanding some uneasiness, and minor protests, about putting American citizens in concentration camps. As in most wars, however, the fervor of patriotic righteousness devoured its minority of dissenters.

This fervor was constantly promoted on the American homefront. Grade-school children went on scrap drives, saved tin foil, bought savings stamps, and helped in the family "victory garden," a backyard fruit-and-vegetable patch designed to free food production for the war effort and to encourage full participation in the national struggle. High-school students might join paramilitary drill teams or wrap bandages as Red Cross volunteers. Housewives went into factories in large numbers, working on assembly lines, in arsenals, or in offices. Local service clubs formed air-raid-warden squads or organized war-bond drives. In town meetings and along flag-festooned parade routes big cities and small towns proclaimed their united support for total victory.

From Hollywood came a flood of war movies, simplistic but appealing stories of heroism and virtue struggling against treachery—and winning. The many warriors of Sunset Strip—John Wayne, Alan Ladd, Randolph Scott, Brian Donleavy—reassured Americans of the nobility of their cause and the inevitability of their victory. Betty Grable, Veronica Lake, and Rita Hayworth made their own contributions to morale.

For the American middle class the sense of national unity effectively compensated for wartime hardship, not the least of which was strict rationing of a broad variety of foods and consumer goods. Horsemeat appeared on some dinner tables. Leg paint replaced nylon stockings. Yellow-colored margarine pretended to be butter. Automobile production stopped, tires and gasoline were in limited supply. Yet the army of middle-class consumers hardly uttered a protest. Organized labor abandoned its precious right to strike. The harmony of common purpose pervaded the land.

Yet the phenomenon of united war effort should not obscure the diversity of experience, the enormously complex impact that World War II had on American society. In particular, the social history of families reflected substantial changes. The uprooting and resettlement of so many families obviously shattered long-settled patterns of residence. Millions of fathers were taken from the home. Social flux affected marriages, the birth rate, divorces. The number of marriages rose sharply during wartime, many of them entered into in haste under the pressures of imminent separation. The nation's population increased by 6.5 million during the war years. Yet in 1946, the year after the war ended, divorces soared to 610,000, the highest level in American history to that point.

Thus the American nuclear family, traditional backbone of the social structure, underwent significant alteration. Opportunity and good fortune on the road to middle-class happiness beckoned many. Others were permanently affected by the sights and sounds of distant places and returned home with new ideas. The war left irreparable scars on those many families whose lost sons would remain forever young in the frozen uniformed photos on the mantlepiece. The war experiences of Americans, all along the human range from joy to tragedy, remain fresh for the generation before yours.

THE AMERICAN CENTURY
Henry Luce

For most Americans, World War II began with the attack on Pearl Harbor, and the purpose of the war was simply to defeat the enemy. But to some of its leaders, the war had larger meaning. In the following article, written just after the United States entered the war, Henry Luce, then publisher and owner of Time-Life, defined the war in terms of an American mission—creating an American century.

To what extent do you think this sense of America's destiny and responsibility toward the world exists today? Do you know many people now who share Luce's perceptions and beliefs? Are they younger or older people? Is there a generational difference in your own family on questions of foreign affairs?

We Americans are unhappy. We are not happy about America. We are not happy about ourselves in relation to America. We are nervous—or gloomy—or apathetic.

. . .

There is one fundamental issue which faces America as it faces no other nation. It is an issue peculiar to America and peculiar to America in the 20th Century—now. It is deeper even than the immediate issue of War. If America meets it correctly, then, despite hosts of dangers and difficulties, we can look forward and move forward to a future worthy of men, with peace in our hearts.

If we dodge the issue, we shall flounder for ten or 20 or 30 bitter years in a chartless and meaningless series of disasters.

The purpose of this article is to state that issue, and its solution, as candidly and as completely as possible.

. . .

. . . We are *not* in a war to defend American territory. We are in a war to defend and even to promote, encourage and incite so-called democratic principles throughout the world.

What circumstances led Luce to this conclusion? Do you agree?

. . .

The big, important point to be made here is simply that the complete opportunity of leadership is *ours*. Like most great creative opportunities, it is an opportunity enveloped in stupendous difficulties and dangers. If we don't want it, if we refuse to take it, the responsibility of refusal is also ours, and ours alone.

What does "leadership" mean in this context?

World War II stirred the patriotic fervor of many Americans—a sentiment that endured long after the war ended. What has happened to cause some contemporary Americans to distrust this sentiment?

• • •

In the field of national policy, the fundamental trouble with America has been, and is, that whereas their nation became in the 20th Century the most powerful and the most vital nation in the world, nevertheless Americans were unable to accommodate themselves spiritually and practically to that fact. Hence they have failed to play their part as a world power—a failure which has had disastrous consequences for themselves and for all mankind. And the cure is this: to accept wholeheartedly our duty and our opportunity as the most powerful and vital nation in the world and in consequence to exert upon the world the full impact of our influence, for such purposes as we see fit and by such means as we see fit.

What are the implications of the last sentence?

168

Two Experiences in the Combat Zone
CHARLES E. KELLY and JAMES J. FAHEY

Have you ever talked to soldiers about their wartime experiences? Some will tell you a great deal, but for others the horror was too great, the memories too personal. The war changed many people who fought in it. It uprooted them from their hometown and neighborhood and introduced them to new lands and customs. For some, the army provided a chance for adventure and the close comradeship that comes with shared danger. (After the war, veterans' organizations became their social clubs.) For many the war meant that they would never be the same again.

As you read the following selections, think about the way that World War II influenced your family and your community. Was any member of your family in the war? What effect has that experience had on his or her attitudes toward war and peace and patriotism?

KELLY: HEROISM IN WAR

Leaving the Salerno beach fifty feet behind me, I pumped my knees up and down in a sort of dog trot, moving straight ahead. That first rush took me past a dead G.I., lying peacefully, as if asleep, with his head on his pack, his rifle by his side. I pulled my eyes away and told myself, *Don't let that worry you.*

Then came a big drainage ditch with G.I.'s lying down inside of it. "Come on! It ain't deep! Jump!" I jumped, only to find the water and slime up to my eyes. The bottom was oozy; my feet sank into it, and I was weighted down by ammunition. I let go of my automatic rifle, but as soon as I dropped it, I felt lonely and lost, and ducked my head under to find it. Groping around, I got my hand on it. There was a small tree handy and, using one of its branches, I pulled myself out of the muck, and so to the other side.

There is no rhyme or reason to how the mind of a soldier in battle works. There I was charging into Italy, passing dead men and coming close to drowning in a ditch, and, after cleaning my rifle as best I could, all I could think about was whether or not the photographs in my wallet had been ruined.

I took them out, tried to wipe them off on the grass, and waved them back and forth to stir up a little air to dry them.

Machine-gun bullets were boring into the ground in front of me and, at intervals, when the blup-blup of their impact came too close together, I hit the dirt. Those machine guns blazed away at us and mopped up our staff sergeant. He went down with bullets in his head.

I kept right on moving forward, and the next time I looked around to check my position, I was alone. The orders I'd heard back on shipboard had gone out of my mind. All I remembered was hearing somebody say, "When you get on the beach, keep moving forward."

Hopping over a wall and following a little path, I jumped over another wall into a clump of thorn bushes. Machine-gun bullets were streaking up and down the path I had

Do you think this preoccupation with insignificant details serves a purpose in combat?

169

just left, so I lay down in those bushes and played dead until the fire slackened. Finally I found a break through the thorns and, at the end of the break, a row of our men dug in. They were from two of our outfits, all mixed up together.

Once more, I started looking for my outfit. After a while I got tired of going along doubled up and stooping over, so I stood up and started walking. I decided I was thirsty, and stopped at a farmhouse well to get a drink. There were grapes and peaches around, and I stuffed some of them into me. I passed deserted farms and houses until they all ran together in my mind and I couldn't tell one from the other. Finally I figured I had walked about eight hours, and must be about twelve miles inland. Turning around, I saw a highway, and started to walk along it heading back in the direction from which I had come. Then, in the distance, German medium Mark IV tanks hove in sight. I dived into a ditch, squinted along my BAR—Browning automatic rifle—and began to fire as they came close, but the slugs from my gun made no impression on them. I was aiming at the tanks' slit openings, but there is so much noise and racket inside one of those things that the Heinies probably didn't hear me. They rumbled and clanked by, and I kept on walking down the highway, coming at last to a little creek, where I drank, took off my shoes and bathed my feet. My toes were stuck together from the sea water I'd waded through back at the Salerno beach. I washed my socks to get the salt out of them and put the same socks back on, keeping my extra ones in reserve.

How does this differ from the war movies?

I put in about fifteen minutes trying to remember the things I was supposed to have had firmly fixed in my head when we landed on the beach. Finally I remembered what our detail was supposed to do. I could see the mountain Lieutenant O'Leary had told

Look at the faces of these young men who have just registered for the draft. How do you explain their enthusiasm? Do you agree with the theory that, whatever sorrow and hardship it brought, World War II was the last time that the United States was united on anything? Can it be true that people "enjoy" war? Is this only a male instinct?

us about. He had called it Mountain Forty-two and we were supposed to take it. So I started toward it.

After climbing for a while, I came to a winery and found the first battalion of our regiment dug in there and all around it in the open fields. I wanted to ask them where my outfit was, but their trigger fingers were too itchy; they were shooting at sounds and dimly seen movements, and it wasn't any time to be dropping in unannounced to tear a social herring with them. So I dug in behind a bush and went to sleep.

It would have been nice to fill my canteen with water before I started again, but my canteen had picked up a bullet hole somewhere along the way. I hadn't known about that bullet before, although it must have given quite a jerk when it ripped through. I tried to rub the sleep from my eyes and walk down the highway. Both sides had infiltrated into and behind each other, so that you had to be on the alert each minute and watch every moving thing on each side of you.

German bullets were zipping around like high-velocity bees, but I finally found my outfit dug in, in spattered, shallow holes. They greeted me with, "Where the hell have you been?"

When I reported to Lieutenant O'Leary, he said, "I was sure they'd got you."

Every once in a while a shell landed near us, but they didn't do any real damage.

After a time we started down the road, and ran into a little Italian boy, who said, "Germans. Germans. Germans." My pal, La Bue, spoke to him in Italian, but the kid was frightened and didn't make much sense.

While La Bue was bickering with him, Lieutenant O'Leary shouted, "Here come some Heinie scout cars! Get off the road!"

We dived for cover and the scout cars opened fire. Bullets and fragments of shells bounced from our rifles, and two of us were hit. All of a sudden, one of our boys got his bazooka on his shoulder and let go with a tremendous, crashing "Boom!" and immediately afterward one of our men jumped up on a wall beside the road, leaped like a frog to the top of one of those panzer wagons and dropped his hand grenade into it. That particular scout car stopped then and there. The others speeded up, trying to get past us, when a company of our antitankers we hadn't seen up to that time went into action with its 57-mm. cannon. It was chancy stuff, for if that 57-mm. had missed its target, it would have gotten us. But as it was, everything worked out nice and clean and efficient. The bazooka kept on booming, and, quicker than it seemed possible, that whole small reconnaissance detachment was knocked out.

The place was a shambles. Scout cars were going up in flames. Tires were burning with a rubbery stink, and bodies were burning too. One German leaped out and started to run. When we went after him, he put his revolver to his head and killed himself. We had thought that only the Japs did that, and for a moment I was surprised and shocked.

Then a deep-rooted G.I. habit asserted itself. A moment before, hell had been popping on that stretch of road. Now, two seconds later, all we thought of was souvenirs. Milky Holland found a German Lüger. Looking back at it, I can remember no feeling about the German dead except curiosity. We were impersonal about them; to us they were just bundles of rags.

About two hours afterward, things were so quiet that some of us sneaked off into the near-by town, but we weren't relaxed and casual, and we took our rifles and sidearms with us. The townspeople were out waving at us and offering us water, wine and fruit. La Bue, a kid named Survilo and I had a yen to see the inside of an Italian jail. A woman had told us it was where they kept the Fascist sympathizers. The leading Fascist citizen of the town was in there, mad as blazes and yelling his head off behind the bars. La Bue listened to him for a while, then got mad himself and tried to reach through the bars and tickle him with the end of a bayonet. The Fascist really sounded off then.

When we came out, we saw some pretty Italian girls. La Bue made a date with one of them—the procedure following the same line as if we had been back in Pittsburgh's North Side. He asked her if she could get a couple of friends for us. Smiling, she said she could, and, feeling that we had accomplished something important, we went back to our bivouac.

But, just as they sometimes do in the North Side of Pittsburgh, our plans laid an egg. Platoon Sgt. Zerk Robertson pointed to a town named Altavilla, five or six miles away, and said, "See that town over there? That's where I'm going, and I want some volunteers to go with me. I'm taking the second platoon and some sixty-millimeter mortars." La Bue looked at me, and I looked at him, and we thought of our dates, but there wasn't anything we could do about it, and presently we were walking out along the highway.

How do you explain this impersonality?

Have you ever heard anyone say war was the best time of his life? Why did he feel this way?

By the time American troops landed at Salerno, the locale of Commando Kelly's story, the Italians had surrendered. American soldiers, expecting nothing more than a pleasant walk up the Italian coast, met stiff German resistance instead. Does the experience of shared danger in battle tend to produce exaggerated patriotism?

Was fighting in the Pacific more bitter because of the hardships induced by the rugged terrain? Was racism a factor as well?

FAHEY: FEAR IN THE SOUTH PACIFIC

July 15, 1943: We returned from our prowl up the Slot in search of Jap ships but nothing happened. I guess the Japs are licking their wounds. . . .

. . . Fighting the Japs is like fighting a wild animal. The troops said that the Japs are as tough and fierce as they come; the Jap is not afraid to die, it is an honor to die for the Emperor, he is their God.

A lot of the fighting is done at night and you can smell the Japs 25 yards away. The jungle is very hot and humid and drains the strength quickly. The jungle is also very think; you could be right next to a Jap and yet you could not see him. The Japs also have Jap women with them. The Japs watch from coconut trees in the daytime and then when it becomes dark they sneak into your foxhole and cut your throat or throw in a hand grenade. A 200 lb. soldier was pulled from his foxhole and killed in short time. You also hear all sorts of noises made by the animals and you think it is the Japs. This is too much for some men and they crack up.

They say the Japs also have some Imperial Marines who are 6 ft. 4" tall. The Japs are experts at jungle fighting and they know all the tricks. You would hardly believe the tricks they use. In the darkness, for instance, they like to throw dirt in your eyes and then attack you. Many of our troops get killed learning their tricks. The Japs take all kinds of chances, they love to die. Our troops are advancing slowly, it is a very savage campaign. Very few Japs surrender, they die fighting, even when the situation is hopeless.

How do you explain the more ideological, almost hysterical bias toward the enemy in this article?

What patriotic attitudes might this war experience produce?

173

State of the Nation
John Dos Passos

The war meant movement—both the movement of troops to training camps and the migration of war workers and their families to industrial and port cities. Perhaps your family participated in this wartime migration. In the section that follows, John Dos Passos describes some of the tensions and difficulties caused by wartime migration into a Southern city. Was the war the real cause of this tension, or were there deeper causes? Does war lead to progress and prosperity, or does it cause the opposite? Are there any traces of social and economic change brought about in your own community as a result of war?

The bus rumbles down the sunny empty highway through the rusty valleys and the bare rainwashed fields and the scraggly woods and the hills the color of oakleaves that are the landscape of winter in the southeast states. Inside, the air is dense with packed bodies and stale cigarette smoke. There's a smell of babies and an occasional sick flavor from the exhaust. The seats are all full. Somewhere in the back a baby is squalling. A line of men and women stands swaying in the aisle. Behind me two men are talking about jobs in singsong voices pitched deep in their chests.

"What's it like down there?" one is asking the other.

"Ain't too bad if you kin stand that bunch of loudmouthed foremen ... If you look crosseyed at one of them guards he'll reach out and yank off your badge and you're through and that's all there is to it."

"Well, I've worked in about all of 'em."

"Say, ain't I seen you somewheres before?"

"I dunno. Might have been on this bus. I been on this bus a thousand times."

. . .

A TOWN OUTGROWS ITSELF

We are in the city now. The bus is swinging out of the traffic of the crowded main street round the low gray building of the bus station, and comes to a stop in the middle of a milling crowd: soldiers, sailors, stout women with bundled up babies, lanky backwoodsmen with hats tipped over their brows and a cheek full of chewingtobacco, hatless young men in lightcolored sports shirts open at the neck, countrymen with creased red necks and well-washed overalls, cigarsmoking stocky men in business suits in pastel shades, girls in bright dresses with carefully curled hair piled up on their heads and highheeled shoes and bloodred fingernails, withered nutbrown old people with glasses, carrying ruptured suitcases, broadshouldered men in oilstained khaki with shiny brown helmets

In terms of age, sex, and social class, what groups are represented in this cross section of war-industry workers?

174

on their heads, negroes in flappy jackets and pegtop pants and little felt hats with turned-up brims, teenage boys in jockey caps, here and there a flustered negro woman dragging behind her a string of white-eyed children. Gradually the passengers are groping their way down the steep steps out of the bus and melting into the crowd.

Out on the streets every other man seems to be in work clothes. There are girls in twos and threes in slacks and overalls. Waiting for the light at a crossing a pinkfaced youth who's dangling a welder's helmet on a strap from the crook of his arm turns laughing to the man who hailed him. "I jes' got tired an' quit." Ragged families from the hills and the piney woods stroll staring straight ahead of them along the sidewalks towing flocks of little kids with flaxen hair and dirty faces. In front of a window full of brightcolored rayon socks in erratic designs a young man with glasses meets two girls in slacks. "We missed you yesterday," they say. "I was sick. I didn't go in. Anyway, I've got me a new job . . . more money."

How did the war affect the character of the city?

The mouldering old Gulf seaport with its ancient dusty elegance of tall shuttered windows under mansard roofs and iron lace overgrown with vines, and scaling colonnades shaded by great trees, looks trampled and battered like a city that's been taken by storm. Sidewalks are crowded. Gutters are stacked with litter that drifts back and forth in the brisk spring wind. Garbage cans are overflowing. Frame houses on treeshaded streets bulge with men in shirtsleeves who spill out onto the porches and trampled grassplots and stand in knots at the streetcorners. There's still talk of lodginghouses where they rent "hot beds." (Men work in three shifts. Why shouldn't they sleep in three shifts?) Cues wait outside of movies and lunchrooms. The trailer army has filled all the open lots with its regular ranks. In cluttered backyards people camp out in tents and chickenhouses and shelters tacked together out of packingcases.

Was your city a war-industry city? Are there any evidences of wartime buildings left?

In the outskirts in every direction you find acres and acres raw with new building, open fields skinned to the bare clay, elevations gashed with muddy roads and gnawed out by the powershovels and the bulldozers. There long lines of small houses, some decently planned on the "American standard" model and some mere boxes with a square brick chimney on the center, miles of dormitories, great squares of temporary structures are knocked together from day to day by a mob of construction workers in a smell of paint and freshsawed pine lumber and tobacco juice and sweat. Along the river for miles has risen a confusion of new yards from which men, women, and boys ebb and flow three times a day. Here and there are whole city blocks piled with wreckage and junk as if ancient cranky warehouses and superannuated stores had caved in out of their own rottenness under the impact of the violence of the new effort. Over it all the Gulf mist, heavy with smoke of soft coal, hangs in streaks, and glittering the training planes endlessly circle above the airfields.

RIFFRAFF

To be doing something towards winning the war, to be making some money, to learn a trade, men and women have been pouring into the city for more than a year now; tenants from dusty shacks set on stilts above the bare eroded earth in the midst of the cotton and the scraggly corn, small farmers and trappers from halfcultivated patches in the piney woods, millhands from the industrial towns in the northern part of the state, garage men, fillingstation attendants, storekeepers, drugclerks from crossroads settlements, longshore fishermen and oystermen, negroes off plantations who've never seen any town but the county seat on Saturday afternoon, white families who've lived all their lives off tobacco and "white meat" and cornpone in cranky cabins forgotten in the hills.

For them everything's new and wonderful. They can make more spot cash in a month than they saw before in half a year. They can buy radios, they can go to the pictures, they can go to beerparlors, bowl, shoot craps, bet on the ponies. Everywhere they rub elbows with foreigners from every state in the Union. Housekeeping in a trailer with electric light and running water is a dazzling luxury to a woman who's lived all her life in a cabin with half-inch chinks between the splintered boards of the floor. There are street cars and busses to take you anywhere you want to go. At night the streets are bright with electric light. Girls can go to beautyparlors, get their nails manicured, buy readymade dresses. In the backwoods a girl who's reached puberty feels she's a woman. She's never worried much about restraining her feelings when she had any. Is it any wonder that they can't stay home at dusk when the streets fill up with hungry boys in uniform?

What longer-range effects did the war have by changing society this way?

Some 27 million people moved during the war, mostly to urban areas to be near factories turning out war goods. To meet the severe housing shortage that developed, trailer camps like this one in Nashville sprang up. How might native townspeople have reacted to this influx of newcomers?

"It's quite dreadful," says the man with his collar around backwards, in answer to my question. He is a thinfaced rustylooking man in black with darkringed dark eyes who sits rocking in a rocking chair as he talks. "We are quite exercised about the problems these newcomers raise for the city . . . Juvenile delinquency, illegitimate babies, venereal disease . . . they are what we call the riffraff. I've seen them in their homes when I was travelling about the state inspecting C.C.C. camps for the government. They live in an astonishing state of degradation, they have no ambition. They put in a few measly crops, hoe their corn a little, but they have no habits of regular work. Most of them would rather freeze than chop a little wood. Most of the time they just sit around taking snuff and smoking. You see little children four and five years old smoking stubs of cigars. It's *Tobacco Road* and what was that other book? . . . *Grapes of Wrath*. People say those books are overdrawn, but they are not . . . They aren't exaggerated a bit. No wonder there's absenteeism . . . They've never worked regularly in their lives . . . They live in a daze. Nothing affects them, they don't want anything. These awful trailer camps and filthy tent colonies, they seem dreadful to us, but they like it like that. They think it's fine. They don't know any different."

What is this man really reacting to?

"Don't you think malnutrition might have something to do with their state of mind?" He was strangely inattentive to my question. A smell of frying fish had begun to fill the bare front room of the rectory. Somewhere out back a little bell had tinkled. The man with his collar around backwards began to stir uneasily in his chair. "I'm afraid I'm keeping you from your supper," I said, getting to my feet. "Yes," he said hastily. I thanked him and said goodbye. As I was going out the door he added, "Of course the people who come to my church, whom you were asking about, are foremen, skilled mechanics, good union men, they are a much better element. These other people are riffraff."

Waiting for the bus at the streetcorner in front of one of the better trailer camps that has clean white gravel spread over the ground, and neat wooden platforms beside each shiny trailer for use as a front stoop, I get to talking to a young man in a leather jacket.

Casual love affairs or marriages entered into hastily before soldiers left for overseas duty were common during the war. Crowded housing conditions, pregnancies, and forced separations often further strained relations. What other factors might have contributed to the high postwar divorce rate?

He's just worked four hours overtime because the other fellow didn't get there to relieve him at his machine. He's tired. You can tell by his breath that he's just had a couple or three beers. He's beefing because of the state regulations limiting the sale of whiskey and cutting out juke boxes in beer parlors. When a man's tired, he says, he needs relaxation. Works better next day. What's the use of dancing if you can't have a drink? What's the use of drinking if you can't dance? If this sort of thing keeps up he's going to pick up and move some place where things are wide open. Meanwhile several busses so jammed with soldiers from the airfield there's no more room, have passed us by. Hell, he groans, might as well go get him another beer, and he trots back into the silent "Dine and Dance" joint across the street.

• • •

"And now they've unloaded the race problem on us," mumbled the Mediator. "We were gettin' along all right until they stirred that up on us. We were givin' the colored folks the best break we could."

"Ain't never no trouble," said the roofer, "unless somebody stirs it up."

"Washington kicked off and the politicians down here are runnin' with the ball . . . White supremacy's a gold mine for 'em."

"As if we didn't have enough troubles organizin' this pile of raw muleskinners into decent union men and citizens," cried out the man in the stetson hat, "without having these longhaired wiseacres come down from Washington to stir up the race question . . . You know as well as I do that there isn't a white man in the South who isn't willing to die for the principle of segregation." He paused. All the men in the room silently nodded their heads. "Hell, we were jogglin' along all right before they sprung that on us. Sure, we have colored men in the unions in the building trades; the bricklayers even had colored officers in some of their locals."

"It's a thing you just have to go easy on," spoke up the Mediator. "Most white mechanics down here 'ud rather have a colored helper than a white helper, but when a colored man gets a notch up above them, they don't like it . . . Ain't a white man in the South'll stand for it. We tried that once in reconstruction days . . . I know of two of those niggers that fair practices board ordered upgraded who are dead niggers today. A piece of iron just fell on 'em."

"If they'd only just concentrate on givin' the negro a square deal within his own sphere most of the liberalminded people in the South would go along."

"There are small towns out here where all the young white men have gone to the army or war industry, and where the old men are all deputy sheriffs with guns slapped on their hips." The Mediator was talking in his slow drawling voice. "The people in those little towns are scared. If some day a drunken nigger made a pass at a white woman all hell 'ud break loose. Now there ain't nothin' going to happen, we know there ain't nothin' goin' to happen, but, mister, you tell your friends up North that this ain't no time to rock the boat."

"We've got our friends in the industrial unions to thank for that," said the young man in the stetson hat, spitting out his words savagely. "They came down here when we had the whole coast organized solid and put in their oar. They beat us at an election in this one yard . . . they got the negroes to vote for 'em, but they couldn't get 'em to join their union. What kind of labor politics is that? They've only got nine hundred members to this day, out of thousands. That's not majority rule . . . That doesn't sound like democracy to me."

What do you think of the argument that segregation and equal economic opportunity can coexist?

A few days before in a mining town in the northern part of the state I'd had lunch with a young college man from North Carolina, who had given me in a slow serious voice the industrial union side of the race question. They knew it was a difficult matter, he'd said, but they had decided to face it squarely. At first the employers down here had hired negro labor to break the white unions, but now that the negroes were joining up the employers were trying to hire all white men. On the whole the negroes had stuck to their locals through hard times better than the whites. In locals where they'd faced the issue squarely . . . equal rights for all . . . there had been very little trouble, even in locals made up of country boys from the farms. He told me of one local right in the black belt where they had tried it without having any real trouble, but the strain on the organizer, who was a Southern boy, had been terrific. He'd gone to a hospital with a nervous breakdown. I laughed. He didn't. It wasn't easy, he went on unsmilingly, but prejudice was something that tended to die away if nobody stirred it up. The cure was firmness and courage —meet it head on.

I told him about a meeting I'd drifted into in the basement of a colored church in a war industry town in the North. It was a meeting to protest against the separate dormitory the government was erecting for colored people. Quietlooking elderly negroes were sitting on cane chairs round an oldfashioned coal stove listening to the booming oratory of a preacher from the city. In a voice stirring as a roll of drums he invoked the Four Freedoms and asked how this country could fight for democracy in the rest of the world while there was still discrimination and segregation for thirteen million of our citizens at home. A lawyer had talked about the Constitution and said that now was the time for negroes to rise up and insist that they would no longer be treated as secondclass citizens. If they were called upon to send their sons and brothers to die for their country they had the right to demand equal rights everywhere throughout the broad land. Very much stirred, the listeners had whispered fervent amens at every pause. A young labor organizer had gotten up and said that such injustices made him ashamed to be a white man.

I was asking whether, perhaps, if only as a matter of tactics, it would not be better to work for fair play, equal wages, equal living conditions, first. Wasn't trying to break up segregation that way an infringement of the liberty of white men who didn't want to mix with negroes? After all, white men had rights, too.

Does this argument seem valid today?

"We have found," the young man said quietly, "that to get fair play for poor whites we've got to fight for equal rights for poor negroes. Of course we have to use tact, a great deal of tact. But in the unions, at least, the question has to be met head on."

If poor whites actually benefit from black advancement, why do they seem to resent it so much?

TWENTY-FIVE YEARS BEHIND THE TIMES

And all the while, by every bus and train the new people, white and black, pour into the city. As fast as a new block of housing is finished, it's jampacked. As soon as a new bus is put into service, it's weighed down with passengers. The schools are too full of

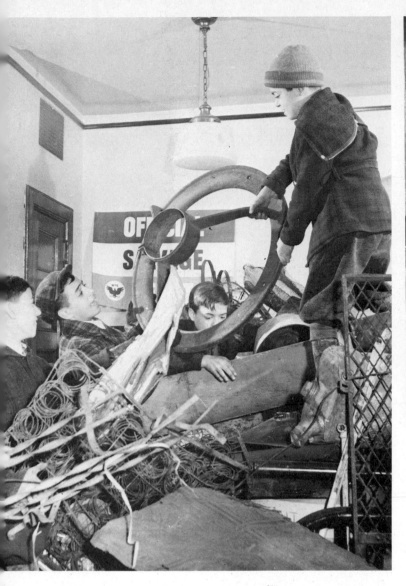

Both Germany and Japan fatally miscalculated this country's ability to quickly and effectively mobilize the homefront for the production of war goods. Every American's aid was enlisted. Children went on scrap drives to collect rubber and metals—resources in short supply due to Japanese control of Pacific sources. Women—adopting the government-inspired image of "Rosie the Riveter"—cut their hair, donned overalls, and went to work in factories, thereby freeing men for the battlefront. Did a member of your family participate in the homefront effort? How?

children. The restaurants are too full of eaters. If you try to go to see a doctor, you find the waitingroom full and a long line of people straggling down the hall. There's no room in the hospitals for the women who are going to have babies. "So far we've been lucky," the health officers say with terror in their voices, "not to have had an epidemic. But we've got our fingers crossed."

Lines of men wait outside of every conceivable office. If you get to see the mayor in the City Hall, you find him, a certain desperation under his bland exterior, desperately calling up Washington to try to pry loose some sewer pipe. The housing project has attended to the plumbing within its domain. The army has attended to these matters within its camps, but nobody has thought of how the new projects are to be linked up with the watermains and sewers of the city.

Do economic booms create as many problems as they solve?

If you go to see the personnel director of one of the big yards—he used to be a football coach—you find him fuming because he can't get the old team spirit into his employees. "What can you do when workingmen are making such big wages they don't give a damn?"

If you ask a labor man why management and labor can't get together to take some action about absenteeism and labor turnover, he snaps back at you: "Management down here won't talk to labor. The men running these yards are twenty-five years behind the times."

"I try to tell the president of one of these concerns," says the Government Man, "that he ought to set up a modern labor relations department and he just gives me a kind of oily grin and says, 'Oh go 'long—you get it all out of a book.'"

179

This is Lucille Ball as a pinup during World War II. Why were pinups so important to the fighting men? Were they demeaning to women? How would you compare this photo with a typical *Playboy* centerfold of today? What does this tell you about changing attitudes toward women? What else does it tell you?

The Government Man's office is under continual siege. Today two very pretty girls in overalls with magnificent hairdos and long sharp red polished nails have been waiting all morning to tell their story. Meanwhile, they tell it to a sympathetic telephone girl. They are welders. They want a release from this company so that they can go somewhere else where they can get more money. The mean old company won't see it their way. Can't the government do something about it? A group of farmboys is complaining that the local police won't let them run their cars without getting local plates. They can't get local plates until they get paid at the end of the week. Without their cars they can't get to work. Can't the government do something about it? In the hall some very black

What effect did the war have on the social position of women in the short run and in the long run?

negroes are hunched in a group leaning against the white marble sheathing of the wall of the officebuilding. They are appealing to Caesar. At the personnel office they've been told that if they quit their jobs they'll have to leave town. They want Uncle Sam to say if it's true. No, it's not true, not yet.

"It's incredible," says the Government Man when his office is finally clear. "Labor turnover in this town has reached twenty-five percent a quarter. That means every man Jack of 'em changed his job in a year. It's rugged individualism, all right. What they do is come into town and get some training, then when they've qualified for the lowest rate of skilled work they go and get 'em a job somewhere else. They can say they've had experience and can get in at a higher rate. After they've worked there a while, they move to some other outfit and get taken on in a higher category still, and they don't know a damn thing about the work because they spend all their time on the bus travelling around. It's the same thing with the foremen and executives. Before any one of them has a chance to learn his work he's snatched off somewhere else. I can't keep anybody in my office. Don't know anything about organizing industry, but they all get big jobs in management. It's upgrading for fair. It's very nice, but nobody stays any place long enough to learn his job. It's a nightmare."

And still . . . the office is in a tall building. We both happen to look out the window at the same time. Across a welter of sunblackened roofs we can see in the slanting afternoon sunlight the rows of great cranes and the staging and the cradled hulls and beyond, in the brown strip of river, packed rows of new tankers, some splotched with yellow and red, some shining with the light gray of their last coat of paint. In spite of turmoil and confusion, ships are getting built, ships, ships, ships.

What effect would this high turnover have on labor unions? on the quality of workmanship? on prices?

A Choice of Weapons
Gordon Parks

The United States Armed Forces were segregated during World War II. At that time black soldiers had to face subtle and direct prejudice everywhere they went. There were many racial incidents and one major race riot in Detroit in these years. The following is an account of some of the problems faced by one black man, Gordon Parks. He writes of his bitter experiences as a press corps member assigned to an all-black air force unit during the war. What did black men and women learn from the war? How did their experiences contribute to the civil rights movement of the 1950s and 1960s? Would you have had as much patience as Gordon Parks demonstrated?

The hot air smelled of gasoline and planes when I arrived at Selfridge Field the next morning. Though it was early the sprawling air base was alive with men and all kinds of machines, from jeeps to P-40 fighter ships. A sergeant met me at the gate in a command car; and, as we halted at company headquarters, a squadron of fighter ships thundered up into the hot sky. I stood marveling at the climbing ships, finding pleasure in the fact that black boys were inside them. And, thinking back to Richard Wright's *Native Son,* I recalled the Negro boy's remark when he witnessed a similar sight: "Look at those white boys fly," he had said in a special sort of awe. Now I was thinking the same thing about these black boys as they flashed above the earth like giant birds.

Why was aviation so long a domain of whites only?

• • •

We spent our weekends in Detroit. And Paradise Valley, a Negro section of the city, opened its arms wide to the nattily uniformed pilots and officers. They were already heroes to these people who had never seen black boys with wings on their chests before. There was no shortage of women; they came from miles around—"in furs, Fords and Cadillacs," Tony used to crow in delight. The problem was to pick wisely from the multitude. Tony was cocky, proud and brazen with good humor; and he was like a one-eyed dog in a sausage factory after two weeks at the base. A very unpretty woman approached him one night at a bar, but Tony, his sights fixed on something more choice, ignored her. Hours later, when we were leaving the bar loaded and broke, the woman passed us and got into a beautiful new Cadillac. Tony stopped in his tracks. Then, walking up to the woman, he tipped his hat. "Baby," he said, "you look like King Kong, but this car and those furs you've got on are a natural gas. Move over, honey. Let Tony baby drive this thing back to camp." She smiled, moved over and we journeyed out to Selfridge in style.

As the training went into fall, the men's attitude began to change. The fun was about over now. And the talk of women and the joking gave way to more serious things. Racial tensions began to have an effect on their actions and thinking. There were several incidents of white enlisted men on the base not saluting Negro officers. And black soldiers in combat were writing back about being segregated in barracks and mess halls in the war zones. The Negro newspapers were filled with stories about the black men being turned from the factory gates when war plants cried desperately for more help. The Pittsburgh *Courier* carried a long piece about Negro soldiers being assigned to menial labor. And there was a front-page article about an army band playing "God Bless America" when the white soldiers boarded the troopships; then, when Negroes went up the gangplank, the band switched to "The Darktown Strutters' Ball."

How does the Dos Passos article support this claim?

And one Sunday night a race riot erupted in Detroit. Fighting spread all over the city; twenty-five Negroes and nine whites were killed and hundreds of both races were injured. The black man was beginning to meet humiliation with violence. White supremacy had become as much an enemy as "blood" and "race" doctrines of the Nazis. Vindictiveness was slowly spreading through the air base. One could feel it in the air, in the mess halls, the barracks and the ready huts.

What were these "race" doctrines? Why didn't American whites perceive the parallel?

Once, after I returned from a trip to Washington, I found a note Tony had left for me. It read:

Dear Gordon,

Sorry to miss you but I'm on my way to Steubenville with Judy Edwards' body. As you probably heard, poor Judy spun in and I had to take his body all the way to Detroit because "there are no facilities" for handling Negro dead up there at Oscoda. It's about three hundred miles from Oscoda to Detroit, and in a goddamn Army ambulance you can imagine how long it took us to get there. Even as I write this to you, my feelings keep swinging from a murderous rage to frustration. How could anybody do anything like this?

His body was lying wrapped in a tarpaulin in the back of the ambulance; and I had trouble accepting the fact that he was dead, for every time I looked back there, the body seemed to move. I now wonder if the doctors at the hospital had examined him, since this would have required them to touch him too. By the time night had fallen I felt so badly that all I could say was "Judy, I'm sorry. . . . I'm sorry. . . ." We have all suffered some brutal indignities from the whites in this country but this was the final indignity of all. All during the trip I was in an emotional state, alternately talking to the driver and quietly crying for Judy, for his family, for the country and for myself. I felt shame and revulsion for having to wear the uniform I had on. The driver seemed to be caught up in the same mood. We were two of the loneliest soldiers in the world.

What ironies in the black man's position in this country does this letter bring out?

I won't tell his folks about this trip because it will just hurt them more. At least to them he was a hero and I'll make sure that when I arrive in Steubenville everyone knows it. The whole dirty business will come into even sharper focus when they lower him into the grave. He'll get an honor guard (a white one), the rifle fire and all the trappings. See you when I get back.

Tony

Despite changes, have you heard any Vietnam War veterans express similar bitterness?

I stuffed the letter into my pocket and walked over to the airstrip. The night was clear and cold and the stars seemed lower than usual. The fighter ships lined up on the quiet field were ghostly. I walked along beside them, noted the names stenciled in white block letters on the cockpits: Gleed, Pruitt, Tresville, Knox, Bright, Walker and many others. How many of these names will be on little white crosses this time next year? I wondered. At least the 332nd would go into battle with pilots who had faced the enemy before. This would be more of a chance than the 99th Squadron was allowed; for, unlike the white pilots, they had gone into their first battle without one seasoned pilot to lead them. The costly pattern of segregation had arranged a lonely death for some of these men—even over enemy territory. Hitler's Luftwaffe must have laughed when they screamed into the formations of the *schwarz* boys—knowing there wasn't an experienced fighter amongst them.

What argument against segregation is exposed here?

• • •

A little after mid-December an order came from the Pentagon halting all furloughs. We knew what this meant. Any day now we would be going overseas. A new tempo hit the base; the men rushed about, restless, patting one another's backs, awaiting moving orders. They came one morning about a week before Christmas. That afternoon Colonel Davis called me to headquarters. "We're about to pull out," he said, "and your traveling papers are not in order."

"What's wrong with them?" I asked.

When blacks did participate in air units, they were usually assigned the job of protecting the bomber planes that brought destruction like this to many German and Italian cities. Over eighty black pilots won the Distinguished Flying Cross for their service during the war. Have history books given adequate coverage to black accomplishments of this sort?

"You'll have to take that up with Washington. I'd advise you to fly there. We'll probably be leaving before they can get word back here to you."

I packed the battle gear that had been issued to me that morning, took a bus to Detroit, then a plane to Washington; I arrived there late that evening. Stryker had left the OWI [Office of War Information] by now and had gone to work in New York for the Standard Oil Co. In fact, just about everyone I knew there had gone; the rest were preparing to leave. Besides, it was a weekend and no officials were around. I didn't know where to turn. The one man I did reach had developed a strange case of laryngitis, and was unable to talk, he said. Finally in desperation I tried to reach Elmer Davis, head of the OWI, but he was away on a trip. I fretted through Saturday and Sunday. Then the first thing Monday morning I went to see Ted Poston, a friend of mine in the OWI press section. He had heard the rumors. And Ted put things in their true perspective: "There's some Southern gentlemen and conservative Republicans on Capitol Hill who don't like the idea of giving this kind of publicity to Negro soldiers."

Why did they fear publicity?

I was shocked—and so was Ted—but there wasn't much we could do about it. The next day I reached Elmer Davis by telephone and told him my story. He listened attentively. When I finished he said, "Don't worry, Gordon, I'll be in touch with the Pentagon this afternoon. You report there tomorrow. I'm sure everything will be all right."

That night, on the Howard University campus, I met Captain Lee Rayford and Lieutenant Walter Lawson, two pilots from the 99th Fighter Squadron. They had returned to the States after completing their required number of missions. Captain Rayford was the holder of the Purple Heart, the Distinguished Flying Cross, the Croix de Guerre, the Air Medal, and the Yugoslav Red Star. He had been shot up over Austria by a Messerschmitt 109. Both of them could have remained Stateside as instructors. Instead they had

184

volunteered to go back to the war zone. We ate dinner together, and since they had to go to the Pentagon the next day we agreed to meet and go together.

We had no sooner boarded the bus and seated ourselves behind the driver than his voice came at us, metallic and demanding. "If you fellas wanta ride into Virginyuh, you gotta go to the rear." We looked at one another questioningly, deciding in our silence not to move. The driver stood up and faced us, a scrawny disheveled man with tobacco-stained teeth and a hawk nose. The armpits of his uniform were discolored from sweat. "You all heard what I said. This bus ain't goin' nowhere till you all go to the back where you belong."

"We intend going to Virginia in the seats we're in," Lee said with finality.

"Okay, if you ain't back there in one minute I'm callin' the MP's and havin' you put off."

"You'd better start calling right now," Lee replied.

Was the driver's action legal?

Two white Air Force captains and a major were seated across the aisle from us and I noticed that they stirred uncomfortably. Several other whites were scattered in the near-empty bus and an elderly Negro woman sat at the rear. I watched her through the rear-view mirror. She had half risen from her seat; there was courage, dignity and anger in every line of her small body. Her look demanded that we stay there, and I was determined not to disappoint her. The bus had become dead quiet while the driver stood glowering at us.

"Fellows." One of the young white captains was speaking now. "We know how you feel about this," he said, his voice cloaked in false camaraderie, "but the major has an appointment at the Pentagon in a half hour. He wonders if you would mind moving back so that we can be on our way?"

My two friends were outranked. But there were no bars on my shoulders. The American eagle on my officer's cap was as large and significant as his or the major's. I took a good look at the old woman in the rear. She was standing now, gripping the seat ahead of her. Then, borrowing the captain's icy politeness, I stood and addressed the major. "Sir," I said, "as you can see, these men are fighter pilots. They have completed their missions but they have volunteered for more duty at the front. Would you like to order your fellow officers to the rear? They have no intention of moving otherwise." My anger was rising, so I sat back down.

The bus driver stood watching us until the major finally spoke to him. "Drive on," he said. "Can't you tell when you're licked?" The driver cursed under his breath, threw himself into the seat and slammed in the gears and we lurched off toward Virginia. "Hallelujah!" the Negro woman shouted from the rear. "Hallelujah!" Her voice rang with pathos and triumph. "Thank God we don't have to sit in the back of our P-38's," Lawson sighed as we got off the bus.

What aspects of the civil rights movement of the 1960s does this incident foreshadow?

• • •

Our plane took off in a blinding rainstorm—and it landed in another one at Norfolk, Virginia. A taxi took me to the ferry landing where I would cross over into Newport News. I sat there in the waiting room for an hour on top of my battle gear among a boisterous group of white enlisted men. Four Negro soldiers were huddled in a nearby corner. Two of them were propped against each other sleeping. Most of the white boys seemed to be making a festivity of these last hours. But there was a sort of emptiness attached to their laughing and drinking. Obviously they were headed for some departure point. It's all to hide the fear, I thought. Their faces were so young.

We filed out when the ferry whistled. It was still raining and we stood near the edge of the dock watching the boat fasten into the slip. Through the wetness I noticed a sign reading COLORED PASSENGERS and another one reading WHITES ONLY. The four black soldiers moved automatically to the colored side, and so did I. How ironic, I thought; such nonsense would not stop until we were in enemy territory.

After all the outgoing passengers were off and the trucks and cars had rumbled past, we started forward. Then I saw a Negro girl step from the ferry. She had been standing in the section marked for cars; now she was in the direct line of the white enlisted men, who stampeded to the boat screaming at the tops of their voices. I saw the girl fall beneath them into the mud and water. The four Negro soldiers also saw her go down. The five of us rushed to her rescue. She was knocked down several times before we could get to her and pull her out of the scrambling mob.

"You lousy white bastards!" one of the Negro soldiers yelled. "If I only had a gun!" Tears were in his eyes, hysteria in his voice. A long knife was glistening in his hands.

"Soldier!" I shouted above the noise, letting him get a look at my officer's cap. "Put that knife away!"

He glared at me fiercely for a second. "But you saw what they did!"

"Yes, I saw, but we're outnumbered ten to one! You can't fight all of them. Get on the boat!" He looked at me sullenly for another moment, then moved off. We cleaned the mud from the girl's coat and she walked away without a word. Only proud anger glistened on her black face. Then the four of us joined the soldier I had ordered away. He was standing still tense beneath the sign reading "colored passengers."

"Sorry, soldier," I said. "We wouldn't have had a chance against a mob like that. You realize that, don't you?"

"If I gotta die, I'd just as soon do it where I got real cause to." His tone was resolute. I had to answer. I was tempted to hand him the bit about the future and all that, but the future was too uncertain. The yelling was even louder now on the other side of the boat. "Sons-of-bitches," he muttered under his breath.

"Good luck," I said to them as we parted on the other shore. "So long," they said— except the one I had spoken to—then they moved off into the darkness and rain again. I turned away, feeling I had somehow let him down.

"Colored move to the rear!" The voice met me again when I got on the bus with some of the white enlisted men. Sick of trouble, I made my way to the back and sat down; I was the only Negro aboard. Some of the whites were standing, but I had four empty seats around me. "Gordy! My God, it's Gordy!" a voice rang out above the noise. And suddenly a soldier was rushing back toward me. "Bud!" I shouted, getting to my feet only to be knocked back to my seat by his bear hug. It was Bud Hallender, a husky man I had played basketball with back in St. Paul. Now he was down beside me, slapping my back and wringing my hands.

"You all cain't ride back there with that nigra! Move back up front where you belong!" Bud ignored the command; now he was telling the others I was the co-captain of his basketball team, his friend.

"You all hear me? You cain't ride back there with that nigra!"

"Go screw yourself!" Bud shouted back. "Drive on or we'll throw you off this god-damned crate and drive it ourselves!" Laughter rocked the bus. The driver plopped down into his seat without another word and drove off toward the heart of town. And Bud and I talked excitedly of a time and place where things had been different. Finally, at the terminal we wished each other a jovial goodbye.

• • •

Tony and I went out for some fresh air the next night. "It's hard to believe but we've had trouble right here on this base," he said as we walked along, "so we'd better stay in this area."

"What kind of trouble?"

"The same old jazz. One of our ground crewmen was beaten up by some white paratroopers night before last. Then they've tried to segregate us at the base's movie house. Everyone's in a hell of a mood." We became suddenly quiet as we circled the area.

A shot sounded nearby and the two of us stopped in our tracks. Then there was another shot. Someone seemed to be returning the fire. "We'd better get in. Sounds like trouble," Tony said. Our barracks had already gone dark when we entered it. Several men were at the windows with guns looking out cautiously into the night. When all was quiet again, the lights went back on and the gambling and the letter writing and the drinking started again. New orders came the following morning. We would take to the boat two days earlier than had been proposed. I was happy about this. There seemed to be less danger at sea than on this troubled base.

Colonel Davis sent for me just before noon. I hurried anxiously to his office. No more trouble, I hoped; it was too close to sailing time. But when he looked up at me his face was calm. It was, after all, some routine matter he would speak about, I thought.

"I'm sorry. Your papers are not in order. A final call from the Pentagon has come through. You will not be able to embark with us."

"This is ridiculous," I said. "Can't you do something? Someone in Washington is trying to prevent coverage of your group overseas, Colonel. This is the first Negro fighter group. It's history. It has to be covered. Can't you protest in some way, Colonel?"

"There's nothing, absolutely nothing I can do. The orders are from the Pentagon. They cannot be rescinded. I'm terribly sorry."

I had lost. And suddenly anesthetized to the colonel and all that was around him, I

Does violent confrontation have a legitimate place in solving racial problems?

What does this incident show about the solidity of white opinion on racial issues in the 1940s?

What do you know about black fighting groups in World War II? In other wars?

turned and started out. "You are aware that you are sworn to the strictest of secrecy about what you have seen or learned here," he was saying as he followed me to the door. "You realize the dangers of any slip."

"Yes, I understand, Colonel."

"It is even possible to detain you until we are overseas under such conditions. But I am sure you won't discuss our movements with anyone."

"I won't. Don't worry. I want to forget the whole thing as quickly as possible." I rushed back toward the barracks, angry and disgusted. I couldn't bring myself to say goodbye to the pilots again. I packed quickly and waited for the command car the colonel had ordered for me.

The pilots were readying themselves for the boat when the car arrived; and I slipped through the rear door without even a backward glance. At five o'clock the next morning, after wiring Sally, I boarded a plane for Washington. I would change planes there and go on to New York, where I would wait for my wife and children. The thought of even stopping in this city irked me. I wouldn't live there again if they gave me the White House rent free, I thought as the plane roared down the runway.

We began circling over Washington at dawn; and far below I could see the landing

This all-black infantry battalion represents only a small fraction of the half-million blacks who saw overseas service in World War II. How did wartime experiences at home and abroad help fuel the civil rights struggles of the 1960s?

field, lying like small strips of cardboard under a wispy path of cloud. Further out in the distance the monuments of the city shone milk-white in the winter sunlight and the water in the mall sparkled like an oblong jewel between the sculptured trees; there was the Capitol standing quiet and strong on one end and the Lincoln Memorial set on the high quarter of the opposite slope. What a beautiful sight to be wed to such human ugliness, I thought. And as we dropped lower I could see the tops of the stores, theaters, and restaurants whose doors were still closed to me.

I thought back to the fighter pilots. They would soon be far out to sea, sailing toward war and death, ignoring at least temporarily, their differences with the land they were leaving to defend. This was the price for a questionable equality.

What irony of symbolism is he pointing out here?

LIFE IN THE CAMPS

The locking up of Japanese-Americans in concentration camps during World War II was in many ways a logical extension of the anti-Oriental racism that had existed on the West Coast since the arrival of the first Chinese immigrants in the 1840s. Japanese laborers began to arrive in California in the decade following the Exclusion Act of 1882, which barred further Chinese immigration. Despite their record of good citizenship and hard work in menial tasks, the first generation of Japanese-Americans endured similar discrimination: the "Gentlemen's Agreement" of 1907 ended Japanese immigration. Many of the Nisei, the second generation of Japanese-Americans, born and brought up in the United States in the period between the two world wars, became substantial businesspeople and property owners. Nevertheless, in the wake of Japan's attack on Pearl Harbor in December 1941, an outpouring of bigotry and fear persuaded officials in California and Washington to "relocate" the Nisei. Ultimately ten "relocation camps" were established in remote areas, from California to Arkansas. Losing their homes and businesses, the Nisei and their children, charged with no crimes and denied legal recourse, became prisoners of war in their own country. The following letters reflect life in the camps.

Left Fresno at 8:55 this morning and reached the Assembly Center at about 9:10 A.M. We first stopped at the registrar's office to be checked and registered. Our bags and pockets were searched, to my surprise. For what? I don't know. Luckily we all passed. I mean nothing was taken from us. Then our baggage was inspected from corner to corner. What a feeling I had when they went through our personal belongings. . . .

When I first entered our room, I became sick to my stomach. There were seven beds in the room and no furniture nor any partitions to separate the males and the females of the family. I just sat on the bed, staring at the bare wall. For a while I couldn't speak nor smile. Well, after getting over with my shock, I started to get the baggage in. . . .

Then we wanted to know where our rest rooms were. This was too much for me. There is no privacy. I just can't explain how it is, but it's worse than a country privy. After it's been used a couple of times, there is a whole stack of flies. Once you open the door the flies can be seen buzzing around; it is like a nest of bees. We just couldn't go in there, so we excavated. The hospital being facilitated with flush toilets, we sneaked in. Then we tried the showers, which are not so bad except that there is no privacy. Well that's that for the day's happening.

As to what I think of camp life; I think it's hell. That's the only word I could think of to describe it.

What would your reaction have been?

What do you think of the term "relocation" as a description of the experience recounted here?

189

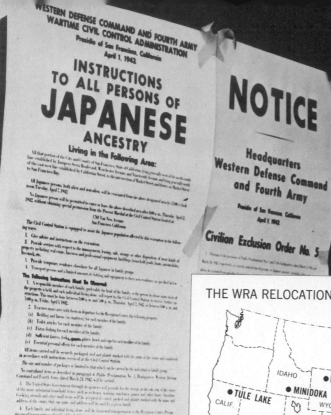

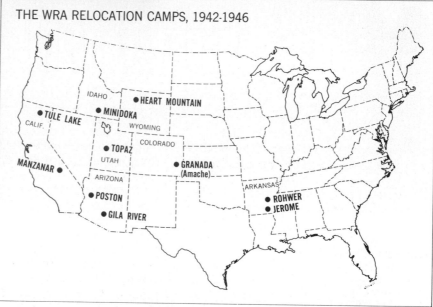

THE WRA RELOCATION CAMPS, 1942-1946

There are going to be a lot of Japs who are going to say, "Oh, yes, we're good Americans and we want to do everything you say," but those are the fellows I suspect the most.

Lt. Gen. John L. DeWitt, commander
of the evacuation effort

What we hate to recall is not so much the hardships that the war and Evacuation brought to us but the vast sense of alienation we suffered when we were like the man without a country.
Kats Kunitsugu, "Evacuation—the Pain Remains,"
Pacific Citizen, Dec. 20–27, 1968

Every Nisei . . . was extremely annoyed when he was reminded by some visiting Caucasian that he had been placed in the assembly center "for his own protection." Also, without exception, everyone was highly indignant at the practice of focusing floodlights from twelve watchtowers on camp every night from twilight to dawn. When informed by the administration that the searchlights had been installed to protect us from outsiders who might leap over the fence to injure us, his usual retort was: "Why should the lights be focused on the barracks and not on the outer fence as a logical procedure?" Similarly, there was keen resentment against the barbed-wire fence surrounding camp and many a time I watched a novice throwing rocks at it to discover if the wires were actually charged.

No systematic study was made of the attitudes of little children but the narrating of a few stray incidents might be of some aid in identifying them. One afternoon in late June, I heard a great commotion behind my barrack and on investigation perceived a group of twelve boys about six to ten years of age shouldering wooden guns and attacking a "Japanese fort" while lustily singing "Anchors Aweigh." . . . Similarly, in the blackout of May 24, little children raced down our street yelling at the top of their lungs: "Turn off your lights! The Japs are coming!"

A Nisei mother once told me with tears in her eyes of her six-year-old son who insisted on her "taking him back to America." The little boy had been taken to Japan about two years ago but was so unhappy there that she was compelled to return to California with him. Soon afterwards they were evacuated to Santa Anita, and the little boy in the absence of his Caucasian playmates was convinced that he was still in Japan and kept on entreating his mother to "take him back to America." To reassure him that he was in America she took him to the information center in her district and pointed to the American flag but he could not be consoled because Charlie and Jimmie, his Caucasian playmates, were not there with him in camp.

It is also interesting to note that whenever little children sang songs these were not Japanese folksongs but typically American songs like "God Bless America," "My Country 'Tis of Thee," "My Old Kentucky Home," "Row, Row, Row Your Boat," "Jesus Loves Me," and other songs known to every American child. The "Americanness" of the Sansei may serve to identify the character of their Nisei parents.

When 1,500 work orders were sent out by the Personnel Office to U.S. citizens above the age of sixteen a day before the camouflage project was opened, approximately 800 were reported to have refused to work. Some excused themselves by claiming that they were allergic to the dye on burlap strips or to the lint which fell off from them, but at least half of that number was said to have refused on principle. They felt that they were really "prisoners of war" and that the U.S. government had no right to appeal to them to aid in the war effort on a patriotic note. The battle cry during the camouflage strike of June 16–17 seemed to be: Give us the treatment accorded other American citizens and we will gladly cooperate in completing the number of nets requested by the U.S. Army. . . .

If your parents were members of an ethnic group at war with the United States, did they fear any repercussions? Did they question why only Japanese-Americans were being involved?

What unjust aspect of the internment is the author indicating here?

Assignment 7

AN INTERVIEW: YOUR FAMILY AND WORLD WAR II

Like the chapter on the depression of the 1930s, this chapter on World War II was chosen because of our assumption that the war was an event of such major consequence that it touched the lives of nearly everyone. Yet, as the readings attempt to illustrate, the effects of the war on people were not as uniform as might be expected. At the same time that soldiers were dying on distant Pacific islands, men unemployed through most of the thirties found steady work.

Your assignment is to interview members of your family about their experiences in the war, at home and abroad. For many people this may well dredge up feelings of pain and terror; you must therefore be sensitive in deciding what is an appropriate line of questioning. Try to discover the ways in which the war affected your family and how existence in the early 1940s contrasted with life in the 1930s. Your investigation should come to some conclusion on the changes that the war brought in terms of economic and social conditions, place of residence, political convictions, opportunities gained, and hardships suffered. Then, after completing your interviews, write a brief preliminary report on your findings, to be incorporated later into your research paper.

BIBLIOGRAPHIC NOTE

The literature on World War II military campaigns and specific battles is enormous. You should be able to find accounts of any particular wartime military episode that is related to your family's experiences. Two of the best accounts of soldiers' experiences in combat are *The Story of G.I. Joe* (1945) by Ernie Pyle, a wartime correspondent, and *The Naked and the Dead* (1948) by Norman Mailer, the brilliant American novelist.

The history of the homefront is still inadequately written. But see Richard Polenberg's collection, *America at War: The Home Front, 1941–1945* (1968) and his *War and Society: The United States 1941–1945* (1972). Fun to read is Richard R. Lingeman, *Don't You Know There's a War On?* (1970). Several excellent works have recently appeared on the Japanese-American internment camps, including Roger Daniels, *Concentration Camps USA* (1972).

eight

The Postwar Era: Your Times

You live in a time of accelerating and bewildering change. During your lifetime technological advances, economic fluctuations, and international crises have had a significant effect on the way you live. If you were born in 1960, you can probably remember the war in Vietnam, the antiwar protests, and at least some of the assassinations of our leaders—John Kennedy, Robert Kennedy, and Martin Luther King, among them. You certainly can recall the first man on the moon, the Watergate scandals, and the first energy crisis, and you may have some memories of the sit-ins and protest marches of the civil rights movement and the violence that broke out in our decaying inner cities. Whether you remember or not, these events and other have influenced your lives.

Most Americans, including probably your parents, emerged from the crisis of World War II with optimism about the future and great confidence in the superiority of the American way of life. But within three years after the war the wartime alliance with the Soviet Union had dissolved into a cold war filled with tension and distrust. The country found itself in the strange and ironical position of sending aid to its former enemies, Germany and Japan, in order to oppose its former ally, the Soviet Union. Then in 1950 fighting broke out in Korea against communist forces, and American men once more had to go half way round the world to participate in a war that, it soon became apparent, neither side could win.

Few people protested the war in Korea, but some Americans imagined that subversive agents were trying to undermine American democracy. Right-wing sympathizers often confused liberals with Communists and any criticism with subversion. In the mid-fifties Senator Joseph McCarthy led a witch hunt designed to ferret out Communists in government, but he succeeded only in threatening the basic American right of free speech.

Despite McCarthy, however, the fifties were a time of complacency and conformity. Most people narrowed their concerns to finding a secure job and accumulating the material evidences of the good life—a home in the suburbs, two cars, and other status symbols. But beneath the placid surface of life flowed currents of discontent. For one thing, the prosperity of the fifties was never equally shared by all classes. Blacks and other minorities, who have always received a small amount of the wealth, continued to suffer, but so did an even larger number of whites, particularly in rural areas. This "other America," as sociologist Michael Harrington dubbed the dispossessed, were especially hard hit by the recessions that America experienced throughout the fifties. And the pride of all Americans was battered by the news in 1957 that the Russians had launched the first space vehicle. Suddenly it seemed we were no longer number one in the world.

The narrow victory of John F. Kennedy over Richard Nixon in 1960 seemed to signal a new era of idealism and change, even if, in retrospect, little that was fundamental actually changed. The civil rights movement, using tactics of sit-ins, protest marches, and boycotts, achieved some victories, but the economic status of the majority of blacks was not improved substantially. The Peace Corps, VISTA, and all the other agencies of Kennedy's New Frontier and Lyndon Johnson's Great Society failed to eliminate poverty either in the United States or in the underdeveloped nations of the world.

The idealism and the faith in change of many of the youth of the 1960s seems to have marked them apart from the young people of the 1950s and perhaps of the 1970s as well. Much of the idealism and optimism of young and old alike was dissipated, however, in the late 1960s in protesting a senseless war in Vietnam. For a time it seemed that the entire nation would be torn apart by hatred and violence. The protesters succeeded in dissuading Lyndon Johnson from running for a second term in 1968 only to have to endure five more years of the war's escalation under Richard Nixon.

With the enthusiasms and fires of the sixties gone, many Americans viewed with alarm the series of crises that the seventies brought. No sooner were American troops withdrawn from Vietnam in 1973 than a political scandal broke that forced the resignation of the President. Coupled with this political instability were economic troubles, brought on partly by the sustained war effort and partly by the country's dependence on costly Middle Eastern oil. No one knew quite how to deal with the unprecedented situation of simultaneous inflation and rising unemployment.

From the perspective of the late 1970s the future seems hard to predict, though certain contemporary social trends do provide some clues. Our problems will certainly be compounded by the continuing growth in the number of Americans. Though the birth rate has declined, average life expectancy has increased because of advances in modern medicine. This has resulted not simply in more Americans but in an older society on the average. As a result, some contend, American society may well become more conservative, less willing to innovate.

Innovation may be exactly what is needed, however, to meet such pressing social problems as decaying urban areas. The problem of the cities stems largely from another social trend of recent years—middle-class flight from cities to suburbs. Such class mobility is the realization of the American Dream for some. But for those left behind— the poor, many of whom suffer as well from discrimination—it represents a nightmare. Unable to support with taxes such basic social services as sanitation, education, hospital care, and police protection, the inner-city poor are likely to suffer even more in the future from disease, ignorance, and crime if the trend continues.

In the past the escape route from such poverty was through more education to achieve a better-paying job. But that route is no longer as open as it once was. Aside from the fact that education has become prohibitively expensive, the economy seems less able today to provide suitable jobs for those who do have an education. The result may be a frozen class structure and a worsening of the trend toward a widening spread of income between rich and poor. Ironically, the apparent solution to this problem, more economic expansion, brings with it another whole set of problems—pollution, ecological imbalance, and the exhaustion of finite resources. Material progress is also usually accompanied by various social problems such as alcoholism and a rise in consumer debt. We may have to trade some potential for upward mobility, then, for a more secure natural and social environment.

The decades ahead will not be easy ones if contemporary trends are an indication of the future. But Americans are as a rule an optimistic lot. For many the past has been good, the present, filled with reminders of how far they have come. And few of the dissatisfied seriously entertain the idea of emigrating. However awesome its problems, America remains today, in dream if not in reality, what it meant to most of its immigrants: the New World Eden, with riches to be sought, where mankind would someday perfect itself.

The material in this chapter seeks to provide you with a basis for defining your relationship with contemporary society. As you read through the articles sketching the events and trends of the last three decades, try to analyze them in terms of how they may affect your own life today or sometime in the future. What leaves you optimistic and what depresses you? Do you agree with some who find the present stimulating and challenging? Or are the critics who predict strife and technological depersonalization more accurate? How has America done since you have been alive?

A Generation Of Bureaucrats

William H. Whyte

Part of the folklore of American society is the notion of the self-made man, the idea that if you work hard you can be a success, you can rise to become president of the company or even President of the United States. But during the 1950s colleges produced a generation of students who seemed to be more concerned with security than with opportunity. These students apparently did not want to be President, just a middle-range executive with a good pension.

The following article was written by a man who graduated from college in the 1930s. He is critical of the generation of the 1950s for wanting to be bureaucrats, rather than innovators, for accepting the system rather than trying to change it. He assumes that those seeking a business career are male—an assumption that clearly would not be made today. Ironically, within a decade after he wrote at least some college students did take up his challenge. They dropped out of society, formed communes, and in other ways became critical of the establishment, especially the "military-industrial complex." How would you characterize your generation? What does this article tell you about the power of the large corporation? Can any amount of protest alter that power?

When I was a college senior in 1939, we used to sing a plaintive song about going out into the "cold, cold world." It wasn't really so very cold then, but we did enjoy meditating on the fraughtness of it all. It was a big break we were facing, we told ourselves, and those of us who were going to try our luck in the commercial world could be patronizing toward those who were going on to graduate work or academic life. We were taking the leap.

Seniors still sing the song, but somehow the old note of portent is gone. There is no leap left to take. The union between the world of organization and the college has been so cemented that today's seniors can see a continuity between the college and the life thereafter that we never did. Come graduation, they do not go outside to a hostile world; they transfer.

Do you see a gap between college and "life," or will working be just a continuation of what you are doing at present?

For the senior who is headed for the corporation it is almost as if it were part of one master scheme. The locale shifts; the training continues, for at the same time that the colleges have been changing their curriculum to suit the corporation, the corporation has responded by setting up its own campuses and classrooms. By now the two have been so well molded that it's difficult to tell where one leaves off and the other begins.

The descent, every spring, of the corporations' recruiters has now become a built-in feature of campus life. If the college is large and its placement director efficient, the processing operation is visibly impressive. I have never been able to erase from my mind the memory of an ordinary day at Purdue's placement center. It is probably the largest and most effective placement operation in the country, yet, much as in a well-run group clinic, there seemed hardly any activity. In the main room some students were quietly

196

Is it significant that all these workers are women? Does this have anything to do with the Women's Movement? How does this type of work compare to the work usually done by women (and by men) a century ago? Is "satisfaction" possible from such work? Or does it only offer "survival"? Is this scene a metaphor for our times?

studying company literature arranged on the tables for them; others were checking the interview timetables to find what recruiter they would see and to which cubicle he was assigned; at the central filing desk college employees were sorting the hundreds of names of men who had registered for placement. Except for a murmur from the row of cubicles there was little to indicate that scores of young men were, every hour on the half hour, making the decisions that would determine their whole future life.

Someone from a less organized era might conclude that the standardization of this machinery—and the standardized future it portends—would repel students. It does not. For the median senior this is the optimum future; it meshes so closely with his own aspirations that it is almost as if the corporation was planned in response to an attitude poll.

Because they are the largest single group, the corporation-bound seniors are the most visible manifestation of their generation's values. But in essentials their contemporaries headed for other occupations respond to the same urges. The lawyers, the doctors, the scientists—their occupations are also subject to the same centralization, the same trend to group work and to bureaucratization. And so are the young men who will enter them. Whatever their many differences, in one great respect they are all of a piece: more than any generation in memory, theirs will be a generation of bureaucrats.

They are, above all, conservative. Their inclination to accept the status quo does not necessarily mean that in the historic sweep of ideas they are conservative—in the more classical sense of conservatism, it could be argued that the seniors will be, in effect if not by design, agents of revolution. But this is a matter we must leave to later historians. For the immediate present, at any rate, what ideological ferment college men exhibit is not in the direction of basic change.

What conditions in the 1950s contributed to this conservatism? Do such conditions exist today?

This shows most clearly in their attitude toward politics. It used to be axiomatic that young men moved to the left end of the spectrum in revolt against their fathers and then, as the years went on, moved slowly to the right. A lot of people still believe this is true, and many businessmen fear that twenty years of the New Deal hopelessly corrupted our youth into radicalism. After the election of 1952 businessmen became somewhat more cheerful, but many are still apprehensive, and whenever a poll indicates that students don't realize that business makes only about 6 per cent profit, there is a flurry of demands for some new crusade to rescue our youth from socialistic tendencies.

If the seniors do any moving, however, it will be from dead center. Liberal groups have almost disappeared from the campus, and what few remain are anemic. There has been no noticeable activity at the other end of the spectrum either. When William Buckley, Jr., produced *God and Man at Yale*, some people thought this signaled the emergence of a strong right-wing movement among the young men. The militancy, however, has not proved particularly contagious; when the McCarthy issue roused and divided their elders, undergraduates seemed somewhat bored with it all.

Their conservatism is passive. No cause seizes them, and nothing so exuberant or willfully iconoclastic as the Veterans of Future Wars has reappeared. There are Democrats and Republicans, and at election time there is the usual flurry of rallies, but in comparison with the agitation of the thirties no one seems to care too much one way or the other. There has been personal unrest—the suspense over the prospect of military service assures this—but it rarely gets resolved into a thought-out protest. Come spring and students may start whacking each other over the head or roughing up the townees and thereby cause a rush of concern over the wild younger generation. But there is no real revolution in them, and the next day they likely as not will be found with their feet firmly on the ground in the recruiters' cubicles.

Are there issues worth protesting about today?

• • •

In judging a college generation, one usually bases his judgment on how much it varies from one's own, and presumably superior, class, and I must confess that I find myself tempted to do so. Yet I do not think my generation has any license to damn the acquiescence of seniors as a weakening of intellectual fiber. It is easy for us to forget that if earlier generations were less content with society, there was a great deal less to be contented about. In the intervening years the economy has changed enormously, and even in retrospect the senior can hardly be expected to share former discontents. Society is not out of joint for him, and if he acquiesces it is not out of fear that he does so. He does not want to rebel against the status quo because he really likes it—and his elders, it might be added, are not suggesting anything bold and new to rebel *for*.

Does the present quiet on campus indicate a liking for the status quo?

• • •

More than before, there is a tremendous interest in techniques. Having no quarrel with society, they prefer to table the subject of ends and concentrate instead on means. Not what or why but *how* interests them, and any evangelical strain they have they can sublimate; once they have equated the common weal with organization—a task the curriculum makes easy—they will let the organization worry about goals. "These men do not question the system," an economics professor says of them, approvingly. "They want to get in there and lubricate and make them run better. They will be technicians of the society, not innovators."

The attitude of men majoring in social science is particularly revealing on this score. Not so very long ago, the younger social scientist was apt to see his discipline as a vehicle for protest about society as well as the study of it. The seniors that set the fashion for

The percentage of the nation's seventeen year olds graduating from high school, and college graduates as a percentage of twenty-three year olds. Current forecasts indicate that educational growth will slow down over the next decade.

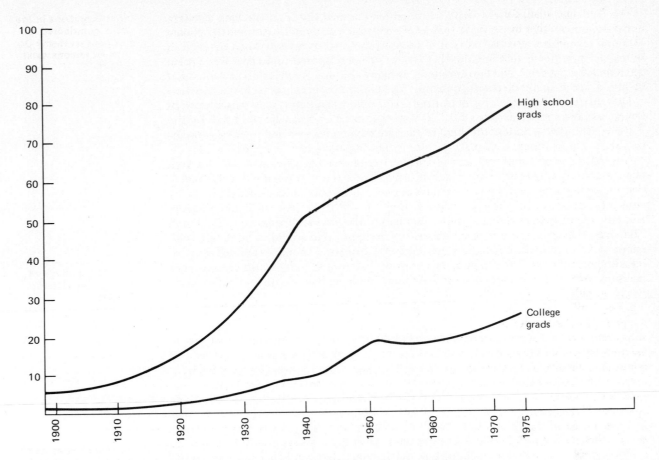

him were frequently angry men, and many of the big studies of the twenties and thirties —Robert and Helen Lynd's *Middletown,* for example—did not conceal strong opinions about the inequities in the social structure. But this is now old hat: it is the "bleeding-heart" school to the younger men (and to some not so young, too), for they do not wish to protest; they wish to collaborate. Reflecting the growing reconciliation with middle-class values that has affected all types of intellectuals, they are turning more and more to an interest in methodology, particularly the techniques of measurement. Older social scientists who have done studies on broad social problems find that the younger men are comparatively uninterested in the problems themselves. When the discussion period comes, the questions the younger men ask are on the technical points; not the what, or why, but the how.

Which are more important—why questions or how questions?

The urge to be a technician, a collaborator, shows most markedly in the kind of jobs seniors prefer. They want to work for somebody else. Paradoxically, the old dream of independence through a business of one's own is held almost exclusively by factory workers—the one group, as a number of sociologists have reported, least able to fulfill it. Even at the bull-session level college seniors do not affect it, and when recruiting time comes around they make the preference clear. Consistently, placement officers find that of the men who intend to go into business—roughly one half of the class—less than 5 per cent express any desire to be an entrepreneur. About 15 to 20 per cent plan to go into their fathers' business. Of the rest, most have one simple goal: the big corporation.

• • •

It is not simply for security that they take the vows. Far more than their predecessors they understand bigness. My contemporaries, fearful of anonymity, used to talk of "being lost" in a big corporation. This did not prevent us from joining corporations, to be sure, but verbally, at least, it was fashionable to view the organization way with misgivings. Today this would show a want of sophistication. With many of the liberals who fifteen years ago helped stimulate the undergraduate distrust of bigness now busy writing tracts in praise of bigness, the ideological underpinnings for the debate have crumbled.

The fact that a majority of seniors headed for business shy from the idea of being entrepreneurs is only in part due to fear of economic risk. Seniors can put the choice in moral terms also, and the portrait of the entrepreneur as a young man detailed in postwar fiction preaches a sermon that seniors are predisposed to accept. What price bitch goddess Success? The entrepreneur, as many see him, is a selfish type motivated by greed, and he is, furthermore, unhappy. The big-time operator as sketched in fiction eventually so loses stomach for enterprise that he finds happiness only when he stops being an entrepreneur, forsakes "21," El Morocco, and the boss's wife and heads for the country. Citing such fiction, the student can moralize on his aversion to entrepreneurship. His heel quotient, he explains, is simply not big enough.

Not that he is afraid of risk, the senior can argue. Far from being afraid of taking chances, he is simply looking for the *best* place to take them in. Small business is small because of nepotism and the roll-top desk outlook, the argument goes; big business, by contrast, has borrowed the tools of science and made them pay off. It has its great laboratories, its market-research departments, and the time and patience to use them. The odds, then, favor the man who joins big business. "We wouldn't hesitate to risk adopting new industrial techniques and products," explains a proponent of this calculated-risk theory, "but we would do it only after we had subjected it to tests of engineers, pre-testing in the market and that kind of thing." With big business, in short, risk-taking would be a cinch.

What is the image of the big corporation today?

• • •

. . . One recruiter went through three hundred interviews without one senior's mentioning salary, and the experience is not unusual. Indeed, sometimes seniors react as if a large income and security were antithetical. As some small companies have found to their amazement, the offer of a sales job netting $15,000 at the end of two years is often turned down in favor of an equivalent one with a large company netting $8,000. Along with the $8,000 job, the senior says in justification, goes a pension plan and other benefits. He could, of course, buy himself some rather handsome annuities with the extra $7,000 the small company offers, but this alternative does not suggest itself readily.

When seniors are put to speculating how much money they would like to make twenty or thirty years hence, they cite what they feel are modest figures. Back in forty-nine it was $10,000. Since then the rising cost of living has taken it up higher, but the median doesn't usually surpass $15,000. For the most part seniors do not like to talk of the future in terms of the dollar—on several occasions I have been politely lectured by someone for so much as bringing the point up.

In popular fiction, . . . heroes aren't any less materialistic than they used to be, but they are decidedly more sanctimonious about it. So with seniors. While they talk little about money, they talk a great deal about the good life. This life is, first of all, calm and ordered. Many a senior confesses that he's thought of a career in teaching, but as he talks it appears that it is not so much that he likes teaching itself as the sort of life he associates with it—there is a touch of elms and quiet streets in the picture. For the good life is equable; it is a nice place out in the suburbs, a wife and three children, one, maybe two cars (you know, a little knock-about for the wife to run down to the station in), and a summer place up at the lake or out on the Cape, and, later, a good college education for the children. It is not, seniors explain, the money that counts.

Is the good life still thought of in material terms?

They have been getting more and more relaxed on the matter each year. In the immediate postwar years they were somewhat nervous about the chances for the good life. They seemed almost psychotic on the subject of a depression, and when they explained a preference for the big corporation they did so largely on the grounds of security. When I talked to students in 1949, on almost every campus I heard one recurring theme: adventure was all very well, but it was smarter to make a compromise in order to get a depression-proof sanctuary. "I don't think A T & T is very exciting," one senior put it, "but that's the company I'd like to join. If a depression comes there will always be an A T & T." (Another favorite was the food industry: people always have

Is avoidance of risk taking and concern for security a fault, as the author implies? Why or why not?

Occupations: What we did and what we do

In 1870, out of every 100 people in the United States, 10 years and older . . .

Farmers 24

Farm women 24

Urban housewives 19

Miners or factory workers 9

Students 6

Traders and financiers 3

Transportation workers 2

Professionals (teachers, doctors, etc) 2

Construction workers 3

Domestics and other personal-service workers 4

Unemployed 2

Government employees 1

Retired people 1

Now, out of every 100 people 16 years and older . . .

Farmers 3

All housewives and househusbands 21

Miners or factory workers 13

Traders ("middle men" and their employees) 11

Students 5

Other self-employed people 5

Armed-service men and women 2

Transportation and utility workers 3

Financiers and real-estate brokers 3

Construction workers 3

Professionals 9

Unemployed 3

Domestic and other personal-service workers 1

Government employees 9

Retired and disabled people 9

Note: A century ago, 10-year-olds frequently entered the labor force; now the figure used by statisticians is 16.

to eat.) Corporation recruiters were unsettled to find that seniors seemed primarily interested in such things as pension benefits and retirement programs.

Seven years of continuing prosperity have made a great difference. Students are still interested in security but they no longer see it as a matter of security *versus* opportunity. Now, when they explain their choice, it is that the corporation is security *and* opportunity both. . . .

. . . When they talk about security they like to make the point that it is the psychic kind of security that interests them most. They want to be of service. Occasionally, their description of service borders on the mawkish, as though the goal was simply to defend the little people, but underneath there is real concern. Seniors want to do something *worth while*.

This worth-whileness needs some qualification. To listen to seniors talk, one would assume that there has been an upsurge of seniors heading toward such service careers as the ministry. There is no evidence of such a rush. The public variety of service doesn't attract either. Seniors scarcely mention politics as a career and even for the more aseptic forms of public service they show little enthusiasm; the number aiming for the foreign services or the civil services has been declining, and this decline was well under way before the Washington investigations.

If they are going to be worth while, seniors want to be worth while with other people. Their ideal of service is a gregarious one—the kind of service you do others right in the midst of them and not once removed. A student at a round-table discussion on the pursuit of happiness put it this way: "People who are just selfish and wrapped up in themselves have the most trouble. And people who are interested in other people . . . are the type of person that is not too much concerned with security. Somehow the security is provided in the things they do, and they are able to reach out beyond themselves."

• • •

The bureaucrat as hero is new to America, and older, conventional dreams of glory do linger on—the lawyer brilliantly turning the tables in cross-examination, the young scientist discovering the secret in the microscope late at night. Even in corporations' institutional advertising there is some cultural lag—many an ad still shows us the young man dreaming by himself of new frontiers as he looks up at a star or a rainbow or a beautiful hunk of alto-cumulus clouds. But slowly the young man at the microscope is being joined by other young men at microscopes; instead of one lone man dreaming, there are three or four young men. Year by year, our folklore is catching up with the needs of organization man.

• • •

Seniors do not deny that the lone researcher or the entrepreneur can also serve others. But neither do they think much about it. Their impulses, their training, the whole climate of the times, incline them to work that is tangibly social. Whether as a member of a corporation, a group medicine clinic, or a law factory, they see the collective as the best vehicle for service.

To a degree, of course, this is a self-ennobling apologia for seeking the comfortable life —and were they thoroughly consistent they would more actively recognize that public service is social too. But it is not mere rationalization; the senior is quite genuine in believing that while all collective effort may be worth while, some kinds are more so. The organization-bound senior can argue that he is going to the main tent, the place where each foot pound of his energy will go the farthest in helping people. Like the young man of the Middle Ages who went off to join holy orders, he is off for the center of society.

Why do you think the '50s generation valued the company man above the rugged individualist? Does your generation think the same way?

KNOX COUNTY, KENTUCKY: THE OTHER AMERICA
John Fetterman

The aspirations of college men defined the outlook and concerns of one segment of the population in the fifties, the well-to-do middle class. But there was another large part of the population, the working poor, that had quite different concerns. Although the 1960s were a time of relative prosperity, poverty was a pressing problem, though largely unrecognized and unacknowledged.

When the dimensions of poverty in this country were finally exposed in the 1960s, the region called "Appalachia" came to symbolize all the worst aspects of the problem. Knox County, in eastern Kentucky, is in that region. Although the area contains fabled amounts of prized energy resources, especially coal, the sad and debilitating evidences of poverty and suffering are everywhere evident. Corporate mining interests are largely at fault. The profits reaped from the area have gone elsewhere, leaving both land and people scarred by their encounter with "progress."

The following article exposes some of the social and economic costs of this progress. Is welfare the solution to such technologically induced poverty? Given our economic system of private enterprise for profit, can poverty ever be eliminated?

There are eight million mountaineers left in Appalachia. Many are leaving. But some are staying—in determination or in despair. Knox County is not the worst of the mountain counties. Nor is it the best. It is merely the county where one day they dedicated a courthouse and where one day a decision was made to visit a place called Stinking Creek.

The Kentucky Department of Commerce and the Knox County Chamber of Commerce have caused to be published a bold little booklet extolling "Industrial Resources, Barbourville, Kentucky." It reveals that the 1960 census credited Knox County with 25,258 living souls, of whom 3,211 live in Barbourville, the county seat. It further advises that 1,187 men and 1,511 women are available as a labor supply.

Barbourville, the booklet says, is 493 miles from Chicago, 388 miles from Detroit, and 829 miles from New York. The study makes the statement, "The inhabitants of Knox County are primarily engaged in agriculture."

We shall see.

The booklet also makes other information available to interested industrial planners:

• The average weekly earnings during 1961 were $51.89 for all industries and $47.20 for manufacturing. During the same period the state average was $83.44 for all industries and $96.07 for manufacturing.

• In 1960, per capita income for Knox County was $501; per capita income for Kentucky was $1,573, far below the national average of $2,223. Knox County ranked 119th among Kentucky's 120 counties and Kentucky ranked 46th among the 50 states.

- The largest employer in Barbourville is a firm which manufactures brassieres and employs around 150 people.

- Knox County operates on an annual budget of something over $125,000.

- The net assessed value of property in Knox County was given as $14,331,725.

Why is poverty a continuing problem in the richest country in the world?

But Knox County is not primarily in the agricultural business, nor is it in the timber business or the coal business, or the brassiere business: Knox County, like all counties of Appalachia, is in the welfare business. And business is great.

Of the 6,500 dwelling units, only 10 percent have plumbing, and about 6 percent of the 20,625 acres of crop land is in good condition. More than 64 percent of the population receives some kind of welfare assistance—not counting medical aid. About half of the lunches in the school lunch programs are served free, because children cannot pay the price of ten cents.

. . .

In Knox County the collecting of welfare benefits has far outstripped the manufacture of brassieres as the backbone of the economy.

Perhaps the most basic and interesting of all the phenomena of the welfare county is the surplus-commodity program. Its administration is simple. A family gets itself approved, is issued a card, and from then on it collects its fair share of the nation's food bounty once a month.

In Knox County, as this is written, 8,461 people enjoy these benefits. The surplus commodities are distributed in a dingy little building on the eastern outskirts of the city to ragtag descendants of men who would fight to the death rather than "be beholden to any man."

In a year, a quarter of a million Kentuckians were given 56,000,000 pounds of surplus foodstuffs that had an estimated wholesale value of around $13,000,000. The recipient families draw a monthly average of around 100 pounds of powdered milk, rice, meal, flour, lard, dried eggs, butter, canned beef and pork, cheese, beans, peanut butter, and occasional cans of fruit.

The commodity food programs are administered on the local level and are regarded with horror by students of political science for the simple reason that the control of food

Some people live in rural America today very much the way they have lived for a century. Except for an ancient automobile and one or two other items, their lives are almost untouched by the modern world.

204

can lead to the control of votes. Charges and denials, innuendoes and inefficiency, are handmaidens of the program.

As for the commodities themselves, most are of high quality. Unattractively packaged by the United States Department of Agriculture in brown boxes or stenciled tin cans, the contents are first rate. The beef and pork, cooked in big iron skillets on wood-burning stoves, is delicious. And so is the cheese, which the occasional visitor "bums" for a lunch up a hollow. The peanut butter is also very good. Many mountaineers dislike the rice and do not know how to prepare it. But they all know what to do with the lard, since frying in deep grease is standard procedure.

But children grow tired of the "commodity food," and rebel. Some mountaineers use the food to trade. Some feed it to the hogs. Others wisely use the commodities as a way to vary their diet of biscuits, coffee, garden beans, corn, and boiled or fried pork.

Stinking Creek is . . . a part of Knox County. It is neither the best nor the worst part. It is typical of nothing, because every hollow of the thousands in eastern Kentucky bears its own particular characteristics dictated by the nature and size of the creek that drains it, the families that settled it, and the particular array of welfare programs that sustain it.

· · ·

Stinking Creek is not a community. It is an area of steep slopes and narrow bottoms sprinkled with homes that range from neat painted clapboard houses—some of them even boasting an inside bathroom—to tottering, sagging little shacks. Each home is a little society unto itself, and many families find they have little in common with their neighbors. They differ in their religion, morals, ethics, and their attitudes toward the welfare program. Family bloodlines are complicated; and although there is a deep feeling of attachment to one's "kin," there is little sense of community unity.

The head-hanging shyness and suspiciousness often credited to the mountaineer are merely his generations-old habit of keeping his nose out of other people's business. Outward signs of love—even between husband and wife—are rare. When affection is shown, it almost always is for the "baby" of the family or for the oldest member.

Mountain homes, those of the very poor, follow a pattern. A room in front, one or two double beds, and a sagging couch in front of a television set being paid for from welfare checks; another room directly behind, full of beds, dark and musty and always with the feeling of dampness; a small room or a lean-to used as a kitchen with a wood- or coal-burning stove, a rickety table, wooden shelves for storing things, and a collection of often-repaired chairs. There are door facings at all the doors, but rarely are there doors. Some doorways modestly boast faded strips of cotton material that can be pulled together for a semblance of privacy.

There is a smell of poverty that is characteristic of many houses along Stinking Creek: a flat, weary, penetrating aroma of seasoned and rotting wood, unwashed clothing and bodies. But the smell of poverty is strangely similar to the smell of prosperous mountain farm homes. Some find it overwhelmingly insufferable. Others find in the flat, strong smell of human bodies a sense of permanence, of enduring things. After several days in the hollows, an elevator filled with ladies in town for a convention is unbearable. The entrapped reek of oils and perfumes and powders can be more nauseating than anything encountered in Stinking Creek—or in any hollow.

An outhouse has a stench of its own, of course. But these are neither an invention of, nor peculiar to, the mountains. Outhouses by the thousands are found in other rural areas across our nation—and even in our cities—and they are often regarded as "quaint." It is customary, however, to gasp in disgust at a two-holer in Appalachia as though it were a temple erected to some god of moral degeneration.

The mountaineer is what he is simply because he was born what he is. Each hollow has its moonshine peddlers and loose women and lazy men and complaining women. And each hollow has its courageous men and determined women who battle hopeless odds to bring their broods to a better life. But the best way to know something of Stinking Creek—and thereby something of Appalachia—is to meet and talk with and learn to know some of the people who live there. Not to study them with the idea of categorizing them into meaningless groups, but to sit and listen.

· · ·

Those who would attempt to separate the citizens of Stinking Creek into two groups could do no better than repeat the words of Golden Slusher:

Does welfare help the poor, or does it in fact hurt them by masking the causes of poverty and treating merely symptoms?

"What don't work is drawin'."

The majority are "drawin'." They draw welfare checks or commodities or both, and these are the basis of their economic security. The balance are working—for the time being.

Golden Slusher was working. It was a blowing, snowy day, and the warmth from his small coal fireplace was welcome. Slusher is a muscular, quiet man in his forties, and not a talker. But he is hospitable and willing to share his fireplace on a wintry day. The Slushers had no children. Mrs. Slusher, a small, wiry, dark-haired woman, sat silently back near the edge of the circular yellow glow from the fireplace. Nearer the fire sat Mrs. Slusher's mother, Mrs. Betty Smallwood, who is eighty-six and who sits and rocks and silently recollects, and complains of her heart.

Golden Slusher knows better than to try to farm as his ancestors did. The soil on the ridges above Pigeon Creek is thin and sandy and heavy with gravel. It contains little clay, and cannot retain moisture. The plant-food content is low. There is no level land along the banks of Pigeon Creek.

Golden Slusher is a logger. He arises before dawn, goes to the woods over in Bell County, hitches up the mules he keeps there, and all day strains his still-powerful muscles to drag out the logs that keep him alive—and off the welfare rolls.

"I ain't drawin'. I'm loggin'," he repeats.

But not many men have his stamina.

It is always easiest to talk with the old people, of whom there are many. They know the creek well, and have a serenity from long years of living with the hills, and an instinctive politeness. Most of the old men once worked in the deep mines. The mines killed many of them and maimed many more. To those who worked and lived, the mines left memories that will not die until the last old man dies.

There are many such old men on Stinking Creek. Ed Sizemore and Frank Patterson are two of them.

Ed Sizemore . . . had his own private coal mine. It was only a small outcropping of coal on the hillside behind his house. But Ed could take a wheelbarrow back there, pick around in the hole he had dug, and return with his own private coal supply. But he doesn't do that much anymore because his back hurts. "If I bend my back it gives me such miseries I can't stand it," he said. He went to work in the mines when he was fourteen, and stayed there until about a year ago.

His present age is a matter of dispute between him and the federal government. Ed is trying to get social security.

Stinking Creek runs directly behind Ed Sizemore's house. A huge boulder sits on the bank to deflect the torrent when the creek is swollen from the spring rains. So far, the boulder has saved his house from each succeeding flood. "It turns the tide right back into the creek," Ed said.

He massaged the small of his back through his loosely fitting overalls, and tried to tell of his difficulties with federal authority. "I don't get a dime from the government," he said. Hurt filled his pale blue eyes. He shuffled his blocky figure beneath the folds of the overalls. "Oh, I got a little compensation when I got hurt. I'm going in front of the doctors agin 'fore long. One's a social-security doctor, too. I got plenty in that social security. Buddy, I worked years and years before social security ever thought of coming in. I was working when the man brought that card up to me for me to sign.

"I said, 'What is it?' It was all green to me.

"I put up most of my life in a mine. I made my living in a hill and raised fourteen kids. Under the union I made good—twenty-five or thirty a day. Under a scab mine you had to really work to get ten a shift.

"Hit'll be a year the sixteenth of this month since I was hurt. I'm old enough to retire, as far as that goes. They sent and got fifty-four as my age. I'm 'way older than that. My mother ought to know my age. Well, I was sixty-two years old two years ago, but they wouldn't have it that way. I just let it go for then. I seen I couldn't do no better.

"The govermint ought to see to a man when he's down and out. But they are hardest on the man who put it in, in the world. He can put it in, but he can't get it out. And nobody in this whole county helped me."

Ed Sizemore remembers the mines well, but not with fondness. Like most old miners, he had a horror that his sons would follow him into the mines. One son did. "Me and

Is it the failure of individuals or of the economic system that makes welfare necessary? What does this man think?

206

Each slice of this economic pie represents one–fifth of all American families and the percentage of the total income each fifth gets. The whole pie keeps getting bigger. The average family income in 1929 ($6,861) has doubled to $13,622. All figures are in 1974 dollars— that is, corrected for inflation. But the chart shows a persistent maldistribution of income despite some change. The biggest shift was the drop in the richest fifth from 54.4 percent of income in 1929 to the present 41 percent. But the lowest fifth's share rose only from 3.8 percent in 1929 to 5.4 percent now.

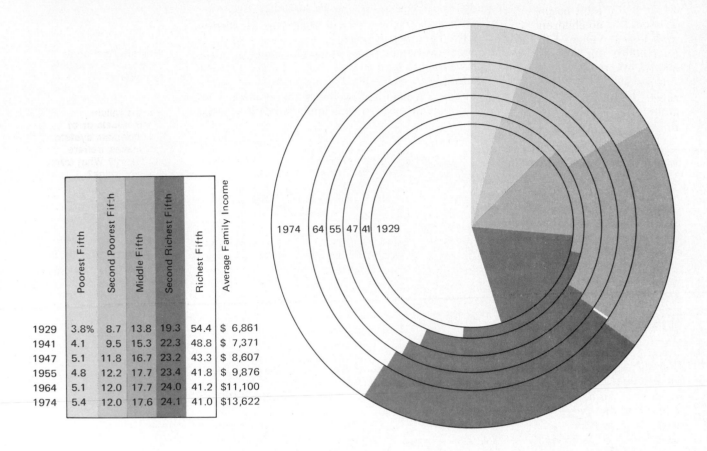

	Poorest Fifth	Second Poorest Fifth	Middle Fifth	Second Richest Fifth	Richest Fifth	Average Family Income
1929	3.8%	8.7	13.8	19.3	54.4	$ 6,861
1941	4.1	9.5	15.3	22.3	48.8	$ 7,371
1947	5.1	11.8	16.7	23.2	43.3	$ 8,607
1955	4.8	12.2	17.7	23.4	41.8	$ 9,876
1964	5.1	12.0	17.7	24.0	41.2	$11,100
1974	5.4	12.0	17.6	24.1	41.0	$13,622

one of my boys worked a seam together oncet. I tried and tried to get him not to go back in. He finally quit and went to Detroit. He runs a 'dozer up there."

Ed Sizemore was injured while "robbing" a mine, a practice that has left many a body entombed forever beneath the mountains. As the old deep miners worked farther and farther into a seam, they left pillars of coal to support the treacherous roof of the mine. After the coal was all taken out, the miners would begin to "rob" the mine—take out the supporting pillars. Starting with the pillar farthest back in the mine, they would salvage all that was left, working their way back to the mine mouth and ready to flee for the opening at the first sign of a fault in the roof.

Mining, Ed said, was dangerous enough without having to rob the seams. "The electric cable, for one thing, could kill you deader than thunder, and it did kill some. I done most my mining in Leslie County. You'd lay on your side or get on your knees, anyway you can get to get at the coal. We was robbing. Getting the last of it."

Ed Sizemore cocked his head to look across the creek, and was silent for a long time. Perhaps he was reliving the day when the mine roof came crashing down and put the miseries in his back. But when he turned back, he did not mention robbing a mine again.

His first wife died twenty-three years ago, and that was when he bought his forty acres on Stinking Creek. He quickly remarried. "I couldn't rest easy working in the mines with the kids home by theirself. So I married her. She help me raise them.

"This is a good spot to live. In forty-seven I had this whole bottom in sweet taters big as your two fists from a goose egg up. They just rot in the ground, but I had enough left for the winter. I had two big mares, and I had some old time getting them up that hill out of the tide when the rains come."

The smell of beans cooking had been coming from the house. Now Ed's wife, a

What social cost of progress do these passages underline? Is progress worth the price?

pleasant woman with a broad smile, came to the kitchen door, made an almost imperceptible signal, and Ed Sizemore eased toward the house.

"Come back any time you take a notion," he said.

Frank Patterson . . . was sitting on a log in the sunshine up by the road near his house. The spot is the last place you can turn a car without climbing all the way to the head of the hollow, and the road was muddy from a recent rain. Frank's unblinking eyes were fixed on the camera. He shoved his hat back a bit on his head and said evenly, "Put under that picture, 'Frank Patterson who's lived eighty-two years!' "

In eighty-two years, he has done about everything a man can do on Stinking Creek. He let his eyes sweep across the hills. "I used to farm all those hills 'till I got wore out . . . and the hills got wore out . . . no timber . . . no nothin'."

The Pattersons are a big family—or a big "generation," as mountain people it. They came to the hollow early, crossing the shallow place in the Cumberland River, then

Why are rural areas especially susceptible to poverty?

For every critic who emphasizes poverty, there is a champion of American progress. Yet even progress has its price. The American Dream, magnet for millions, was sustained by hope. And material progress, particularly over the past generation, has certainly provided more abundance than our ancestors could have imagined. At the same time, the scenes of destruction and congestion are all about us. Where is it to lead? Should we call a halt to economic growth? What do you think would happen if we did?

turning northeastward into the Stinking Creek watershed. The first Patterson was "old man" John Patterson, Frank's grandfather.

"There wasn't no record kept of nobody," Frank said. "But John Patterson was the first in. He fought in the old Revolution War and didn't die 'til after I was married. John was old enough to be using a walking cane, and I was about twenty when he died. He was a big tall fellow. Weighed about one seventy-five. He farmed and hunted. John had eight children. My notion is he came from Tennessee. John married a Golden, Polly Ann Golden. They used to live up the hill there."

The old man, John Patterson, who had come to live upon his land given him for his service against the British, did leave a large "generation." There are many Pattersons in the hollow.

Frank is the oldest Patterson now. And the family records are in his head.

"My daddy was James, or Jim. Jim lived to eighty-four, and my mother was a Taylor. There were nine of us children." Frank and a sister are the only survivors of that family.

As was the custom, the family land was divided among the children, then among the children's children, until the vast mountain holdings dwindled to tiny plots.

"My mother aired [was heir to] three hundred acres of land, and we divided it up. John had one hundred acres at Messer and sold it out. I own this little bit of property here where I'm livin'."

Frank waved a bony hand toward the bottom below his house, a wide space beside the creek where a square, concrete block one-room school now sits. The name of the school is Erose.

"The county paid me $150 for that bottom. I tried to get out of selling it, but they forced me to. That was going on thirty year ago."

Mrs. Patterson is a small woman, gray and prim, friendly and frank. Her tiny body appears to be buried in layers of cotton petticoats, skirts, and an apron. Her dark eyes are alert and inquisitive. The best single word to describe her, perhaps, is "sweet." If a woman were needed to personify the perfect mountain grandmother, Mrs. Patterson would make an excellent candidate. The Pattersons were sitting on the porch of their sturdy, ancient house. The yard is surrounded by its "palings," a fence of slender slats that encircles and protects the yard.

• • •

Mrs. Patterson spoke softly and slowly, sometimes pausing to knit her pale brow in concentration, as though she wanted to make sure there would be no inaccuracies: "Lord, I'm seventy-five, and I was Mary Jane Mills. My generation of Mills' lived in Clay County."

Frank interrupted. "I think we got eighty grandchildren."

Mrs. Patterson's voice was patient and firm: "We got sixty-eight grandchildren and thirty-three great-grandchildren. We got a big generation." Mrs. Patterson smoothed her cotton apron. "It don't hurt nobody to tell what you think," she said, "I think there's a lot around here that'll write and try to get more added on their check. Some are getting $64 and up that away. We hain't. They claimed we drawed too much to get commodities. You ain't allowed to sell a calf unless you turn it in and they cut your check down. And we ain't got no way to get out of here to buy. I just shop around these little places—I call them peanut stores."

She said most of the young people are gone. "People have just quit lookin' for work around here and went off hunting for jobs. There ain't nothin' around here to work at. We got two children still live here on the creek. The rest scattered over the whole known world, 'peers like to me. Some in Clay County, some in Bell County, some in Dayton, some in Cleveland."

Is the trend toward the movement away from the land by the younger people a healthy one? Why or why not?

So Mrs. Patterson runs her four-room house for only her husband now, and they live in apparent mountain comfort on their old-age benefits. "We draw $55 apiece every month."

"We git some out of there," Frank said, waving toward the small garden just outside the paling fence. "I own, in all, sixty acres." There is coal under the land, but Frank, like most mountaineers, considers it a curse rather than a blessing. "There's plenty coal here," he said. "There's a seven-foot vein. But most of the coal around here was sold out years ago. They sold mineral rights sixty years ago at least.

"Here we are sittin' on millions in coal, oil, and gas. They claim there's a pocket of oil and gas forty miles square in here. Over on Red Bird you can hear that gas a-squealin' before you get within half a mile of it. They struck oil, and it run just like water 'till they plugged it up.

What do you think he means by this?

"It don't do this country no good."

210

DEMONSTRATING IN MISSISSIPPI
Anne Moody

The 1960s were a time of demonstrations, sit-ins, and protest marches. The first wave of this social turmoil was the civil rights movement, which may be said to have begun in Montgomery, Alabama, in 1955 when a black woman refused to give up her seat on a segregated bus and a young black Baptist minister named Martin Luther King led the black community in protest. Sit-ins, freedom rides, and other forms of demonstrations spread across the South eventually leading to the desegregation of buses, restaurants, and schools. Initially, however, the protests met with massive resistance and violence. The next essay is the autobiographical account of a black college student during the violent summer of 1963. Were the results of the demonstrations worth the violence?

A few weeks after I got involved with the Tougaloo chapter of the NAACP, they organized a demonstration at the state fair in Jackson. Just before it was to come off, Medgar Evers came to campus and gave a big hearty speech about how "Jackson was gonna move." Tougaloo sent four picketers to the fair, and one of them was Dave Jones. Because he was chosen to be the spokesman for the group, he was the first to be interviewed on TV. That evening when the demonstration was televised on all the news programs, it seemed as though every girl in the dorm was down in the lounge in front of the set. They were all shooting off about how they would take part in the next demonstration. The girl Dave was now seeing was running all around talking about how good he looked.

Dave and the other demonstrators had been arrested and were to be bailed out around eight that night. By eight-thirty a lot of us were sitting outside on the dormitory steps awaiting their arrival, and they still hadn't shown up. One of the girls had just gone inside to call the NAACP headquarters in Jackson, when suddenly two police cars came speeding through the campus. Students came running from every building. Within minutes the police cars were completely surrounded, blocked in from every direction. There were two cops in the front seat of each car. They looked frightened to death of us. When the students got out of the cars, they were hugged, kissed, and congratulated for well over an hour. All during this time the cops remained in their seats behind locked doors. Finally someone started singing "We Shall Overcome," and everyone joined in. When we finished singing, someone suggested we go to the football field and have a big rally. In minutes every student was on the football field singing all kinds of freedom songs, giving testimonies as to what we were going to do, and praying and carrying on something terrible. The rally ended at twelve-thirty and by this time, all the students were ready to tear Jackson to pieces.

The following evening Medgar Evers again came to campus to, as he put it, "get some of Tougaloo's spirit and try and spread it around all over Jackson." He gave us a good pep talk and said we would be called upon from time to time to demonstrate.

In mid-September I was back on campus. But didn't very much happen until February when the NAACP held its annual convention in Jackson. They were having a whole lot of interesting speakers: Jackie Robinson, Floyd Patterson, Curt Flood, Margaretta Belafonte, and many others. I wouldn't have missed it for anything. I was so excited that I sent one of the leaflets home to Mama and asked her to come.

Three days later I got a letter from Mama with dried-up tears on it, forbidding me to go to the convention. It went on for more than six pages. She said if I didn't stop that shit she would come to Tougaloo and kill me herself. She told me about the time I last visited her, on Thanksgiving, and she had picked me up at the bus station. She said the sheriff had been by, telling her I was messing around with that NAACP group. She said he told her if I didn't stop it, I could not come back there any more. He said that they didn't need any of those NAACP people messing around in Centreville. She ended the letter by saying that she had burned the leaflet I sent her. "Please don't send any more of that stuff here. I don't want nothing to happen to us here," she said. "If you keep that up, you will never be able to come home again."

Why were students generally more enthusiastic about civil rights than their elders, who had probably suffered more from discrimination?

I was so damn mad after her letter, I felt like taking the NAACP convention to Centreville. I think I would have, if it had been in my power to do so. The remainder of the week I thought of nothing except going to the convention. I didn't know exactly what to do about it. I didn't want Mama or anyone at home to get hurt because of me.

I had felt something was wrong when I was home. During the four days I was there, Mama had tried to do everything she could to keep me in the house. When I said I was going to see some of my old classmates, she pretended she was sick and said I would have to cook. I knew she was acting strangely, but I hadn't known why. I thought Mama just wanted me to spend most of my time with her, since this was only the second time I had been home since I entered college as a freshman.

Things kept running through my mind after that letter from Mama. My mind was so active, I couldn't sleep at night. I remembered the one time I did leave the house to go to the post office. I had walked past a bunch of white men on the street on my way through town and one said, "Is that the gal goin' to Tougaloo?" He acted kind of mad or something, and I didn't know what was going on. I got a creepy feeling, so I hurried home. When I told Mama about it, she just said, "A lotta people don't like that school." I knew what she meant. Just before I went to Tougaloo, they had housed the Freedom Riders there. The school was being criticized by whites throughout the state.

I had become very friendly with my social science professor, John Salter, who was in charge of NAACP activities on campus. All during the year, while the NAACP conducted a boycott of the downtown stores in Jackson, I had been one of Salter's most faithful canvassers and church speakers. During the last week of school, he told me that sit-in demonstrations were about to start in Jackson and that he wanted me to be the spokesman for a team that would sit-in at Woolworth's lunch counter. The two other demonstrators would be classmates of mine, Memphis and Pearlena. Pearlena was a dedicated NAACP worker, but Memphis had not been very involved in the Movement on campus. It seemed that the organization had had a rough time finding students who were in a position to go to jail. I had nothing to lose one way or the other. Around ten o'clock the morning of the demonstrations, NAACP headquarters alerted the news services. As a result, the police department was also informed, but neither the policemen nor the newsmen knew exactly where or when the demonstrations would start. They stationed themselves along Capitol Street and waited.

To divert attention from the sit-in at Woolworth's, the picketing started at J. C. Penney's a good fifteen minutes before. The pickets were allowed to walk up and down in front of the store three or four times before they were arrested, At exactly 11 A.M., Pearlena, Memphis, and I entered Woolworth's from the rear entrance. We separated as soon as we stepped into the store, and made small purchases from various counters. Pearlena had given Memphis her watch. He was to let us know when it was 11:14. At 11:14 we were to join him near the lunch counter and at exactly 11:15 we were to take seats at it.

What theory lay behind nonviolent tactics? How were they supposed to accomplish civil rights objectives?

Seconds before 11:15 we were occupying three seats at the previously segregated Woolworth's lunch counter. In the beginning the waitresses seemed to ignore us, as if they really didn't know what was going on. Our waitress walked past us a couple of times before she noticed we had started to write our own orders down and realized we wanted service. She asked us what we wanted. We began to read to her from our order slips. She told us that we would be served at the back counter, which was for Negroes.

"We would like to be served here," I said.

The protests of the early 1960s were focused on civil rights, particularly on the traditionally racist institutions of the South. Courageous and energetic people, many of them young, threw themselves into demonstrations and voting drives. Only later would the focus shift to racist patterns in the North and elsewhere, and by then the nation's attention had drifted to other concerns and crises. To what extent was the civil rights movement successful in altering the social and political life of the South? Has the economic stiuation changed? What prevented further change? In what ways is the political consciousness of the 1960s related to your sense of politics today? Why does the enormous Washington demonstration which heard Martin Luther King's "I Have A Dream" speech in 1963 seem so out of character today?

213

The waitress started to repeat what she had said, then stopped in the middle of the sentence. She turned the lights out behind the counter, and she and the other waitresses almost ran to the back of the store, deserting all their white customers. I guess they thought that violence would start immediately after the whites at the counter realized what was going on. There were five or six other people at the counter. A couple of them just got up and walked away. A girl sitting next to me finished her banana split before leaving. A middle-aged white woman who had not yet been served rose from her seat and came over to us. "I'd like to stay here with you," she said, "but my husband is waiting."

The newsmen came in just as she was leaving. They must have discovered what was going on shortly after some of the people began to leave the store. One of the newsmen ran behind the woman who spoke to us and asked her to identify herself. She refused to give her name, but said she was a native of Vicksburg and a former resident of California. When asked why she had said what she had said to us, she replied, "I am in sympathy with the Negro movement." By this time a crowd of cameramen and reporters had gathered around us taking pictures and asking questions, such as Where were we from? Why did we sit-in? What organization sponsored it? Were we students? From what school? How were we classified?

In the 1960s the media were often accused of causing dissent. What part did the media play?

I told them that we were all students at Tougaloo College, that we were represented by no particular organization, and that we planned to stay there even after the store closed. "All we want is service," was my reply to one of them. After they had finished probing for about twenty minutes, they were almost ready to leave.

At noon, students from a nearby white high school started pouring in to Woolworth's. When they first saw us they were sort of surprised. They didn't know how to react. A few started to heckle and the newsmen became interested again. Then the white students started chanting all kinds of anti-Negro slogans. We were called a little bit of everything. The rest of the seats except the three we were occupying had been roped off to prevent others from sitting down. A couple of the boys took one end of the rope and made it into a hangman's noose. Several attempts were made to put it around our necks. The crowds grew as more students and adults came in for lunch.

We kept our eyes straight forward and did not look at the crowd except for occasional glances to see what was going on. All of a sudden I saw a face I remembered—the drunkard from the bus station sit-in. My eyes lingered on him just long enough for us to recognize each other. Today he was drunk too, so I don't think he remembered where he had seen me before. He took out a knife, opened it, put it in his pocket, and then began to pace the floor. At this point, I told Memphis and Pearlena what was going on. Memphis suggested that we pray. We bowed our heads, and all hell broke loose. A man rushed forward, threw Memphis from his seat, and slapped my face. Then another man who worked in the store threw me against an adjoining counter.

Down on my knees on the floor, I saw Memphis lying near the lunch counter with blood running out of the corners of his mouth. As he tried to protect his face, the man who'd thrown him down kept kicking him against the head. If he had worn hard-soled shoes instead of sneakers, the first kick probably would have killed Memphis. Finally a man dressed in plain clothes identified himself as a police officer and arrested Memphis and his attacker.

Pearlena had been thrown to the floor. She and I got back on our stools after Memphis was arrested. There were some white Tougaloo teachers in the crowd. They asked Pearlena and me if we wanted to leave. They said that things were getting too rough. We didn't know what to do. While we were trying to make up our minds, we were joined by Joan Trumpauer. Now there were three of us and we were integrated. The crowd began to chant, "Communists, Communists, Communists." Some old man in the crowd ordered the students to take us off the stools.

Why, almost ten years after the heyday of McCarthyism, was "Communism" still a scare word used to brand people and causes?

"Which one should I get first?" a big husky boy said.

"That white nigger," the old man said.

The boy lifted Joan from the counter by her waist and carried her out of the store. Simultaneously, I was snatched from my stool by two high school students. I was dragged about thirty feet toward the door by my hair when someone made them turn me loose. As I was getting up off the floor, I saw Joan coming back inside. We started back to the center of the counter to join Pearlena. Lois Chaffee, a white Tougaloo faculty member, was now sitting next to her. So Joan and I just climbed across the rope at the front end of the counter and sat down. There were now four of us, two whites and two Negroes, all women. The mob started smearing us with ketchup, mustard, sugar, pies, and everything on the counter. Soon Joan and I were joined by John Salter, but the moment he sat down he was hit on the jaw with what appeared to be brass knuckles. Blood gushed from his face and someone threw salt into the open wound. Ed King, Tougaloo's chaplain, rushed to him.

At the other end of the counter, Lois and Pearlena were joined by George Raymond, a CORE field worker and a student from Jackson State College. Then a Negro high school boy sat down next to me. The mob took spray paint from the counter and sprayed it on the new demonstrators. The high school student had on a white shirt; the word "nigger" was written on his back with red spray paint.

We sat there for three hours taking a beating when the manager decided to close the store because the mob had begun to go wild with stuff from other counters. He begged and begged everyone to leave. But even after fifteen minutes of begging, no one budged. They would not leave until we did. Then Dr. Beittel, the president of Tougaloo College, came running in. He said he had just heard what was happening.

About ninety policemen were standing outside the store; they had been watching the whole thing through the windows, but had not come in to stop the mob or do anything. President Beittel went outside and asked Captain Ray to come and escort us out. The captain refused, stating the manager had to invite him in before he could enter the premises, so Dr. Beittel himself brought us out. He had told the police that they had better protect us after we were outside the store. When we got outside, the policemen formed a single line that blocked the mob from us. However, they were allowed to throw at us everything they had collected. Within ten minutes, we were picked up by Reverend King in his station wagon and taken to the NAACP headquarters on Lynch Street.

After the sit-in, all I could think of was how sick Mississippi whites were. They believed so much in the segregated Southern way of life, they would kill to preserve it. I sat there in the NAACP office and thought of how many times they had killed when this way of life was threatened. I knew that the killing had just begun. "Many more will die before it is over with," I thought. Before the sit-in, I had always hated the whites in Mississippi. Now I knew it was impossible for me to hate sickness. The whites had a disease, an incurable disease in its final stage. What were our chances against such a disease? I thought of the students, the young Negroes who had just begun to protest, as young interns. When these young interns got older, I thought, they would be the best doctors in the world for social problems.

Were the 1960s the final stages of the disease of racism?

• • •

Mass rallies had [soon] come to be an every night event, and at each one the NAACP had begun to build up Medgar Evers. Somehow I had the feeling that they wanted him to become for Mississippi what Martin Luther King had been in Alabama. They were well on the way to achieving that, too.

After the rally on Tuesday, June 11, I had to stay in Jackson. I had missed the ride back to campus. Dave Dennis, the CORE field secretary for Mississippi, and his wife put me up for the night. We were watching TV around twelve-thirty, when a special news bulletin interrupted the program. It said, "Jackson NAACP leader Medgar Evers has just been shot."

We didn't believe what we were hearing. We just sat there staring at the TV screen. It was unbelievable. Just an hour or so earlier we were all with him. The next bulletin announced that he had died in the hospital soon after the shooting. We didn't know what to say or do. All night we tried to figure out what had happened, who did it, who was next, and it still didn't seem real.

First thing the next morning we turned on the TV. It showed films taken shortly after Medgar was shot in his driveway. We saw the pool of blood where he had fallen. We saw his wife sobbing almost hysterically as she tried to tell what had happened. Without even having breakfast, we headed for the NAACP headquarters. When we got there, they were trying to organize a march to protest Medgar's death. Newsmen, investigators, and reporters flooded the office. College and high school students and a few adults sat in the auditorium waiting to march.

Of the civil rights leaders of the 1960s, how many survive today?

• • •

The Sunday following Medgar's funeral, Reverend Ed King organized an integrated church-visiting team of six of us from the college. Another team was organized by a group in Jackson. Five or six churches were hit that day, including Governor Ross Barnett's. At each one they had prepared for our visit with armed policemen, paddy wagons, and dogs—which would be used in case we refused to leave after "ushers" had read us the prepared resolutions. There were about eight of these ushers at each church, and they were never exactly the usherly type. They were more on the order of Al Capone. I think this must have been the first time any of these men had worn a flower in his lapel. When we were asked to leave, we did. We were never even allowed to get past the first step.

A group of us decided that we would go to church again the next Sunday. This time we were quite successful. These visits had not been publicized as the first ones were, and they were not really expecting us. We went first to a Church of Christ, where we were greeted by the regular ushers. After reading us the same resolution we had heard last week, they offered to give us cab fare to the Negro extension of the church. Just as we had refused and were walking away, an old lady stopped us. "We'll sit with you," she said.

We walked back to the ushers with her and her family. "Please let them in, Mr. Calloway. We'll sit with them," the old lady said.

"Mrs. Dixon, the church has decided what is to be done. A resolution has been passed, and we are to abide by it."

"Who are we to decide such a thing? This is a house of God, and God is to make all of the decisions. He is the judge of us all," the lady said.

The ushers got angrier then and threatened to call the police if we didn't leave. We decided to go.

"We appreciate very much what you've done," I said to the old lady.

As we walked away from the church, we noticed the family leaving by a side entrance. The old lady was waving to us.

Two blocks from the church, we were picked up by Ed King's wife, Jeanette. She drove us to an Episcopal church. She had previously left the other two girls from our team there. She circled the block a couple of times, but we didn't see them anywhere. I suggested that we try the church. "Maybe they got in," I said. Mrs. King waited in the car for us. We walked up to the front of the church. There were no ushers to be seen. Apparently, services had already started. When we walked inside, we were greeted by two ushers who stood at the rear.

"May we help you?" one said.

"Yes," I said. "We would like to worship with you today."

"Will you sign the guest list, please, and we will show you to your seats," said the other.

I stood there for a good five minutes before I was able to compose myself. I had never prayed with white people in a white church before. We signed the guest list and were then escorted to two seats behind the other two girls in our team. We had all gotten in. The church service was completed without one incident. It was as normal as any church service. However, it was by no means normal to me. I was sitting there thinking any moment God would strike the life out of me. I recognized some of the whites, sitting around me in that church. If they were praying to the same God I was, then even God, I thought, was against me.

When the services were over the minister invited us to visit again. He said it as if he meant it, and I began to have a little hope.

Many churches in the South still remain segregated. Does this mean that the civil rights movement failed there?

On the whole have the conditions of blacks improved since the early 1960s?

What Happened to the Class of '65?

Michael Medved and David Wallechinsky

Ten years seems like a long time, especially when you are eighteen, but the years from 1965 to 1975 were filled with a great many horrible and dramatic events. Everyone tries at some point in his or her life to recapture the past, one reason, perhaps, that high school and college reunions are so well attended. The two authors of this article, graduates of a high school in an affluent suburb of Los Angeles, decided to record the experiences of their high-school class, and with those some of the events of the ten tumultuous years after they graduated. They uncovered some success stories and some accounts of failure, as you might expect. All reveal something of the tenor of their times. How many of the events recalled do you remember? Were these years, as one of their teachers remarked, "the saddest years of the century"?

The *Time* magazine article back in January 1965 was the biggest thing that had ever hit the Palisades. For weeks this quiet, comfortable corner of suburban Los Angeles was astir with controversy over what had been said, what had been implied. In the $100,000 homes, behind the broad lawns and carefully tended palms, the text of the article was debated over breakfast and dinner. And on the brand-new open-air campus of Palisades High School, the two thousand students chattered and worried and bragged, enjoying their place at the center of the stage.

For *Time* had selected this high school, and this senior class of '65, as the focus for its cover story on TODAY'S TEENAGERS. "In the mid-1960's," *Time* enthused, "smarter, subtler, and more sophisticated kids are pouring into and out of more expert, exacting and experimental schools." What better place to illustrate this trend than Palisades High School? The Los Angeles Board of Education had lavished $8 million on the construction of this stylish red brick facility in a secluded canyon overlooking the Pacific. The school was designed to attract the best teachers, and to service the most privileged students, in the city of Los Angeles. The neighborhoods that fed into Palisades High—Brentwood, Bel Air, Pacific Palisades—represented the sort of affluence that all America was striving to achieve. In one of the *Time* article's most controversial passages, a member of the high school faculty commented sardonically on this rarefied atmosphere:

> "These are the students' cars," says English Teacher Jeanne Hernandez, pointing to a fast collection of "wheels" ranging up to Jags, "and these are the teachers' cars," pointing to a sedate group of compacts and the like. "It's so lush here that it's unreal," she says. "After a while you feel like a missionary in the tropics. If you don't get out, you go native."

When we talked with her ten years later, Mrs. Hernandez was still marveling over the wealth of Palisades parents. "The principal at that time," she recalls, "was giving us the figure of forty-two thousand dollars for median income. I don't know how it was computed. But that's what he read to us at one of those new-term indoctrination meetings. It was so shocking that all you could hear was the concerted sound of indrawn breath."

It was only to be expected that this sort of background would produce a sense of isolation and security. Our Palisades classmates viewed the other stories in that January issue of *Time* as entertaining, perhaps, but hardly relevant to their day-to-day affairs. The big news of the week was the inauguration of President Lyndon Johnson, following his landslide victory over Barry Goldwater in the November elections. "The Great Society," Johnson declared in his inaugural, "is the excitement of becoming—always becoming... Is a new world coming? We welcome it—and we will bend it to the hope of man." Meanwhile, the Reverend Dr. Martin Luther King, Jr., announced that his 1965 civil rights drive would focus on the town of Selma, Alabama. Buddhist monks were demonstrating against the United States in faraway Vietnam. Winston Churchill had just died in England at the age of ninety, and *Time* devoted three pages to an article on his life. Hollywood marked the passing of another sort of greatness, as Jeanette MacDonald was honored with an enormous funeral. In sports, quarterback Y. A. Tittle of the New York Giants announced his retirement after seventeen years in professional football. And the newest hit of the TV season was *The Man from U.N.C.L.E.*, starring Robert Vaughan as the suave Napoleon Solo. Yet not even a discussion of this superhero could take our attention from *Time*'s detailed description of the social cliques, campus personalities and generational trends observed at Palisades High School.

Do political and social events help mark time for you, or do you rely more on personal memories?

There had always been a sense of celebrity and excitement about our group; we had known we were special even before *Time* told us so. Part of it was no doubt the Hollywood influence; the children of personalities such as Betty Hutton, Karl Malden, Henry Miller, Sterling Hayden, James Arness and Irving Wallace were highly visible on campus. Then there were the expectations of parents, teachers and now the press: we were part of the healthiest, most beautiful, best-educated and most affluent generation in the history of the world. We were, in fact, the natural leaders of that generation. Never mind *Time*'s dark hints about drinking, sexual promiscuity and unbridled hedonism in the Palisades senior class. We were the children of destiny, and we would make our way successfully through dangerous and uncharted seas. We were, as the article promised in its subtitle, "on the fringe of a golden era."

That era did not begin auspiciously. A month after graduation came the Watts riot, just fifteen miles from where we lived, and with it, America's first season of urban unrest. That same summer the Johnson Administration began the big American build-up in Vietnam. Then, in 1966, our old school was in the news again. It was *Newsweek* this time which did a special story on Palisades High, and the growing drug problem in the class that had followed us. Gone were the balmy, tranquil days of '65. With the draft calls rising and the first stirrings of student discontent, *Newsweek* found "something clearly amiss in Paradise" and wondered, somewhat implausibly, whether the Palisades might not become "a WASP Watts."

In the years that followed, through all the upheavals in sex, politics and life styles, our group was always at the forefront, always riding the crest of the wave. In the late sixties, when social commentators around the country began hailing the pioneers of an Aquarian Age, we had no question whom they had in mind. In his best-selling 1970 book, *The Greening of America*, Professor Charles Reich proclaimed "a great change" among "the bright, sensitive children of the affluent middle class." Specifically, this change centered on "the college class of 1969, which entered as freshmen in the fall of 1965" —once again, our class. "There is a revolution coming," Reich announced. "It will originate with the individual and with culture and it will change the political structure only as its final act.... This is the revolution of the new generation.... At the heart of everything is what we shall call a change of consciousness. This means a 'new head'— a new way of living—a new man."

How do you view the generation of the 1960s—as unrealistic dreamers or as models for your own generation?

Whatever happened to that "new man" who was supposed to change America? After ten years of intense publicity, he seemed to have slipped from sight. From the sober vantage point of 1976, how could we trace the "revolutionary" history of our generation?

...

THE KENNEDY ASSASSINATION

As members of the class of '65 we felt we were the Leaders of Tomorrow and expected that we would someday change the world. We knew that the future of mankind hung in the balance. We had gone through the Cuban missile crisis together—many of us in our parents' fallout shelters—just weeks after arriving at Palisades High School. Yet our first real confrontation with the fact that all stories do not have happy endings, and that bright promises are not always fulfilled, came that moment in junior year when we heard that the President had been shot. It was a nightmare of brief duration, and after a few days we returned to our classes, dances, debates and football games. Yet that November day foreshadowed the difficult days that lay ahead, and our universe could never again be entirely secure.

JEFF STOLPER: A RECOLLECTION OF THE EVENT AND REFLECTION ON TODAY

I was in the eleventh grade. I had Study Hall third or fourth period—I can't remember which. I was in the library with a friend of mine. He had just ordered his new surfboard a couple of weeks before and was supposed to pick it up that day. He snuck out of the library, which you're not supposed to do, over to the phone booth in the administration building. He came back and said, "I just heard something really weird. Kennedy has been shot. You know, people in the attendance office are crying."

I said, "Naw, it's got to be something else. They must have been sneezing or something." Then one of the monitors from the administration building came in, and talked to us over to the side. She said, "Yeah, everybody in there is crying. He was shot." At that time you'd never heard of anybody being shot except on TV. You remembered that cowboys being shot would get up afterwards. You figured that he was probably shot, but that he'd recover.

Sure enough, the announcement came over the PA system from the principal that he had been shot. They didn't say how bad it was. I remember now that it must have been third period, because I had gym fourth period that year. By the time I got to the gym they were changing in the locker room and the announcement came over that he was

The Presidency of John Fitzgerald Kennedy began with promises of political and social renaissance and ended in tragic martyrdom. His personality, looks, and rhetoric aroused a generation and raised expectations everywhere. Even now, so many years after his death, Kennedy's charisma still somehow touches many Americans. Do you feel this? How do you perceive JFK's importance in recent American history?

dead. Nobody in the gym could hear it. The rumors were that he died and Johnson had a heart attack and died. Then it was that he died and that Johnson had a heart attack but didn't die. No one knew what the story was until we got to lunch.

I remember Mr. Thomas was my gym teacher. He walked out of the gym office with a bag of basketballs and mumbled one or two words that no one could understand. He dropped the balls on the ground, went inside and left us out there on our own to do whatever we wanted to do. I didn't feel like doing anything. Most of the people I knew didn't feel like doing anything.

Then lunch period came around. Naturally, everybody was talking about what had happened and the possibilities of being attacked by Russia. You know, nuclear war and the whole bit. Later some people were joking around, but it wasn't the time to joke around. It was a sad event. It was something that the whole country experienced together. You know, that people *do* get killed, people *do* die. Life can be hard. I guess it was probably the first time that everybody in that high school experienced one feeling together.

In your opinion did the assassination strengthen the nation or undermine the confidence of its people?

. . .

If I had to choose, I'd rather go to high school when we did than go back as a student today. In our time a lot of things were a challenge. The bit with long hair was a real challenge that I enjoyed. Even the idea of avoiding the draft was a big challenge for me. There's no draft today. Breaking down the resistance of the opposite sex so they'd do what you wanted—that was a much bigger challenge when we went to school.

It's hard to say if the kids today are having a lot of fun. I think they're maturing faster because of all the freedom that is thrown upon them. There's a lot of dope floating around. I know that they don't go to the Bay Theatre. There's no more Sports Nights. The dances that I've seen, nobody dances.

Times are tougher now. It's harder to get a job. The kids in high school feel that. I always talk with my students and ask them what their plans are. Every one of those students has some sort of plan and some sort of goal set up. I have a lot of kids whose parents have been laid off work. They know that they've got to go out and face the world, and what it's really like. I don't think we had that problem when we were seniors.

Do you agree with his analysis of your generation?

I'd say that the whole country has lost some of its innocence. When we went to school, Kennedy was probably one of the biggest heroes. We had the Beatles and the Rolling Stones. Today the big hero is Superfly. It's a very different thing.

A lot of people from our class had a very tough time. I think some of them just peaked too early. They were trying so hard to achieve that number-one status in high school. By the time they got rolling into college, they had probably burned themselves out.

I never had that problem. I graduated way down in our class, and never felt the pressure that other people felt. I could never have pictured myself going back to Palisades to teach. I never had any desire! But once I started teaching, I was happy to be back at the old school. I enjoy it very much, although I still consider myself to be somewhat rebellious and hope to continue to stand up for what I feel is right.

. . .

THE WAR

Since 1965, nothing has disrupted the lives of so many young American males as the U.S. government's attempts to field an army in Southeast Asia. The youth of most strata of society responded with either obedient resignation or patriotic fervor. Palisades graduates, however, knew that they had options. More often than not, their parents gave them financial support so they could go to school and enjoy II-S deferments. When they finally finished college, more money was available to pay one of the many draft lawyers who specialized in protecting young men from the not very selective Selective Service. With the help of legal counsel it was possible to win I-Y medical deferments, which were temporary, or the coveted IV-F deferments, which were permanent.

There were exceptions, and some men, like Jon Wilson, did in fact fight in Vietnam. But the number of Pali graduates who actually entered the armed services is disproportionately small. Not one member of the Palisades class of '65 lost his life in Indochina.

Why was draft evasion by deferment more widely accepted in the Vietnam War than in previous wars?

To many Americans, it seemed like the war in Vietnam would never end. Do you recall the demonstrations, and the often violent confrontations? Why was the reaction so different during World War II? What effect did the antiwar movement have on the civil rights movement? What significance do you attach to the photograph of the final evacuation of Saigon?

221

After I graduated I went to the University of California at Santa Cruz. I was very solitary that year. It turned out that one of the few people I saw was Lee Grossman, my old friend from high school and junior high. I remember walking in the woods with him and talking about philosophy. He explained Sartre to me, *Being and Nothingness,* and made it all seem very clear.

That summer I worked in a Headstart program and became very involved in the whole peace-march circuit and antiwar activities. In October of '67 I decided to let myself be arrested as part of the protest at the Oakland Induction Center. There were three hundred other people who were arrested that day, including Joan Baez. My parents understood what I was doing, and I think they respected me for it.

I was in jail for twenty days in the same room with seventy other women. I nearly went crazy! For one seven-day period they fed us nothing but bread and evaporated milk. We were given a list of thirty-six rules: how to tuck in our blankets, where to place our pillow, how to put our shoes at the foot of the bed. We were rarely allowed to change our clothes, shower or change our sheets. I learned what it's like to be in a situation where someone else has all the power, and you have nothing ... nothing, and they have everything.

I also had my first exposure to lesbianism. There were three or four regular prisoners who had become men. They wore their hair a certain way, walked a certain way, wore their uniforms with their handkerchiefs in their pockets, and they had boys' names. One of them was really cute—you could see getting a crush on her.

I remember on the last day they gave us all our mail. I opened up a letter from my younger sister and the colors just burst out. She had written on stationery with flowers and butterflies. I hadn't realized that I had missed color so much.

After I got out of jail I moved in with a guy. It was my first real love relationship, but we didn't get along. All the time I was becoming more and more disillusioned. I knew I had done everything I could to stop the war, but no one paid any attention. The war was marching forward, so in 1969 I quit school. I traveled around Europe and the Middle East for two years and spent some time in a kibbutz in Israel. By this time I had become a vegetarian and I was already interested in Eastern religions and reading heavily.

When I got back to the U.S. I lived for a while on a farm in Connecticut, and at this same time I began taking drugs. I took everything that came my way: LSD, mescaline, psilocybin and peyote. It was not good for my body, but I don't regret it. I'm glad I was part of the hippie movement; I think it changed me a lot.

I started doing a lot of yoga, and after a while I stopped taking drugs. I met a man who had just gotten back from India, where he had been living with a yoga teacher. This man was a musician and an astrologer—an interesting person. He had run away from home when he was fourteen and he never finished high school. I started traveling with him, and I started my period of craziness. Intense craziness. I had had my spiritual awakening and I didn't know how to balance it with the rest of life. I was extremely blissful. It was wonderful, just wonderful. I gave everything away—all my possessions. I was oblivious to everything except my own joy. But it was crazy in that I didn't have touch with reality. I had lost touch with the fact that all of us are God—not just me.

· · ·

Did war resistance end the war in Vietnam, or did it end for reasons unrelated to protest?

Are drugs and/or religion still looked upon as an answer to life's problems?

REUNION

On Saturday night, December 27, 1975, the Palisades class of '65 held its gala reunion. Exactly ten years, six months and twenty-two days had elapsed since the date of our graduation from high school. The scene of the reunion was a huge banquet room in the Lobster House restaurant in LA's Marina del Rey. For months in advance, Pali alumni had sent their $8 reservations to the treasurer of the reunion committee, Harvey Bookstein. Another committee member, Jeff Stolper, had arranged for a professional disc jockey to play old records from the early sixties as part of the evening's entertainment. The restaurant prepared meatballs, cocktail franks and other hors d'oeuvres, while David Wallace made a special trip to a produce market to provide snacks for our vegetarian classmates.

Over three hundred people attended this event—a hundred more than expected by the reunion committee. Questionnaires had gone out to everyone on the class mailing list, and the responses offered some intriguing statistics. For example, 61 percent of the women are now married, but only 48 percent of the men, and 64 percent of our married classmates have children. Only half of the women who are married described their primary occupation as "housewife"; nevertheless, "housewife" was the most common occupation listed by members of the class. The others most frequently mentioned were "teacher" (13 percent) and "lawyer" (10 percent). Attorneys seemed to be particularly overrepresented among the people who actually attended the reunion, and at times the gathering had the flavor of a Bar Association cocktail party. Fully 9 percent of the survey respondents were still students, including an impressive number of women who had recently returned to school. We were astonished as we reviewed some of the more personal comments and statistics from the questionnaires. An amazing 11 percent of our class admitted to an arrest record, and in nearly all cases this involved either political or drug-related charges. Eighteen individuals from the class of '65 reported histories of psychiatric hospitalization.

· · ·

. . . Thinking back on our project, we got out our battered copy of *Time* magazine with the article about Palisades High School, and recalled their rosy predictions of "a golden era." "Teenagers today," that article concluded, "do not think of themselves as 'knights in shining chinos' riding forth on rockets to save the universe. But even the coolest of them know that their careers could be almost that fantastic." *Time* had been right about our wide-ranging possibilities, but had not foreseen the fact that we might be paralyzed by them. With the experts of the world waiting expectantly for glorious achievements, how could we possibly disappoint them? And so we struggled forward, constantly shifting our choices, plagued by chronic indecision, searching in vain for a fate that might be worthy of us. Our former teacher Jean O'Brien may have been right when she called the period from '65 to '75 "the saddest years of the century." Perhaps that was the real reason for our sense of loss as we looked back. But when in human history have the bright hopes of seventeen ever been satisfied—least of all by the age of twenty-seven? We reminded ourselves that we were still young, and that unwritten chapters lay ahead.

Do you agree with those social commentators who argue that all the "revolutions" of the 1960s came to nothing? Why or why not?

THE FUTURE OF THE FAMILY
ALVIN TOFFLER

Throughout this book we have stressed the impact of the family on self-perception and have shown, in turn, the many historical forces that have left their imprint on the family through the years. But today many observers suggest that the family as we have known it will soon disappear. A rising divorce rate and declining birth rate are two signs of this possible trend. Working mothers and an increasing number of couples living together without being married also seem to threaten the family. In the following essay Alvin Toffler suggests some of the ways the family may change in the future. If the family is the cornerstone of American democracy, what will happen to the country if the family really changes?

The family has been called the "giant shock absorber" of society—the place to which the bruised and battered individual returns after doing battle with the world, the one stable point in an increasingly flux-filled environment. As the super-industrial revolution unfolds, this "shock absorber" will come in for some shocks of its own.

Social critics have a field day speculating about the family. The family is "near the point of complete extinction," says Ferdinand Lundberg, author of *The Coming World Transformation.* "The family is dead except for the first year or two of child raising," according to psychoanalyst William Wolf. "This will be its only function." Pessimists tell us the family is racing toward oblivion—but seldom tell us what will take its place.

Family optimists, in contrast, contend that the family, having existed all this time, will continue to exist. Some go so far as to argue that the family is in for a Golden Age. As leisure spreads, they theorize, families will spend more time together and will derive great satisfaction from joint activity. "The family that plays together, stays together," etc.

A more sophisticated view holds that the very turbulence of tomorrow will drive people deeper into their families. "People will marry for stable structure," says Dr. Irwin M. Greenberg, Professor of Psychiatry at the Albert Einstein College of Medicine. According to this view, the family serves as one's "portable roots," anchoring one against the storm of change. In short, the more transient and novel the environment, the more important the family will become.

It may be that both sides in this debate are wrong. For the future is more open than it might appear. The family may neither vanish *nor* enter upon a new Golden Age. It may—and this is far more likely—break up, shatter, only to come together again in weird and novel ways.

Does your generation still consider marriage an important institution?

Traditionally, the nuclear family has been the most valued institution in American culture, in theory if not always in reality. Does the family have a future as well as a history? What are the forces in contemporary life that are breaking down its central place in our culture?

THE MYSTIQUE OF MOTHERHOOD

The most obviously upsetting force likely to strike the family in the decades immediately ahead will be the impact of the new birth technology. The ability to pre-set the sex of one's baby, or even to "program" its IQ, looks and personality traits, must now be regarded as a real possibility. Embryo implants, babies grown *in vitro*, the ability to swallow a pill and guarantee oneself twins or triplets or, even more, the ability to walk into a "babytorium" and actually purchase embryos—all this reaches so far beyond any previous human experience that one needs to look at the future through the eyes of the poet or painter, rather than those of the sociologist or conventional philosopher.

It is regarded as somehow unscholarly, even frivolous, to discuss these matters. Yet advances in science and technology, or in reproductive biology alone, could, within a short time, smash all orthodox ideas about the family and its responsibilities. When babies can be grown in a laboratory jar what happens to the very notion of maternity? And what happens to the self-image of the female in societies which, since the very beginnings of man, have taught her that her primary mission is the propagation of and nurture of the race?

Few social scientists have begun as yet to concern themselves with such questions. One who has is psychiatrist Hyman G. Weitzen, director of Neuropsychiatric Service at Polyclinic Hospital in New York. The cycle of birth, Dr. Weitzen suggests, "fulfills for most women a major creative need . . . Most women are proud of their ability to bear children . . . The special aura that glorifies the pregnant woman has figured largely in the art and literature of both East and West."

What happens to the cult of motherhood, Weitzen asks, if "her offspring might literally not be hers, but that of a genetically 'superior' ovum, implanted in her womb from

Is becoming a mother or father as important to your generation as it was to your parents' generation?

225

another woman, or even grown in a Petri dish?" If women are to be important at all, he suggests, it will no longer be because they alone can bear children. If nothing else, we are about to kill off the mystique of motherhood.

. . .

If a couple can actually purchase an embryo, then parenthood becomes a legal, not a biological matter. Unless such transactions are tightly controlled, one can imagine such grotesqueries as a couple buying an embryo, raising it *in vitro*, then buying another in the name of the first, as though for a trust fund. In that case, they might be regarded as legal "grandparents" before their first child is out of its infancy. We shall need a whole new vocabulary to describe kinship ties.

Why did parents have children in the past? Is this motivation still prevalent?

Furthermore, if embryos are for sale, can a corporation buy one? Can it buy ten thousand? Can it resell them? And if not a corporation, how about a noncommercial research laboratory? If we buy and sell living embryos, are we back to a new form of slavery? Such are the nightmarish questions soon to be debated by us. To continue to think of the family, therefore, in purely conventional terms is to defy all reason.

Faced by rapid social change and the staggering implications of the scientific revolution, super-industrial man may be forced to experiment with novel family forms. Innovative minorities can be expected to try out a colorful variety of family arrangements. They will begin by tinkering with existing forms.

THE STREAMLINED FAMILY

One simple thing they will do is streamline the family. The typical pre-industrial family not only had a good many children, but numerous other dependents as well—grandparents, uncles, aunts, and cousins. Such "extended" families were well suited for survival in slow-paced agricultural societies. But such families are hard to transport or transplant. They are immobile.

Industrialism demanded masses of workers ready and able to move off the land in pursuit of jobs, and to move again whenever necessary. Thus the extended family gradually shed its excess weight and the so-called "nuclear" family emerged—a stripped-down, portable family unit consisting only of parents and a small set of children. This new style family, far more mobile than the traditional extended family, became the standard model in all the industrial countries.

Super-industrialism, however, the next stage of ecotechnological development, requires even higher mobility. Thus we may expect many among the people of the future to carry the streamlining process a step further by remaining childless, cutting the family down to its most elemental components, a man and a woman.

. . .

A compromise may be the postponement of children, rather than childlessness. Men and women today are often torn in conflict between a commitment to career and a commitment to children. In the future, many couples will sidestep this problem by deferring the entire task of raising children until after retirement.

This may strike people of the present as odd. Yet once childbearing is broken away from its biological base, nothing more than tradition suggests having children at an early age. Why not wait, and buy your embryos later, after your work career is over? Thus childlessness is likely to spread among young and middle-aged couples; sexagenarians who raise infants may be far more common. The post-retirement family could become a recognized social institution.

Do you see any problems with late-in-life childrearing?

BIO-PARENTS AND PRO-PARENTS

If a smaller number of families raise children, however, why do the children have to be their own? Why not a system under which "professional parents" take on the childrearing function for others?

Raising children, after all, requires skills that are by no means universal. We don't let

The Median Age Level Is Rising

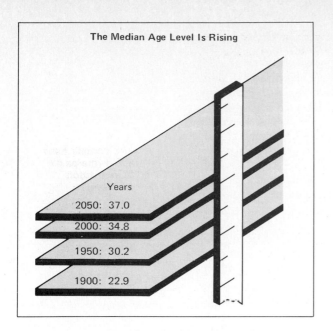

Years
2050: 37.0
2000: 34.8
1950: 30.2
1900: 22.9

The Percentage of People Over 65 Is Increasing

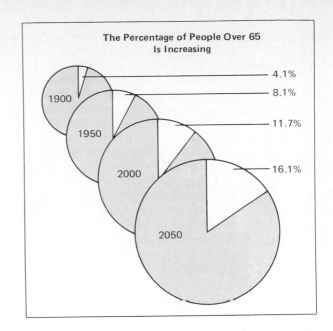

1900 — 4.1%
1950 — 8.1%
2000 — 11.7%
2050 — 16.1%

More People Under 35 are living alone more are divorced and more are staying single

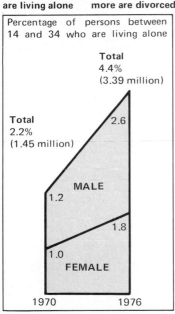

Percentage of persons between 14 and 34 who are living alone

Total 4.4% (3.39 million)

2.6

Total 2.2% (1.45 million)

MALE
1.2
1.8

1.0
FEMALE

1970   1976

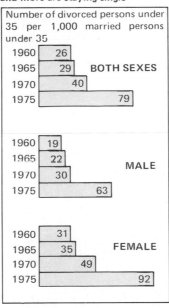

Number of divorced persons under 35 per 1,000 married persons under 35

BOTH SEXES
1960 — 26
1965 — 29
1970 — 40
1975 — 79

MALE
1960 — 19
1965 — 22
1970 — 30
1975 — 63

FEMALE
1960 — 31
1965 — 35
1970 — 49
1975 — 92

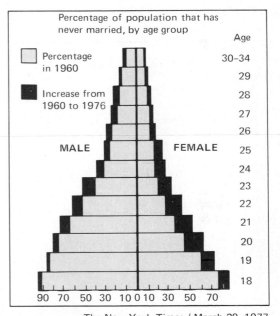

Percentage of population that has never married, by age group

☐ Percentage in 1960
■ Increase from 1960 to 1976

MALE   FEMALE

Age
30–34
29
28
27
26
25
24
23
22
21
20
19
18

90 70 50 30 10 0 10 30 50 70

Source: Bureau of the Census

The New York Times / March 20, 1977

"just anyone" perform brain surgery or, for that matter, sell stocks and bonds. Even the lowest ranking civil servant is required to pass tests proving competence. Yet we allow virtually anyone, almost without regard for mental or moral qualification, to try his or her hand at raising young human beings, so long as these humans are biological offspring. Despite the increasing complexity of the task, parenthood remains the greatest single preserve of the amateur.

• • •

Parental professionals would not be therapists, but actual family units assigned to, and well paid for, rearing children. Such families might be multi-generational by design, offering children in them an opportunity to observe and learn from a variety of adult models, as was the case in the old farm homestead. With the adults paid to be professional parents, they would be freed of the occupational necessity to relocate repeatedly. Such families would take in new children as old ones "graduate" so that age-segregation would be minimized.

Should parenthood become professionalized?

Quite a different alternative lies in the communal family. As transience increases the loneliness and alienation in society, we can anticipate increasing experimentation with various forms of group marriage. The banding together of several adults and children into a single "family" provides a kind of insurance against isolation. Even if one or two members of the household leave, the remaining members have one another. Communes are springing up modeled after those described by psychologist B. F. Skinner in *Walden Two* and by novelist Robert Rimmer in *The Harrad Experiment* and *Proposition 31*. In the latter work, Rimmer seriously proposes the legalization of a "corporate family" in which from three to six adults adopt a single name, live and raise children in common, and legally incorporate to obtain certain economic and tax advantages.

• • •

Still another type of family unit likely to win adherents in the future might be called the "geriatric commune"—a group marriage of elderly people drawn together in a common search for companionship and assistance. Disengaged from the productive economy that makes mobility necessary, they will settle in a single place, band together, pool funds, collectively hire domestic or nursing help, and proceed—within limits—to have the "time of their lives."

Communalism runs counter to the pressure for ever greater geographical and social mobility generated by the thrust toward super-industrialism. It presupposes groups of people who "stay put." For this reason, communal experiments will first proliferate among those in the society who are free from the industrial discipline—the retired population, the young, the dropouts, the students, as well as among self-employed professional and technical people. Later, when advanced technology and information systems make it possible for much of the work of society to be done at home via computer-telecommunication hookups, communalism will become feasible for larger numbers.

Is communal living still as popular among the young as it was a decade ago? Why or why not?

We shall, however, also see many more "family" units consisting of a single unmarried adult and one or more children. Nor will all of these adults be women. It is already possible in some places for unmarried men to adopt children. In 1965 in Oregon, for example, a thirty-eight-year-old musician named Tony Piazza became the first unmarried man in that state, and perhaps in the United States, to be granted the right to adopt a baby. Courts are more readily granting custody to divorced fathers, too. In London, photographer Michael Cooper, married at twenty and divorced soon after, won the right to raise his infant son, and expressed an interest in adopting other children. Observing that he did not particularly wish to remarry, but that he liked children, Cooper mused aloud: "I wish you could just ask beautiful women to have babies for you. Or any woman you liked, or who had something you admired. Ideally, I'd like a big house full of children —all different colors, shapes and sizes." Romantic? Unmanly? Perhaps. Yet attitudes like these will be widely held by men in the future.

Are men as suited as women for childrearing?

• • •

As homosexuality becomes more socially acceptable, we may even begin to find families based on homosexual "marriages" with the partners adopting children. Whether these children would be of the same or opposite sex remains to be seen. But the rapidity with which homosexuality is winning respectability in the techno-societies distinctly points in this direction. In Holland not long ago a Catholic priest "married" two homosexuals, explaining to critics that "they are among the faithful to be helped." England has rewritten its relevant legislation; homosexual relations between consenting adults are no longer considered a crime. And in the United States a meeting of Episcopal clergymen concluded publicly that homosexuality might, under certain circumstances, be adjudged "good." The day may also come when a court decides that a couple of stable, well educated homosexuals might make decent "parents."

We might also see the gradual relaxation of bars against polygamy. Polygamous families exist even now, more widely than generally believed, in the midst of "normal" society. Writer Ben Merson, after visiting several such families in Utah where polygamy is still regarded as essential by certain Mormon fundamentalists, estimated that there are some 30,000 people living in underground family units of this type in the United States. As sexual attitudes loosen up, as property rights become less important because of rising affluence, the social repression of polygamy may come to be regarded as irrational. This shift may be facilitated by the very mobility that compels men to spend considerable time away from their present homes. The old male fantasy of the Captain's Paradise may become a reality for some, although it is likely that, under such circumstances, the wives left behind will demand extramarital sexual rights. Yesterday's "captain" would hardly consider this possibility. Tomorrow's may feel quite differently about it.

Still another family form is even now springing up in our midst, a novel childrearing unit that I call the "aggregate family"—a family based on relationships between divorced and remarried couples, in which all the children become part of "one big family." Though sociologists have paid little attention as yet to this phenomenon, it is already so prevalent that it formed the basis for a hilarious scene in a recent American movie entitled *Divorce American Style*. We may expect aggregate families to take on increasing importance in the decades ahead.

Childless marriage, professional parenthood, post-retirement childrearing, corporate families, communes, geriatric group marriages, homosexual family units, polygamy— these, then, are a few of the family forms and practices with which innovative minorities will experiment in the decades ahead. Not all of us, however, will be willing to participate in such experimentation. What of the majority?

Are sexual attitudes really loosening up?

Do you have any clear ideas about the world these children will inherit at age thirty? Is it possible that they will be socialized by different institutions and concepts than those that shaped you? To what extent are traditional vehicles like the nuclear family, religious training, public schools, and gender-based sex roles outmoded? Do you find more value in continuity or change?

Minorities experiment; majorities cling to the forms of the past. It is safe to say that large numbers of people will refuse to jettison the conventional idea of marriage or the familiar family forms. They will, no doubt, continue searching for happiness within the orthodox format. Yet, even they will be forced to innovate in the end, for the odds against success may prove overwhelming.

The orthodox format presupposes that two young people will "find" one another and marry. It presupposes that the two will fulfill certain psychological needs in one another, and that the two personalities will develop over the years, more or less in tandem, so that they continue to fulfill each other's needs. It further presupposes that this process will last "until death do us part."

These expectations are built deeply into our culture. It is no longer respectable, as it once was, to marry for anything but love. Love has changed from a peripheral concern of the family into its primary justification. Indeed, the pursuit of love through family life has become, for many, the very purpose of life itself.

Love, however, is defined in terms of this notion of shared growth. It is seen as a beautiful mesh of complementary needs, flowing into and out of one another, fulfilling the loved ones, and producing feelings of warmth, tenderness and devotion. Unhappy husbands often complain that they have "left their wives behind" in terms of social, educational or intellectual growth. Partners in successful marriages are said to "grow together."

This "parallel development" theory of love carries endorsement from marriage counsellors, psychologists and sociologists. Thus, says sociologist Nelson Foote, a specialist on the family, the quality of the relationship between husband and wife is dependent upon "the degree of matching in their phases of distinct but comparable development."

If love is a product of shared growth, however, and we are to measure success in marriage by the degree to which matched development actually occurs, it becomes possible to make a strong and ominous prediction about the future.

It is possible to demonstrate that, even in a relatively stagnant society, the mathematical odds are heavily stacked against any couple achieving this ideal of parallel growth. The odds for success positively plummet, however, when the rate of change in society accelerates, as it now is doing. In a fast-moving society, in which many things change, not once, but repeatedly, in which the husband moves up and down a variety of economic and social scales, in which the family is again and again torn loose from home and community, in which individuals move further from their parents, further from the religion of origin, and further from traditional values, it is almost miraculous if two people develop at anything like comparable rates.

If, at the same time, average life expectancy rises from, say, fifty to seventy years, thereby lengthening the term during which this acrobatic feat of matched development is supposed to be maintained, the odds against success become absolutely astronomical. Thus, Nelson Foote writes with wry understatement: "To expect a marriage to last indefinitely under modern conditions is to expect a lot." To ask love to last indefinitely is to expect even more. Transience and novelty are both in league against it.

Is the idea of marriage as a lifetime commitment still held widely among your friends?

TEMPORARY MARRIAGE

It is this change in the statistical odds against love that accounts for the high divorce and separation rates in most of the techno-societies. The faster the rate of change and the longer the life span, the worse these odds grow. Something has to crack.

In point of fact, of course, something has already cracked—and it is the old insistence on permanence. Millions of men and women now adopt what appears to them to be a sensible and conservative strategy. Rather than opting for some offbeat variety of the family, they marry conventionally, they attempt to make it "work," and then, when the paths of the partners diverge beyond an acceptable point, they divorce or depart. Most of them go on to search for a new partner whose developmental stage, at that moment, matches their own.

As human relationships grow more transient and modular, the pursuit of love becomes, if anything, more frenzied. But the temporal expectations change. As conventional marriage proves itself less and less capable of delivering on its promise of lifelong

While traditional attitudes toward sex and marriage still prevail in some parts of the nation, public tolerance toward manners and morals has expanded at enormous speed within a very short time. "Living in sin" has given way to the benign and familiar "living together." Evidence of premarital and extramarital sex, trial marriages, and common-law associations abounds. Can you contrast the more permissive climate of today with the attitudes of your parents' generation? Are they comfortable with today's attitudes? Are you? Why do you think there has been so much change in this regard over the past decade?

love, therefore, we can anticipate open public acceptance of temporary marriages. Instead of wedding "until death us do part," couples will enter into matrimony knowing from the first that the relationship is likely to be short-lived.

They will know, too, that when the paths of husband and wife diverge, when there is too great a discrepancy in developmental stages, they may call it quits—without shock or embarrassment, perhaps even without some of the pain that goes with divorce today. And when the opportunity presents itself, they will marry again ... and again ... and again.

Serial marriage—a pattern of successive temporary marriages—is cut to order for the Age of Transience in which all man's relationships, all his ties with the environment, shrink in duration. It is the natural, the inevitable outgrowth of a social order in which automobiles are rented, dolls traded in, and dresses discarded after one-time use. It is the mainstream marriage pattern of tomorrow.

How might a conservationist retort to this analogy between our throwaway habits and marriage?

• • •

MARRIAGE TRAJECTORIES

As serial marriages become more common, we shall begin to characterize people not in terms of their present marital status, but in terms of their marriage career or "trajectory." This trajectory will be formed by the decisions they make at certain vital turning points in their lives.

For most people, the first such juncture will arrive in youth, when they enter into "trial marriage." Even now the young people of the United States and Europe are

231

engaged in a mass experiment with probationary marriage, with or without benefit of ceremony. The staidest of United States universities are beginning to wink at the practice of co-ed housekeeping among their students. Acceptance of trial marriage is even growing among certain religious philosophers. Thus we hear the German theologian Siegfried Keil of Marburg University urge what he terms "recognized premarriage." In Canada, Father Jacques Lazure has publicly proposed "probationary marriages" of three to eighteen months.

In the past, social pressures and lack of money restricted experimentation with trial marriage to a relative handful. In the future, both these limiting forces will evaporate. Trial marriage will be the first step in the serial marriage "careers" that millions will pursue.

Are trial marriages a good idea? Why or why not?

A second critical life juncture for the people of the future will occur when the trial marriage ends. At this point, couples may choose to formalize their relationship and stay together into the next stage. Or they may terminate it and seek out new partners. In either case, they will then face several options. They may prefer to go childless. They may choose to have, adopt or "buy" one or more children. They may decide to raise these children themselves or to farm them out to professional parents. Such decisions will be made, by and large, in the early twenties—by which time many young adults will already be well into their second marriages.

A third significant turning point in the marital career will come, as it does today, when the children finally leave home. The end of parenthood proves excruciating for many, particularly women who, once the children are gone, find themselves without a *raison d'être*. Even today divorces result from the failure of the couple to adapt to this traumatic break in continuity.

Among the more conventional couples of tomorrow who choose to raise their own children in the time-honored fashion, this will continue to be a particularly painful time. It will, however, strike earlier. Young people today already leave home sooner than their counterparts a generation ago. They will probably depart even earlier tomorrow. Masses of youngsters will move off, whether into trial marriage or not, in their mid-teens. Thus we may anticipate that the middle and late thirties will be another important breakpoint in the marital careers of millions. Many at that juncture will enter into their third marriage.

This third marriage will bring together two people for what could well turn out to be the longest uninterrupted stretch of matrimony in their lives—from, say, the late thirties until one of the partners dies. This may, in fact, turn out to be the only "real" marriage, the basis of the only truly durable marital relationship. During this time two mature people, presumably with well-matched interests and complementary psychological needs, and with a sense of being at comparable stages of personality development, will be able to look forward to a relationship with a decent statistical probability of enduring.

Not all these marriages will survive until death, however, for the family will still face a fourth crisis point. This will come, as it does now for so many, when one or both of the partners retire from work. The abrupt change in daily routine brought about by this development places great strain on the couple. Some couples will go the path of the post-retirement family, choosing this moment to begin the task of raising children. This may overcome for them the vacuum that so many couples now face after reaching the end of their occupational lives. (Today many women go to work when they finish raising children; tomorrow many will reverse that pattern, working first and childrearing next.) Other couples will overcome the crisis of retirement in other ways, fashioning both together a new set of habits, interests and activities. Still others will find the transition too difficult, and will simply sever their ties and enter the pool of "in-betweens"—the floating reserve of temporarily unmarried persons.

Toffler's four-stage marriage pattern makes certain assumptions about women. Might an early and sustained career orientation by women alter this pattern?

• • •

Children in this super-industrial society will grow up with an ever enlarging circle of what might be called "semi-siblings"—a whole clan of boys and girls brought into the world by their successive sets of parents. What becomes of such "aggregate" families will be fascinating to observe. Semi-sibs may turn out to be like cousins, today. They may help one another professionally or in time of need. But they will also present the society with novel problems. Should semi-sibs marry, for example?

Surely, the whole relationship of the child to the family will be dramatically altered. Except perhaps in communal groupings, the family will lose what little remains of its power to transmit values to the younger generation. This will further accelerate the pace of change and intensify the problems that go with it.

What social institution besides the family is qualified to transmit values?

232

A REVIEW: YOU AND SOCIAL FORCES

Before you begin to put your materials together for writing your family history, try your hand at a brief autobiographical statement that attempts to relate your own experience since early childhood to the major social forces of your lifetime. Break down what you consider to be the important themes of this chapter (e.g., the nature and variety of available work, political and social protest, progress and problems in the area of the environment, the family, racism, class structure, etc.). Write a brief commentary on the effect of these forces in the shaping of your own life.

After completing this, you may want to review the section "Researching and Writing Your Family History," before putting your notes in order. You may also find it useful to reread each of the chapter assignments to refresh your memory. Try to decide what periods or events or personalities or historical forces have over the long run been most instrumental in creating the situation that you and your family confront today.

BIBLIOGRAPHIC NOTE

The post war era is a vast period with a vast literature. A good introduction is Robert D. Marcus and David Burner, editors, *America Since 1945* (1972). For American foreign policy, especially with respect to the Soviet Union, Walter La Faber's *America, Russia, and the Cold War, 1945–1975* (1976) is interesting reading.

Many works related to the topics of social history covered in this chapter are also available. For the culture of poverty, two works in particular are recommended: Michael Harrington's *The Other America* (1962) and Oscar Lewis' *La Vida* (1966). For a history of the civil rights movement in the 1950s and early 1960s, see Anthony Lewis' *Portrait of a Decade: The Second American Revolution* (1964). A good, general social history of the past decade can be found in William O'Neill, *Coming Apart: An Informal History of the 1960s* (1971). And, for essays on the future of the family, see *The Nuclear Family in Crisis* (1972), edited by Michael Gordon.

About the Authors

Jim Watts is Associate Professor of History at the City College of New York, where he has taught since 1965. Because of an ongoing interest in experimental modes of teaching history, he has participated in the production of history courses over radio and television and has made historical films. He was awarded a National Endowment for the Humanities Younger Humanist Fellowship for the 1973–1974 academic year to develop cross-disciplinary approaches to historical studies.

Allen F. Davis is Professor of History at Temple University, where he has taught since 1968. He is the author of *Spearheads for Reform: The Social Settlements and the Progressive Movement* and *American Heroine: The Life and Legend of Jane Addams*—the latter, winner of the 1974 Christopher Award. In addition, he has edited or coedited several books, including *Conflict and Consensus in American History,* and has served as Executive Secretary for the American Studies Association.

A Note On The Type

The text of this book is set in Caledonia, designed by W. A. Dwiggins. It belongs to the family of printing types called "modern face" by printers—a term used to mark the change in style of type-letters that occurred about 1800. Caledonia borders on the general design of Scotch Modern, but is more freely drawn than that letter.

Appendix

Materials for Research and Writing

The materials in this section should be used only as they are useful to you. The assignments in the text suggest some of the ways that you can use them to your best advantage. You can familiarize yourself with the techniques of researching and writing your family's history by reading the first essay in this section. The three pieces that follow, one a transcription of an interview with an old Russian emigré and the others student papers recording their research into their own families' histories, are intended to offer you models to follow for interviewing and writing. You may use the questions, charts, and questionnaires that end this section as aids in interviewing family members and writing up results. Do not think that you must fill in every space, answer every question, retrieve every bit of requested information. Instead, select what seems most pertinent to your investigations. As you uncover documents and conduct your oral interviews, return to this section to refresh your memory. Questions and possible areas or information that you rejected or overlooked the first time through may seem on second glance necessary to your work.

Researching and Writing Your Family History

Below are some suggestions about how to proceed to search for your family history. Not all of the suggestions will be useful to you; some of the suggestions may take longer to apply than the time you have in your class to do your project. But searching for your ancestors and studying your family history can become a lifetime hobby. You, or a member of your family, may want to continue your search after the school year is over.

The task of the historian is to collect as much information as possible about a person, an event, or a movement; to sift the relevant from the irrelevant, to organize the surviving data; and then to interpret the evidence by writing a story that attempts to make sense out of the past. Of course, the past can never be recaptured or reconstructed exactly. The information available is always incomplete and often contradictory, since witnesses remember the same event differently. In addition each historian approaches the evidence with a particular point of view and purpose. All history is necessarily subjective, therefore, but that is why it is interesting and important.

There is a special thrill in coming across an old letter written when your grandmother was a young girl, in discovering the name of an ancestor in a census record, or in talking about what life was like sixty years ago with a great-aunt. It is a thrill of recognition, a realization that you have made a personal connection with the past. But going beyond that flash of recognition—learning how to interpret and understand this past—is a more difficult task.

As you acquire information about your family, you will need to devise a systematic way to organize your notes. Otherwise, you will end up with many bits and pieces of paper with incomplete information, and you may have a difficult time locating the notes you need. There are several charts and forms in this Appendix, but you will need to supplement them with blank sheets of the same size. If you take all of your notes on the same size paper and label each sheet carefully, they will be easier to organize. *Write on only one side of the paper.* This may seem like a waste, but when you spread your notes on a table or even on the floor, writing on the back may easily be lost. *Take notes carefully and be complete.* When you are copying a document or recording data from a gravestone or from a court record, take notes as if you were never going to see the document again—in many cases you probably will not. Make sure you record complete references to the sources you use so that you, or someone else, can retrace your steps. If it is a book, you need the author, place, and date of publication, the complete title, and the specific pages. If you are using a court document, you usually need a volume number and a number for the document in addition to the date. If it is a gravestone, you might give directions for finding the cemetery. (Locating a single stone in a large cemetery can be an all-day job.) Most libraries and courthouses now have photocopy machines, and for a small charge you can get an exact copy of a document or a page from a book. This saves time and eliminates the possibility of error, but be sure to write the source on each photocopy. Make a list of those sources consulted that contained no information useful to your project. This will prevent a second trip to the same source at a later date. *Above all be careful, be organized, and be clear.*

If you start with yourself, you will discover that you already know something about your family's history (probably more than you realize). When and where were you born? When and where were your brothers and sisters, parents and grandparents born? How many times have you moved? Can you reconstruct in your mind the appearance of the house in which you lived at ten? Where did everyone sleep? Where did the family sit at the table? Taking notes of things you cannot remember may be useful, since you can later ask a relative.

INTERVIEWING RELATIVES

After you have written down all the information about your family that you can remember, it is time to approach other family members—your parents, grandparents, uncles and aunts, or anyone who survives and is able to talk to you. It is amazing how much about your family you can learn and how far back in time you can go. If you have a grandmother who is eighty years old and she remembers things her grandmother told her about her childhood, you may be able to recover an oral tradition that goes back to the early part of the nineteenth century. A word of caution is in order before you begin your interviewing.

Interviewing is a delicate art at best. Although it has special benefits, interviewing one's parents and grandparents also may cause special problems. The family should be informed of the purpose of this project so that fears of embarrassment or invasion of privacy can be allayed. Assurance must be given that no use beyond the classroom is contemplated and, if you think it necessary, a commitment can be made for prior clearance before the paper is submitted.

Talking to relatives about your family's history can be a rewarding experience, but you should use your judgment and common sense about the most effective way to approach them. The best interviewers are those who have an interest in their subject and have done a careful job of preparation before they begin to interview. You should begin by doing as much research as possible before you conduct your interviews, utilizing what you have learned from the earlier chapters of this book. The next step is to gather as much useful information as you can by asking specific questions of your parents and grandparents: place of birth, date of marriage, grandmother's maiden name, and so on. It is probably better to fill out the questionnaires at the end of this Appendix yourself rather than to ask your relatives to do it, because forms have a tendency to stifle talk rather than stimulate it.

As you move to the more substantive questions, it is usually best to structure your interview loosely. Reading a list of prepared questions will be stilted and formal, so use the suggested questions and topics as guides only. (Of course, being fairly unstructured in your interview does not mean being unprepared.) Try to ask open-ended questions that stimulate, rather than questions that can only be answered by yes or no or questions so broad that they inhibit a response. Thus, instead of asking, "Was the depression economically difficult for you?" try inquiring, "Where did you work and how much were you paid?" Or, instead of the nonspecific question, "Where were you during World War II?" try asking, "What was the single most significant thing that happened to you during the war?" Moreover, a simple question like "What do you remember eating for Sunday dinner when you were a child?" may yield surprising information on family structure, standard of living, the role of religion, and so on. Be ready to ask follow-up questions, and be flexible enough to alter your plan and pursue a topic that you had not considered.

Do not overlook mundane topics, since you may later be able to use the information in your analysis. Seemingly inconsequential details may be of significance—holiday traditions, for instance, or the role of music in the home. If your ancestors were born in hospitals, who paid the bill? If not, who delivered the child, and what reciprocal gestures were expected as a result? In other words, concentrate on the areas of life your relatives know best, not their opinion of world leaders, unless of course they actually knew those famous people.

Your major role as interviewer is to listen carefully—not an easy job—and to act as a guide and director of the conversation. Try not to let your own preconceived ideas influence your questions or your responses to answers, and do not assume that your parents and grandparents share your value system. Guard against overly sophisticated questions; try to keep them simple and direct.

If you have a tape recorder readily available, it may prove useful, but tape may not be the best way to record your interviews. The machine, reproducing every detail of what is said, may frighten or inhibit some people. Transcribing the tapes at a later time can also be very difficult. Some interviewers prefer to take brief notes during the interview, and then to write up a summary and impressions immediately afterward. Whatever method you choose for recording your interview, try to make the situation as natural and relaxed as possible. The length of time you can talk at one session will vary, depending on the age and personality of the person to whom you are talking, as well as on your attitude and mood. Most interviewers find that two hours is the absolute maximum for one interview session. Several short sessions may be more effective than one long session, because that gives you time in between to go over what has been accomplished, to fill in gaps, to formulate new questions. If a relative lives a long distance from you, or if all of your sources of information are far away, questions may be sent through the mail. Letters are a poor substitute for face-to-face conversations, however, and consequently the facts-by-mail approach should be supplemented by interviews the next time you return home.

Human memory is often unpredictable and unreliable, especially as people grow older. The documents, pictures, and clippings you have collected should help trigger memories and establish a time sequence. Remember that you are interested in general trends, thoughts, feelings, and overall meaning more than in establishing and confirming each fact. Being a historian is in some ways like playing detective, but beware of overplaying the role. Most families have stories or legends about the family's past that have been passed from one generation to another. It is important to try to separate fact from myth, but legends and stories can also be important. As you proceed in a flexible and open manner, you will learn a great deal. You will also acquire a new understanding and appreciation for your own heritage.

Some useful books on interviewing and oral history are:

1. Brady, John. *The Craft of Interviewing.* Cincinnati, Ohio: Writers Digest, 1976.

2. Gordon, Raymond L. *Interviewing: Strategy, Techniques and Tactics.* Homewood, Ill.: Dorsey Press, 1969.

3. Sherwood, Hugh C. *The Journalistic Interview.* New York: Harper & Row, 1972. Designed for the journalist but useful for anyone doing interviewing.

4. Wigginton, Eliot. *Foxfire.* 3 vols. New York: Anchor Press/Doubleday, 1972, 1973, 1975. Contains interviews of long-time residents of rural Georgia conducted by high-school students.

Most history books are based on research in written records. Diaries, letters, newspapers, and reports are the stuff out of which written history is created. You may never have thought about it, but every family has its own archives where primary sources for family history can be found. Perhaps in an old box, a trunk, a desk drawer, or a file cabinet in your parents' and grandparents' homes you may find papers and memorabilia from the past. How much has been saved and how useful it is will vary a great deal from one family to another, but in addition to an oral tradition almost all families preserve some of the following written records and physical artifacts.

BIRTH RECORDS

Not only do birth certificates provide the official record of an individual's date and place of birth, but they often give the age, occupation, and birthplaces of both parents as well as the mother's maiden name. A birth certificate for your father may reveal that the first name he always used was really his middle name, or that your grandfather was born in Ireland and was a carpenter and your mother was born in Massachusetts. There may be an official record of birth in the town or city where you or your ancestor was born. Sometimes for recent births you may have to supply proof of relationship to obtain the official document. In some cases, when an official record was not made or the original record has been destroyed, church records, school records, family Bible records, or the testimony of relatives may be taken in place of the official record. Of course, people born in other countries and immigrating at an early age may not know exactly when they were born. If you find a birth certificate that contradicts the information on a cemetery stone or in an obituary, the official birth certificate is usually the most accurate.

DEATH CERTIFICATES

These are also official documents and contain information on parents, including the maiden name of the mother of the deceased, cause of death, and usually place and date of death.

MARRIAGE CERTIFICATES

These will give you correct names of both partners, where they were born, and the place and date of marriage. Both death and marriage certificates are recorded and can usually be obtained for a small fee, but first you have to know when and where the event took place.

NATURALIZATION PAPERS

In addition to the date and place of birth, such papers record the nationality as well as the age, and/or date of arrival in the United States and the date of naturalization, and in some cases the parents' names. If you cannot find these papers and know that an ancestor was naturalized, it is possible to locate the records, but it is often a difficult task. The records for those naturalized before 1840 are available at the National Archives and at Federal Records Centers. Some other records, especially for the New England states 1789–1906, are in the National Archives. Records of state and local courts are available in the state archives or occasionally in county court houses. After 1906 there was a regular and complicated procedure established that included a formal petition and examination and a certificate of naturalization. These records are usually difficult to obtain if less than fifty years old. Remember that many immigrants were not naturalized, but that children born in America were automatically citizens.

DISCHARGE PAPERS FROM THE ARMED FORCES

These often give date and place of birth or of induction as well as the highest rank achieved, number of years served, military unit, and discharge date and place.

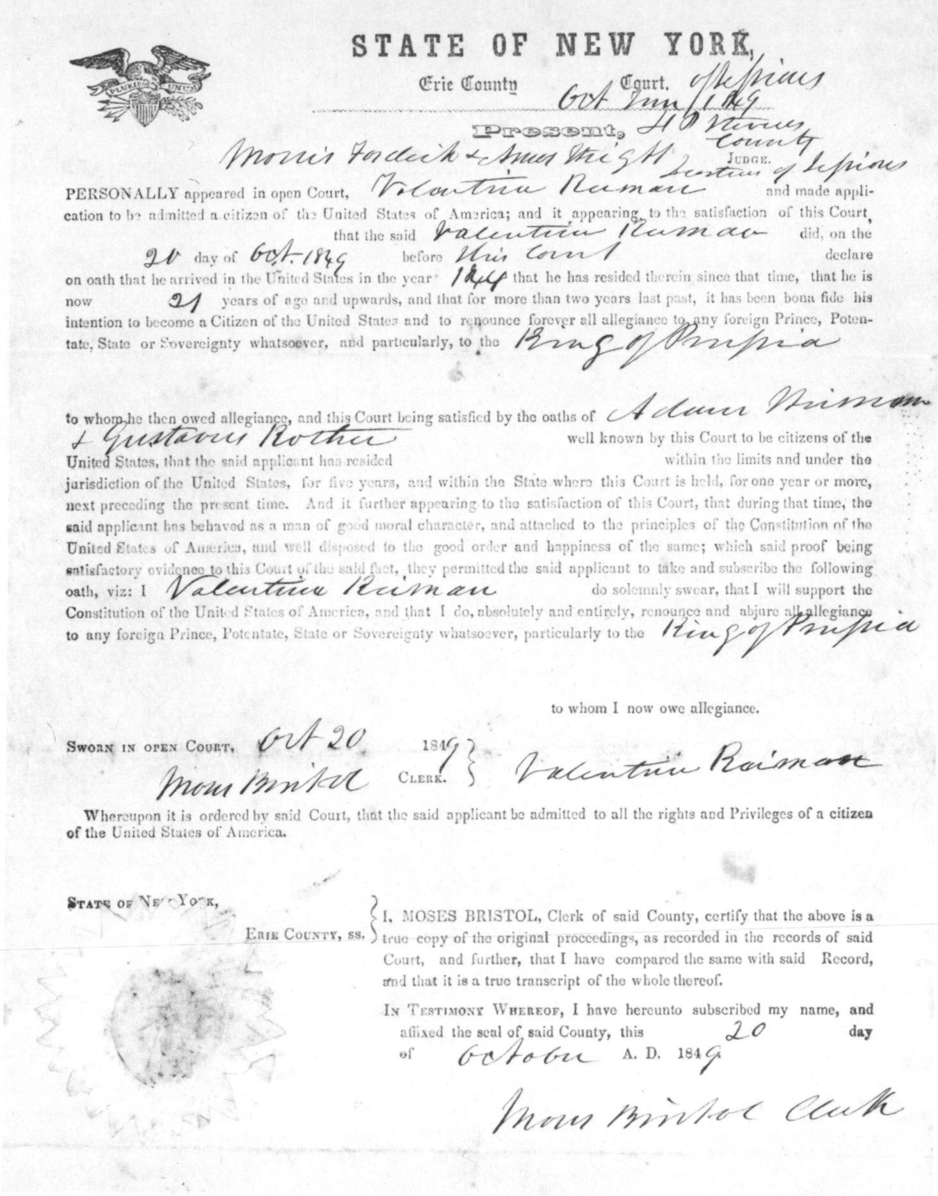

STATE OF NEW YORK,

Erie County

[handwritten court heading]

Present, *[handwritten]*

PERSONALLY appeared in open Court, *Valentine Raiman* and made application to be admitted a citizen of the United States of America; and it appearing to the satisfaction of this Court, that the said *Valentine Raiman* did, on the *20* day of *Oct 1849* before this Court declare on oath that he arrived in the United States in the year *1844* that he has resided therein since that time, that he is now *21* years of age and upwards, and that for more than two years last past, it has been bona fide his intention to become a Citizen of the United States and to renounce forever all allegiance to any foreign Prince, Potentate, State or Sovereignty whatsoever, and particularly, to the *King of Prussia*

to whom he then owed allegiance, and this Court being satisfied by the oaths of *Adam Wisman + Gustavus Rother* well known by this Court to be citizens of the United States, that the said applicant has resided within the limits and under the jurisdiction of the United States, for five years, and within the State where this Court is held, for one year or more, next preceding the present time. And it further appearing to the satisfaction of this Court, that during that time, the said applicant has behaved as a man of good moral character, and attached to the principles of the Constitution of the United States of America, and well disposed to the good order and happiness of the same; which said proof being satisfactory evidence to this Court of the said fact, they permitted the said applicant to take and subscribe the following oath, viz: I *Valentine Raiman* do solemnly swear, that I will support the Constitution of the United States of America, and that I do, absolutely and entirely, renounce and abjure all allegiance to any foreign Prince, Potentate, State or Sovereignty whatsoever, particularly to the *King of Prussia*

to whom I now owe allegiance.

SWORN IN OPEN COURT, *Oct 20* 1849

Moses Bristol CLERK. *Valentine Raiman*

Whereupon it is ordered by said Court, that the said applicant be admitted to all the rights and Privileges of a citizen of the United States of America.

STATE OF NEW YORK,
ERIE COUNTY, ss.

I, MOSES BRISTOL, Clerk of said County, certify that the above is a true copy of the original proceedings, as recorded in the records of said Court, and further, that I have compared the same with said Record, and that it is a true transcript of the whole thereof.

IN TESTIMONY WHEREOF, I have hereunto subscribed my name, and affixed the seal of said County, this *20* day of *October* A. D. 184*9*

Moses Bristol Clerk

Here is an excellent example of a document which carries great meaning. Read it closely, and see if you can sense the emotions which the German immigrant must have felt on that day. Why do you think the courts insisted on the specific renunciation of past allegiances? Which of your ancestors went through this process? If you could determine where, and about when, perhaps you could obtain your own family record.

LETTERS, DIARIES, ACCOUNT BOOKS, ETC.

We know a great deal about some American families because they left a large amount of material behind. The Adams family of Massachusetts, for example, which produced two Presidents and several scholars, diplomats, and businessmen, left an enormous volume of letters, diaries, and other writings that have enabled historians to reconstruct the family's history in great detail over several generations. The letters of a less famous Georgia family have recently been published in Robert Manson Myers, ed., *Children of Pride* (New Haven, Conn.: Yale University Press, 1972). Most families have not saved the letters written among family members, but perhaps you will be lucky and come across the love letters written between your grandfather and grandmother before they were married, or the account book kept by an ancestor who was a storekeeper or blacksmith, or the diary of someone who fought in the Civil War. If you should discover some interesting family letters or a diary, you should contact your local or state historical society. Most archives and historical societies are becoming increasingly interested in preserving the papers of anonymous people. They might be interested in copying the papers and would usually return the originals to you.

Even if you cannot find a trunk full of old letters, you may be able to find a few items that have been tucked away in a drawer or perhaps in an old book. There might even be some letters written by you when you were a child, or a postcard mailed home by your father.

FAMILY BIBLES

Many nineteenth-century families owned a family Bible. Sometimes these were large and elaborate, but at other times they were smaller in size. Often these Bibles contained a place to record births, deaths, and marriages. Usually the family records section was placed between the Old and New Testaments, but it could be in the front or in the back or the entries could be written wherever there was a blank space. You need to be something of a detective to analyze these records. If the dates go back before the date

Family Bibles and, less frequently, samplers are great research prizes, since traditionally they contained basic family records. You should inquire, perhaps of the oldest surviving member of your family, about the record-keeping habits of the past. Is there an old Bible hidden away somewhere? Which of your ancestors did needlework? Have you ever seen a sampler?

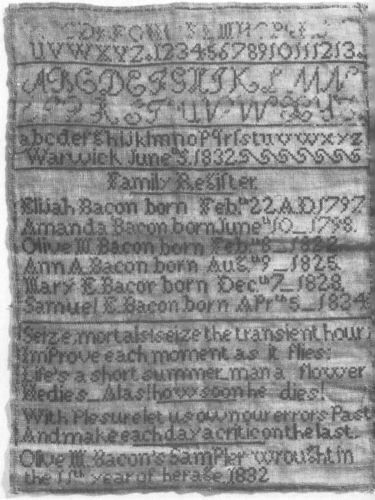

the Bible was printed and all the handwriting is the same, you know they were added later. Someone wrote the information at a later date, probably from memory, and therefore there may be possibilities of inaccuracies. If you find a family Bible in the possession of a relative, ask for a photocopy of the family information for your records. Family Bibles were often used as a hiding place for valuable letters and papers, so look carefully. Family information was often written or pasted into dictionaries and other such books, and these may be profitably investigated as well.

NEWSPAPER CLIPPINGS, DEEDS, DIPLOMAS, ETC.

Many families clip news items that relate to the family—the story of a wedding, an obituary, or perhaps a fiftieth wedding anniversary. Look for these in desk drawers, in scrapbooks, or wherever valuable things are kept in the house. You may also find high-school or Sunday-school certificates or deeds of purchase for a house. There may be old school yearbooks, dance programs, or accounts of sporting events. All of these things had significance for a relative, and if he or she is still alive they may trigger a memory that can lead to an interesting story. Again, do not overlook the books in the house, some of which may have inscriptions, notes, or other writings. Speaking of books, cookbooks should not be overlooked. Sometimes cookbooks or recipes may have been passed down from mother to daughter and may give you some idea of the meals served in your grandmother's house.

OTHER OBJECTS IN THE HOME

As you browse through the attic or the basement of your own home or that of a grandparent, think of yourself as an archeologist uncovering the remnants of another civilization. Perhaps you will find an old radio or phonograph, a flatiron that was heated on top of a stove, or a chamber pot and pitcher that recall a day before indoor plumbing. In the basement you may find old canning jars or bottles, possibly a coal hod, or even a horse harness. Maybe your family has preserved quilts or tablecloths from an earlier time, or a sampler that has the record of a family cross-stitched into the cloth. Perhaps there is a silver spoon with initials on it, or a table that was a wedding gift to great-grandparents. Are there pieces of furniture or dishes that have been cherished by several generations? Can you find out the stories that go with them?

The following books may be useful in identifying objects and aiding your thoughts about the way people lived with those objects:

1. Cotter, John. *Aboveground Archeology*. Washington, D.C.: U.S. Government Printing Office, 1975. This is available for 60 cents by writing to the Government Printing Office, Washington, D.C. 20402.
2. Winchester, Alice. *How to Know American Antiques*. New York: Signet, 1951. This work identifies the age and style of furniture and other objects.
3. Munsey, Cecil. *Illustrated Guide to Collecting Bottles*. New York: Hawthorn, 1970.
4. The Sears, Roebuck and Montgomery Ward catalogues. Two that have been republished: the *1897 Sears Catalogue*. New York: Chelsea House, 1968; and the *1927 Sears Catalogue*. New York: Crown, 1970. These may prove useful in identifying objects you find, and they may also help to stimulate the memory of those you are interviewing.
5. Andrew, Wayne. *Architecture, Ambition and Americans*. New York: Harper & Row, 1955. Changing architectural styles are discussed in a lively style.
6. Editors of *Life. America's Arts and Skills*. New York: Time-Life Books, 1968. This well-illustrated book includes discussion of architecture, tools, and furniture.

PHOTOGRAPHS

Almost every family can document at least a portion of its history with photographs. Some families may even have home movies that date from the 1940s and 1950s. There may be old daguerreotypes or tintypes from the middle of the nineteenth century tucked away in grandfather's bureau drawers. Or there may be some old stereograph photos—two identical images that were viewed through a stereoscope to give the illusion of three dimensions.

Perhaps you can find a family album from the late nineteenth century; covered with rich red cloth, such an album was usually placed next to the family Bible in the middle-class Victorian home and contained pictures of stern-looking ancestors. The family

Midnineteenth-century daguerreotypes of a newly married couple.

Julia Maloney Sullivan Hughes (1859–1959) was born in County Cork, Ireland and emigrated to the United States at the age of thirteen, never to return to Ireland. She spent over fifty years "in service" in middle-class homes in and around New York City. Twice widowed, she lived until the age of 100, spending her last thirty years in Oswego, N.Y. in the home of her daughter Mary and son-in-law James F. Watts. In this picture, taken in the mid-1930s, she holds her grandson, Jim, coeditor of this book.

A stereograph view from the 1880s.

album was a prized possession in many homes, especially when the family was separated by great distances. Sons and daughters, aunts and uncles moved to the city or to the West, but they could be recalled by studying their pictures. Unfortunately many families did not take the time to give names to the portraits (since at the time everyone knew who they were), so that today many people are anonymous. There are often many clues for your family history in these albums and perhaps there is a grandmother or great-aunt who will still remember some of the faces. But even if you cannot tell exactly who they are, you can still learn something of their personalities and the time in which they lived by studying the clothes they wore and the poses they affected.

Not every family has preserved nineteenth-century photos, but almost every family has snapshots of twentieth-century events—family picnics, school pictures, weddings. Most families seem to take pictures on vacations or during holidays. Perhaps you can take a lesson from the unlabeled pictures from the past and help your parents or grandparents label their pictures. Even pictures taken over a ten- or twenty-year period will allow you to study changing styles in dress, hair, automobiles, and home furnishings.

Some useful books to consult in interpreting such photos are:

1. Akeret, Robert. *Photoanalysis: How to Interpret the Hidden Psychological Meaning of Personal and Public Photographs.* New York: Pocket Books, 1973.

Families separated by distance often exchanged snapshots as a means of staying in touch. These were sent by a woman in Nova Scotia, Alice Burns (pictured at left), to her niece Elizabeth in Boston. Her two sons are among the group at right. Perhaps some of your relatives have collected similar shots over the years.

2. Taft, Robert. *Photography and the American Scene.* 1938. Reprint. New York: Dover, 1964.
3. Welling, William. *Collector's Guide to Nineteenth Century Photographs.* New York: Collier, 1976.

WRITING TO RELATIVES

As you look through your family archives, you may need to write to relatives living in distant places. Be polite, explain why you are interested in information on the family, and what use you are going to make of it. Keep your requests simple, at least in the first letter. Since elderly people often have difficulty with their eyesight, you should probably type or print your letter. Enclose a self-addressed stamped envelope to make the reply as easy as possible.

You may discover in writing to relatives that someone in your family has prepared a genealogy. It may be a few pages of handwritten notes recording births and deaths, or it may be an elaborate, published book tracing many branches of the family to the original immigrant ancestor. But you should not accept the facts as accurate just because they are written or even published. Use whatever information you can find, but check the facts whenever you can and remember that family history is more than genealogy.

SOURCES IN THE COMMUNITY

The best place to start your study of your own family is with yourself and those relatives who are still alive. The next place to go is to the sources preserved by the family. (These two stages can often go on simultaneously.) Eventually you will exhaust the resources of your family archives and you will need to look to more public sources.

CEMETERIES

Gravestones are fascinating to study even if you have no knowledge of the people buried beneath them. The triumphs and tragedies, the human stories of another era, are all preserved in stone. There is a special thrill if you can locate the gravestone of a great-

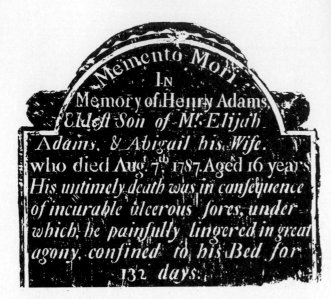

Memento Mori.
In
Memory of Henry Adams,
Eldest Son of M.ʳ Elijah
Adams, & Abigail his Wife.
who died Aug. 7.ᵗʰ 1787. Aged 16 years
His untimely death was in consequence
of incurable ulcerous sores, under
which, he painfully lingered in great
agony, confined to his Bed for
132 days.

Where are your ancestors buried? Are they interred in different places, perhaps indicating the family's migratory history? What information is recorded on the tombstones you have seen? Can simple birth and death dates lead you to such additional information as obituaries, birth certificates, and names and addresses of ancestors?

grandparent. Gravestones can also sometimes provide valuable genealogical information not available elsewhere. If you know where your ancestors lived (the most important clue for unlocking the secrets of the past generations), you may well be able to find where they are buried, although not everyone was buried near where he or she lived. The smaller the town, city, borough, or parish, or the closer you can pinpoint a residence in a rural county, the easier it will be to find an ancestor's grave. A detailed topographical map will help you in your search, but you still may look through several cemeteries before finding the stones you are looking for. Some you will never find, but the search itself is part of the fun. Gravestones may vary from the simple slate markers of the eighteenth and early nineteenth centuries to the more elaborate and ornamental granite and marble stones of a later period. The inscriptions and carvings can sometimes give you a clue as to the occupation of the deceased and even how he or she died. They can also tell you something about people's religious beliefs and their attitudes toward death in a particular time. Many early stones contained hand-carved death's heads, cherubs, urns, and willows. One early and fairly common rhyme was:

> As you are now,
> So once was I;
> As I am now,
> So you must be.
> So prepare for death
> And follow me.

A popular hobby is gravestone rubbing. You can try this with some very simple equipment, but remember the best results come from the old slate stones (usually those before 1810), though the technique can be used on later stones. You will need a roll of masking tape, a large pad or roll of paper, and a box of black lumber-marking wax crayons. Clean the stone, tape the paper over the stone, and then, using the side of the crayon, rub until the image comes through. Usually you will have to go over the stone several times. If you prefer to photograph the stones, go over the inscription with white chalk to make it more legible in the picture. A slow, black and white film such as Kodak Panatomic X will give you the best results.

Sometimes the data on the gravestone are inaccurate because the stones were erected years after the deaths. You may also discover that the dates are not always exact: "Died in the sixty-eighth year of his age," or "Died at age sixty-seven years, seven months, and two days" are both common inscriptions. Sometimes the cemetery records in the custodian's or the town clerk's office may be more accurate and complete than the cemetery stone itself. The inscriptions from many cemeteries have been copied and placed in historical societies or in genealogical libraries.

Some useful books in reconnoitering cemeteries are:

1. Newman, John J. *Cemetery Transcribing: Preparations and Procedures.* Technical Leaflet 9. American Association of State and Local History, 1315 Eighth Avenue, South Nashville, Tenn. 37203. 50 cents.

A typical death certificate. Notice that you can learn the father's and mother's names and birthplaces from such certificates.

2. Gillon, Edmund Vincent, Jr., *Early New England Gravestone Rubbings*. New York: Dover, 1966.

VITAL RECORDS

The official records of birth, marriage, divorce, and death usually are recorded by the town, city, borough, or occasionally the county. Sometimes the older records are compiled and are also available at the library or archives of a state. If you know the town where an ancestor died or was born, you may write for assistance to the town clerk or the city archivist, giving as much information as you have (the more exact the information, the more likely you will be successful). You should always enclose a stamped self-addressed envelope and offer to pay a reasonable fee for the search. If you are not sure exactly where to write, you may write to the Superintendent of Documents, U.S. Government Printing Office, Washington, D.C. 20402 for three pamphlets: *Where to Write for Birth and Death Records*, DHEW Pub. No. HRA 75–1142: *Where to Write for Marriage Records*, DHEW Pub. No. HSM 72–1144; and *Where to Write for Divorce Records*, DHEW Pub. No. HRA 75–1145 (Public Health Service Publications 630A, 630B, 630C). For old records, consult the state-by-state list in an article by Harold Clarke Durrell, *New England Historical and Genealogical Register* 90 (January 1936), 9–31. There is also a good list in *How to Trace Your Family Tree* (Garden City: Dolphin, 1975), compiled by the staff of the American Genealogical Research Institute.

OBITUARIES

Your ancestors may not have been important enough to have an obituary in the *New York Times*, though it may be worth your while to check the *New York Times Index*. Some libraries also have indexes to obituaries in other newspapers, including the *Boston Transcript, 1875–1930*. A more likely source is the local newspaper in the community where your ancestor lived. Ordinary people often are given extensive obituaries in the local press.

CHURCH RECORDS

In many communities the churches kept records of births, deaths, and marriages, as well as records of who joined the church. Unlike vital records, these are often hard to locate. If you have located a town where an ancestor lived and can find no vital records, try to locate the pastor of the church to which he or she may have belonged. Some church records have been collected. There is a good chapter in Gilbert Doane, *Searching for Your Ancestors* (New York: Bantam, 1974), which lists references and depositories.

LAND RECORDS

The record of the purchase and the sale of land is another valuable source for those tracing the history of their family. Some of the early records also include the former residence of the buyer, and this can be a valuable clue. These records are usually kept at the town or city level, but in some states they may be at the county court house, and the older records may have been collected in the state archives. You may want to write to local or state historical and genealogical societies for additional information. As in the case of vital records and church records, you may discover that many records have been destroyed by fires and other disasters.

MAPS

A good map may be an invaluable source for finding where your ancestors lived and for locating cemeteries and villages. The detailed geodetic survey maps available for most parts of the country can be useful. But even more valuable are the old maps kept in historical societies that can give you information about a town or city as it existed a century ago. Sometimes these maps include the owner of a farm or store and, in a city, the numbers for each block.

WILLS AND PROBATE RECORDS

Various documents in probate courts (usually at the county courthouse in the county where your ancestors lived) can be useful in tracing your family and finding interesting information about them. Wills and papers relating to the settling of an estate usually give the names of the heirs, but along with the probate records there often are inventories of the estate of the deceased. These documents list both the objects and the property owned by the ancestor, allowing you to reconstruct the interior of his or her house and to imagine life in another era. If you cannot get to the county seat, clerks of probate courts will usually supply any documents relating to the settling of a particular individual's estate if you have the date of death. There usually is a small fee. Wills and probate records may also be filed with land records.

CITY DIRECTORIES

Most cities of even moderate size publish directories and have done so since the early part of the nineteenth century. These list the place of residence and the business of most people living in the city. The directories can help you tell when someone moved into and left a particular place. Local historical societies, public libraries, and city archives usually have files of these directories. There currently is a microfilm project which will copy all directories before 1840. Some states also publish directories listing the town officers and the businesses in the various towns and cities.

COUNTY AND CITY HISTORIES

There was a great flurry of interest in local history after the centennial, and many cities, towns, and counties prepared histories that are often useful if you know where your ancestors lived in 1880 or 1890. Often these local histories give information on the various families then residing there, and one did not always need to be prominent to get into one of these histories. Sometimes they are accompanied by biographical volumes that again might prove useful in your search, but remember many of these books were financed by those who had their biographies included. Local histories can usually be found in town and county libraries as well as in state historical society libraries and in such major libraries as the Newberry Library in Chicago, the New York Public Library, and the Library of Congress.

PENSION RECORDS

If you had an ancestor who served in a war the chances are good that there is some record of his service or of a pension granted to him or his widow in the National Archives. Often in order to substantiate a claim, a considerable amount of family information was given. For veterans of the Revolution, Indian Wars, the War of 1812, and the Mexican, Civil, and Spanish American wars, you can write for information, but first you need the proper forms. It may be helpful to read *Military Service Records in the National Archives of the United States* (General Information Leaflet No. #7), or send directly for forms to Military Service Records, National Archives, Washington, D.C. 20408. World War I and World War II records should be requested at the United States Veterans' office in your state, but these records rarely have family information.

CENSUS RECORDS

The national census, taken every ten years beginning in 1790, can be useful in tracing your ancestors, but there are limitations to its usefulness. Some states such as New York have also taken censuses, and these can also be valuable. The 1900 national census and those after that date are open selectively for genealogical research on your own family. If the person listed in the census is still alive, that person has to apply for the records. If the person is dead, then a next of kin may apply. Information and forms can be secured by writing to Application of Search of Census Records, BC600 Personal Census Service Branch, Bureau of the Census, Pittsburg, Kans. 66732. The 1890 census was almost completely destroyed by fire. The censuses from 1790 through 1840 list only the name of the head of the household and certain other facts about those other people living in the house. For example, the 1790 census lists the name of the head of the family, the number of free white males over sixteen, the number of free white males under sixteen, the number of free white females, the number of free black persons, and the number of slaves. The 1790 census has been published for ten of the thirteen original colonies plus Maine and Vermont, and copies can be located in state historical societies and most major research libraries. The 1820 census lists the head of the family, the number of free white males and females under ten, the number of free white males ten to sixteen, the number of white males and females sixteen to eighteen, the number of free white males and females eighteen to twenty-six, twenty-six to forty-five, and over forty-five. It also includes statistics on the number of naturalized aliens, the number of persons engaged in agriculture, commerce, and manufacturing, the number of free blacks and slaves, and the number of persons except Indians not taxed.

The most useful censuses are those from 1850 to 1880, all of which list the name and age of everyone in the household. They also list the value of property and professions of those over fifteen. The 1880 census gives name, age, sex, color of each person, the relationship of each person to the head of the household, and the place of birth of the mother and father of the person listed. This last item alone can provide the clue that can lead you back at least one more generation. The 1900 census can also be valuable because it lists the birthplaces of parents, and if immigrants, the year of immigration and naturalization.

The census is on microfilm in the National Archives in Washington, and there are

This is an example of a page from the 1850 census.

copies at many other locations such as Federal Records Centers and many libraries. In order to find your ancestors in the census, you need to know where they were living in the year of the census. If they lived in a large city, you need to know the ward or it will be a long search. City maps can help if you have the street address. The census, like any document, is not always accurate; people were missed in 1850 just as they were in 1970. The census taker often misspelled names or got the age of a child wrong. Even when you have all the necessary information, you may search through the microfilm reels for hours before coming across your ancestor, but as Alex Haley recalls, there is a special thrill in actually finding your own people in the official census records.

RECORDS OF THE CHURCH OF JESUS CHRIST OF LATTER DAY SAINTS

Many church records are possible sources of information on family history, but the Church of Jesus Christ of Latter Day Saints in Salt Lake City, Utah, has special resources. The Mormons believe that the family will survive in the future paradise, so every Mormon is obligated to trace his or her ancestry as far back as possible. For this reason the church has copied vital records, land records, probate records, family Bibles, and other material of all kinds from all over the world, but especially from the United States and Europe. There are more than 1 million reels of microfilm in the vaults in Salt Lake City. You can consult many of these records if you go there. You also can consult many records at branch libraries, and some material can be researched for you. For information, write to The Genealogical Department, Church of Jesus Christ of Latter Day Saints, 50 East North Temple Street, Salt Lake City, Utah 84150.

BOOKS FOR MORE INFORMATION

There are thousands of books and articles written about the science of genealogy. If you become seriously interested in tracing your family's history, you will want to consult some of them. The following titles suggest places where you might start:

1. *Genealogy Beginners Manual.* This pamphlet was prepared by the staff of the Newberry Library, 60 West Walton Street, Chicago, Ill. 60610.

2. *How to Trace Your Family Tree.* American Genealogical Research Staff. Garden City: Dolphin, 1975.

3. Doane, Gilbert H. *Searching for Your Ancestors.* New York: Bantam, 1974.

4. Everton, George B., et al. *The Handybook for Genealogists.* Logan, Utah: Everton, 1971.

5. Williams, Ethel W. *Know Your Ancestors.* Rutland, Vt.: Charles E. Tuttle, 1960.

6. *Tracing Your Ancestors in Canada.* Available from Information, Ottawa, Ontario, Canada.

7. Rottenberg, Dan. *Finding Our Fathers: A Guidebook to Jewish Genealogy.* New York: Random House, 1977.

8. Walker, James Dent. *Black Genealogy: How to Begin.* Available from Georgia Center for Continuing Education, Athens, Ga. 30602.

9. Greenwood, Val D. *Researcher's Guide to American Genealogy.* Baltimore: Genealogical Publishing Co., 1974.

TRACING IMMIGRANTS FROM OVERSEAS

If you cannot find naturalization papers or other records relating to your immigrant ancestors, perhaps you can find your ancestor's name on a passenger list. The more information you have about date of arrival, port of entry, and the name of the vessel, the more likely you are to be successful. The passenger list records are not complete. Many have been destroyed; for example, there were two fires in San Francisco making it difficult to trace people who landed in that city, but see Louis J. Rasmussen, *San Francisco Passenger Lists,* 4 vols. (Ship 'N Rail Series, San Francisco Historic Records, 1976). The records in the National Archives go back as far as 1798, but most relate to the period from 1825 to 1945. A useful guide is Harold Lancour, *A Bibliography of Ships' Passenger Lists, 1538–1825: Being a Guide to Published Lists of Early Immi-*

grants to North America (New York: New York Public Library, 1963). For later records see the very useful book *Guide to Genealogical Records in the National Archives* (Washington, D.C.: U.S. Government Printing Office, 1964). The best records seem to be for New York, Boston, Philadelphia, and Baltimore. Not to be overlooked are the records of travelers' aid societies that often helped recent arrivals. The Philadelphia Jewish Archives Center (625 Walnut Street), for example, has records kept by a travelers' aid society for Jewish immigrants arriving in Philadelphia (with many going on to other cities) from 1885 to 1920. Slaves coming into the United States or to the American colonies were not listed by name, as Alex Haley discovered, but listed only by the number on each ship.

TRACING YOUR ANCESTORS WHILE OVERSEAS

If some day you want to search for your ancestors in Ireland, Italy, Sweden, or England, you should make sure you have done all the work possible in the United States before you go. Perhaps you still have relatives in the village your ancestors came from; that makes the task easier and more pleasant. Just as in tracing your ancestors on this side of the Atlantic, your task is made easier if you know the village or place that your ancestors came from. You might want to consult Leslie G. Pine, *The Genealogist's Encyclopedia* (New York: Weybright and Talley, 1969), which lists archives and record depositories in many countries; also *Genealogical Research: Methods and Sources*, 2 vols. (Washington, D.C.: American Society of Genealogists, 1960, 1971); and Dan Rottenberg, *Finding Our Fathers.* If you go to Europe or Africa, you should not expect to find too much. Remember, it took Alex Haley a great deal of time, money, and luck to find his African roots.

A WORD OR TWO OF WARNING

Beware of the letter that offers to provide your family with a coat of arms or to trace your family tree for a fee. What you are likely to receive is a pamphlet containing the origins of your name and perhaps a few famous people who share the name with you, with no effort to prove your connections to those people; or you may get an expensive coat of arms that in all probability has no connection to your family. If you must hire someone to trace your family history, write to the Board of Certification of Genealogists, 1307 New Hampshire Avenue N.W., Washington, D.C. 20036.

TRACING YOUR FAMILY HISTORY IF ADOPTED

If you are adopted or an orphan your problems are obviously complicated. Some states, however, are beginning to open up adoption records in response to the growing concern on the part of many adopted children about their real parents. There are many successful stories of adopted children who have found their roots, so that even though difficult, the search is not impossible. Two books which describe the search of adopted or illegitimate children for their families are: Betty Jean Lifton, *Twice Born: Memoirs of an Adopted Daughter* (New York: Penguin, 1976); and Rod McKuen, *Finding My Father: One Man's Search for Identity* (New York: Coward, 1976).

ETHNIC GROUPS

Many people will discover that the trail of their ancestors disappears after a generation or two, and many others will find it impossible to recover the name of that first immigrant who came to America. But we all can discover the ethnic mix in our backgrounds, and with a little research and a lot of imagination, we can reconstruct what it must have been like for our ancestors.

The references listed below may be of some help. The list is by no means complete, but many of the books contain extensive bibliographies.

GENERAL ACCOUNTS

Carlson, Lewis H. and George A. Colburn, eds. *In Their Place: White America Defines Her Minorities, 1850–1950.* New York: Wiley, 1972. Essays on Indians, Afro-Americans, Chicanos, Chinese, Japanese, Jews, and immigration policy.

Coleman, Terry. *Going to America.* Garden City, N.Y.: Anchor, 1973.

Davis, Allen F. and Mark H. Haller, eds. *The Peoples of Philadelphia: A History of Ethnic Groups and Lower Class Life, 1790–1940.* Philadelphia: Temple University Press, 1973. Essays on blacks, Jews, Poles, Irish, and Italians.

Dinnerstein, Leonard and Frederic C. Jaher. *The Aliens: A History of Ethnic Minorities in America.* New York: Appleton-Century-Crofts, 1970. Essays on many ethnic groups.

———and David M. Reimers. *Ethnic Americans: A History of Immigration and Assimilation.* New York: Dodd, Mead, 1975.

Handlin, Oscar, ed. *Children of the Uprooted.* New York: Grosset & Dunlap, 1966. An anthology.

Hansen, Marcus Lee. *Atlantic Migration, 1607–1860.* 1940. Reprint. Gloucester, Mass.: Peter Smith, n.d. Mostly on the European background.

Herberg, Will. *Protestant, Catholic, Jew.* rev. ed. Garden City, N.Y.: Doubleday/Anchor, 1955. An essay on the major American religious groups.

Morison, Samuel Eliot. *The European Discovery of America: The Northern Voyages.* New York: Oxford University Press, 1971. Deals with the expansion of Europe and the voyages of discovery.

Novotny, Ann. *Strangers at the Door: Ellis Island, Castle Garden, and the Great Migration to America.* Riverside, Conn.: Chatham, 1971. Illustrated account of immigration.

Palmer, Robert R. and Joel Colton. *The History of the Modern World.* 5th ed. New York: Knopf, 1977.

RACIAL AND ETHNIC GROUPS

Afro-Americans

Curtin, Philip D. *The Atlantic Slave Trade: A Census.* Madison: University of Wisconsin Press, 1969.

Fishel, Leslie H., Jr., and Benjamin Quarles. *The Negro American: A Brief Documentary History.* rev ed. Glenview, Ill.: Scott Foresman, 1970.

Franklin, John Hope. *From Slavery to Freedom.* 4th ed. New York: Random House, 1974.

Gutman, Herbert G. *The Black Family in Slavery & Freedom, 1750–1925.* New York: Pantheon, 1976.

Haley, Alex. *Roots: The Saga of an American Family.* Garden City: Doubleday, 1976. Fiction but still a fascinating story.

Meier, August, and Elliott M. Rudwick, eds. *The Making of Black America.* Studies in American Negro Life Series. New York: Atheneum, 1969.

American Indians

Brandon, William. *The American Heritage Book of the Indians.* New York: Dell, 1964.

Driver, Harold E. *Indians of North America.* 2d ed. Chicago: University of Chicago Press, 1969.

Josephy, Alvin M., Jr. *The Indian Heritage of America.* New York: Knopf, 1968.

Levine, Stuart and Nancy O. Lurie. *The American Indian Today.* Deland, Fla.: Everett-Edwards, 1968.

Spicer, Edward. *A Short History of the Indians of the United States.* New York: Van Nostrand Reinhold, 1969.

Armenians

Vartan, Malcolm H. *Armenians in America.* New York: Pilgrim Press, 1919.

British (English, Scotch, Scotch-Irish, Welsh)

Berthoff, Rowland T. *British Immigrants in Industrial America, 1789–1950.* 1953. Reprint. New York: Russell & Russell, 1970.

Graham, Ian C. *Colonists from Scotland: Emigration to the United States, 1707–1783.* Ithaca, N.Y.: Cornell University Press, 1956.

Leyburn, James G. *The Scotch-Irish: A Social History.* 1944. Reprint. Chapel Hill: University of North Carolina Press, 1962.

Chinese

Cooledge, Mary R. *Chinese Immigration.* New York: Holt, 1909.

Sandmeyer, E. C. *The Anti-Chinese Movement in California.* Urbana, Ill.: University of Illinois Press, 1939.

Czechs

Capek, Thomas. *The Czechs in America.* 1920. Reprint. American Immigration Collection Series, no. 1. New York: Arno Press, 1969.

Dutch

Lucas, Henry S. *Netherlanders in America: Dutch Immigration to the United States and Canada, 1789–1950.* Ann Arbor: University of Michigan Press, 1955.

French-Canadians

Ducharme, Jacques. *Shadows of the Trees: The Story of French-Canadians in New England.* New York: Harper & Row, 1943.

Wade, Mason. *The French Canadians, 1760–1945.* New York: Macmillan, 1955.

Germans

O'Connor, Richard. *The German-Americans.* Boston: Little, Brown, 1968.

Rothan, Emmet H. *The German Catholic Immigrant in the United States, 1830–1860.* Washington, D.C.: Catholic University of America Press, 1946.

Schrader, Frederick F. *The Germans in the Making of America.* 1924. Reprint. Americana Series, no. 47. New York: Haskell House, 1972.

Greeks

Saloutos, Theodore. *The Greeks in the United States.* Cambridge, Mass.: Harvard University Press, 1964.

Hungarians

Lengyel, Emil. *Americans from Hungary.* 1948. Reprint. Westport, Conn.: Greenwood Press, n.d.

Irish

Clark, Dennis. *The Irish in Philadelphia: Ten Generations of Urban Experience.* Philadelphia: Temple University Press, 1974.

Handlin, Oscar. *Boston's Immigrants: A Study in Acculturation.* rev. ed. Cambridge, Mass.: Harvard University Press, 1959.

Schrier, Arnold. *Ireland and the American Emigration, 1850–1900.* 1958. Reprint. New York: Russell & Russell, 1970.

Wittke, Carl. *The Irish in America.* 1956. Reprint. New York: Russell & Russell, 1970.

Italians

Barzini, Luigi. *The Italians.* New York: Atheneum, 1964.

Covello, Leonard. *The Social Background of the Italo-American School Child.* New York: Humanities Press, 1967.

Gambino, Richard. *Blood of My Blood.* New York: Doubleday, 1974.

Gans, Herbert J. *The Urban Villagers: Group and Class in the Life of Italo-Americans.* New York: Free Press, 1962.

Nelli, Humbert S. *The Italians in Chicago, 1880–1930: A Study in Ethnic Mobility.* New York: Oxford University Press, 1973.

Japanese

Ichihashi, Yamato. *Japanese in the United States.* 1932. Reprint. American Immigration Collection Series, no. 1. New York: Arno Press, 1969.

Kitano, Harry H. *Japanese Americans: The Evolution of a Subculture.* Englewood Cliffs, N.J.: Prentice-Hall, 1969.

Jews

Handlin, Oscar. *Adventure in Freedom.* 1954. Reprint. American History and Culture in the Twentieth Century Series. Port Washington, N.Y.: Kennikat Press, 1971.

Howe, Irving. *World of Our Fathers: The Journey of the East European Jews to America and the Life They Found and Made.* New York: Harcourt Brace Jovanovich, 1976.

Rischin, Moses. *The Promised City: New York's Jews, 1870–1914.* Cambridge, Mass.: Harvard University Press, 1962.

Schoener, Allon. *Portal to America: The Lower East Side, 1870–1925.* New York: Holt, Rinehart and Winston, 1967.

Sklare, Marshall, ed. *The Jews: Social Patterns of an American Group.* New York: Free Press, 1958.

Mexicans

Gamio, Manuel. *Mexican Immigration to the United States.* 1930. Reprint. American Immigration Collection Series, no. 1. New York: Arno Press, 1969.

McWilliams, Carey. *North from Mexico: The Spanish-Speaking People of the United States.* 1949. Reprint. Westport, Conn.: Greenwood Press, 1961.

Samora, Julian, ed. *La Raza: Forgotten Americans.* Notre Dame, Ind.: University of Notre Dame Press, 1966.

Norwegians

Blegen, Theodore C. *Norwegian Migration to America, 1825–1860.* 1931. Reprint. American Immigration Collection Series, no. 1. New York: Arno Press, 1969.

Poles

Fox, Paul. *The Poles in America.* 1922. Reprint. American Immigration Collection Series, no. 2. New York: Arno Press, 1970.

Thomas, William I., and Znaniecki, Florian. *The Polish Peasant in Europe and America.* 5 vols., 1918–1920. Reprint in 2 vols. New York: Octagon, 1971.

Puerto Ricans

Lewis, Oscar. *La Vida: A Puerto Rican Family in the Culture of Poverty, San Juan and New York.* New York: Random House, 1966.

Padilla, Elena. *Up from Puerto Rico.* New York: Columbia University Press, 1958.

Russians

Davis, Jerome. *The Russian Immigrant.* 1922. Reprint. American Immigration Collection Series, no. 2. New York: Arno Press, 1970.

Slavs

Balch, Emily G. *Our Slavic Fellow Citizens.* 1910. Reprint. American Immigration Collection Series, no. 1. New York: Arno Press, 1969.

Swedes

Janson, Florence E. *The Background of Swedish Immigration, 1840–1930.* 1931. Reprint. American Immigration Collection Series, no. 2. New York: Arno Press, 1970.

Syrians

Hitti, Philip. *The Syrians in America.* New York: Holt, Rinehart and Winston, 1924.

Ukrainians

Halich, Wasyl. *Ukrainians in the United States.* 1937. Reprint. American Immigration Series, no. 2. New York: Arno Press, 1970.

A RUSSIAN IMMIGRANT REMEMBERS *

Isadore Ross

I was born in 1899 in T-Tiev-Kiev-Guberini, Russia. My parents, three brothers, two sisters, and myself lived in a one-room house made from lime and straw. Our house was built by my father, and we slept, cooked, ate, and did business there. My parents sold whiskey. They would buy it in bottles and sell it in shots. This was illegal. My father also used to sell cows and sheep to eke out a living.

At the age of six, my father wrapped me in a talis and took me to Cheddar. It was about a mile and a half from the village I lived in. School was in the city and there were about forty kids in it. Both Jews and Christians lived in my village. We made mud pies, went swimming in the creek, and stole fruit from the trees. I used to take the stolen fruit to school and sell it for a button. We played games with the buttons. The Christian kids used to beat me and steal my lunch. There was much anti-Semitism.

My father died when I was twelve, leaving my mother penniless. She continued making whiskey for a living, but then a gentile wanted 10 rubles as a bribe. She didn't have it, so he squealed. She was arrested and after pleading guilty was put in jail for three months. While she was in jail, uncles and aunts saw to it that she had kosher food.

When I was fourteen years old, I was apprenticed to a wagon shop. I was small and not too strong. It was hard to pick up the tools. I was paid six dollars a year and got room and board. At night I went to school. . . . [Jews] could not own property unless they paid very high taxes. They were also not allowed to sell whiskey. If a Jew owned a saloon, he had to buy it under a Christian name and couldn't work behind the counter. There were a few Jews who were better off. They were able to sell wheat and corn. My family was not so well off. We had no relatives in the village.

In 1914, when I was sixteen years old, I was drafted into the army. You are told to report and let a doctor examine you. If you're healthy they take you. I was told to report sixty miles away in Kiev. It was the first time I had ever been to a big city. I had never seen people dressed up or seen a train station. When I was a kid, there was one pair of boots for all five children to share. It was the first time I had had my own shoes. From Kiev we went to Moscow. This was very exciting. It took about two days overnight in a train. There were about 160 of us boys. We went to the barracks where there were tents. I was shocked to see a really big city. I went to a Russian bath and got a haircut. All my beautiful curly hair was cut off. The army gave us clothes. Mine were too big and I found a Jewish tailor who made the clothes fit better. The officers noticed how well I looked. The next day I noticed the officers watching me. They took us to training drill and showed us how to run, jump, and use a gun. Some boys rebelled. I made up my mind: if I had to be a soldier, I'd be a good one. I was determined to succeed. We were paid the equivalent of ten cents a week. We were told how to salute the officers according to their rank. We'd sit on the floor, and the officers would question us. I knew the answers after a few times. When the others didn't know, they'd say, "Ask Yitzak." After a week of this we were taken to the barracks inside a building. Training continued every day. Training was for six weeks. This was wartime though, and after five weeks we prepared to be shipped to the front. We were lined up and called alphabetically. After three days

*Transcript in Philadelphia Jewish Archives.

they still hadn't called my name. I felt bewildered and didn't know what to think of it. One morning I was called into the office. The officer said, "Yitzak, go to the main office and try your gun; turn in your clothes and you'll get new clothes; get your pay." I got forty cents pay for four weeks.

Then I came back to him and he said, "Yitzak, now you come with me." I went out to a horse-driven Russian carriage. This was my first ride, and we went to his home about twenty minutes away. When we arrived at his home I was amazed to see a beautiful two-story home. I had never seen anything like it in my life and I didn't know what to look at first. He introduced me to his parents and to his sister, who was going to college. He then took me to the kitchen downstairs and introduced me to the servants. When we went to his room, he said, "You're going to be my 'geskick' [orderly] and take care of my clothes." Later he took me upstairs and showed me my room: I thought it was a room for the czar! It was nicely furnished with a map of the world on one wall and pictures of czars of the past on another. The third wall had pictures of different opera stars, actors, and actresses, and the fourth was lined with pictures of famous writers— Dostoevsky among them. It took me three to four weeks to figure out all the different people. This was certainly a different world!

I managed to do my job as an orderly and had breakfast each morning with the officer. He once told me I couldn't go into town for four weeks because it was wartime and I was supposed to be in training. After the four weeks, though, I went into town. I had no idea of where to go first and I ended up in a beautiful park on Zubovsky Boulevard. In this park I met some soldiers who were Russian and Jewish, as I was. We became acquainted and started talking. They noticed that I was a greenhorn, and they took me out to movies, concerts, and so forth. . . . They were all from different towns and one had been in my town for over a year.

At four o'clock I had to be home. At six o'clock we had dinner fit for a king—meat, kasha, borscht, black bread, vegetables, vodka, and other drinks. After dinner I used to go with the officer to shows and dances. At the dances there were mostly nurses, and the officer would say, "Yitzak, get a girl to dance with." Of course I did and we danced the mazurka. I was a great dancer! As poor as I was, I had gone to the village dances. The officer was very proud of me, and one nurse wouldn't leave me alone. She gave me her name and added that her father was Jewish.

I went often to these dances, and for this five-month period of my life I was very happy. Then one morning we were sitting at the breakfast table and the officer said to me, "Yitzak, I have some bad news for you. You and I have to go to the front." I felt awful. I read in the paper every day that many were getting killed. He told me to get a gun and my equipment and clothes. I had been living and dressing like a civilian, so he sent me to his tailor. About a week later we left. The trains were packed with soldiers. We were all going to the front. We left Moscow at eight o'clock at night and arrived ten o'clock the next morning at Baronovitch, a Russian city on the German border.

The first thing we did was to dig ditches. A few hours later the shooting started. This lasted for a few days, and every day for two hours the shooting stopped to let us clean up the wounded and the killed. I was at the officer's side all of the time. One day there was a big fight with much shooting. My leg felt very warm. I had been wounded; beside me, my officer was lying dead. I was so upset. He was like a brother to me; he was so good to me. They took the dead and wounded away.

The Red Cross put us on trains, treated us, and stuffed us into the hospital in Moscow. This was the first time I saw a hospital. I was there for about four weeks with a broken leg. . . .

When I was ready to be discharged the nurse said to me, "Yitzak, you are going to be sent to a new regiment, but we'll give you five or six days to recuperate." A few days before I was to leave we heard, in the nighttime, a lot of noise, a lot of shooting. We didn't know what had happened. In the morning all the doctors had disappeared. They were in the czar's army. Only the nurses were left, and we still didn't know what had happened. We looked outside and saw and heard people crying and screaming and still lots of shooting. This was the beginning of the Russian Revolution of 1917.

We saw lots of people lying in the streets. We were afraid to go out from the hospital. The next morning we saw the Communists carrying signs ordering everyone to come to Red Square because Lenin was coming from Petrograd to speak. The next morning those of us who were discharged went to Red Square. We found thousands and thousands of people there ahead of us. Lenin showed up on the platform with a red flag in his hand. He greeted us, saying, "Hello, comrades." Then he started to talk. "I just came from

Petrograd, and I want to report to all of you that we got rid of the whole czar's family; we shot them all and burned their bodies." The Communists clapped. Lenin continued, "I left Trotsky in command of Petrograd and I'm going to remain in Moscow to put that city in order. We arranged headquarters in every district in Moscow, and we asked all the soldiers from every regiment to report to any district they wished." I also reported to a certain district.

When I came to my district there were hundreds of soldiers already there, waiting for orders. . . . I knew that this wasn't going to be the end of my duties, so I decided to leave Moscow and try to return to my home state of Kiev. When I came to the train station in Moscow, I found thousands of soldiers but no trains. We waited and waited. Some trains came but none to take me to Kiev, so I had to wait another day. Finally, a train pulled in that was going to Odessa, which was in the direction of Kiev. This train was full of soldiers with many on the roofs and many on the locomotive. I jumped onto the roof. It was bitter cold and the ride to Kiev took three-and-one-half days. On the way we stopped at little stations and picked up food. The train finally reached Kiev, and I jumped off the roof of the train and went into the train station.

The station in Kiev, like the one in Moscow, was filled with soldiers. I found a place to sit and made plans to reach my little town, seven to eight hours away. I had to wait three days until a train would take me to Pogrovich, the station near my home town. When I arrived in Pogrovich I didn't know what to do. There was no transportation to my home, so I decided to walk. Other soldiers joined me on the way.

When I arrived at my little town, T-Tiev, the town was dead. No one was in the streets and the windows were boarded up. I knew in my head what had happened; a few days before they had had a pogrom. I was planning to go to my mother's house, but I was afraid because she lived near the village. I walked into the city to the house of my girlfriend, Reba. I had met Reba at dancing school when I was fifteen and she was fourteen. We were just kids.

When I knocked on the door of the house they were afraid to open the door. Reba finally opened the door, and everyone started crying. They told me that fifty people had been killed. I decided to remain in the house a couple of days. When things quieted down I went back to see my family. I hadn't seen them for almost three years. Things became normal and more quiet for a little while—but not for too long.

Reba's family and mine thought we ought to get married. They set the date for the wedding and made all the preparations. The time was April. At the night of the wedding everyone was in the synagogue. While the rabbi performed the ceremony under the "chupa," some bandits came in. My wedding became like a scene from "Fiddler on the Roof." Some guests were killed, and we all ran in different directions. We had no idea of where to go until I decided that we would go to a village where I had lived once before with the Christians.

We came to the house of a woman who used to take care of us when we were kids. We stayed in the stable. The dogs started barking, and the woman came out to find out why. She opened the stable door and saw us still dressed in our wedding clothes. When she recognized me, she yelled, "Oh my God, Yitzak, I raised you." I told her what had happened, but she already knew. Her son was one of those killing the Jews.

She then said, "This is not the place for you," and she took us about a block from the stable. There we came across a large hole, about eight feet deep with a stepladder inside. "Here, maybe you'll be safe." She was a good woman. The hole was damp and cold and at nighttime she used to bring us food and water. In the evening we heard shooting and screaming while we were lying in this hole.

One night when she brought us some food, she told me that her neighbor had seen my brother lying wounded near the lake. My wife and I didn't know what to do. I wanted to help my fifteen-year-old brother, Sulik. My wife was afraid to be alone, and thought I would be killed. She refused to let me go. About an hour later she then said to me, "Maybe you should go."

I walked up the stepladder alone, and I went to look for my brother. When I finally found him, he was lying in the dirt in a pool of blood. He could hardly talk. I moved him away to a clean place on the grass. I then went to the lake, took off my jacket and hat, and got some water for my brother. Using the jacket as a rag, I cleaned him up. His shoulder was all chopped up. There were no bullet marks; apparently he had been beaten. I then took off my shirt and tried to bandage him. He was still bleeding when I picked him up. I put him on my shoulders and took him to an empty, dilapidated barn. I left him there, and that was the last time I ever saw my brother.

When I returned to the shelter my wife was very afraid, and she cried when I told her what had happened. The next day the kind woman gave us the report that the city was completely destroyed. The bullies had left, and everything was quiet. She thought it best that we leave because she was afraid that her sons would come home and find us. My body was covered with blood and I was stripped to the waist, so the woman gave me some clothes for our journey. . . .

Finally, we reached Pliskov. We found the town in bad shape, although there were survivors, about 200 of them. Some survivors agreed to help us find a safe place to go to, and we got together and planned for our immediate future. We decided to try to go to Poglovitch, a city about fifteen miles from Pliskov, and from there get a train to Odessa. . . .

We waited a couple of days. Then the stationmaster told us he expected some trains at midnight with a train to Odessa for us. He told us to be ready when the train pulled in because it would be full of Red Army soldiers. And it was. They were all over the roofs and on the back platform. About half of the cars were coal and freight trains, and we had no choice except to sit on top of one of these.

Four or five hours later we reached Odessa and were met right away by a group set up to aid the refugees. We were both very dirty and black from coal. They took us to a synagogue, cleaned us up, and gave us new clothes. The next day some of the social workers asked us if we had any relatives in Odessa. I had a sister living there, but I didn't know her address. Many of the other refugees had relatives here, too, and they were located very quickly. They found my sister, Fanya, and she took my wife and I to her home.

Fanya lived in an apartment, owned a laundry business, and had two children. We were happy to be with her two little boys as we had been married for almost three years and had no children of our own. For the next six or seven months we stayed with my sister until we heard that the bandits were near Odessa. After hearing this news we decided to leave immediately because our lives would be endangered. So we made plans to get to the city nearest the Rumanian border. We left Odessa by train and traveled from station to station until we reached the Russian-Rumanian border. . . .

To cross the border one would have to go across a very stormy body of water, a "nester." The man paid to take the refugees across put them all in little canoes. Many of these canoes capsized, and many people drowned. . . . About sixty of us went into the canoes, and we were very fortunate to make it across the border. [While making the crossing] we heard people screaming; some ice had broken through, and many refugees had fallen through to their deaths.

We spent three days at a small town called Dabroven and were aided by the Jews. Then we rode to Keshinkol, a larger city. Again we were placed in a synagogue, and there were people waiting for us when we arrived. This synagogue was our shelter for a few months. We decided to stay here for a while and I, along with other men my age, went to look for a job. Many of us found work in a brick factory. We pushed the wheelbarrows full of sand and bricks. We made about forty bricks each day. We did not get paid but could buy things very cheaply. Berries and grapes sold for one cent per five pounds. For our labor we received a large room for me and my wife to stay in. It was like a warehouse, wet and cold with absolutely no heat. We obtained some lumber and made ourselves a bed, which was more like a bench. Besides my wife and I, there were four others in this room. Outside in the yard I built a barbecue pit. This is where we cooked all of our meals. We had enough food to eat because everything was very cheap. We stayed in this place for a while.

In the meantime, HIAS, a social [agency], got in touch with my brothers and sisters in America. I had no idea where they lived but HIAS found them with just their names. In a little while we started receiving letters with a few dollars and the necessary papers to get us to America. . . .

In the meantime we went to Bucharest to get our visas. It took a few months but we finally got our visas. But we didn't have enough money for a passenger ship. HIAS suggested that we take any kind of ship that we could, so we boarded a freighter headed for America. There were sixty to seventy refugees on board, and as soon as we got on we became sick. The ship was dirty, smelly, and dilapidated. We couldn't do anything about it. We had to take anything we could. As soon as the ship started to move, my wife got sick. It was a freight boat and stopped at many ports on the way to America. We were forty-six days on the sea, and we were sick the whole time. Finally we came to American waters. We could see the Statue of Liberty and felt happy. We landed at Ellis Island, where both my sisters, Rachel and Mary, were waiting for us. They took us to their apartment in Coney Island and we met one of my sisters' children, three gorgeous girls. We were very happy because we didn't have this kind of family feeling in the old country anymore. I loved the children. When they started calling us Uncle and Tante, it was something new. We were in a new country without knowing the language, but there was love around us. My plan was to go to Philadelphia to live. I had two brothers and another sister living there. We stayed in New York for a few days and then took the train to Philadelphia. Already, though, I was in love with the children and felt that I was leaving something behind in New York.

My family lived in North Philadelphia. We came to them and sat around talking. At that time my wife and I had been married for four years. We wanted to have a baby but we hadn't been able to. In the family was a little baby, six months old, and my heart went out to her. We were happy to be where we were going to live for a while, at last. That night there was so much going around in my head that I couldn't sleep. The next morning, the door opened and a little girl, six years old, stuck her head in the doorway. She wanted to see who was there. I took her in my arms and she got scared. She didn't know who we were. She was my brother's little girl, Katie. At breakfast, we met my brother's son, who was fourteen and very clever. He started asking us how the ship had been built, and what the ocean was like, and what fishes we had seen. I was ready to tell them where we had come from. We talked and talked. Later my sister came over and took us to Wilmington where her oldest daughter had just had her first baby. Her daughter was around twenty-two. I was twenty-five. She called us Uncle and Tante. It was a thrill for me. After a few days we went back to Philadelphia and I started looking for a job. We stayed at my brother's house at this time. Finally I found a job in Buds.

The job was a good one. I was getting paid fifty-six cents an hour. The foreman of my floor was a Russian, and the other workers were all from Europe. There were very few Americans. They spoke my language and I was happy. While I was working, my heart was already home on those kids. I wanted to finish the job quickly to get home to them.

After a couple of weeks, I got myself an apartment on the same street as my brother had for nine dollars a month. I figured with that rent, I would save fifteen to twenty dollars a week, and I'd be a rich man. I worked and I saved and we got a little better apartment. I never used to go home directly from work, though. I would always go to my brother's or sister's and see the kids first. We lived on Marston Street and life was good to us. In about five or six months I had saved enough to pay my brother back for all the clothes he bought for my wife and I when we first came here....

"My Family's History Begins in Edmondson, Arkansas"

Norene Dove

LIFE IN THE SOUTH

My family's history begins in Edmondson, Arkansas. Edmondson is a one-horse town that could easily be missed or overlooked upon passing through. Population at the last count was 212 and that count I am sure included dogs, chickens, cows, and other living animals. My parents' ancestors had come to Edmondson in the late 1800s. They were able to buy a small farm with money they had saved up as sharecroppers. In this one-horse town that was without any of the conveniences necessary if a person desired to live a normal, healthy life, my mother and father and later their five children were born. My father was born in 1916 and my mother in 1918. They both lived and worked on their parents' farms until they were married. The change in Edmondson from the time of my parents' childhood up until we left was minimal. Edmondson is still without (1) a hospital, (2) doctors, (3) public transportation, (4) industries, (5) paved streets, (6) shopping areas and department stores for the most part, and (7) any of the social institutions found in other towns and cities. Memphis, which was thirty miles away, was the closest city.

My mother and father were married in January 1938. They started out with a small house and twenty-five acres of land that had been left to my father by his father. Compared to some of the other blacks in Edmondson they were pretty lucky and well off. The Great Depression of the thirties affected the entire world, but the people of Edmondson suffered tremendously from it. Many of them fled to the North while others, who could not get their fare, found themselves in servitude, with white farm owners as their overseers. Both my mother and my father lacked extensive educational careers. My father had left school when he was in the eighth grade because his help was needed on the farm. My mother had gone as long as the school system in Edmondson permitted and that was only to the ninth grade. So with hardly any education, no skills other than those associated with farming, and no money to buy equipment necessary to make their first crop, the nightmare began. Like many other blacks, they entered into a semisharecropping agreement with one of the larger white farmers who, together with a few other whites, had succeeded in maintaining complete control over the entire black community.

The black people in Edmondson were mainly of one social class except for the two teachers and the preachers who, although they too were farmers, felt a little superior because of their part-time positions. Most of the people in the community had (1) similar moral attitudes, (2) lots of religious and racial affiliations, (3) no political or economic influence, and (4) little or no formal schooling. Most of them either owned small plots of land or hired themselves out to white farmers, who sometimes permitted them to cultivate small portions of their land. Though there were whites who had economic investments in Edmondson, hardly any of them lived in the predominantly black Edmondson. Those who did live there lived within their own little world and dared the blacks to cross their path.

There were three stores, which were white-owned and -operated, in Edmondson.

They sold everything from food and clothing to farm supplies and drugs. Housed in one of these three stores were the post office and a small stand where one could buy whiskey, wine, and beer. The stores were located on the only paved street in Edmondson. These stores not only functioned to provide the people of Edmondson a place in which to shop, but you often found many of the black males congregated on their steps, discussing crops and on some occasions talking about the good life that was available in the North. The store owners discouraged the use of money by their customers to purchase goods. Most of them did not have money anyway. The store owners readily charged and kept annual accounts for their customers, gladly settling with them after their crops were gathered. Since no records were being kept by the purchasers, they often found themselves having to pay for goods that they had not purchased.

The people in Edmondson depended on the cotton economy as a source of income. My parents, though they owned a small farm, could not compete with the large, white-owned and -operated farms surrounding them. Because of the inadequate rules and regulations governing the banks and credit unions, they were not permitted to borrow money to make a profit on their crops. They had to indebt themselves to a white farmer, who often managed to claim the entire profit made from a single crop. Each year before planting time my family was given what I will call an allowance. Most of the money was spent for purchases of farm supplies and what was left, which was usually minimal, went toward purchases of clothing and food that was not raised on the farm. After the receipt of this allowance, which did not vary with an increase in family size, there was no other source of income within our household until the end of the year when the crops had been gathered. If the family consisted of many members (and it usually did), the members were often very hungry and without sufficient clothing. Whether the crops were good or bad had little effect upon the plight of my family, who had planted and gathered the crops. The crops, after they were gathered, were turned over to the white suppliers. They sold the crops in Memphis and, often without telling my parents how much the crops sold for, gave them that which was left after all of the incurred expenses had been deducted. Since my parents had not kept their own records or were ignorant about selling prices in Memphis, they often received just enough money to keep them going until they received their next allowance.

In this type of system, it was impossible for them to ever conceive of getting ahead. Not only were the people of Edmondson being exploited individually, they were being denied the right to develop or improve their community. None of the money that was made from the many hours spent in the fields by the people was being invested in the community to make life easier or more fulfilling for them and future generations.

There were only a few places in the South where a black man dared go to bring charges against his white exploiters and Edmondson was not among those places. There was no judicial system in Edmondson. The systems outside town were useful and helpful only for those who were politically and economically in control, and this definitely did not include the poor black farmers. People in the community as a whole were not allowed to vote or to express any of their personal beliefs about many local politicians, who were always white. Occasionally teachers were permitted to vote as long as they voted for the candidate favored by the whites controlling the school system.

The denial of intelligence, ambition, health, education, and economic achievement motivated my parents to move to Cleveland. After having spent the majority of their lives working hard on a farm that no longer belonged to them and having nothing to show for their hard work, they decided to move. They had hopes of a better life for their children if not for themselves.

In September of 1960 we moved to Cleveland, Ohio.

LIFE IN THE NORTH

The North offered my family, if not a totally different life, a more favorable one. In spite of considerable discrimination, it offered them more economic opportunities, more security as citizens, and greater freedom as human beings. Many of my parents' relatives and friends had moved to Cleveland during or after World War I. The fact that they were not completely alone in Cleveland did much to help them adjust without too much unhappiness about the familiar places and friends they had left behind.

My parents had come to Cleveland with a few personal objects and very little money. They did not have enough money to secure a place of their own. My mother's brother permitted us to live with him until we could do better. My uncle at the time lived in a very large, dilapidated apartment building in one of Cleveland's many ghettos. It appeared that among the many people in the building every Southern state in the Union was represented except Arkansas. My family came to their aid by expanding their representation. All of the people were black and appeared to be in no better shape than the black people we had left behind. My uncle had two children of his own, to whom he was acting as both mother and father, since their mother had left for work one morning and never returned home. Although the outside of the building wasn't pleasant to look at, the inside really wasn't that bad. I should say that it wasn't that way until after my mother spent many hours on her hands and knees scrubbing the floors, washing walls, and making it what she considered livable. My mother had always been a fanatic when it came to housework and that apparent need that she had to keep everything spotless created a lot of discomfort for me throughout my entire childhood. There were five rooms in my uncle's apartment, which now served as accommodations for eleven people. During the time that we stayed in his apartment, there was always a fuss at night as to who was sleeping where.

My father managed to get a job working for Ford Motor Company on an assembly line. Although his salary was as much in one week as our entire allowance had been for several months in the South, it wasn't enough to buy the house that my mother was constantly saying we needed. After we had been in Cleveland about nine months my mother decided to go to work in order to get her children out of that neighborhood before they turned bad. Most of the kids including myself attended an all-black school about two blocks away from home. Naturally we walked to school and en route we often had fights with the kids from other blocks who thought or acted as if they were better than us, and occasionally kids from different neighborhoods would try to coax us to try drugs. It was when my younger brother reported these happenings to my mother that she developed an intense dislike for the neighborhood and everyone in it. She complained about how the people in the neighborhood didn't try to look after their children or how they showed a lack of interest about the vicinity in which they lived in general. On several occasions she took it upon herself to act as the sanitation department and cleaned up the entire court surrounding our building.

My mother was also unhappy with the school that we had to attend because, for reasons that were known only by the board of education, it was open for only four hours each day. On nights that we did not have homework she complained and told us that if we only knew how badly she had wanted to go to school and wasn't permitted to do so, we would show a little more concern about school and try to do our best at all times. On a few occasions she made calls to our teachers verifying whether or not we had homework.

During the week our neighborhood was relatively quiet. Most of the adults worked during the day on jobs that left them fatigued by the end of the day and ready for little other than their beds when they returned home. All of the children, if they were of school age, attended school. When we were not in school, we spent the remainder of our time outside in front of the building or strolling around downtown, window shopping, making sure we arrived home before our parents did. Unlike other children in nearby neighborhoods, we could never afford to go to the movies or participate in any activity that required money. There were no free recreational facilities made available for us, so we had little else to do but stroll around town. On Saturday nights it seemed that practically everyone was awake and sort of celebrating. My mother objected and did not permit us to participate in the celebrating. She termed the behavior of the people outrageous and refused to get involved or participate. My father on the other hand seemed to enjoy the loud laughter, the music, and the arguments that usually ended in fights.

The burning and stealing that resulted from the riots of the sixties proved to be a little bit too much for my parents, and besides, our entire neighborhood was almost burned down. When the streets were declared safe again, my parents went out and found a house in a neighborhood that had been, up until blacks began to move in, totally white. My mother for one solid year never stopped thanking the Lord for having answered her prayers.

Partially because she was so wrapped up in her new home, my mother did not find adjusting in the new neighborhood difficult. For myself and the other children it took quite a while to get used to our new peers, both black and white. We didn't seem to have much in common with the blacks or the whites. We had previously lived in areas that were racially and culturally homogeneous; therefore, it was difficult for us to identify with the whites or the blacks who appeared to be imitating their white peers. My mother, as she has always done in the past, came to our rescue. Although we knew we could not afford it, my mother insisted that all five of us join the community center where we took music, swimming, and dancing lessons. She also made sure that those that were young enough were sent off to camp each summer. This new mode of living that mother had adopted for the family put a big strain on my father's wallet. Though my father had since gotten a raise and a promotion, he could not financially afford to live the type of life that my mother had decided upon for the family. He eventually had to take a second job as a cab driver. He really did not seem to mind it that much because all of the other black men in our neighborhood at one time or another worked two jobs in order to maintain the standard of living they had adopted. Most of them tried to give the appearance of being middle class, but this was far from the real truth. None of the workers in our neighborhood held positions that, according to American standards, entitled them to middle-class status. Because they were black they were kept out of certain industries. Most of them were confined because of their educational background to skilled and semiskilled occupations that were unattractive to white workers. In Cleveland, as in other cities in the North, many employers believed that black people are inferior as workers except for dirty, heavy, hot, or otherwise unattractive jobs. In Cleveland, as in the South, the chances of a black man in our neighborhood achieving vocational success and social recognition were minimal. The aspiration that was present in both my father and mother did little to change their position in society but it had a great impact on all of their children. All of their children except me have finished college and are, according to American standards, holding white-collar jobs and would, if they were not black, be allowed to participate in America's economic and social prosperity.

I attended a racially mixed high school. This was beneficial in that it exposed me to people that were of different cultural and economic backgrounds. Some of the children were from families that were economically well off and some were from families that were less fortunate than my parents. Although there was no law that said blacks were not to intermingle with people of other races as there had been in the South, other nonblack groups just avoided the black population, letting it exist separately in its designated black neighborhoods. The school was structurally superior to the one that I had attended in Arkansas, but there was no encouragement for vocational or academic achievement given from the teachers who were predominantly white. The encouragement and aspiration that I possess can be attributed to both my parents and the racist society in which I have been forced to live. The society taught me early in life how important the color of my skin is and my parents taught me that if I was to minimize the obstacles that would present themselves because of my skin color, I would have to work harder and surpass those who desire white over black. It never seemed to bother my parents that they were never able to go on a vacation or that the only place they were really accepted or recognized was within the walls of their black neighborhood.

My mother seemed pretty content as long as she could afford to buy the material conveniences that are enjoyed by the genuinely successful and economically fixed American middle class. My mother never gave up hopes of going back to school. When she could find the time she would attend the Y.W.C.A., taking whatever course they had available at the time. She was forever buying some kind of book that someone had told her about or one that she had heard about in her travels back and forth to work. Because of her active participation in the block unit and numerous church affairs, she seldom got a chance to read any of them. My father, on the other hand, when he was not working, either watched television or tried to engage in a conversation about the local politicians when he could get a listener. The children of the family did not fancy talking about that because it was far removed from poor working-class people. The year that I graduated from high school, my mother became very ill and had to quit work. Unlike my other sisters and brothers, I did not receive a scholarship. Because of the financial situation that had gotten worse since mother had left her job, I was unable to go to college. Depressed about not being able to go to college and my parents' financial situation, I decided to come to New York where I could make some fast money to help my parents and go to college with the rest.

In New York I lived with my father's sister and got a job as a file clerk in the telephone company, making $70 a week. I soon found out that I was not going to be able to help my parents very much, and as for school, I would have to work a long time on that salary. During my stay at the telephone company I experienced what I feel many working-class people experience. The job that I had was meaningless and extremely boring. I had no interest whatsoever in my job. The only meaning that it had was that it provided me with a source of weekly income. Realizing that I could not mentally or physically endure a lifetime of paper pushing, I decided to save as much as possible for the day that I could return to school. On the salary that I was making it took several years. But for me, returning to school was my only hope and salvation. In September 1972 I entered college in hopes of learning to deal with or understand the "society" which I am forced to live in but, because I'm black, have little chance of ever entering.

Biography of a Grandmother

Linda K. Schilke

Kathryn Harriet deNeui was born July 23, 1888, at Aplington, Iowa, the third child and second daughter of Hendrick Peter and Catherine Taatje (Dallmann) deNeui. On that day, her father entered in his diary, "Tippie had a calf. Katie was born." Although his wife wryly teased that, for him, this was the order of importance of the two events, Hendrick loved his children deeply. An example of this love occurred when Kathryn was five, and her parents, German/Dutch immigrant farmers, decided to move to South Dakota with their five children. The trip was made in the boxcar of a train, and the baby developed pneumonia. To complicate matters, the rest of the children had whooping cough. No doctor was available, and despite his parents' efforts, the child's condition grew worse, and he died as his mother attempted to remove the phlegm from his throat. Hendrick felt the loss deeply and later said he had felt like digging the little body out of the ground with his bare hands. The deNeuis settled on a farm near Tyndall, South Dakota, where three more boys and a girl, who died in infancy, were born.

Kathryn was known as Kitty or, more commonly, Kate. She attended grades one through eight in a one-room country schoolhouse a number of miles from her home, where she learned reading, writing, and arithmetic. . . . After graduating from the eighth grade, Kate stayed at home to help on the farm. Few people went on to high school in the farming community, and the deNeui children were no exception. Besides her work in the house, Kate spent long hours in the fields, harvesting corn and other crops. When her older sister, Anne, married in 1910, Kate was the only girl left to help her mother. This she did willingly, seemingly getting along quite well with her parents.

Although life on the farm was hard, the young people managed to have a good time. . . . Plays and programs were produced by both students and adults at the schoolhouse, and the accordian and harmonica were great favorites in accompaniment to singing. Box and candy socials were held to raise money for the school, each girl hoping the "right guy" would win the bid for her gaily decorated box. Taffy pulls, corn popping, and parlor games took place at house parties. In the winter, Kate and her friends would go skating on a nearby lake or bobsledding on the hills. Transportation during these winter months was provided by horses hitched to a bobsled or wagonbox on runners, which was piled deep with straw. Lap robes made of cow or horsehide and lined with wool covered the riders, keeping them warm.

• • •

Kate had many friends with whom she exchanged pictures; several of these friendships lasted throughout her life. One friend, Bessie Bambas, signed Kate's autograph book: "To knit and spin was once a girl's employment, but now to dress and have a beau is all a girl's enjoyment." Kate evidently thought Bessie's advice was sound; she became engaged to the local schoolteacher, then boarding at the deNeui home. For an unknown reason, this engagement was broken off, but the empty spot in her life was soon filled.

As early as October of 1911,* Kate had met a young Dutch immigrant named Herman Hoekman. The oldest son of Meyne and Wilhelmina (Martyn) Hoekman, Herman had come to America with a brother and friend in search of better opportunities. They found employment on the various farms around Tyndall, Herman especially seeking work with English-speaking farmers so that he could learn the language more easily. For a time, Herman went farther west, but returned, perhaps drawn by his attraction for Kate. He came courting with his horse, Prince, and a buggy, and at night, after leaving Kate, he would tie the reins around the whip socket and fall asleep, trusting Prince to bring him safely home.

Kate and Herman were married on January 7, 1915, in a double ceremony with her younger brother, John, and his fiancée, Anne Temple. Their wedding trip consisted of a 250-mile journey to Wilmot, South Dakota, where Herman had rented a farm. There they joined the newly formed First Baptist Church of Corona, Herman helping on the building construction.

On September 22, 1916, their first child, a girl, was born, Wilhelmina Gertrude (Gert). Kathryn Pearl (Kay) was born two years later on October 21, 1918. In both births, Kate was assisted by the family physician, Dr. Harris. When Kay was a year old, the Hoekmans moved to a farm outside Corona, South Dakota, which Herman had bought. Soon after, on December 13, 1920, a third daughter, Florence Jane, was born. Herman tried to contact Dr. Harris, but his efforts were futile. The doctor was out on house calls, and when he returned, he overlooked the message concerning Kate's labor. The woman who usually helped Kate during her births, Mrs. Loof, was not available either, and Herman, frantic by this time, delivered the baby, who came feet first, alone. The birth was successful and drew Herman and Kate closer together.

Just over three years later, on February 20, 1924, a fourth child, Maynard Henry, was born, this time with the aid of a doctor. As farmers need sons, the birth of the boy was a time of great rejoicing. Gert was in school at the time, and Kay and Florence had been taken over to the neighbor's, where they made valentines from wallpaper samples and popped corn to bring home to their mom. When they found a new baby brother awaiting them, Florence offered him a kernel of corn, but Kate quickly vetoed this gesture.

Kate's life on the farm was hard, as she had little in the way of modern conveniences. Her greatest setback was the lack of a cistern where soft, filtered rainwater could be collected and kept. All the other farms had cisterns, but for some reason, Herman, who was a bit of a procrastinator, never built her one. Soft water was necessary for washing clothes and hair, and Kate gathered what she could in barrels under the eaves of the house. This water was siphoned off by hose through a window to fifty-gallon vinegar barrels kept in the cellar and saved for laundry. In the winter, snow would be melted, and in the spring, the melting snow would be ladled from roadside ditches into buckets and carried to the house. A majority of the time, soft water was not available, and Kate would have to break down the chemicals in the hard well water by adding lye to it. The chemicals, rising to the surface of the water, would be skimmed off, and the water was then put in a washboiler to heat. The washing machine and wringer were hand-powered; a stick, connected to a dolly inside the machine and pushed back and forth, caused the machine to agitate the wash. All laundry was done in the same water, whites first, colors second, and the dirtiest overalls and work clothes last. They were rinsed in a separate tub and rolled through a wringer. Clothes were hung outside to dry all year long. This process was difficult in the winter, the clothes often freezing before they could be put on the line. Although the freezing process took much of the moisture from the clothes, the heaviest things often were not dry by the time they were brought into the house. They would then be placed on lines hung from hooks in the kitchen. When dry, they were ironed with a flatiron heated on the stove. Although this reconstituted hard water was hard on the clothes and difficult to use, Kate was always proud of her whites.

The soap for the laundry was made at butchering time. The fat from a pig was cut to pieces and put in a large black kettle over a fire in the yard. When the lard was rendered out of the cracklings, both were cooked with lye and water and allowed to harden in boxes. Cut into bars, this concoction made a fairly good soap.

Butchering took place in the fall, with a couple of families joining in the work. Herman usually slaughtered a cow and a pig, and Kate would can most of the meat in jars she had prepared in the washboiler. She also made different kinds of sausage. A great favorite was liver sausage, which she made by grinding the liver and parts of the head with spices.

*The earliest his autograph appears in Kate's book.

Kate, with the help of her girls as they grew older, churned her own butter. The Hoekmans had no ice house, as did many of the other farmers, so the butter and milk were placed in a bucket and put down the well to keep them cold and sweet. The cellar was also cool, and home-canned fruits and vegetables were stored there. A corner was allotted to potatoes, which Herman dug with a fork and Kate and the children picked up and put into burlap sacks. Kate always had a big kitchen garden, and cabbage, parsnips, turnips, carrots, and other root vegetables were also stored in the cellar. During the winter, these vegetables were covered with newspapers and quilts to keep them from freezing. She also grew beans and tomatoes, lettuce and radishes, for use in summer salads, cucumbers, from which she made several kinds of pickles, and some peas, although she did not have the patience it took to raise many of them. She made plum jam with plums from her own trees, chokecherry jam from chokecherries which grew in the coulees in the pasture and applesauce and apple butter from apples bought nearby. During the 1920s, she bought cases of strawberries and made jam which would go on bread for school lunches.

Kate never liked to cook much, though good at it, but she did like to bake. She had to contend with an old, beat-up, black cook stove, which, because it blackened the walls of the kitchen, caused the need for repapering every year; nevertheless, she turned out delicious baked goods. She baked her own bread and had an excellent recipe for dough-nuts which would be rolled in sugar, placed in a huge coffeepot or the roaster, and hung in the cellarway. When she had to feed twelve men during the hot threshing time, she would bake early in the morning so that the stove would be cool by dinnertime. She took great pride in the dinners she served these men, plucking chickens and polishing her best silver the day before, making special sugar cookies with raisin filling, and setting the table with a white tablecloth and her best china, pink Depression glass. She considerately set up washtubs and towels outside for the men to use.

Using advanced methods, Kate was a leader in chicken raising. She early discovered that brooding hens, the method used by most people, were unreliable, and she acquired an incubator, which she set up in the living room. Made of wood, it held 500 eggs in four trays and was steam-heated by a kerosene lamp under a tray of water. When returning home, Kate would look for the light in the window, worried that it had gone out and that the eggs might be chilled. X-marks were placed on one end of each egg, and it was turned regularly to prevent the chick from sticking to the shell. After the chicks were hatched, they were placed in the brooder coop, which was disinfected with lye and water, then filled with clean straw and gravel. Kate kept 200 to 250 roosters and as many hens. She found that Leghorns laid the most eggs, so a majority were these, but she also kept Rhode Island Reds and Plymouth Rocks, meatier breeds of chicken, for butchering. She sold hatching eggs, using the money she made to buy the weekly groceries. At the end of the summer, she would sell the roosters for money to buy her children school clothes. Scarves, sweaters, socks, shoes, overshoes, long-legged underwear (which the girls wore through ninth grade, much to their chagrin), and material for dresses, which was then fourteen cents a yard, came from the rooster money. Kate owned a treadle sewing machine and, during the summer, sewed all her girls' clothes. She was also adept at cutting down used clothes, given them by neighbors more fortunate than they, to fit members of her own family.

Besides her work in the house, Kate had her share of the chores to do, especially during the summer when Herman was busy in the fields. She had to feed and milk the cows, carry feed to the chickens, and slop to the pigs. Although Kate had her children to help her, she did not have the patience to teach them to do difficult tasks, finding it easier to do them herself and give them the easier, more menial jobs. The girls did not learn to cook or sew at home, though Kay did learn to bake.

In addition to her busy everyday life, Kate had family worries, especially when her children were small. In the fall of 1924, when Maynard was a baby, Florence, 3, and Kay, 5, all three developed whooping cough. Kate did the best she could to keep them comfortable. She moved a crib into the kitchen so that they could be warm, while she watched them as she worked. She placed Kay and Florence on kitchen chairs facing each other with a Vapo-lamp between them. This was a kerosene lamp with a stand above it supporting a bowl filled with a solution called Vapo-cresoline. A quilt placed over the girls caught the fumes and created a congestion-relieving atmosphere. The whooping cough lasted a long time. In mid-December, Florence developed a high fever and severe pains in her side. When she did not recover after a few days, she was taken to the doctor, who diagnosed appendicitis. She still had the whooping cough, and the doctors were afraid if she was given ether, she would develop pneumonia. It soon became evident that she would die if not operated on; administering the ether, they removed her appendix, which had ruptured in two places, on her fourth birthday. She was coughing so much that the stitches ripped out of the incision, and a pus pocket formed on her intestine. She almost died, and was left so weak by the ordeal that she had to relearn to walk. Kate was by Florence's bedside most of the three weeks she was hospitalized; Florence remembers her crying and praying for God's help as she leaned her head on her hand.

• • •

Herman and Kate's family was not as destitute as some people during the Depression. There was always plenty of milk, cream, bread, eggs, and potatoes, and they never went hungry. Kate usually fixed potatoes and eggs or oatmeal for breakfast, potatoes and meat, as long as it lasted between butcherings, for dinner, and potatoes and eggs for supper. Herman loved to fish and was good at it; his catches added to the meals. Kate would divide a jar of canned fruit between her four children for two school lunches, while she and Herman went without. Throughout these years, the Hoekmans always had a carpet on the living room floor and a big case of books. They were proud and refused to go on "relief," no matter how hard-pressed they became. The greatest hardship during this time was the lack of fuel. During the 1920s, Kate had kept fires in the kitchen, the living room, and her downstairs bedroom. Fire had to be restricted to the kitchen during the hard times, the other rooms becoming extremely cold. Kate would find frost on her counterpane when she woke in the morning, the temperature in the room reaching as low as ten degrees below zero! The cold had a negative effect on her health; she developed bronchitis and severe coughing spells. In spite of her problems, Kate tried to make her family as comfortable as possible. Before sending the children to bed, she would wrap a heated iron or brick or a hot water bottle in towels and place it between the sheets in an attempt to warm them. In the mornings, she, or the first person to rise, would serve the rest of the family hot tea in bed.

Kate was more conscious of the lack of money than her children were and in later years said she wished she could have given them the things she had wanted to. She did give them lots of love and concern. She was inventive in thinking of recreation for the girls, showing them how to make playhouses by stringing binder twine from tree to tree and how to play ball with a board used for a bat. When Kay broke a hole in her doll's head, Kate mended it by pasting adhesive tape over it and painting hair on the doll which covered the tape. To Kay, the doll seemed as good as new.

Although she did not have much money to work with, Kate tried to make Christmas a special time. The Hoekmans always had a green tree, which Kate would help the children to decorate with paper chains, popcorn, and candles. She tried to have something for each of them and, one year, sat up late sewing beautiful new doll's clothes for the girls. She always managed to have a new dress ready for each of the girls for the Sunday School Christmas program. Kate often sewed pretty and original costumes, either from material or, more often, crepe paper, for various holiday programs put on at her children's school.

Kate could also enter into the sorrows of her children. Once, when a favorite puppy was killed by a truck, she cried right along with them. She loved pets, especially cats, and had several over the years, including one named Pausha, her special cat.

Life was not entirely work for Kate. Her parents had retired about the time of her marriage and moved to Milbank, while John and Anne had moved to Ortonville, Minnesota. Another brother, Henry, and his wife, Nora, lived in Twin Brooks. All these towns being within twenty miles of each other, the deNeuis often got together at Kate's parents' home for a visit, while their children amused themselves with ghost stories in the parlor. Kate and Herman also invented a game for the children, using different languages for dogs, cats, calves, and pigs. Through these animals they would imaginatively project their thoughts, amusing each other and their children. They would sing, too, as they went about their work, Herman's Dutch songs especially amusing the family.

Both Herman and Kate valued education and tried to give their children the best schooling they could afford. They saw education as a stepping stone to a better life and urged their children to do well and get ahead so that they would not have "to grovel all your life like we did." Since there was no high school in Corona when Gert was ready to begin, she was sent to Milbank. Even at that time, schooling beyond the eighth grade was not customary among the farming families, and Gert was the first person from their Baptist Church to graduate from high school. By 1934, a school had been erected in

Corona, but after two years there, Florence and Kay followed their sister to Milbank where they could take business courses and home economics. They stayed with their grandmother, getting home only for holidays and special occasions.

• • •

Kate and Herman had an active religious life. Devotions were held before every meal, Kate reading the Bible and leading in prayer before breakfast and Herman doing the same at dinner and supper. Kate felt her responsibility as the Christian nurturer of her children. . . . She would kneel and pray earnestly for her children and friends and was always happy to feel her prayers were answered. The Hoekmans seldom missed the three church services a week, unless it were during the busiest part of the summer.

• • •

Throughout her life, Kate had a love for beautiful things. In her later life, she collected and displayed china and decorative elephants. She loved to be out in nature, where she saw and felt God's love and might. As she called her family's attention to a beautiful sunrise or sunset or a majestic thundercloud, she was reminded of God's Word: "The heavens are telling the glory of God; and the firmament proclaims his handiwork." She loved to be by a lake or to go boat riding. She saw beauty in rocks, which she collected from her trips and cemented into a beautiful pyramidal rock garden. Her appreciation for nature came forth most clearly in her love for flowers. Both on the farm and after she had retired to town, she had beautiful flower gardens with every variety of flower imaginable, though she especially liked petunias. She had a green thumb, and plants multiplied and spread under her touch. She spent many happy hours in her garden, planning changes to increase its beauty from year to year. She realized that her garden was the loveliest in town and took great pride in it and the compliments she received for it.

• • •

Kathryn deNeui Hoekman died July 20, 1971, three days short of her eighty-third birthday, and was buried in the Corona Baptist Cemetery beside her husband and baby daughter. Living all but four years of her life under the influence and guidance of her parents and husband and never working outside of the home, Kate did not develop self-confidence, although she was an extremely capable person. This lack of self-assurance and impatience were her two greatest faults. These faults were far outweighed, however, by the rich heritage she left her descendants of love, hard work, struggle, respect for education, creativity, a love for the beauty of nature, and, above all, a deep belief, love, and trust in God. She died deeply beloved by her children, grandchildren, and friends.

Sketching Your Family:
Questions and Questionnaires

Note: The following questions are suggestions only. You may want to ask them of yourself and your relatives, but they do not exhaust the possibilities, and not every question may apply to your particular situation.

BASIC INFORMATION

When were you born? How old were you when you married? When did you move to your present residence? Why? What kinds of work have you done?

RACE ETHNICITY

To what racial or ethnic group do you belong? When did you begin to think of yourself as a member of this group? Why? How did this identification influence you? In what ways is your group primarily defined—by religion, ancestry, skin color, or language? Are there general limitations imposed on your group by society? What? How are they imposed? In what economic and social class are most members of your group found? Why? What are society's stereotypes of your group? What stereotypes does your group hold of other groups?

EDUCATION

How many years of schooling have you had? How was your education important in your life? Did you have more schooling than your parents? Did you "do well" in school? How did that affect your life? What do you remember about your teachers?

COMMUNICATION

What are your sources of information about the world outside your community? What folklore about your family or group do you know? What outsider has been most widely respected in your family in the last ten years? Why?

CLASS, STATUS, AND MOBILITY

How do you define your social class—working class, middle class, professional class, country club set, other? What characteristics put you in this class? How do your social contacts influence your life? What contacts do you have with people in other classes? Is your social class different from that of your parents? If so, how was it changed? Is formal education most important in social mobility, that is, moving up in social class? If not, what is? What places outside your community have the reputation for offering a better life? Could you improve your social-class position if you tried? How? What do you like/dislike about your place in society?

STATE, LAW, AND POLITICAL LIFE

What rights does citizenship give you? What burdens come with citizenship? In what areas does the state provide you services? Through what officials are you in contact with the state (e.g., policemen, politicians, tax collectors)? Are representatives of the state generally from the same economic and social class as you? What kinds of laws affect your life? Do you think the law favors any individual or group? How? Where are the political decisions made that affect your life? What kinds of people run for political offices? Could you approach political officials about your problems successfully? How much does voting mean to you? Would you run for office?

RELIGION

Have you always belonged to the same denomination? Do you go to church only for services? If not, what else have you done at church? Are most members of your church in about the same social and economic position as you? Have religious ideas taught to you ever been in conflict with the general beliefs or practices of society in things like morality, science, and individual rights? How did religion affect the way you were brought up, and the way that you brought up your children?

COMMUNITY

What makes up your community besides just being a group of people living near each other? Why did you choose to live in this community? What basic needs are not satisfied within your community (e.g., employment, health care, education, recreation)? Why not? Does your community have control of its own development? Is your community also an ethnic, racial, religious, or political unit? How have your community's leaders achieved their positions as leaders?

VOLUNTARY ASSOCIATIONS

To what voluntary associations do you belong? Why? How is membership limited? What does membership provide for you? In what ways are other members similar to you (e.g., in terms of race/ethnicity, religion, social class, income, life style)? Would you like your children to belong to this association too? Why?

ECONOMIC CONDITIONS

To what economic class do you belong? What percentage of your income goes for necessities? Is your place in the economic order the result of what you do for a living? Why do you do the job you do? How much training did you have for it? Have you always done the same thing? If not, why did you switch jobs? Are you in about the same economic situation as your parents and grandparents? How many members of your family work full time? How many people give you orders on your job? Have you ever had people working under you? What would you do if you lost your job? Are charge accounts and credit cards a help or hindrance to the economic health of your family? What determines who gets the best jobs and higher incomes in society? Do you believe that most working people are treated fairly by society?

THE FAMILY

Who lived in your household when you were a child (or when you were a parent)? How large were the living quarters? What factors determined who would live in the household? How many brothers and sisters did you have? Do you all still live near each other? Why or why not? Did your family surroundings provide privacy? Who had the most influence in making family decisions? Who had the least? Why? Were all members of the family expected to bring money home? To what age were children supported financially? Who controlled the outflow of money? How much of your "education" came at home? What customs or values were passed on to you? What was the origin of these customs and values? Did you attempt to bring up your children in the same way? What was the religious function of your family? With whom did you have fun in your free time? How?

The Whys and Hows of Writing Your Paper

Any individual's past is the essence of the millions.
—ALEX HALEY

This book has tried to help you relate your personal past to a larger history. The main question it has posed is: What is there in your own history that has brought you to your present position? We believe it is important to ask that question because an investigation of the longer-range historical forces that have influenced you may explain a great deal more about yourself than immediate, short-range factors.

A key event in the past that may well tell you much about your present position is your ancestors' uprooting and resettlement in America. Hopefully, you have already learned something about this often heroic chapter of your family's history. Do you have a theory now about why they came across the ocean? Surely, except for the Africans and others who came in chains, hope for a better life was a motivation. Perhaps they came to escape anti-Semitic outrages or famine, like the eastern European Jews and the Irish; or perhaps to flee from war and conscription, like the Germans. There were, of course, many other reasons: Religious persecution drove out many, including the Puritans, the earliest European-Americans. And, class oppression uprooted southern European and Asian peasants, from Greece to China. In general, then, they left because the societies in which they were born were inflexible, with children following parents in the same class positions, living the same lives, held by the same traditional bonds of culture. The changes that migration brought (or failed to bring) should be illuminating to you, especially through the comparisons with the present that this information should invite. Why, for instance, do most Americans now stay in school so much longer than past generations did? How has home life changed in the last three generations of your family's history? What has happened to your family's standard of living over the past fifty years? How do you account for the changes?

This series of questions attempts to uncover the structure of contemporary American society by asking you to retrace the path by which you arrived at your position in it. Your investigation is an *historical* one because it leads you to understand the attitudes and values taught you throughout childhood as the outcome of your ancestors' experiences in a particular historical epoch. Ultimately, the question you should try to answer is whether history has been rewarding or alienating for you and your family. To find out requires some careful thinking and planning during the course of your research.

First, you should decide on the scope of your paper, that is, how much you want to do in relation to what is expected of you in your course. Is it enough, for example, for you to write a paper focusing on a particular aspect of family living to gain some insight into the influence of history? Or should your paper be a fuller, more traditional effort?

Although you need not follow either model, let us assume for now that you are interested in writing a detailed description and analysis. The first suggestion is that you thoroughly familiarize yourself with the information that you have accumulated. Review all of your material a few times. Two or three hours spent in mastering the data will permit you to go on to the next step.

A series of questions must be asked of the material, since the isolated facts you have collected are virtually useless until some framework of meaning is given to them. Some of the facts must be emphasized and others discarded, and those emphasized must be put into a sequence that produces some conclusion. The essence of planning lies in deciding which questions are to be asked of the historical record and which problems are to be solved. Familiarity with your research materials should reveal some major areas of inquiry. Perhaps you have discovered one especially interesting and influential person in your family who might provide a focal point for your essay. Or, possibly, there was a crucial incident—a move, a crisis, an accomplishment, a disaster—that you can use as a key. If you can pinpoint neither a person nor an event, try thinking in terms of the social factors discussed in this book. For example, place of residence may seem to be important, so that you can concentrate on the interactions between your ancestors and their locality: their coming, settlement, development through time, and assumption of position in the local social structure. Racism, war, economic class, or any other large historical force that may turn up throughout your research into the past two or three generations of your family can form the basis for structuring the family's history.

This structure, to reiterate, will be developed by the questions you pose. Your assumptions about what was most important in your family's history will be closely related to your hypothesis, that is, the historical argument you are making. You may initially develop a hypothesis that, when applied to your facts, loses its appeal. There may be too little evidence to support your theory (or too much counterevidence), thus forcing you to modify the hypothesis. This process is not unusual, and, in any case, the resulting argument is very much strengthened by it. As you look at your research notes, the important evidence is whatever helps you to explain the questions that you are interested in having answered. But, exercise care in determining the validity of the data before you.

The product of your efforts should be an essay that is organized around a central hypothesis, accounts for change over time, clearly identifies the causes of the change, and seeks to analyze the larger historical meanings associated with the family's story. As you measure your family's progress—in economic advancement, social mobility, educational change, political involvement—remember that your task is not to glorify or to condemn the past, but to understand it. Understanding your historical legacy, in turn, allows you some insight into those economic and social forces most significant to your existence. Or, as Sören Kierkegaard, the existentialist philosopher, expressed it, "One has to live life in the present but can only understand life from its history."

Genealogical Charts

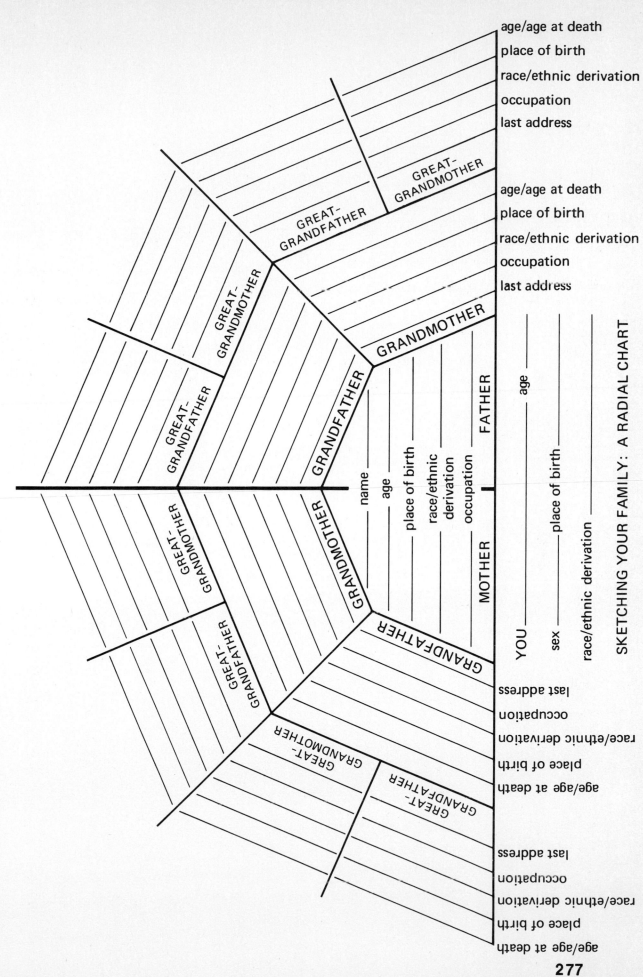

SKETCHING YOUR FAMILY: A RADIAL CHART

GREAT-GRANDMOTHER
age/age at death
place of birth
race/ethnic derivation
occupation
last address

GREAT-GRANDFATHER

GREAT-GRANDMOTHER

GRANDMOTHER
age/age at death
place of birth
race/ethnic derivation
occupation
last address

GREAT-GRANDFATHER

GRANDFATHER

FATHER
age

YOU
name
age
place of birth
race/ethnic
derivation
occupation

sex
place of birth
race/ethnic derivation

MOTHER

GREAT-GRANDMOTHER

GRANDMOTHER

GREAT-GRANDFATHER

GRANDFATHER
last address
occupation
race/ethnic derivation
place of birth
age/age at death

GREAT-GRANDMOTHER

GREAT-GRANDFATHER
last address
occupation
race/ethnic derivation
place of birth
age/age at death

277

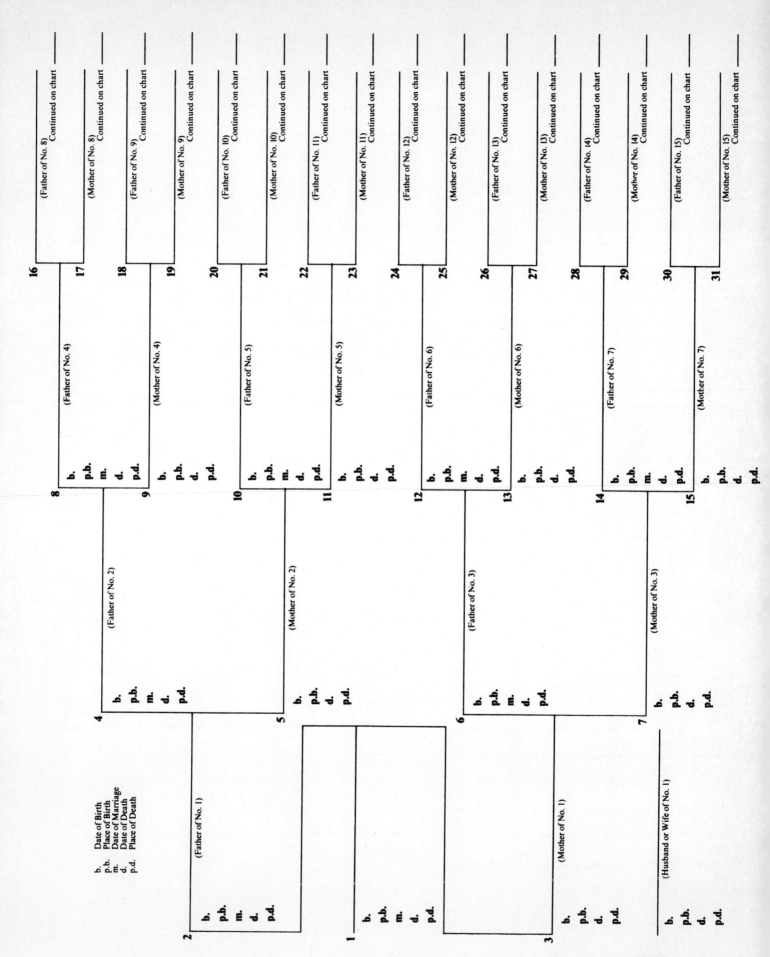

b.   Date of Birth
p.b.   Place of Birth
m.   Date of Marriage
d.   Date of Death
p.d.   Place of Death

2 (Father of No. 1)
b.
p.b.
m.
d.
p.d.

1
b.
p.b.
m.
d.
p.d.

3 (Mother of No. 1)
b.
p.b.
d.
p.d.

(Husband or Wife of No. 1)
b.
p.b.
d.
p.d.

4 (Father of No. 2)
b.
p.b.
m.
d.
p.d.

5 (Mother of No. 2)
b.
p.b.
d.
p.d.

6 (Father of No. 3)
b.
p.b.
m.
d.
p.d.

7 (Mother of No. 3)
b.
p.b.
d.
p.d.

8 (Father of No. 4)
b.
p.b.
m.
d.
p.d.

9 (Mother of No. 4)
b.
p.b.
d.
p.d.

10 (Father of No. 5)
b.
p.b.
m.
d.
p.d.

11 (Mother of No. 5)
b.
p.b.
d.
p.d.

12 (Father of No. 6)
b.
p.b.
m.
d.
p.d.

13 (Mother of No. 6)
b.
p.b.
d.
p.d.

14 (Father of No. 7)
b.
p.b.
m.
d.
p.d.

15 (Mother of No. 7)
b.
p.b.
d.
p.d.

16 (Father of No. 8) Continued on chart
17 (Mother of No. 8) Continued on chart
18 (Father of No. 9) Continued on chart
19 (Mother of No. 9) Continued on chart
20 (Father of No. 10) Continued on chart
21 (Mother of No. 10) Continued on chart
22 (Father of No. 11) Continued on chart
23 (Mother of No. 11) Continued on chart
24 (Father of No. 12) Continued on chart
25 (Mother of No. 12) Continued on chart
26 (Father of No. 13) Continued on chart
27 (Mother of No. 13) Continued on chart
28 (Father of No. 14) Continued on chart
29 (Mother of No. 14) Continued on chart
30 (Father of No. 15) Continued on chart
31 (Mother of No. 15) Continued on chart

YOURSELF

name _____ age/date of birth _____

home address _____ city/state _____

place of birth _____ citizenship _____

number of siblings _____ their ages _____

places of residence since birth

_____ years there _____ left in 19 _____

_____ years there _____ left in 19 _____

_____ years there _____ left in 19 _____

_____ years there _____ left in 19 _____

religion _____ same as parents _____

leisure time activities _____

_____

_____

number of hours of television watching averaged each week _____

military service _____

_____

racial/ethnic identification (if any) _____

languages spoken in the home _____

your social and economic class _____

_____

_____

_____

advantages/disadvantages of your education to this point _____

_____

_____

_____

_____

job/career choice after graduation _____

_____

_____

YOUR FATHER

name _____ age _____

place of birth _____ date of birth _____

schooling (years) _____ vocational training (in) _____
occupations

1. _____ where _____ when _____

2. _____ where _____ when _____

3. _____ where _____ when _____

approximate income level _____

all residence movements

from _____ to _____ when _____ why _____ how _____

from _____ to _____ when _____ why _____ how _____

from _____ to _____ when _____ why _____ how _____

religion _____

political/social affiliations _____

leisure-time activities _____

military service (length, rank, experiences, recollections) _____

_____

date and place of marriage to your mother _____

age of bride _____ age of groom _____

previous or subsequent marriages _____

number of children of this marriage _____ of other marriages _____

number of people living in the home now

adults _____ children under 18 _____

frequency of contact with relatives _____

associations with ethnic derivation _____

_____

general attitudes toward American life as fulfilling expectations _____

_____

recollections of childhood _____

_____

specific information regarding his own parents _____

_____

YOUR MOTHER

name (inc. maiden name) _____ age _____

place of birth_____ date of birth _____

schooling (years) _____ vocational training (in)_____
occupations

1. _____ where _____ when _____

2. _____ where _____ when _____

3. _____ where _____ when _____

approximate income level _____

all residence movements up to marriage

from _____ to _____ when _____ why _____ how _____

from _____ to _____ when _____ why _____ how _____

from _____ to _____ when _____ why _____ how _____

religion_____

political/social affiliations _____

leisure-time activities _____

_____

date and place of marriage to your father_____

  age of bride _____ age of groom_____

  previous or subsequent marriages _____

  number of children of this marriage _____ of other marriages_____

associations with ethnic derivation _____

_____

_____

general attitudes toward contemporary women's movement_____

_____

_____

general attitudes toward American life as fulfilling expectations _____

_____

_____

recollections of childhood _____

_____

specific information regarding her own parents_____

_____

282

YOUR FATHER'S FATHER

name_____ age/age at death _____

place of birth_____ date of birth _____

schooling (years) _____ vocational training (in)_____
occupations

1._____ where _____ when _____

2._____ where _____ when _____

3._____ where _____ when _____

all migrations (movement of the family residence)

from _____ to _____ when _____ why _____ how _____

from _____ to _____ when _____ why _____ how _____

from _____ to _____ when _____ why _____ how _____

religion_____

political/social affiliations _____

leisure-time activities _____

_____

date and place of marriage to your father's mother _____

age of groom _____ age of bride _____

previous or subsequent marriages _____

image of homeland after leaving (if immigrant to United States); or, image of area of identification (e.g., Africa)_____

_____

_____

_____

length of contact with old country after leaving _____

general attitudes toward American life as fulfilling expectations _____

_____

recollections of childhood _____

_____

_____

_____

specific information regarding his own parents_____

_____

YOUR FATHER'S MOTHER

name _____ age/age at death _____

place of birth _____ date of birth _____

schooling (years) _____ vocational training (in) _____
occupations

1. _____ where _____ when _____

2. _____ where _____ when _____

3. _____ where _____ when _____

all migrations (movement of the family residence)

from _____ to _____ when _____ why _____ how _____

from _____ to _____ when _____ why _____ how _____

from _____ to _____ when _____ why _____ how _____

religion _____

political/social affiliations _____

leisure-time activities _____

_____

date and place of marriage to your father's father _____

  age of bride _____ age of groom_____

  previous or subsequent marriages _____

image of homeland after leaving (if immigrant to United States); or, image of area of identification (e.g., Africa) _____

_____

_____

  length of contact with old country after leaving _____

general attitudes toward American life as fulfilling expectations _____

_____

_____

recollections of childhood _____

_____

_____

specific information regarding her own parents _____

_____

YOUR MOTHER'S FATHER

name_____ age/age at death _____

place of birth_____ date of birth _____

schooling (years) _____ vocational training (in)_____
occupations

1. _____ where _____ when _____

2. _____ where _____ when _____

3. _____ where _____ when _____

all migrations (movement of the family residence)

from _____ to _____ when _____ why _____ how _____

from _____ to _____ when _____ why _____ how _____

from _____ to _____ when _____ why _____ how _____

religion_____

political/social affiliations _____

leisure-time activities _____

_____

date and place of marriage to your mother's mother _____

age of groom _____ age of bride _____

previous or subsequent marriages _____

image of homeland after leaving (if immigrant to United States); or, image of area of identification (e.g., Africa) _____

_____

_____

_____

length of contact with old country after leaving _____

general attitudes toward American life as fulfilling expectations _____

_____

_____

_____

recollections of childhood _____

_____

_____

specific information regarding his own parents_____

_____

_____

YOUR MOTHER'S MOTHER

name _____ age/age at death _____

place of birth _____ date of birth _____

schooling (years) _____ vocational training (in) _____
occupations

1. _____ where _____ when _____

2. _____ where _____ when _____

3. _____ where _____ when _____

all migrations (movement of the family residence)

from _____ to _____ when _____ why _____ how _____

from _____ to _____ when _____ why _____ how _____

from _____ to _____ when _____ why _____ how _____

religion _____

political/social affiliations _____

leisure-time activities _____
_____

date and place of marriage to your mother's father _____

age of bride _____ age of groom _____

previous or subsequent marriages _____

image of homeland after leaving (if immigrant to United States); or, image of area of identification (e.g., Africa) _____
_____
_____
_____

length of contact with old country after leaving _____

general attitudes toward American life as fulfilling expectations _____
_____
_____

recollections of childhood _____
_____
_____

specific information regarding her own parents _____
_____
_____
_____

A STEP-PARENT

name_____ age_____

place of birth_____ date of birth_____

schooling (years)_____ vocational training (in)_____

occupations

1. _____ where_____ when_____

2. _____ where_____ when_____

3. _____ where_____ when_____

all residence movements

from_____ to_____ when_____ why_____ how_____

from_____ to_____ when_____ why_____ how_____

from_____ to_____ when_____ why_____ how_____

religion_____

political/social affiliations_____

leisure-time activities_____

_____

married to your_____

date and place of marriage_____

age of groom_____ age of bride_____

previous or subsequent marriages_____

associations with ethnic derivation_____

_____

_____

_____

general attitudes toward American life as fulfilling expectations_____

_____

_____

recollections of childhood_____

_____

_____

specific information regarding his or her own parents_____

_____

_____

SIBLINGS OF YOUR FATHER AND YOUR MOTHER

father's siblings

name _____ age/age at death _____ present hometown _____

name _____ age/age at death _____ present hometown _____

name _____ age/age at death _____ present hometown _____

name _____ age/age at death _____ present hometown _____

occupations _____

_____

_____

_____

_____

_____

frequency of contact with your own family _____

_____

_____

_____

_____

mother's siblings

name _____ age/age at death _____ present hometown _____

name _____ age/age at death _____ present hometown _____

name _____ age/age at death _____ present hometown _____

name _____ age/age at death _____ present hometown _____

occupations _____

_____

_____

_____

_____

_____

frequency of contact with your own family _____

_____

_____

_____

_____